A CONCISE TEXTBOOK ON

Human Psychology

Dr. Sarabjeet Kaur
BHMS, MD (Hom) Psychiatry

B. Jain Publishers Pvt. Ltd.
USA—EUROPE—INDIA

A CONCISE TEXTBOOK ON HUMAN PSYCHOLOGY

First Edition: 2008
7th Impression: 20|20 !

> **NOTE FROM THE PUBLISHERS**
> Any information given in this book is not intended to be taken as a replacement for medical advice. Any person with a condition requiring medical attention should consult a qualified practitioner or therapist.

Published by Kuldeep Jain for
B. JAIN PUBLISHERS (P) LTD.
D-157, Sector-63, NOIDA-201307, U.P. (INDIA)
Tel.: +91-120-4933333 • *Email:* info@bjain.com
Website: **www.bjain.com**
Registered office: 1921/10, Chuna Mandi, Pahargani,
New Delhi-110 055 (India)

Printed in India

ISBN: 978-81-319-0333-9

Contents

Publisher's Note

Since a long time, there was a dire need for a book on psychology which can quench the thirst of all of them aspiring to understand the subject of human psychology.

"A Concise Textbook on Human Psychology" by Dr. Sarabjeet Kaur is a basic book for all who want to know and understand the science of human behaviour.

The author has carved the subject very well and in an interesting format. Beginning from the basic functionality of different parts of brain which determine the human psychology, she subtly enters the arena of human behaviour and covers various aspects like Learning, Memory, Intelligence and Emotions while maintaining a link from one chapter to another. The reader will appreciate the beautiful link she establishes while explaining the finer details of brain function and how they work in response to external stimulation and generate varied ways of reaction.

It is a book for all to have who want to understand human psychology and use the benefit of this knowledge about the complex human counselling. We thank the author for her untiring efforts and dedication, for giving this shape to the book.

Kuldeep Jain
CEO, B. Jain Publishers

Foreword

I am delighted to write a foreword to the book "A Concise Textbook on Human Psychology"
As most psychologists, I am passionate about the study of psychology. I was introduced to the subject at the age of fourteen when I read my first book on the subject, by an international author, which was one of the most extraordinary and absorbing books which served as a foundation for my passion. Today, after having been in this field for over thirty years, training and guiding students, the search for a comprehensive and integrative book by an Indian author on the subject is most welcome.

Dr. Sarabjeet Kaur covers so much information creatively, with invented approaches and new speculation that give insight and wisdom even though the principles remain the same.
The book is easy to read and simply makes perfect sense. It would be hard for anyone to disconnect the wisdom found in every chapter. This concise volume is packed with information boxes, illustrations, diagrams and figures which will help simplify the students learning process.
The last chapter on "Dreams and Dreaming" is a unique feature and should go a long way to help the readers understand the subject thoroughly, a major tool in psychotherapy.

"A Concise Textbook on Human Psychology" is a good integrative text book and reference book covering the entire gamut of the basic knowledge of psychology. It would also be of great help to the teachers, trainers and a broad spectrum of colleges teaching psychology as a part of their subject curriculum.

I am confident that all will benefit by keeping a copy of this book. I congratulate Dr. Sarabjeet Kaur for this fine contribution and commend this book for all those who enter the field of psychology.

Dr. Deepali Kapoor, India
Counselling Psychologist, MA, EdM (Counselling) PhD (Psychology)
Hon. Chairperson, Delhi Commonwealth Women's Association
Hon. Vice President, Core Cancer Foundation
Hon. Counsellor, Breast Cancer Patients Benefit Foundation
Hon. Counsellor, Cancer Patients Aid Association
Consultant, Counselling Psychologist (Oncology), Indraprastha Apollo Hospitals
Consultant, Tata Consultancy Services and Hewitt Associates

Preface

A concise textbook on human psychology has emerged as a result of my deep interest in the subject of human psychology. The main purpose of this book is to help the readers understand the subject of Psychology in better and easier way. Psychology deals with many problems of everyday life and many other things that a person experiences during his lifetime. After going through this book the reader will be in a position to know the cause of those problems and also he will be able to rectify some of the problems, and clear his doubts too.

WRITING FOR A BROAD RANGE OF STUDENTS

I wanted to write a book that students would actually enjoy reading, and I hope the book might find its way into the hands of students from a broad spectrum of colleges. This book would be of immense help to the undergraduates as well as the postgraduate students having psychology as one of their subject.

KEEPING PACE WITH EMERGING KNOWLEDGE

In this book I have attempted to bring readers up-to-date information about this rapidly changing discipline (psychology). Psychology, like other areas of knowledge, has its classic theories and studies which form the basis for the much current work. Students should know about these too, and I have not neglected them.

RESEARCH FOCUS

This book takes psychological science seriously. A student should come out of an introductory psychology class not only with a sense of the basic questions and frameworks for answering them but also with an appreciation for how to obtain psychological knowledge.

INTEGRATIVE APPROACH

Solo-authoring an introductory text is probably presumptive evidence of mental instability (and is clearly a cause of it as well), but I could not have produced this book any other way. As one psychologist puts it, (Holt, 1976), the human psyche is not the handiwork of an obsessive-compulsive God who created cognition on one day, affect on another, motivation on another, and so forth, and made sure that they all stayed neatly in their own territories. Too often our efforts to classify and label, lead us to try to separate the inseparable. The integrative bent of the book stems primarily from the clinical and experimental perspectives as well as the concepts and methods from various psychological traditions. Although the chapters are integrated with one another, each chapter can stand on its own and be understood independently of the others.

ORGANIZATION

The chapters have been organized in a way that would be convenient for the students to follow. A separate chapter on "The Concept of Mind and Schools of Psychology" is introduced for the convenience of the students. Also the last chapter on "Dreams and Dreaming" has been added in this book which will prove quite helpful for the students. All contributors of information on psychology have been given due credit but wherever it has been missed or overlooked I accept my folly for same.

ILLUSTRATION AND DESIGN

Tremendous care has been taken to select and design only those figures and tables that actually contribute to the text and that do not just make the pages look less ominous. The same is true of photo selection; images that would provoke thought have been only added. In some chapters, few informative boxes are also used. Pay attention to the illustrations, tables, and the boxes too, because they are as important as the corresponding discussions in the text.

ANNEXURE

At the end of the book annexure (I to V) are provided. These are added not to increase the bulk of the book; rather they are quite informative for the readers and each reader must go through them.

This book is my first work as an author and I have tried my best to convey the right information in a simplest form and in required details. This book has underwent checking several times by me and by editorial team but some mistakes might remain. While reading if you find any mistake or have any suggestions, I'll be greatful to receive the feedback from you end and the mistakes can be rectified in future editions.

DR. SARABJEET KAUR
B.H.M.S.
(Nehru Homoeopathic Medical College, New Delhi, India)
Ex-House physician (NHMC, New Delhi)
M.D. (Hom) Psychiatry

Acknowledgement

I acknowledge with thanks, to the B. Jain Publishers (P) Ltd., and especially Dr. Rohit Jain for giving me this opportunity. I appreciate their patience and suggestions for making this work possible.

Psychology: An Introduction

ORIGIN OF THE WORD "PSYCHOLOGY"

PSYCHOLOGY AS A SCIENCE
— Experimentation and observation
— Based on principles and laws
— Concepts and terms
— Applied value

HISTORY OF PSYCHOLOGY
— Pre-socratic philosophers
— Greek philosophers
— Aristotle
— Beginning of modern psychology
— Physiology and the mind
— Academic psychology
— Diversification of psychology

RESEARCH METHODS IN PSYCHOLOGY
— Case Studies
— Naturalistic observations
— Survey research
— Quasi-experiments and correlational studies
— Experimental method
— Systematic observation
— Clinical method

VARIOUS SUB-FIELDS OF PSYCHOLOGY
— Clinical psychology
— Counselling psychology
— Experimental psychology
— Physiological psychology
— School and educational psychology
— Industrial psychology
— Organizational psychology
— Developmental psychology
— Social psychology
— Community psychology

RELATED DISCIPLINES AND PRACTICES
— Psychiatry
— Psychoanalysis
— Philosophy

Psychology : An Introduction

Psychology deals with many problems of our everyday life and with many things we have already experienced. Earlier, psychology concentrated on the study of sensory processes, perception, simple learning and memory. Gradually, however, this field expanded to the point that it now covers a range of topics broad enough to touch the lives of all of us. Psychology gives us a rational basis for understanding what we and others do. Psychology is gradually nearing the goal of understanding human behaviour.

ORIGIN OF THE WORD "PSYCHOLOGY"

The word "Psychology" was formed from two Greek words. The first, "Psyche", originally meant "breath" but later acquired the additional meaning "soul", because breathing was thought to indicate that the soul had not yet left the body, and later still (during the seventeenth century) broadened further in meaning to include "mind". The equivalent Latin word "anima", from which the English words "animal" and "animate" are derived, also started life meaning "breath" and later evolved the additional meaning "mind". The second Greek word, "logos", originally meant "word" and later expanded in meaning to include "discourse" and eventually "science". According to its Greek roots, therefore, psychology is literally the "science of the mind".

Later, scientists criticised this because mind could not be observed or experimented upon. Hence, *psychology* was called as the study of conscious behaviour. But this was also criticised when psychoanalysis pointed out that we must try to study unconcious processes because they control our behaviour to a very great extent. Finally, Psychology was defined by **John B. Watson** as the scientific study of human and animal behaviour.

Definition: Psychology is the scientific study of human and animal behaviour.

PSYCHOLOGY AS A SCIENCE

A science is a body of systematized knowledge that is gathered by carefully observing and measuring events. *Erismann* asserted that the natural sciences such as physics or biology, were concerned with explanations, whereas psychology, when attempting to grasp central phenomena of the mental life, had recourse to comprehension or understanding. *Psychology* deals with actual experience and sets out to study this experimentally with exact methods.

Psychologists do experiments and make observations which others can repeat; they obtain data which can be verified by others too. Psychology is a science as it uses the scientific methods, principles and explanations to explain human and animal behaviour. Because it is a science, psychology, is not limited to intuition; it searches the facts.

Psychology is a science, therefore, it follows some general characteristics of science which are as follows:

Experimentation and observation

In Psychology, the whole data is gathered by

experimentation and observation; no reliance is placed on intuition, opinion or belief. Psychologist does experiments, makes observations which others can repeat and verify. Therefore, psychology being empirical is science.

Based on principles and laws

Experimentations and observations are necessary but they are of little use if they do not make some sense. They must be capable of being sumarized by some principles and laws. As psychology is based on certain principles and laws, the whole data is collected and summarized accordingly; so, it is called a science.

Concepts and terms

Another important characteristic of science is definition of the terms and concepts used. Concepts and terms should not be vague and abstract. They should convey the same meaning to all the psychologist. Psychology, as a science, uses operational definition of terms.

Applied value

As all sciences have application in our day-to-day lives in some or the other ways; psychology should also help us to solve everyday life problems. Since, the knowledge of psychology is being applied, today, to each and every activity of human being in the areas of health, industry, school and education; we can very well say that it has applied value in our lives like other sciences. Knowledge of psychology is being increasingly applied but it requires skill and considerable experience.

HISTORY OF PSYCHOLOGY

Although psychology has been recognized as an independent discipline for little more than a century, psychological speculations and practices can be found in the records of most ancient civilizations. The **Ebers papyrus**, an *ancient Egyptian*

document devoted to medical matters dating from before 1500 BC, for example, describes practices strikingly similar to modern hypnosis.

In the history of **Herodotus,** the *world's first history book,* which was completed in about 429 BC. According to Herodotus, the experiment was performed by the ancient *Egyptian Pharaoh Psammetichus, I* in the seventh century BC to determine whether human beings have an inborn capacity for speech, and if so, which particular language is innate. He ordered two infants to be brought up in a remote place by a shepherd who was forbidden to speak in their presence. After two years the children began to speak, and the word that they repeated most often was becos.

Psammetichus concluded that the capacity for speech is inborn and that the innate, natural language of human beings in *Phrygian*.

Psammetichus's experiment was certainly poorly designed and methodologically unsound, but what is striking is that it was a psychological experiment none the less; in its conceptual structure and methodology it is strinkingly similar to the highly regarded experiments of **William H. Thorpe,** who reared birds in isolation from members of their own species in order to discover the innate features of their songs.

Psychology existed for a long time as a branch of Philosophy that was called *"mental philosophy"*. During the eighteenth and nineteenth centuries, developments in the biological sciences began to suggest empirical approaches to some of the problems of mental philosophy and towards the end of the period psychology finally reached maturity and gain its independence as a separate discipline in its own right.

Pre-socratic philosophers

The first systematic investigations of psychological problems were carried out in ancient Greece by the *pre-socratic philosophers* of the sixth and fifth centuries BC. They did not have any concept of an individual soul or mind, but they were the first to understand that the brain plays an important role in mental experience. In particular, they understood that our eyes cannot see and our ears cannot hear without the help of our brains, and by contributing this crucial insight the pre-socratics paved the way for the scientific study of sensation and perception.

The pre-socratics were also the first to develop a theory to explain the fact that people differ from one another not only physically but also psychologically, that is, not only in appearance but also in temperament, or what psychologists now call *personality*.

Greek philosophers

They established two more or less discrete philosophical approaches to psychology. One approach emphasized reason, logic, thought, theory, innate knowledge and a mind distinct from the body.

The other approach emphasized observation, experimentation, environmental learning and unity of body and soul. Much of all future psychology has fallen into one of these two camps.

Aristotle

The views of Aristotle cannot be assigned to either camp. **Aristotle** was a theorist as well as an observer. **Watson** considers him to have been the first psychologist because he tried to present a systematic and integrated view of the function of human mind.

Aristotle thought that form cannot be separated from matter—that a bronze statue, for instance, must have matter in order to have form and vice versa. This unifying concept is present in Aristotle's view of the *"psyche"*, often interpreted as *"soul"* or *"mind"*. Aristotle's *"soul"* includes matter as well as the functioning of the mind. Aristotle's *"psyche"* did not have any religious or supernatural properties.

Beginning of modern psychology

Descartes introduced his dualistic concept of man. He said that the mind or soul is located in the brain, though it has no substance. The body, on the other hand, was thought to have substance, or *"extended"* qualities which, like machines, followed mechanical laws. Descartes further believed that mind can influence the body and the body can influence the mind. He attempted to describe the physiological mechanisms of this interaction. Descartes is often called the first modern psychologist, because psychology would have remained speculative without the introduction and the recognition of physiological factors.

Physiology and the mind

Pierre Flourens demonstrated that certain parts of the brain are directly responsible for certain behavioural functions.

The studies of sensory receptors, nerves, and muscles also contribute much to the understanding of human feelings, thoughts, and activities. **Du Bois-Raymond** demonstrated in 1849 that neural activity is measurable and that it is accompanied by an electrical impulse and **Helmholtz** showed in 1850 that neural conduction requires a specified time. Physiology brought not only physiological data but the scientific method in general to psychology.

Academic psychology

In 1879 the first psychological laboratory was founded by **Wilhelm Wundt** at the *university of Leipzig*. Wundt was trained in medicine, physiology and philosophy. He tried to investigate the mind by studying its concious content and more specifically the elements of sensation, such as intensity, duration and locality. His preferred method was that of *"introspection"*, in which an individual describes his sensations and feelings in discrete, technical terms. Wundt's laboratory became the center of psychological activities. Students came to him from all over the world to investigate problems related to visual perception, hearing, touch and taste, reaction time, word associations and so on.

Diversification of psychology

Unity in psychology was short-lived and existed perhaps only in the early days at Wundt's laboratory. Other psychological schools were soon to follow which emphasized different methods for studying the mind.

Certain psychological schools and systems which evolved around the turn of the century differed not only in methodology, but about the purpose of psychology itself.

There were other applied systems of psychology which contributed to its great diversification. Applied areas such as conditioning, psychoanalysis and mental testing have provided, perhaps as by-products, many psychological theories. In some areas, the theories may have overshadowed experimental verification. Some psychologists feel that their science has been *"oversold to an overwilling public."*

RESEARCH METHODS IN PSYCHOLOGY

The fundamental aim of research in psychology is to discover and understand the nature, functions and phenomena of behaviour and mental experience. Research in psychology, as in any other science, always begins with a question that needs answering; provided that it relates to behaviour or mental experience and is an empirical question that can be tackled by collecting objective evidence, it is a legitimate problem for psychological research. What follows is a brief outline of the main research methods used in psychology.

Case Studies

A **case study is** a relatively primitive research method. In psychology, it involves a detail investigation of a single individual, or occasionally a single social organization. The data reported in *case studies* may be derived from interviews, diaries, case histories, medical records, questionnaires and other psychometric tests or direct observations of behaviour. The findings of case studies can be interesting and valuable, but they often suffer from problems of generalization because individual's response to a particular treatment is not necessarily the same as another's. The accumulation of evidence from a number of case studies, especially if they are reported by independent investigations, can sometimes mitigate this problem.

Naturalistic observations

Naturalistic observations, are widely used in ethological research and less commonly, in certain areas of developmental and social psychology. They involve careful observations and recordings of the behaviour of animals or people in their natural habitats. *Naturalistic observations* are generally non-interactive; in this, the investigator tries to avoid influencing the behaviour that is being observed. It yields important findings about everyday behaviour in natural environments, and it can sometimes serve as a useful corrective to the findings of artificial laboratory studies.

Survey research

Survey research is useful for investigating psychological phenomena in specific sections of a population or in different populations. It is used, in particular, to answer questions about the incidence, prevalence and distribution of mental disorders, behaviour patterns, attitudes, opinions, beliefs and personality characteristics. The most common sources of data in survey research are *interviews* and *questionnaires*. To ensure that the individuals studies are truly representative of the population groups to which they belong, survey researchers use sophisticated methods of sampling. The ideal method of sampling, from a theoretical point of view, is simple random sampling, in which every member of population has an equal chance of inclusion. In practice, simple random sampling is seldom used because of the difficulty in compiling a sampling frame and the further problem of persuading all of the selected subjects to participate in the survey. As a consequence, the most common sampling technique in psychological survey research and also in market research and opinion polling, is quota sampling. This involves selecting individuals more or less arbitrarily to fill predetermined quotas, matching the proportions in the population at large according to age, sex, social class or whatever criteria are thought to be important for research.

Quasi-experiments and correlational studies

Quasi-experiments resemble controlled experiments. They are designed to answer questions about cause and effect, but they lack the full control of conjectured causes and extraneous variables that is characteristic of controlled experiments. Correlational research focuses on non-causal questions about the relationship between variables—intelligence and creativity, introversion and self-esteem, gender and verbal ability and so on. Both of these research methods focus on the relationship between two or more factors over which the investigator has imperfect or non-existent control.

Neither of these research methods can conclusively settle questions about cause and effect, but valuable information about the relationship between variables can often be obtained, and it is sometimes reasonable to draw tentative inferences about probable causal and effects from quasi-experiments.

Experimental method

In **experimental method,** observations take place under controlled conditions. Every experiment is an attempt to discover relationships among certain conditions or events that can change. The *essence of experimental method* is:
1. The experimenter changes or varies the events which are hypothesized to have an effect on the observation.
2. He keeps other conditions constant.
3. He looks for an effect of the change or variation on the system under observation.

Thus, an experimental method aims at establishing cause-effect relationship.

Some important concepts used in experimental method are:

Subject

The man or animal on which the experiment is performed is called the **subject.**

Experimenter

The person who conducts experiment is called **experimenter.**

Variables

A **variable** is an event or condition which can have different values. Variables are of two types:
(a) Independent variables
(b) Dependent variables

Independent variables

These are conditions set or selected by an experimenter to see whether they would have an effect on behaviour. This factor is increased, decreased or withdrawn by the experimenter, e.g., stimulus presented, a drug administered, a new method of training business managers and so on.

Dependent variables

The effect of independent variable is called as the dependent variable or changes that comes about as a result of the changes in the independent variable is called as the dependent variable. Dependent variable is the behaviour of the person and animal in the experiment, it might be the response of the person to the stimulus, a change in behaviour after administration of the drug.

In doing experiments, hypotheses are formulated about the effect of one thing on another, the independent variable is one expected to produce changes in the dependent variable.

Controls

In an experiment, it is important that only the specified independent variables be allowed to change. Factors other than the independent variable which might affect the dependent variable must be held constant.

In an experiment we must control conditions, which would give misleading results. Scientists must be very careful to control their experiments adequately. This is often difficult in psychology

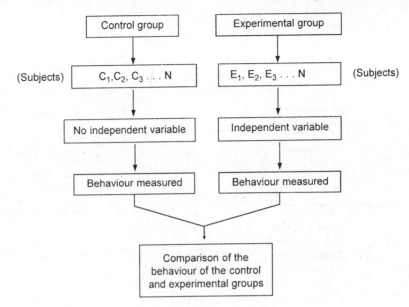

Fig. 1.1 Control group design

because so many factors can influence the behaviour that is being studied. In interpreting experiments, it is important to look for uncontrolled factors which might have affected the results.

There are two kinds of variables which needs to be controlled:

(a) Conditions

(b) Characteristics of the group

Conditions

One has to control the conditions under which experiments are being performed.

Characteristics of the group

The characteristics of the group which are relevant has also to be controlled. The characteristics that are relevant in most psychological experiments on human beings are intelligence, age, sex and personality of the subject.

1. **Control group design:** In this design, the experimenter selects two similiar groups called as the *Experimental group* and the *control group.* In the experimental group Indenpendent variable, is introduced, there is deliberate manipulation of the Independent variable. In the control group the behaviour is observed under normal conditions, no deliber-

ate manipulation of the variable is seen. When a control group design is used, the groups should be equivalent in every way except for the independent variable. This type of design study large group of subjects.

2. **A–B–A Within—Subject Experimental design:** To make sure that the independent variable produced the change in the behaviour, it is often a good idea to see what happens when the independent variable is removed after it has been introduced. The behaviour should go back to *baseline* levels if the independent variable did, in fact, produced the observed changes. This is called an A–B–A within—subjects experimental design. The first 'A' is the baseline condition without the independent variable and the last 'A' refers to the final test of the behaviour without the independent variable. This design is a good one to use when the independent variable does not have a long lasting effect.

Limitations of the experimental method

1. This method *cannot* always be used, especially if the experiment might be dangerous for the subjects.

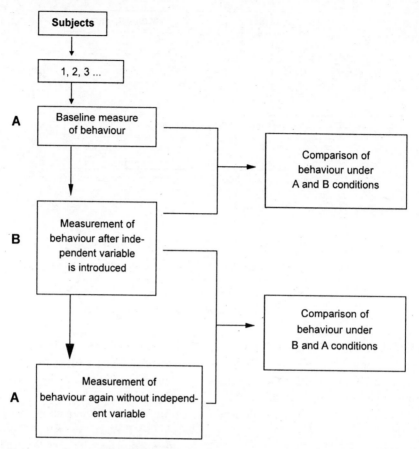

Fig. 1.2 A-B-A within subject experimental design

2. The method is restricted in its application. The conclusions derived from an experiment may be limited to the artificial experimental situation—they may not apply to "*natural*" situations or even to other experimental situation.

3. The method sometimes interferes with the very thing it is trying to measure.

Systematic observation

In this method, researchers do not willfully manipulate the independent variable. Instead, they capitalize on variations that occur naturally. Using this method, the psychologist makes the most *systematic* study of the behaviour that occurs naturally. Many facts of human as well as animal behaviour are learned in this fashion. After making a number of observations, the psychologist can, using certain rules of logic, try to infer the causes of the behaviour being studied.

This method is definitely *not* a substitute for an experimental method but is often applicable where experimentation is impossible. This method can be applied with great ease in studies of public opinion, the effects of advertisement and other mass communication systems on consumer preferences and many other social problems and even in determining the role of such factors as hereditary and environment. For instance, using questionnaires, surveys and interviews, psychologists might study the changes in behaviour patterns of men and women caused by the mass communication. The method of systematic observation tells us what people do and how they differ in their behaviour. The psychologist who uses the method of systematic observation may also seek to find out what causes the observed behaviour, so that he can answer questions about why things happen.

Suppose, for instance, that a psychologist wants to find the general cause of the severe behaviour disorder known as *schizophrenia*. Symptoms of schizophrenia include bizarre or strange patterns of thought and behaviour, inappropriate emotional responses and perhaps hallucinations and delusions. Suppose psychologists who are studying schizophrenia hypothesize that its cause is to be found in the way children are reared by their parents. Using the method of systematic observation, the researchers will probably try to test this hypotheses by comparing the ways in which schizophrenic and normal people were reared. To do this, they will match normal and schizophrenic groups on as many factors—such as age, sex, socioeconomic status, years of schooling, intelligence and so on. Then they look for differences in the rearing practices used by the parents of the *"normals"*. Using precisely this type of strategy, psychologists have found differences; but these differences do not, by themselves, establish causation. All that has been established so far is that differences in rearing go along with schizophrenia. Other factors and their interaction with rearing may be the cause.

Limitations of systematic observation

1. Full control over independent variable is not possible as in the case with the experimental method. Experimenter cannot manipulate the independent variable as per his desires.
2. There is greater possibility of the impact of extraneous variables. If this occurs results would be greatly effected.
3. It tells us what is happening but not why or how a certain type of behaviour occurs. It tells us nothing about cause-effect relationship.

Clinical method

The clinical method is ordinarily used only when people come to psychologists with personal problems. For example, little child refuses to eat, cries all the night and generally makes life miserable for his parents. Problems like these and other kinds too bring people to the clinical psychologist.

The psychologist may administer tests of various kinds—intelligence tests, interest tests, tests of emotional maturity, personality tests and other tests. From these tests and from the biographical information, the psychologist will try to diagnose the problem and treat, or remedy, the difficulty. The tests, the diagnosis and the remedy will differ from case to case. As a method, it combines features of clinical observation, experiment and systematic observation.

Limitations of clinical method

1. Clinical observation does not often provide much scientific information.
2. It is usually too subjective, casual, uncontrolled and lacking in precise measurement.
3. In clinical method, what appear to be cause and effect in one case may not be in another.
4. Even in a single case, it is extremely difficult to sort out the significant causal factors with certainty.

VARIOUS SUB-FIELDS OF PSYCHOLOGY

Psychologists hold an almost endless and pretty varied variety of jobs. Many of them teach in colleges or universities. Some work in hospitals, some in schools, some in penal systems and some psychologists are employed in industry. According to American Psychological Association there are more than 40 subdivisions of psychology. Some of the most commonly known sub-fields are as follows :

Clinical psychology

This is one of the largest subfields of Psychology. **A clinical psychologist** is one who has received specialized training in causation of abnormal behaviour, its diagnosis and often its treatment by psychotherapeutic methods used in the correction of abnormal behaviour.

Clinical Psychologist	Psychiatrist
1. A clinical Psychologist holds a Ph.D. or M.A. degree.	1. A psychiatrist holds a M.D. degree.
2. The Ph.D. clinical Psychologist has taken 4 or 5 years of Post-graduate work in psychology department; the M.A. clinical psychologist has about 2 years of postgraduate work.	2. The psychiatrist has gone to medical school and then completed 3 or 4 years of residency training in psychiatry.
3. The clinical psychologist, who does not have medical training, cannot prescribe drugs to treat behaviour disorders.	3. The psychiatrist prescribe durgs to treat behaviour disorders.

Fig 1.3 Some of the differences between clinical Psychologist and Psychiatrist

- Both provide psychotherapy.
- Both use various techniques to relieve the symptoms of psychological disorders and to help people understand the reasons for their problems.

Fig 1.4 Some similarities between clinical Psychologist and Psychiatrist

They are *"doctors"* who diagnose psychological disorders and treat them by means of psychotherapy. Clinical psychologists are basically attached to mental hospitals or are associated with the department of psychiatry in general hospitals. They also work in close collaboration with neurologists, paediatricians etc. Many of them are attached to schools and colleges.

In clinical psychology, the findings of basic and applied research into the classification, aetiology, diagnosis, treatment and prevention of mental disorders are put to use in an effort to deal with these problems more effectively.

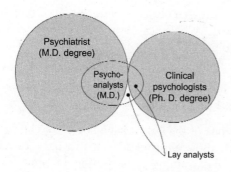

Fig 1.5 Relationships among psychiatrist, clinical psychologists and psychoanalysts

Psychoanalyst

A **psychoanalyst** is a person who uses the particular psychotherapeutic techniques which originated with **Sigmund Freud** and his followers. Anyone who has had the special training required to use these techniques can be a psychoanalyst. Psychoanalysts without M.D. degrees are known as **"Lay analysts"**.

Counselling psychology

It overlaps to a great extent with clinical psychology. The work of counselling psychologist is quite similar to that of the clinical psychologist. **Counselling psychologist** work with individuals whose problems are less serious than those who see a clinical psychologist or a psychiatrist.

Counselling helps individuals with vocational and academic problems; counselling psychologist may use psychotherapy in an attempt to help with these kind of problems. In their practice, counselling psychologist may make extensive use of tests to measure aptitudes, interests and personality characteristics.

These are wide varieties of counselling. Some of them are Vocational educational counselling,

Marriage counselling, Employee counselling, Rehabilitation counselling etc.

Experimental psychology

It is one of the fundamental subfields of psychology. Fundamental because it carries on research and experimental work in many basic aspects of behaviour. These psychologists try to understand the fundamental causes of behaviour. The **experimental psychologist** studies how behaviour is modified and how people retain these modifications, the processing of information in thinking, how human sensory systems work to allow people to experience what is going on around them and factors that urge them on and give direction to behaviour.

The distinguishing characteristics of experimental psychology is that it uses the experimental method as the main tool of investigation.

Experimental psychology is distinguished from other subfields by what it studies—the fundamental processes of learning, memory, thinking, sensation, perception, motivation and emotion.

Physiological psychology

Physiological psychologist are concerned with the relationship of the brain and other biological activity to behaviour. They look for causal events in the organism's physiology, especially the nervous system and its interaction with glands that secrete hormones. Physiological psychologists mostly study animals because physiological experiments cannot ethically be performed with humans.

School and educational psychology

These are two interrelated subfields of psychology. **Educational psychologists** are especially concerned with increasing the efficiency of learning in school by applying their psychological knowledge about learning and motivation to the curriculum.

They are more concerned with general psychological principles underlying the entire process of education. The main question that educational psychology tries to answer are, when to teach, what to teach and how to teach. Educational psychology researches into problems of learning, adjustment and behaviour among school-children is applied in an effort to provide practical help to teachers, parents and children with learning or behaviour problems.

Counselling psychologists who are involved in the testing and guidance of individual students are usually called **school psychologists.** They are more concerned with the problems of individual students than with the general principles of education. Their main task is to help students with various problems to reach full adjustment to the school or college situation. School psychologist's job consists of diagnosing learning difficulties and trying to remedy them. Using tests and information gained from consultations with the student and his or her parents, the school psychologist tries to pinpoint the problem and suggest action to correct it.

Industrial psychology

The application of psychology in industrial and business fields started with the use of psychological tests for selection of the right worker for the right job. **Industrial psychology** can be divided into two most important subdivisions; *Personnel psychology* and *Engineering psychology*.

Industrial psychology is oriented towards fitting the worker to the job, through selection, classification, training and incentives. Industrial psychologists seek to select the right man for right job, whereas the engineering psychologist is oriented chiefly towards fitting the job to the worker by designing appropriate procedures, equipment and work environment.

Organizational psychology

It is a growing subfield of psychology. It began with the work of **F.W. Taylor** and **Frank**

Gilbreth. It is concerned with not only industrial organizations but with any organization where human beings work. Some of the topics covered under organizational psychology includes stress, communication, organizational develop- ment, organizational decision making etc. In **organizational psychology,** research into the well-being and efficiency of people at work and into organizational behaviour is applied to the problems arising in those settings.

Developmental psychology

The main objective of **developmental psychology** is to investigate the changes in human behaviour that accompany changes in age. It is study of human organism from the time of conception to death. Developmental psychologists try to understand complex behaviours by studying their beginnings and the orderly ways in which they change with time.

Developmental psychology has both research and applied aspects. In its effort to obtain a meaningful picture of human development, through its various stages of growth, such as infancy, childhood, adolesence, youth, adulthood and old age, developmental psychology seeks to discover sequential changes in human personality by utilizing specialized techniques. Child psychology is a part of developmental psychology.

Social psychology

Social psychology focuses on the nature of social interaction. Social psychology attempts to determine the manner in which the behaviour of one individual is influenced by other people. This field has particularly benefited from contributions by sociologists. While the research endeavours of people from both disciplines often overlap, the focus of social psychology is typically upon the individual, while the sociologist is primarily concerned with societal institutions.

Social psychology studies the impact of group life on various aspects of individual's behaviour. Some of the major topics which social psychology

studies are interpersonal attraction, social perception, social communication, group attitudes, public opinion, sexual behaviour, social influence, group decision making etc.

Community psychology

Community psychologists apply psychological principles, ideas and points of view that help individuals to solve the social problems and also help them to adapt to their work and living groups.

Some community psychologists are essentially clinical psychologists. They set up programs to reach people in the community who happen to have behaviour problems, or are likely to develop them and who are not presently being served by traditional psychotherapeutic methods. These psychologists are a part of the community mental-health movement. Other community psychologists are more concerned with bringing ideas from the behavioural sciences to bear on community problems. We might call these the *"social-problem community psychologists"*.

Community psychologists often work to encourage certain groups to participate in community decisions, to provide psychological information about effective and health promoting child-rearing practices, or to advise school systems about how to make their curricula meet the needs of community members. To accomplish their aims, social-problem community psychologists sometimes focus on changing community organizations and institutions to help remove the sources of community problems.

RELATED DISCIPLINES AND PRACTICES

It is important to distinguish psychology from a few related practices and professions with which it is often confused.

Psychiatry

As its name suggests, **psychiatry** is a branch of medicine concerned with mental disorders—

their classification, aetiology, diagnosis, treatment and prevention. Anyone intending to qualify as a psychiatrist must first undergo a full medical training and then specialize in psychiatry, which is simply a medical specialization among many others, including cardiology, dermatology, and gynaecology.

Psychology, in contrast, is not a medical specialization and psychologists are not medically trained. Furthermore, most of psychology is concerned with normal behaviour and mental life rather than with mental disorders. A small part of academic psychology is, however, concerned with mental disorders and one of the professions of psychology, clinical psychology involves the treatment of mentally disordered patients. Psychiatrist tend to favour more medically oriented interpretations of mental disorders and more physical forms of treatment than do most clinical psychologists because of their different backgrounds and training.

Psychoanalysis

Psychoanalysis is a theory of mental structure and function and a method of psychotherapy based on the writings of **Sigmund Freud** and his followers. As a theory, psychoanalysis focuses primarily on unconscious mental processes and the various defence mechanisms that people use to repress them. As a therapeutic method, psychoanalysis involves the client in three or more 50-minute sessions per week for several years. During the analytic sessions a number of specialized techniques are used to help the client uncover the repressed thoughts and feelings, to understand why they were repressed and also to accept them conciously.

Psychoanalysts are not necessarily trained in psychology or psychiatry; their training involves undergoing psychoanalysis themselves. Conversely, it is also true to say that most psychologists and psychiatrists have no formal qualifications in psychoanalysis; but many of them are influenced to varying degrees by psychoanalytic ideas and approaches. Most—though by no means all psychologists, on the other hand, hold attitudes towards psychoanalysis ranging from indifference to open hostility.

Philosophy

Many of the problems that non-psychologists assume to fall within the scope of psychology are really philosophical problems. These are questions that must be tackled by rational argument rather than by experiments or observations of behaviour.

Although psychology was once a branch of philosophy called **"mental philosophy"**, the psychological offspring has grown up to be quite distinct in its subject matter from its distinguished philosophical parent. Psychology, in contrast to philosophy, is devoted to empirical questions, that is, questions that can, in principle atleast, be decided by observations of real world facts and events.

The most obvious example is the **mind-body problem**. This problem relates to the puzzling relationship and apparent interaction between mental experiences and the physical world. How can mental experiences such as desires, which are entirely immaterial, produce physical effects like bodily movements—in other words, how can a thought move a muscle? And how can physical injuries to our bodies produce the non-physical mental experiences we call pains? These are irreducibly philosophical questions, inspite of their superficial resemblance to psychological problems, because they could not be solved, even in principle, by empirical investigations of any kind, or atleast that is what most philosophers and psychologists believe.

Factual questions about moral attitudes and behaviour, and how they develop in children, are legitimate topics for psychological research, but questions about how people ought to behave belong to the field of ethics within the discipline of philosophy. It goes almost without saying that psychologists ought to be and generally are, concerned about moral issues that arise in psychological research and practice. ■ ■

CHAPTER 2

The Human Mind and Schools of Psychology

CONCEPT OF MIND
— Views of greek philosophers
— View of the western philosophers
— Views of eastern cultures
— Views of french philosophers

MIND
— Mind-body problem from the standpoint of psychologists
— Mind-body problem from the standpoint of natural science

SCHOOLS OF PSYCHOLOGY
— Structuralism
— Functionalism
— Gestalt psychology
— Behaviourism
— Psychoanalysis

MODERN VIEW POINTS ABOUT PSYCHOLOGY
— Cognitive psychology
— Humanistic psychology
— Behavioural psychology
— Biological psychology
— Social psychology
— Psychoanalytic psychology

The Human Mind and Schools of Psychology

CONCEPT OF MIND

The human mind is customarily viewed as having the capacity to perform such mental functions as thinking, reasoning, planning and decision-making; and of possessing the property of consciousness, as well as producing emotional responses to stimuli.

"The mind is a mental system consisting of a grouping of brain cells, which have the special capability of being able to directly generate thought messages."

Views of greek philosophers

In ancient times, it was commonly believed that the universe consisted only of space and a vast magnitude of atoms in ceaseless motion that interact with one another. A greek philosopher, *Democrites*, who lived around 400 B.C., reasoned that the mind is only a specific grouping of atoms, which interact with each other and with the environment to produce the person's behaviour, and exists only as long as the person is alive.

On the other hand, the ancient greek philosopher *Plato,* who lived during the same time period, proposed that the mind is non-physical and exists independently of the body, before the birth of the person and after the person's death. He believed that the mind not only interacts with the physical world but has access to the pure concepts of a second non-physical world.

Plato viewed the *human psyche* to be comprised of three parts :
*   The element of reason.
*   A spirited or emotional, element.

*   The element of bodily needs, appetites and desires.

He considered the proper relationship between these elements to be one in which the element and the irrational element of desires and appetites.

Aristotle, who also was a renown ancient Greek philosopher and a student of Plato held a belief regarding the mind somewhere between the two. He believed the mind to be a form of the body and not separate from it. However, he regarded the mental properties exhibited by the mind to be a distinct class of properties different from the physical properties of the body.

Another view of mind was held by the Stoic school of philosophy, which became popular around the time the Roman empire flourished. These philosophers believed the living creatures were created from ordinary matter by the infusion of *"pneumata,"* which is derived from the greek word, meaning *"breath"* and translated into the latin word meaning *"spirit".* The observation that life begins with breathing and ceases when breath leaves the body probably gave rise to the Stoic theory. The human spirit, according to this theory, leaves the body at death and rejoins the universal spirit from whence it came. The immortal soul doctrine of various religions is another form of the Stoic theory.

View of the western philosophers

The various kinds of philosophically opposing views of the mind held by the ancient western philosophers are :
*   That it is purely a material, physical substance.

- That it is part of the body, but has properties unlike those of the body.
- That it is non-physical and distinct from the body and continues to exist after death.

Views of eastern cultures

The ancient eastern cultures also formulated view about the human mind and psyche. According to the scriptures of the philosophic religion of Hinduism called the Vedas, the human psyche is comprised of the elements of "Atman", "Manas", "Vijana", and "Buddi".

Atman is the ultimate, true self of a person. It is the essence, or spirit, of an individual, the person's essential core of being, the spark of God within all of us which gives us life. Atman is the observer of all that is happening to a person; all the ideas, all the thoughts and all that is perceived by the person. Atman is seen as being eternal, imperishable, indestructible and self-existent, neither being born nor capable of dying.

Manas is the element whose function is to focus attention on specific stimuli being perceived by the senses. Out of the multitude of stimuli constantly impinging upon the senses, Manas gathers in and directs the attention of the senses to be actually perceived. The selected stimuli are transformed into a particular sensation, image, or sound, while the others are discarded. Manas is the necessary mental faculty required for sense perception. For instance, it is what takes the perceived visual and audible stimuli and turns them into the vision and sound of a bird singing.

Vijana's function is to take the selected perception that Manas has presented to it and make that perception into an actual experience, so that the sight and sound of a bird singing is not just sound and sight, but is something we experience, feel and store in memory and later can recall. Vijana is that which holds together the accumulation of all our experiences into a coherent whole that we consider to be ourselves, the "*I am*" with whom we identify ourselves.

Buddi's function is to reflect upon and evaluate the stored data gained from experience (Vijana) and to make decisions. Buddi gives meaning to that which we have perceived and experienced. It is the awareness or consciousness of oneself and that his or her existence is distinct from other beings and from the environment. In the process of making a choice or decision, Buddi forms judgements by evaluating and discriminating from among all the knowledge and experiences the individual has accumulated.

Views of french philosophers

The seventeenth century French philosopher and mathematician, Rene Descartes considered man to be comprised of two entirely different types of substances:

1. A mental substance.
2. A physical substance

The human brain falls into Descartes' definition of a physical substance, to the extent that it is a tangible substance that responds mechanically to stimuli. The mind corresponds to Descartes' definition of a mental substance, which he considered to be a spiritual, immaterial thinking substance, having the capacity for thought, consciousness and free will.

There were, however, many who disagreed with Descartes that the mind is immaterial, considering it to be part of the brain; and there were others who denied its spirituality, or that it has free will. And even today there are many contrary views held as to the nature of the mind.

Till now, we have seen the various views of different philosophers on the concept of mind. Now, we will be discussing the concept of mind as understood by the psychologist and natural sciences.

MIND

Until a psychology with a scientific orientation was created, psychological inquiry and thinking were concerned with the mind, its substantiality, spirituality and mortality. The mere fact of talking about a mind serves to distinguish it from the body to which it is bound. Thus the theory of mind raises the mind-body problem. Investigation of the mind and its relation to the body was the special task of rational or metaphysical psychology, which was and is a branch of philosophy.

About the middle of the nineteenth century, psychology was detached from philosophy and turned to science and its methods, it considered its subject to be those psychic processes whose totality Wilhelm Wundt sought to embrace in his actualistic concept of mind. The term coined by F.A. Lange, *"Psychology without a soul"*, is on the whole correct for modern scientific psychology. Nevertheless, the question concerning the real essence of the problem of mind persists.

On the whole psychology in so far as it considers itself a *"pure"*, empirical science, cannot decide the problem of mind.

Mind-body problem from the standpoint of psychologists

The *mind-body problem* is rarely defined in detail in contemporary psychology. Nevertheless it is a genuine problem and its existence can be demonstrated.

It can be considered on the basis of the principle of conflict or identity or alternatively by a combination of these two principles.

If it is approached from the principle of conflict (i.e., *dualistically*), the theory of interaction can be used to explain the functional relationship between mental and somatic processes: physiological processes *"cause"* mental correlates and vice versa. Psychosomatic and psychopharmacology are based on this principle; traumatic experiences lead to somatic disorders of a functional and organic nature. Drugs have a specific influence on the mental state.

From the standpoint of the identity principle in contemporary psychology only the physiological-materialistic concepts remain relevant: mental phenomena are derivatives of processes in the muscles, nerves and brain. For the devel-

opment of psychology these assumptions have the advantage that they clearly emphasize the importance of the body as distinct from the metaphysical approach. The solution to the mind-body problem indicated by most authors under the heading of *"identity"* are located in accordance with the distinction made here, *"substantially and functionally"* between the two extreme solutions described above and therefore combine the two principles.

Spinoza defines the mind and body as two attributes, he introduces dualism in the sense of a bilateral theory. **Leibniz's concept of parallelism** can be considered in the same light; he refers to unity in the substance and duality in the function.

Methodical dualism would probably be acceptable as a description of the attitude to the mind-body problem in contemporary psychology: every psychologically relevant process or state must be described, analyzed and interpreted through its physical (neuro-physiological) and psychological (experiential) coordinates.

Mind-body problem from the standpoint of natural science

All over conscious processes and states are dependent on the brain, as is demonstrated by the following facts:

(a) If the brain becomes unable to function as a result of chemical or mechanical influences (narcosis, injury), all psychological activity ceases.

(b) Changes in our brain activity due to the administration of certain substances (alcohol, opium morphine, LSD, etc.) lead to changes in our conscious experience.

(c) Failure of specific areas of the brain results in the breakdown of certain psychological functions. (aphasia, agnosia, alexia, etc.)

(d) There is a phylogenetic and ontogenetic parallel between the development of the brain and mental development. It follows that all forms of conscious experience are based on specific brain processes; brain processes form the indispensable prerequisite for psychological activity.

The mind-body problem can be reduced to two questions: "What happens in the brain when we experience something?" and "What is the causal relationship between psychological and cerebral process?"

The first question can in principle be answered reliably during all conscious experience an enormous number of electrical and chemical processes takes place in the ganglionic cells and fibres of the cerebral cortex (nervous system). The resulting *"excitation constellations"* must be *"specific"*, i.e., a separate excitation constellation corresponds to each individual content of our conscious experience; there must therefore be atleast as many excitation constellations as there are contents of experience.

The answer to the second question is dependent in large measures on the importance attached to the *"difference in nature"* between the two processes; it consists of the fact that the psychological processes are non-physical (they are not made up of atoms and molecules and are largely independent of space and time), while the cerebral processes belong to the organic-material sphere.

The old mind-body theories overlooked this distinction and held that there could be an interaction between physical and mental processes or that they could be two aspects of the same process.

New theories have tried to explain the dependence of psychological processes on cerebral activity and the difference in nature between them by the assumption that conscious experience is an effect of the brain processes but cannot itself act on the latter (*"theory of the ultimate effect,"* Rohracher, 1967).

The natural-scientific approach to the mind-body problem is best reflected in the *"theory of the ultimate effect"*, which fully recognizes the special character of psychological processes—immateriality considerable independence of space and time—as well as the absolute dependence of the psychological processes on the brain. For natural-scientific psychology, the conscious experiences are biological phenomena; they help to maintain life and individuality (e.g. the vital and social drives) as well as cultural progress. The mental processes can be considered as the highest expression of natural developmental and as the ultimate effect of the organic process as a transcendental expression of the material process in immaterial subjective experience. Advantage of this theory lies in the fact that it avoids the logical difficulties inherent in the assumption of a *"feedback"* effect of psychological processes on physical activity.

SCHOOLS OF PSYCHOLOGY

In the first decade of the twentieth century, psychologists came to hold quite different views about the nature of mind and the best ways to study it. About the same time, strong differences of opinion about what psychology should study and how it should study, and should psychology be the study of mind or behaviour; or should both mind and behaviour be included?

Groups of like—minded psychologists, which formed around influential teachers argued for one viewpoint or another. Schools of thought formed around these influential psychologists as their students adopted their ideas. These schools of thought are known as the *schools of psychology;* they set the direction for research on mind and behaviour in the early years of this century. Time has tended to blunt the old arguments somewhat and the early schools have largely passed into history.

Structuralism

Structuralism became the most commonly held view of the early 1900's. It developed primarily out of the works of the German philosophy, professor Wilhelm Wundt, who was formally trained in medicine and physiology and the American philosopher and psychologist William James. It was established at cornell university in the United States by one of Wundt's students, Edward B. Titchener.

Structuralists were mainly concerned with analyzing and explaining conscious human experiences, particularly feelings and sensations.

They were called *"structuralists"* because they attempted to understand human experience by breaking it down into its simplest components or structures. The goal of the structuralists was to find the units or elements which makes up the mind. They thought that as in chemistry, a first step in the study of the mind should be a description of the basic or elementary, units of sensation, image and emotion which compose it. The main method used by the structuralists to discover these elementary units of mind was *"introspection"*.

Subjects were trained to report as objectively as possible; what they experienced in connection with a certain stimulus, disregarding the meanings they had come to associate with the stimulus. For example, a subject might be presented with a coloured light, a tone, or an odour and asked to describe it as minutely as possible. These experiments using introspection have given us a great deal of information about the kinds of sensations people have.

The purpose and significance of these experiments:
Wundt attempted by experimentation to discover the basic elements comprising consciousness. He found two such elements to be *"perception"* and *"apperception."* Perception is the mental process of bringing sensations into the consciousness of a person. Apperception is the mental process of attending to and interpreting the perceived sensations.

Wundt investigated the higher mental process of thinking, memory and cognition, which all involve language. One interesting discovery he made was that the fundamental basic unit of thought is not a word, or other linguistic element, but a *"general impression"* that is independent of words. According to Wundt, in the thought process there is first a general impression. This process of transformation of impressions into words occurs when listening to someone else speak, as well as when a person is formulating in his or her own mind and also in thoughts when he or she is about to speak. Thus, the origin of thoughts are impressions which become verbalized.

Structuralism was also criticised for many things which include:
At times, the act of introspection may change the experience drastically. For example: Introspection regarding anger; if the state is attended to, it tends quickly to disintegrate and may even disappear completely. Thus, the measuring technique interferes with experience, as it does with electrons for the physicist.

Psychologists at different laboratories were not getting comparable results; rather scientists in one laboratory asserted things that contradicted the results of scientists elsewhere. There was also growing concern for the data, which were not accessible to introspection.

Functionalism

Functionalism as a school of psychology started in university of Chicago out of the writings of **John R. Angell**. It was developed by **Harvey Carr** and **Robert S. Woodsworth**.

Functionalism is the philosophical doctrine of James Angell who considers mental phenomena in their dynamic unity as a system of functions (geared to adapting the organism to its environment) for the satisfaction of needs that are biological in origin. Functionalists studied *"what mind and behaviour do"* rather than *"what they are composed of."* Specifically, they were interested in the fact that mind and behaviour are adaptive; they enable an individual to adjust to a changing environment. Instead of limiting themselves to the description and analysis of mind, the functionalists did experiments on the ways in which learning, memory, problem solving and motivation help people and animals adapt to their environments.

According to *James Angell,* the basic principles of functionalism are as follows:

- Functional psychology is the study of mental operations and not mental structures. (For example, the mind remembers; it does not contain a memory).
- Mental processes are not studied as isolated and independent events but as part of the biological activity of the organism. These processes are aspects of the organism's adaptation to the environment and are a product of its evolutionary history. The fact that we are conscious implies that consciousness has adaptive value for our species.
- Functional psychology studies the relation between the environment. There is no meaningful distinction between mind and body; they are part of the same entity.

Functionalism emphasized learning, mental testing and other utilitarian subject matters. Functionalism concerned more with functional interrelationships of variables than with theoretical super structures; accepting both introspective and behaviour data but utilizing mainly the latter, stressing adaptive behaviour and purposive motivated activity.

If this approach is applied to social life, this appears as an organism comprehended through the relationship existing between organs and their functions.

Gestalt psychology

Gestalt psychology was developed into a school of psychology in Germany about 1912 by **Max Wertheimer** and his colleagues **Kurt Koffka** and **Wolfgang Köhler**. It is mainly concerned with how human beings perceive things. The word *"Gestalt"* is german and it means *"form", "shape", "configuration"* or *"pattern of something"*. Gestalt, as used in psychology, denotes that the objects are perceived in the context of their overall form or configuration, not as the sum of their individual elements. For instance, a square is composed of four separate and equal lines connected together at right angles. However, if a person was asked what he sees, he would respond that he sees a square, the whole configuration, not for individual lines. Gestalt psychologists believed that just as a person perceives in terms of the whole object rather than its parts, that human behaviour should be studied as a pattern, not as separate incidents of stimulus and response.

The gestalt psychologists observed that the mind imposes its own interpretation on the sensations it perceives, independent of the stimuli themselves. A good example of this is optical illusion. Two lines of equal length may be drawn in a certain way against a particular background, and made to appear to be unequal. Such optical illusions obviously are not inherent properties of the objects themselves. Thus, it can be concluded that the illusions must be caused by one's mental processes and that the brain does not just passively react to stimuli.

Studies made by gestalt psychologists also showed that the mind can focus attention on one thing and can perceive only one thing or one sensation at a time. They also showed that the mind tends to simplify complex sensual information by grouping together those that have similar characteristics.

For example, if there are seven pieces of fruit in a bowl, of which three are apples and four are oranges, the mind will group the apples together and the oranges together. So, if asked what is in the bowl, one would answer, "three apples and four oranges," not seven pieces of fruit. Although its principles and ideas are still utilized in the studies of perception, and behaviour, gestalt psychology, which began as a revolt against "structuralism," no longer exists today as a separate school.

Behaviourism

It is a radical form of objective psychology in

which all references to introspection and consciousness are rejected in favour of a discussion of psychologically relevant events primarily in terms of stimulus and response. This radical form was first proposed in America by **John B. Watson** in a paper entitled "Psychology as the behaviourist views it." Watson rejected mind as the subject of psychology and insisted that psychology be restricted to the study of behaviour; the observable (or potentially observable) activities of people and animals.

In addition to its focus on behaviour as the proper subject matter of psychology, behaviourism had three important characteristics:

- First was an emphasis on conditioned responses as the elements, or building blocks, of behaviour. Behaviourism, in fact, was somewhat like the structuralism because it maintained that complex processes are compounds of more elementary ones. Its elements however, were conditioned responses rather than sensations, images or emotions. The conditioned responses can be described loosely as a relatively simple learned response to a stimulus. Watson argued that complex human and animal behaviour is made up almost entirely of conditioned responses.
- Second closely related characteristic of behaviourism was its emphasis on learned, rather than unlearned behaviour. It denied the existence of inborn, or innate behavioural tendencies.
- Third characteristic of behaviourism was its focus on animal behaviour. Watson held that there are no essential differences between human and animal behaviour and that we can learn much about our own behaviour from the study of what animals do.

Watsonian behaviourism

The central tenet of behaviourism is, of course, the objectivity of the data to be accepted by science. The facts of observation are to be limited to those of any other science: observable events that can be recorded by an experimenter, often with the aid of precision instruments. The events to be included are, first of all, the antecedent stimuli, and then the consequent responses of muscles and glands. Muscles and glands are the only effectors; there is no additional "mental activity." The behaviourist was also interested in the products of behaviour, which can also be objectively measured. Verbal responses, although produced by muscular movements, are really products of movement, quite as much as words typed on a page or check-marks on a psychological test. This interest in the products of behaviour saved behaviourism from becoming a "muscle-twitch" psychology—an unfavourable description mentioned by Watson in the preface to his psychology from the standpoint of a behaviourist.

The acceptance of verbal responses as behaviour also freed behaviourism from restrictions that would otherwise have been imposed: for instance, it permits the study of dreams, without calling this introspection.

Behaviourism is still very much alive today in psychology. Behaviourism has given birth to the technology of teaching machines, the use of behaviour modification in instructing the mentally retarded and the use of behaviour therapy to treat mental disorders.

Psychoanalysis

The psychoanalytic school was founded in Vienna, Austria, by the psychiatrist **Sigmund Freud.** Contrary to the other schools of psychology, which looked for the external and structural factors to determine the causes of human behaviour, the psychoanalytic school looked for the emotional causes of behaviour, and concerned itself with abnormal behaviour as well as normal.

In the course of his practice with the neurotic patients, Freud developed a theory of behaviour and mind which said that much of what we do and think result from urges, or drives, which seek expression in behaviour and thought. A crucial point about these urges and drives, according to psychoanalytic theory, is that they are hidden from the awareness of the individual; they are, in other words, unconscious. It is the expression of unconscious driver which show up in behaviour and thought.

Freud emphasized that human behaviour is controlled by unconscious forces or behaviour. Human behaviour is largely controlled by only two instincts, namely that of sex and aggression. All human behaviour is caused and expressed because of these two instincts. Psychoanalysis also emphasized that the first six years of life are very important and play a crucial role in the formation of the personality development.

Psychoanalysis received mixed reception. Some welcomed its ideas as revolutionary, others criticised it for being more of an art and less scientific. However, psychoanalytic views, thinking, concepts and explanations still predominate amongst the psychological works.

MODERN VIEW POINTS ABOUT PSYCHOLOGY

Today, except for modern versions of behaviourism and psychoanalysis, the old schools of psychology have disappeared. Some of the points of view about what is important in understanding mental life and behaviour, characterize the present scene; among these are:

Cognitive psychology

Jean Piaget and **Bruner** and **Gagne** have contributed immensely towards the development and our understanding of cognitive psychology. According to them, behaviour and mind are to be understood in terms of the ways in which information from the environment, received through the senses, is processed. **Cognitive psychology** is a branch of psychology that deals with perception, learning and memory, concept formation verbal behaviour and problem solving especially in human beings. Unlike behaviourism, cognitive psychology deals with unobservable mental processes that presumably are composed of particular brain functions.

Although cognitive psychologists now study mental structures and operations, they have not gone back to the introspection methods that were employed by structuralists like Wundt. They still use objective research methods, just as behaviourists do.

Humanistic psychology

Humanistic psychology developed from psychology proper, chiefly from the writings of **Abraham Maslow, Carl Rogers** and **Charlette Bulher.** Humanistic psychology was called as the *"third force"* in psychology by Abraham Maslow. It developed as a reaction to the two dominant schools of thought namely behaviourism and psychoanalysis. According to Maslow both the dominant schools of thought had taken, a very biased view of mankind. Both viewed human behaviour in terms of deterministic and reductionistic principles.

The determination of Freud was characterized in teams of biological principles of instincts, namely the principle of sex and aggressive instinct. Whereas, the determinism of behaviourism was characterized in terms of conditioning principles.

Humanistic psychology believed that human beings are free. They have a *"free choice"* and a *"free will"*. They are not puppets in the forces of nature, environment or instincts. It emphasizes a person's sense of self and each individual's attempts to achieve personal competence and self-esteem.

Humanistic psychology emphasized the

future of human beings. The study of his subjective experiences using phenomenological methods. Humanistic psychology de-emphasized the study of animals. They stressed that no doubt human beings are very much similar to animals but we should study how human beings are different from animals because it is these differences that make man a unique being.

Humanistic psychology emphasized the healthy, positive, creative and uniqueness of individuals.

Behavioural psychology

The current behavioural perspective focuses on the observed behaviour of people or animals and not on their mental processes.

Biological psychology

Psychologists with a biological perspective try to relate people's behaviour and mental events, as observed through their behaviour, to functions of their bodies—especially to the activity of their nervous and glandular system.

Social psychology

Psychologists with a social perspective are interested in the interactions between and among people which influence mind and behaviour.

Psychoanalytic psychology

The current psychoanalytic perspective (or, more broadly, the psychodynamic perspective) focuses, as did its historical forerunner, on the unconscious motives and defense mechanisms which manifest themselves in mental life and behaviour. ■ ■

Biological Basis of Mental Life and Behaviour

NEURONS: BASIC UNITS OF THE NERVOUS SYSTEM
— Anatomy of the neuron
— Firing of a neuron
— Transmission of information between cells

THE ENDOCRINE SYSTEM

THE PERIPHERAL NERVOUS SYSTEM
— The somatic nervous system
— The autonomic nervous system

THE CENTRAL NERVOUS SYSTEM
— Evolution of the central nervous system
— The spinal cord
— The hindbrain
— The midbrain
— The forebrain
— The cerebral cortex

MIND, BRAIN AND GENE
— Species-typical behaviour patterns

Biological Basis of Mental Life and Behaviour

No Historical account of psychology would be complete without mentioning the contributions of medical practitioners to an understanding of the brain as the *"organ of the mind"*. In the late eighteenth century, the German physician **Franz Josef Gall** systematically compared the brains of different species, and definitively established the general fact that higher mental functions were associated with relatively larger and more complex brains.

Psychologists and behavioural scientists are concerned with the study of nervous and endocrine system because there is an intimate relationship between various aspects of our behaviour including thoughts, cognitions etc. and our physiological system. Various behaviour and mental events like memory, learning, perception, motivation, speech etc are greatly influenced by the various processes of the nervous system, most particularly the brain.

The branch of psychology concerned with how activity in nervous system is related to behaviour and experience is called *physiological psychology* which is also called by various other names like *biological psychology, biopsychology, neuropsychology, psychobiology and psychophysiology*.

We begin by examining the neuron, or nerve cell and the way neurons communicate with one another to produce thought, feeling and behaviour.

NEURONS: BASIC UNITS OF THE NERVOUS SYSTEM

Nerve cell, or *neurons,* are the basic units of the nervous system. We think, we feel, we hurt and we want, but we do all these things through the silent, behind-the-scenes activity of neurons, which carry information from cell to cell within the nervous system as well as to and from muscles and organs. The nervous system is composed of three kinds of neurons: sensory neurons, motor neurons, and interneurons.

- **Sensory neurons** (also called *afferents neurons*) transmit information from sensory cells called receptors (that is, cells that receive sensory information) to the brain, either directly or by way of the spinal cord. Thus, sensory neurons might send information to the brain about the sensations perceived as the sunset or a sore throat.
- **Motor neurons** (or *efferent neurons*) transmit commands from the brain to the glands and muscles of the body, most often grabbing a glass of water, and vital bodily functions, such as digestion and heart beat.
- **Interneurons** connect other neurons with one another and comprise the vast majority of neurons in the brain and spinal cord.

Anatomy of the neuron

No two neurons are exactly alike in form, size and shape, but their cellular structure is basically the same. The main part of the neuron is the **cell body,** or *soma*. The cell body includes a nucleus that contains the genetic material of the cell as well as other structures vital to cell functioning.

Like other cells, the neuron is surrounded by a membrane made of lipids (fats) and proteins that transport chemicals across the membrane and receive signals from other cells. Neurons are held in place in much of the nervous system by *glial cells,* which also insulate the neurons from messages not "intended" for them.

Branch like extensions of the cell body, called

and arduous, which helps explain why babies have such poor motor control. As myelination occurs in areas of the nervous system involved in motor action, an infant becomes capable of reaching and pointing. Such developmental achievements can be reversed in *demyelinating* diseases such as multiple sclerosis.

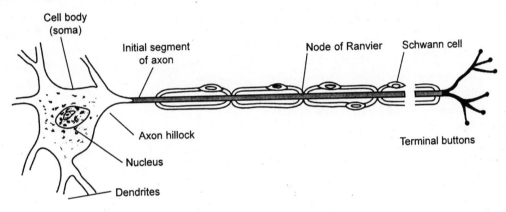

Fig 3.1 Motor neuron with myelinated axon

dendrites, receive information from other cells. The **axon** is a long extension—occasionally as long as several feet—that frequently has two or more offshots, or **collateral branches.**

The axons of all but the shortest neurons in the nervous system are covered with a **myelin sheath,** a tight coat of cells composed primarily of lipids. Myelinated axons give some portions of the brain a white appearance (hence the term *"white matter"*). The "gray matter" of the brain gets its colour from cell bodies, dendrites and unmyelinated axons.

The myelin sheath insulates the axon from chemical or physical stimuli that might interfere with the transmission of nerve impulses, much as the coating of a wire prevents electrical currents from getting crossed. The myelin sheath can also dramatically increase the speed of transmission of messages.

Not all axons are myelinated at birth. The transmission of impulses along these axons is slow

At the end of an axon are **terminal buttons,** which send signals from a neuron to adjacent cells

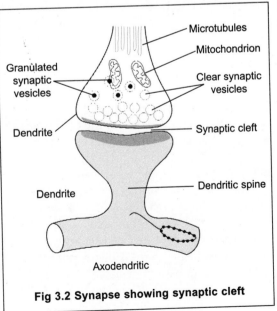

Fig 3.2 Synapse showing synaptic cleft

and are triggered by the electrical impulse that has travelled down the axon. These signals are then typically received by the dendrites or cell bodies of other neurons, although they may also be received by muscle or gland cells. Connections between neurons occur at **synapses**. Two neurons do not actually touch at a synapse, instead, a space exists between the two, called the *synaptic cleft*. Not all synapses actually occur at terminal buttons at the end of an axon; in the brain, many synapses are located directly on it.

Firing of a neuron

Most neurons communicate at the synapse through a process that involves electrical and chemical changes. To understand this process, we examine how neurons function in their normal resting state and the events that lead them to fire.

Resting potential

When a neuron is "at rest", its membrane is *polarized,* like two sides of a battery: inside the membrane is a negative electrical charge, whereas the fluid outside the cell has a positive charge. This polarized state reflects the fact that the cell membrane naturally lets some chemicals in, keeps others out, and actively pumps some in and out.

A combination of chemicals normally exists inside and outside the membrane, the most important of which are sodium (Na^+), potassium (K^+), and chloride (Cl^-) ions. Sodium and chloride ions tends to concentrate on the outside of the cell. The cell membrane of a neuron is typically not permeable to positively charged sodium ions; that is, these ions cannot easily get through the membrane, so they tend to accumulate outside the neuron.

The membrane is also completely impermeable to a variety of negatively charged protein ions inside the cell that are involved in carrying out its basic functions. As a result, the electrical charge is normally more negative on the inside than on the outside of the cell.

This "resting" condition, in which the neuron is not firing, is called the **resting potential**. (It is called a *potential* because the cell has a stored-up source of energy, which has the potential to be used). At its resting potential, the difference between the electrical charge inside and outside the neuron is about −70 millivolts (mV).

Graded potential

When a neuron is stimulated by another, one of two things can happen. The stimulation can reduce the membrane's polarization, decreasing the voltage discrepancy between the inside and the outside. Alternatively, stimulation from another neuron can *increase* polarization.

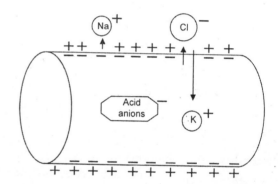

Fig 3.3 Chemical basis of the resting potentials

- A decrease in polarization **(depolarization)** stems from an influx of positive sodium ions. As a result, the charge inside the cell membrane becomes less negative.
- Increasing the electrical difference between the inside and outside of the cell—is called **hyperpolarization.** This condition usually results from an outflow of potassium ions, which are also positively charged, or an influx of negatively charged chloride ions; as a result, the potential across the membrane becomes even more negative.

Most of these brief voltage changes occur at synapses along the neuron's dendrites and cell body, they then spread down the cell membrane like ripples on a pond. These spreading voltage changes, which occur when the neural membrane received a signal from another cell, are called graded potentials, and they have two notable characteristics.

- First, their strength diminishes as they travel along the cell membrane away from the source of the stimulation.
- Second, graded potentials are cumulative, or additive. If a neuron is simultaneously depolarized by +2 mV at one point on a dendrite and hyperpolarized by −2 mV at an adjacent point, the two graded potentials add up to zero and essentially cancel each other out. In contrast, if the membrane of a neuron is depolarized at multiple points, a progressively greater influx of positive ions occurs, producing a "ripple" all the way down the cell body to the axon.

Action potential

If this cumulative electrical "ripple" crosses a certain threshold, depolarizing the membrane at the axon from its resting state of −70 mV to about −50 mV, a sudden change occurs. For a

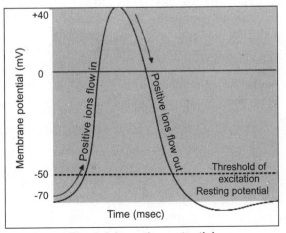

Fig. 3.4 An action potential

flicker of an instant, the membrane is totally permeable to positive sodium ions, which have accumulated outside the membrane. These ions pour in, changing the potential across the membrane to about +40 mV. Thus, the charge on the inside of the cell becomes momentarily positive. An outpouring of positive potassium ions then rapidly restores the neuron to its resting potential, rendering the charge inside the cell negative once again. This entire electrochemical process typically takes less than 2 milliseconds.

The shift in polarity across the membrane and subsequent restoration of the resting potential is called an **action potential**, or the "firing" of the neuron. The action potential rapidly spreads down the length of the axon to the terminal buttons.

Although action potentials seem more dramatic, in many ways the prime movers behind psychological processes are graded potentials. Graded potentials create *new* information at the cellular level by integrating signals from multiple sources (multiple synapses). Action potentials, in contrast, can only pass along information already collected without changing it.

The synapse

Nerve cells contact one another when the terminal arborization of one cell "contacts" the cell body and dendrites of a second cell. Every such contact is a **synapse**. Each branch of the terminal arborization of the first cell ends in a knob like structure called an axon terminal, or **synaptic knob.** The synaptic knobs do not touch the surface of the dendrites or cell bodies but come very close to them, leaving a uniform gap of about 20-30 nanometers (nm). The synaptic vesicles, are believed to contain the specific chemical substances by which one nerve cell excites another at synapses.

Transmission of information between cells

When a nerve impulse travels down on axon, it sets in motion a series of events that can lead to

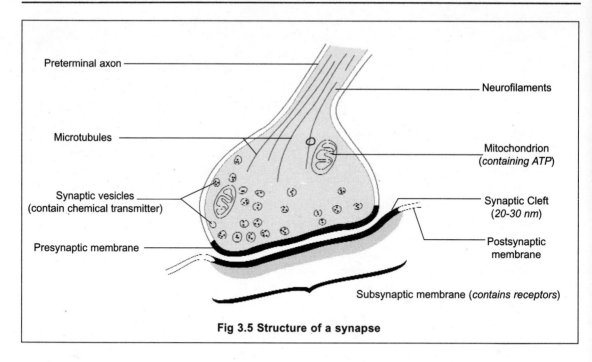

Preterminal axon

Neurofilaments

Microtubules

Mitochondrion
(*containing ATP*)

Synaptic vesicles
(contain chemical transmitter)

Synaptic Cleft
(*20-30 nm*)

Postsynaptic
membrane

Presynaptic membrane

Subsynaptic membrane (*contains receptors*)

Fig 3.5 Structure of a synapse

transmission of information to other cells. The neuron that is sending an impulse is called the presynaptic neuron (that is, *before* the synapse); the cell receiving the impulse is the postsynaptic neuron.

Neurotransmitters and Receptors

Within the terminal buttons of a neuron are small sacs called **synaptic vesicles.** These sacs contain **neurotransmitters** (also called *transmitter substances*), chemicals that transmit information from one cell to another. When the presynaptic neuron fires, the synaptic vesicles in its terminal buttons move toward the cell's membrane (the presynaptic membrane). Some of them adhere to the membrane and break open, releasing neurotransmitters into the synaptic cleft.

Once in the synaptic cleft, some of these chemical molecules then bind with protein molecules in the postsynaptic membrane called **receptors**. Receptors act like locks that can be opened only by particular keys. In this case, the keys are neurotransmitters in the synaptic cleft. When a receptor binds with the neurotransmitter that fits it—in both molecular structure and

electrical charge—the chemical and electrical balance of the postsynaptic cell membrane changes, producing a graded potential a ripple in the neuronal pond.

The effects of neurotransmitters

Neurotransmitters can either *increase* or *decrease* neural firing. **Excitatory neurotransmitters** depolarize the postsynaptic cell membrane, making an action potential more likely. (That is, they *excite* the neuron). In contrast, **inhibitory neurotransmitters** hyperpolarize the membrane (increase its polarization); this reduces the likelihood that the postsynaptic neuron will fire (or *inhibits* firing). Excitatory neurotransmitters thus grease the wheels of neural communication, whereas inhibitory neurotransmitters put on the brakes.

Types of neurotransmitters

A decade ago, researchers only knew of a handful of neurotransmitters. Progress in the understanding of neural transmission has proceeded so rapidly, however, that we know of atleast 75 substances that can transmit messages between neurons. For example,

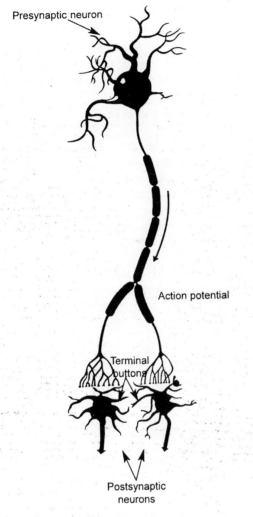

Fig. 3.6 Transmission of nerve impulse

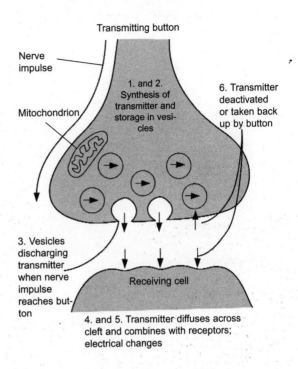

Fig. 3.7 Steps in the chemical transmission of information across a synapse

epinephrine and **norepinephrine** are involved in emotional arousal, particularly fear and anxiety. **Endorphins** are chemicals that elevate mood and reduce pain. Endorphins have a range of effects from the numbness people often feel immediately after tearing a muscle, to the "runner's high" athletes sometimes report after a prolonged period of exercise.

Glutamate and GABA

Glutamate (glutamic acid) and *GABA* (gamma-aminobutyric acid) are two of the most widespread neurotransmitters in the nervous system. Glutamate can excite nearly every neuron in the nervous system, whereas GABA has the opposite effect in the brain, playing an inhibitory role.

Glutamate is involved in many psychological processes, but recent research suggests that it may play an important role in learning (*Blokland, 1997; Izquierdo and Medina, 1997*).

GABA is particularly important in the regulation of anxiety; drugs like valium and alcohol that bind with its receptors tend to reduce anxiety. Low levels of GABA may also be related to both severe depression and mania.

Dopamine

Dopamine has wide ranging effects in the nervous system. Some neural pathways that rely on dopamine are involved in the experience of pleasure and in the learning of behaviours associated with reward. Other dopamine pathways are involved in movement, attention, decision making and other cognitive processes. Abnormally high levels of dopamine in some parts of the brain have been linked to schizophrenia.

L-dopa gets past the blood-brain barrier. The rest affects neurons in the rest of the body and can cause side effects such as nausea, vomiting and shortness of breath. L-dopa can reduce Parkinsonian symptoms, but it can also produce

Transmitter Substance	Some of its known effects
1. Glutamate	1. Excitation of neurons throughout the nervous system.
2. GABA (gamma-aminobutyric acid)	2. Inhibition of neurons in the brain.
3. Gylcene	3. Inhibition of neurons in the spinal cord and lower brain.
4. Dopamine	4. Emotional arousal, pleasure, and reward; voluntary movement; attention.
5. Serotonin	5. Sleep and emotional arousal; aggression; pain regulation.
6. Acetylcholine (Ach)	6. Learning and memory.
7. Epinephrine and norepinephrine	7. Emotional arousal, anxiety, and fear.
8. Endorphins and enkephalins	8. Pain relief and elevation of mood.

Fig. 3.8 Partial list of neurotransmitters

Degeneration of the dopamine—releasing neurons in a *part of the brain called substantia nigra* causes **Parkinson's disease,** a disorder characterized by uncontrollable tremors, a general slowing down and difficulty both initiating behaviour (such as standing up) or stopping movements that are already in progress (such as walking forward).

Although disordered movement is the most visible sign of Parkinson's disease, other symptoms can include depression and a general slowing of thought that parallels the slowing of behaviour. Physicians tried treating these patients with L-dopa, a chemical that readily converts to dopamine and had recently proven effective in treating Parkinson's disease. Dopamine itself cannot be administered because it cannot cross the *blood-brain barrier*, which normally protects the brain from foreign substances in the blood. (The blood-brain barrier results from the fact that the cells in the blood vessels of the brain tend to be so tightly packed that large molecules have difficulty entering).

Unfortunately, only a small percentage of even

disordered thinking or movement disorders other than Parkinson's.

Serotonin

Serotonin serves a variety of functions. It appears to be involved in the regulation of mood, sleep, eating, arousal and pain. Decreased serotonin in the brain is common in severe depression, which often responds to medications that increase serotonin activity. People who are depressed often have trouble sleeping and eating, in part because the disruption of serotonin activity that may accompany depression can also affect these other functions. Serotonin plays an inhibitory role in most sites in the nervous system.

Acetylcholine

Acetylcholine is another neurotransmitter involved in learning and memory. For example, experiments have shown increased ACh activity in rats learning to discriminate one stimulus from another, in comparison to rats in control conditions that do not require learning.

A key piece of evidence liking ACh to

learning and memory is the fact that patients with Alzheimer's disease, which destroys memory, show depletions in ACh. Transplanting tissue rich in ACh has led to markedly improved functioning in learning-impaired rats.

THE ENDOCRINE SYSTEM

The endocrine system is a collection of glands that secrete chemicals directly into the blood-stream; these chemicals are called *hormones*. Like neurotransmitters, hormones bind with receptors in cell membranes, but because they travel through the bloodstream, they can simultaneously activate many cells in the body as long as these cells are equipped with the right receptors. The chemical structure of some hormones is similar or even identical to that of some neurotransmitters. The hormone *adrenalin*, for example, is the same compound as the neurotransmitter epinephrine; similarly the chemical structure of the hormone *noradrenalin* is the same as norepinephrine.

The endocrine system "broadcasts" its signals by releasing hormones into the bloodstream. Its messages are less specific but readily "heard" throughout the body.

Pituitary gland

The pituitary gland is an oval structure about the size

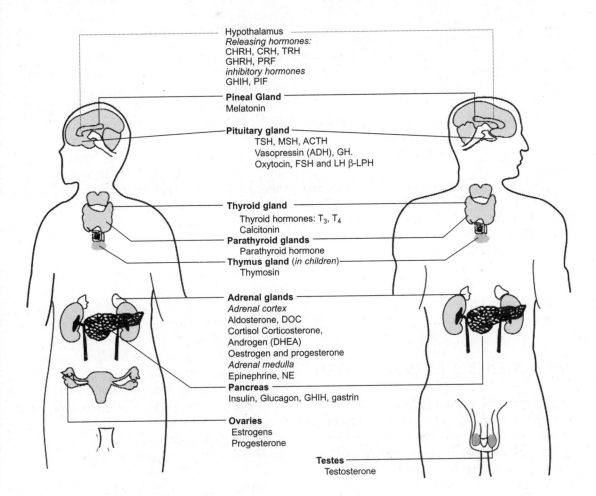

Hypothalamus
Releasing hormones:
CHRH, CRH, TRH
GHRH, PRF
inhibitory hormones
GHIH, PIF

Pineal Gland
Melatonin

Pituitary gland
TSH, MSH, ACTH
Vasopressin (ADH), GH.
Oxytocin, FSH and LH β-LPH

Thyroid gland
Thyroid hormones: T_3, T_4
Calcitonin

Parathyroid glands
Parathyroid hormone

Thymus gland (*in children*)
Thymosin

Adrenal glands
Adrenal cortex
Aldosterone, DOC
Cortisol Corticosterone,
Androgen (DHEA)
Oestrogen and progesterone
Adrenal medulla
Epinephrine, NE

Pancreas
Insulin, Glucagon, GHIH, gastrin

Ovaries
Estrogens
Progesterone

Testes
Testosterone

Fig. 3.9 The major endocrine glands and the hormones they secrete

of a pea that is located in the brain. It is often described as the "master gland" because some of the hormones it release stimulate and regulate the other glands. The pituitary is connected more directly to the central nervous system than any of the other endocrine glands.

Thyroid gland

The thyroid gland, located in the neck, releases a hormone that controls metabolism. The thyroid gland also affects energy levels and mood. People with *hypothyroidism*, or an underactive thyroid, sometimes require artificial replacement of thyroid hormones to relieve sluggishness and depression.

Adrenal glands

These are located above the kidneys. These glands secret adrenalin and other hormones during emergencies.

Pancreas

It is located near the stomach and produces hormones that control blood-sugar level.

Gonads

The gonads influence sexual development and behaviour. The male gonads, or testes, are located in the testicles; the most important hormone they produce is *testosterone*. The female gonads, the *ovaries,* produce *estrogens*. In both sexes, these hormones control secondary sex characteristics such as growth of breasts in females, deepened voice in males, and pubic hair in both sexes.

THE PERIPHERAL NERVOUS SYSTEM

The peripheral nervous system consists of neurons that convey messages to and from the central nervous system. The peripheral nervous system has two subdivisions : the somatic and the autonomic nervous systems.

The somatic nervous system

The *somatic nervous system* transmits sensory information to the central nervous system and carries out its motor commands. Sensory neurons receive information through receptors in the eyes, ears, skin, muscles and other parts of the body such as the tongue. Motor neurons direct the action of skeletal muscles. Because the somatic nervous system is involved in intentional actions, such as standing up or shaking someone's hand, it is sometimes called the *voluntary nervous system*. The somatic nervous system also directs some involuntary or automatic actions, such as adjustments in posture or balance.

The autonomic nervous system

The *autonomic nervous system* conveys information to and from internal bodily structures that carry out basic life processes such as digestion and respiration. It consists of two parts: the sympathetic and the parasympathetic nervous systems. Although these systems work together, their functions are often opposed or complementary. In broadest strokes, one can think of the sympathetic nervous system as an emergency system and the parasympathetic nervous system as a "business-as-usual" system.

Sympathetic nervous system

This system is typically activated in response to threats. Its job is to make the body ready for fight or flight, which it does in several ways. It stops digestion, since diverting blood away from the stomach re-directs the blood to the muscles, which may need extra oxygen for an emergency response. It increases heart rate, dilates the pupils and causes hairs on the body and head to stand erect. It is also involved in other states of intense activation, such as ejaculation in males.

By preparing the organism to respond to emergencies, the sympathetic nervous system serves an important adaptive function. Sometimes, however, the sympathetic cavalry comes to the rescue when least wanted. A surge of

Gland	Hormone(s)	Target tissue	Major function(s)	Hyposecretion	Hypersecretion
Thyroid	Thyroxin	All cells	Raises metabolic rate	Lethargy, retardation	Hyperactivity
Parathyroids	Parathormone (vitamin D)	Intestines, bone, kidney	Increases blood calcium lowers blood phosphate, prevents loss of Ca and P	Hyperactivity, Seizures, Bone deficiencies	Lethargy
Adrenal cortex	Corticoids (steroids)	All cell membranes, liver, gonads	Sodium retention, potassium loss, increased carbohydrate metabolism, glycogen formation, sex hormone effects	Lethargy, fluid retention, weight loss, salt loss	Sexual precocity
Adrenal medulla	Norepinephrine	Heart	Increases heart rate, constricts visceral and peripheral arteries, releases blood glucose, releases ACTH	Unknown	Under stress only
Pancreas	Glucagon Insulin	Liver All cells	Increases blood glucose (constr.) Lowers blood glucose	Unknown Diabetes mellitus	Unknown Hypoglycemia and lethargy
Posterior pituitary	Vasopressin (includes ADH) Oxytocin	Arteries Kidney Uterus & Mammary glands	Raises blood pressure (constr.) Water reabsorption Contraction Milk secretion	Diabetes insipidus	Unknown (hypertension)
Anterior pituitary	Somatotrophic Thyrotrophic Adrenocorticotrophic Follicle-stimulating Luteinizing Lactogenic	Bone Thyroid Adrenal cortex Gonads Gonads Gonads mammary glands	Body growth Thyroxin secretion Corticoid secretion Ova and sperm production Sex hormone production Corpus luteum development and milk production	Dwarfism, acromegaly See thyroid gland See adrenal cortex Sterility Sexual vigor increases Sterility	Giantism Unknown Decreases vigor Unknown
Testes	Androgens	All tissues	Sexual arousal, primary and secondary sex characteristics	Sexual vigor increases	Decreases vigor
Ovaries	Estrogens Progesterone	All tissues Uterus	Sexual arousal, primary and secondary sex characteristics Prepares for embryo, maintains pregnancy	Sexual vigor Sterility	Decreases vigor Unknown
Placenta Pineal	Chorionic Melatonin	Uterus Gonads	Maintains pregnancy Suppress hormone output	Miscarriage Increased sexual vigor	Unknown Decreases vigor

Fig. 3.10 Synopsis of endocrine gland functions

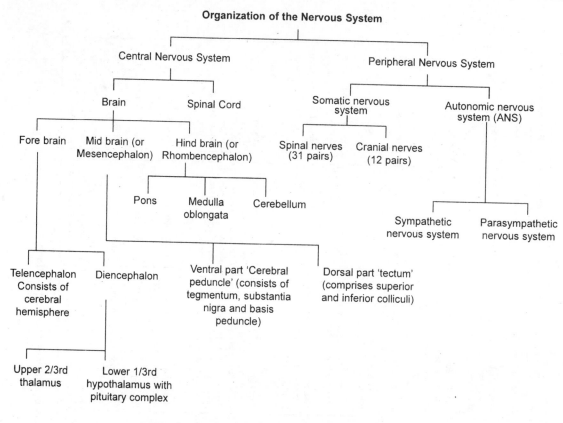

Fig. 3.11 Organization of the Nervous System

anxiety, tremors, sweating, dry mouth and palpitating heart may have helped to prepare our ancestors to flee from a hungry lion, but they are less welcomed when trying to deliver a speech. Similarly physiological reactions occur in panic attacks, which include symptoms such as intense anxiety, tremors and palpitating heart.

Parasympathetic nervous system

This system supports more routine, activities that maintain the body's store of energy, such as regulating blood-sugar levels, secreting saliva and eliminating wastes. It also participates in functions such as regulating heart rate and pupil size. The relationship between the sympathetic and parasympathetic nervous systems is in many ways a balancing act: When an emergency has passed, the parasympathetic nervous system resumes control, reversing sympathetic

responses and returning to the normal business of storing and maintaining resources.

THE CENTRAL NERVOUS SYSTEM

The brain and spinal cord constitute the central nervous system. The human central nervous system is probably the most remarkable feat of electrical engineering ever accomplished.

Evolution of the central nervous system

The human central nervous system, like that of all animals, is like a living fossil record: The further down one goes (almost literally, from the upper layers of the brain down to the spinal cord), the

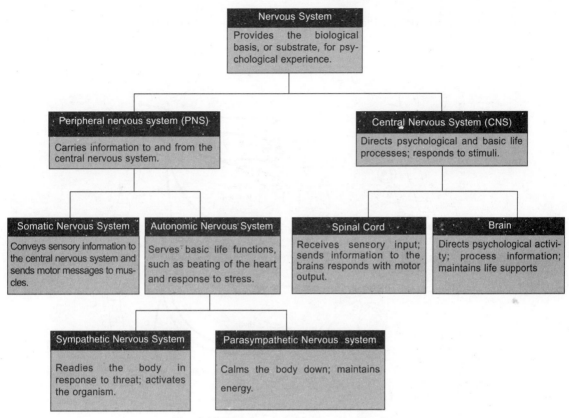

Fig. 3.12 Divisions of the Nervous System

more one sees ancient structures that evolved hundreds of millions of years ago and were shared—and continue to be shared—by most other vertebrates (animals with spinal cords).

It is tempting to think of nature's creatures as arranged on a scale from simple to complex, beginning with organisms like amoebas, then moving up the ladder perhaps to pets and farm animals, and on to the highest form of life, ourselves.

Although the human brain and the brains of its early vertebrate and mammalian ancestors differ dramatically, most of the differences are the result of additions to, rather than replacement of, the original brain structures. Two very important consequences flow from this. The first is, that many neural mechanisms are the same in humans and other animals; others differ across species that have evolved in different directions from common ancestors.

The human brainstem is almost identical to the brainstem of sheep (Kolb & Whishaw, 1996), but the two species differ tremendously in the size, structure and function of their cortex. Much of the sheep's cortex is devoted to processing sensory information, whereas a greater part of the human cortex is involved in forming complex thoughts, perceptions and plans for action.

The second implication is that human psychology bears the distinct imprint of the same relatively primitive structures that guide motivation, learning and behaviour in other animals. This is a sobering thought which led *Freud* to view our extraordinary capacities to love, create and understand ourselves and the universe as a thin veneer (only a few millimeters thick, in fact) over primitive structures that motivate our greatest achievements and our most "inhuman" atrocities; and led *Skinner* to argue that the same laws of learning apply to

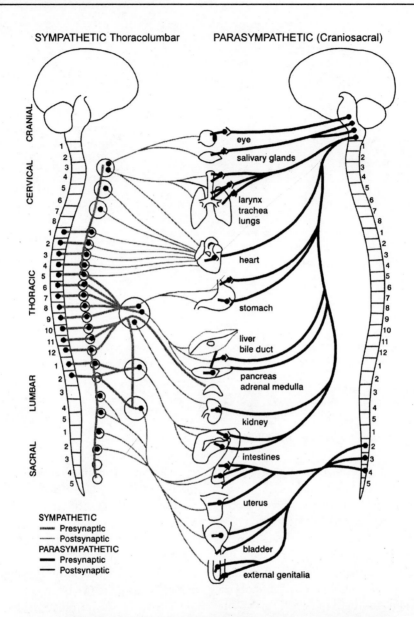

SYMPATHETIC Thoracolumbar   PARASYMPATHETIC (Craniosacral)

Fig. 3.13 Distribution of the parasympathetic (left) and sympathetic (right) divisions of the autonomic nervous system

humans as to other animals.

The human nervous system is thus a set of hierarchically organized structures built layer upon layer over millions of years of evolution. The most primitive centers send information to, and receive information from, higher centers; these higher centers are in turn integrated with,

and regulated by, still more advanced areas of the brain. Behavioural and cognitive precision progressively increases from the lower to the higher and more recently evolved structures. Thus, the spinal cord can respond to a prick of the skin with a reflex without even consulting the brain, but more complex cognitive activity simultaneously occurs as the person makes sense of what has happened. We reflexively withdraw from a pinprick, but if the source is a vaccine injection, we inhibit our response—though often milliseconds later, since information travelling to and from the brain takes neural time. Responding appropriately requires the integrated functioning of structures from the spinal cord up through the cortex.

The spinal cord

As in all vertebrates, neurons in the human spinal cord produce reflexes, as sensory stimulation activates rapid, automatic motor responses. In humans, however, the main function of the *spinal*

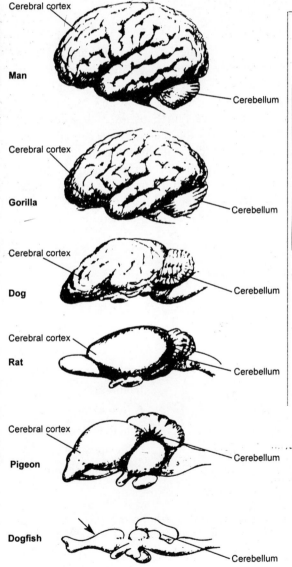

Fig. 3.14 The evolution of the brain

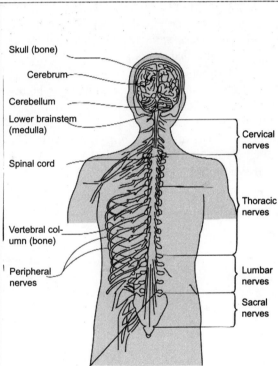

Fig. 3.15 The Spinal cord and segments

cord is to transmit information between the brain and the rest of the body. The spinal cord sends information from sensory neurons in various parts of the body to the brain, and it relays motor commands back to muscles and organs (such as heart and stomach) via motor neurons.

The spinal cord in humans is segmented, with each segment controlling a different part of the body. By and large, the upper segments control the upper parts of the body and the lower segments the lower body. Outside the cord, bundles of axons from the sensory and motor neurons join together to form 31 pairs (from the two sides of the body) of *spinal nerves;* these nerves carry information to and from the spinal cord to the periphery. Inside the spinal cord, other bundles of axons (*spinal tracts,* which comprise much of the white matter of the cord) send impulses to and from the brain, relaying sensory messages and motor commands. (Outside the central nervous system, bundles of axons are usually called *nerves;* within the brain and spinal cord, they are called *tracts.*)

When the spinal cord is severed, the result is loss of feeling and paralysis at all levels below the injury, which can no longer communicate with the brain. Even with less severe lesions, physicians can often pinpoint the location of spinal damage from patient's descriptions of their symptoms alone.

The hindbrain

other animals, hindbrain structures like the brain to the spinal cord, sustain life by controlling the supply of air and blood to cells in the body, and regulate arousal level. With the exception of the cerebellum, which sits at the back of the brain and has a distinct appearance, the structures of the hindbrain merge into one another and perform multiple functions as information passes from one structure to the next on its way to higher brain regions.

Medulla oblongata

Anatomically, the lowest brainstem structure, the *medulla oblongata* (or simply *medulla*), is actually an extension of the spinal cord. Although quite small—about an inch and a half long and three-fourth of an inch wide at its broadest part—the medulla is essential to life, controlling such vital physiological functions as heart beat, circulation and respiration. Neither humans nor other animals can survive destruction of the medulla.

The medulla is the link between the spinal

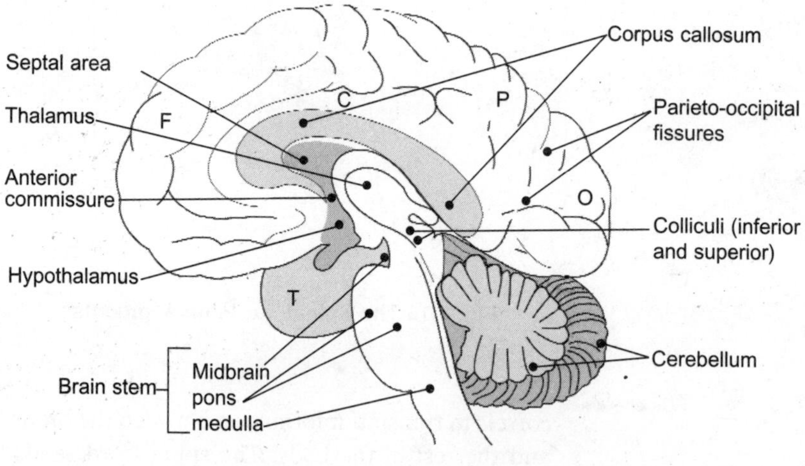

Fig. 3.16 The human brain medial view (brain cut from front to back along longitudinal fissure).

F, frontal lobe;

P, parietal lobe;

O, occipital lobe;

C, cingulate gyrus

Directly above the spinal cord in humans are several structures that comprise the *hindbrain;* the medulla oblongata, cerebellum and parts of the reticular formation. Another small hindbrain region, the *pons,* is not yet well understood, although it may play some role in learning. As in

cord and the rest of the brain. Here, bundles of axons cross over from each side of the body to the opposite side of the brain. As a result, most of the sensations experienced on the right side of the body, as well as the capacity to move the right side, are controlled by the left side of the brain, and vice versa. Thus, if a person has weakness in the left side of the body following a stroke, the damage to the brain was likely on the right side of the brain.

Cerebellum

The *cerebellum* is a large structure at the back of the brain. For decades researchers have believed that the cerebellum is exclusively involved in coordinating smooth, well-sequenced movements (such as riding a bike) and in maintaining balance and posture. Staggering and slurred speech after a few drinks stem in large part from the effects of alcohol on cerebellar functioning. The cerebellum also takes a pounding when the head is repeatedly snapped back in boxing.

More recently, however, researchers using positron emission tomography (PET) and functional magnetic resonance imaging (FMRI) scans have founded the cerebellum to be involved in sensory and cognitive processes as well, such as learning to associate one stimulus (such as sound) with another (such as a puff of air on the eye, which leads to an eyeblink reflex) (*Blaxton 1996; Cabeza 1997*).

Cerebellum receives sensory and other inputs from the spinal cord, brain stem and forebrain; it processes this information and then sends outputs to many parts of the brain to help make our movements precise, coordinated and smooth.

Reticular formation

The *reticular formation* is a diffuse network of neurons that extends from the lowest parts of the medulla in the hindbrain to the upper end of the midbrain. The reticular formation sends axons to many parts of the brain and to the spinal cord. Its major functions are to maintain consciousness, regulate arousal levels, and modulate the activity of neurons throughout the central nervous system. The reticular formation also appears to help higher brain centers to integrate information from different neural pathways by calling attention to their simultaneous activation.

Reticular damage can affect sleep patterns as well as the ability to be alert or attentive. Damage to the reticular formation is a major cause of coma. Infact, humans can lose an entire side of the cerebrum without losing the capacity for consciousness, whereas lesions to the reticular formation can render all the information in the cortex useless.

The inputs to the cortex from lower brain centers involve conscious states of arousal, attention and sleep, as well as the inputs governing simple sensation. The *Brain Stem Reticular Formation* (BSRF) is involved as an *Ascending Reticular Activating System* (ARAS).

Specific Thalamic Projection System

The classic sensory pathways form a *specific thalamic projection system (STPS)* that results in topographically organized sensory input for vision, hearing and the skin senses (somesthesia). There are secondary sensory areas for all three senses, but they are phylogenetically older and are not a part of the STPS.

Diffuse Thalamic Projection System

There are secondary sensory areas for somesthesia, vision and audition. These secondary areas are supplied partly by the *diffuse thalamic projection system (DTPS)*. The DTPS has a more widespread distribution than does the STPS, represents an earlier from of sensory input, and is less "modality specific." Its arousal by auditory stimulation, for example, may result in a change in nerve impulses reaching widespread areas of the brain. The reaction of the cortex to the DTPS is brief compared to its reaction to the ascending reticular activating system. The cortical responses observed have been called "recruiting responses" because the neural activity in areas supplied by the DTPS becomes more regular and synchronized and has a larger amplitude. Recruiting responses are probably caused by excitation reverberating back and forth between the thalamus and cortex. The sensory pathways involved begin with the STPS, which has collateral to diffuse nuclei of the thalamus. These nuclei in turn send fibers to the basal ganglia and to widespread cortical areas. The effect of the DTPS on the secondary sensory areas in particular may serve as a mechanism for selective attention. Certain cells in the secondary areas may be active only when the animal is attending to that specific sensory input. This would form a modality-specific mechanism for attention.

Ascending Reticular Activating System

This system serves the whole cerebral cortex. The *ARAS* originates in the central parts of the medulla, midbrain and diencephalon, as compared to the thalamic projection of the STPS and DTPS. The medulla, midbrain and gray matter of nuclei and short interneurons lie in the central core, surrounded by the white matter of myelinated tracts. Much of this central gray matter is composed of short, many branched, interconnecting cells, called the *brain stem reticular formation (BSRF)*. Part of the BSRF makes up the ARAS. The cells of the ARAS are fired by collateral from the incoming sensory pathways of the STPS. The cells of the ARAS fire through many synapses; the relayed excitation being passed from cell to cell up through the central core of the brain stem reaches all areas of the cerebral cortex. The ARAS excites the cells of the cerebral cortex and lowers their threshold to

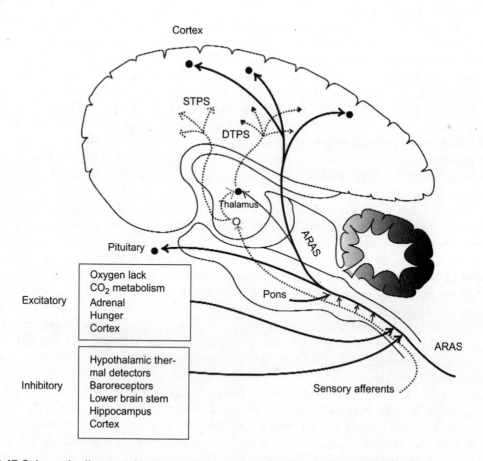

Fig. 3.17 Schematic diagram showing sensory projection to cortex through specific thalamic projection system (STPS), diffuse thalamic projection system (DTPS), and ascending reticular activating system (ARAS)

incoming stimuli from other sources. The main function of the ARAS is to "keep the brain awake." The more active the ARAS, the more aroused and alert is the animal. Quiescence of the ARAS results in a low level of cortical activity, a state of sleep and a higher threshold for the cortex to incoming sensory stimulation.

Descending Reticular Activating System

The cells of the BSRF can regulate muscle tone by exciting or inhibiting extensor stretch reflexes. This can be called a *descending reticular activating system* because of the role of sensory feedback in maintaining states of wakefulness and attention. Perhaps you have noted that your neck muscles ache or your leg muscles are tired after a period of alert, concentrated study, although you have been sitting in a chair the entire time. When the BSRF is active and the cerebral cortex is stimulated by the ARAS, the *DRAS* increases extensor muscle tone. The more the extensor muscles are contracted in maintaining this tone, the greater is the stimulation of kinesthetic receptors—the receptors in muscles that are sensitive to muscle contraction. Excitation from some of these receptors reaches the cerebral cortex and gives rise to sensations of muscle contraction. Excitation from some of these receptors reaches the cerebral cortex and gives rise to sensations of muscle contraction. In the states of alert attention, then, the BSRF activates the cortex via the ARAS and also increases muscle tone. Increased muscle tone fires kinesthetic receptors that feedback excitation to the cerebral cortex, further increasing cortical excitation. Thus the BSRF has both an ascending and a descending activating system.

The midbrain

The *midbrain* surrounds the cerebral aqueduct. Above the aqueduct are found the peashaped colliculi, which are visual and auditory reflex centers. The floor of the midbrain contains tracts of conducting fibres and a few synaptic centers.

The *midbrain* consists of the *tectum* and *tegmentum*. The *tectum* includes structures involved in vision and hearing. These structures largely help humans to orient with visual and auditory stimuli with eye and body movements. When higher brain structures are lesioned, people can often still sense the presence of stimuli, but they cannot identify them. The *tegmentum*, which includes parts of the reticular formation and other neural structures, serves a variety of functions. Many are related to movement; the tegmentum includes the substantia nigra, which deteriorates in Parkinson's disease.

Recent research suggests that these midbrain structures also play an important role in learning to produce behaviours that minimize unpleasant consequences and maximize rewards—a kind of learning studied for years by behaviourists. Neurons deep inside the tectum are part of a system of neurons involved in generating unpleasant feelings and linking them, through learning, to actions that can help the animal escape or avoid them. Chemical or electrical activation of these pathways in rats produces "Freezing" (a characteristic fear response) and efforts to escape. Other *nuclei* in the tegmentum are involved in the experience of pleasure or reward, which is crucial to learning to produce actions that lead to positive consequences.

The forebrain

The *forebrain* which is involved in complex sensory, emotional, cognitive and behavioural processes, consists of the hypothalamus, thalamus and cerebrum. Within the cerebrum are the basal ganglia and limbic system, which are called *subcortical* structures. The outer layers of the cerebrum, or cortex are so complex that a separate section will be devoted to them.

Hypothalamus

Situated in front of the midbrain and adjacent to the pituitary gland is the *hypothalamus*.

Although the hypothalamus accounts for only 0.3 percent of the brain's total weight, this tiny structure helps to regulate behaviours ranging from eating and sleeping to sexual activity and emotional experience. In animals, the hypothalamus is involved in species specific behaviours, such as responses to predators.

The hypothalamus works closely with the pituitary gland and provides a key link between the nervous system and the endocrine system, largely by activating pituitary hormones. When people undergo stressful experiences, the hypothalamus activates the pituitary, which in turn puts the body on alert by sending out hormonal messages.

One of the most important functions of the hypothalamus is *homeostasis*—keeping vital processes such as body temperature, blood-sugar (glucose) level, and metabolism within a fairly narrow range. For example, as people ingest food, the hypothalamus detects a rise in glucose level and responds by shutting off hunger sensations. Chemically blocking glucose receptors (cells that detect glucose levels) in cats can produce ravenous eating, as the hypothalamus attempts to maintain homeostasis in the face of misleading information.

Thalamus

The *thalamus* is a set of nuclei located above the hypothalamus. Its various nuclei perform a number of functions; one of the most important is to provide initial processing of sensory information and to transmit this information to higher brain centers. In some respects the thalamus is like a switchboard for routing information from neurons connected to visual, auditory, taste and touch receptors to appropriate regions of the brain. However, the thalamus plays a much more active role than a simple switchboard. Its function is not only to *route* messages to the appropriate structures but also to *filter* them, highlighting some and de-emphasizing others.

The thalamus is ideally situated for performing this function, since it receives *projections* from several sensory systems, as well as feedback from higher cortical centers in the

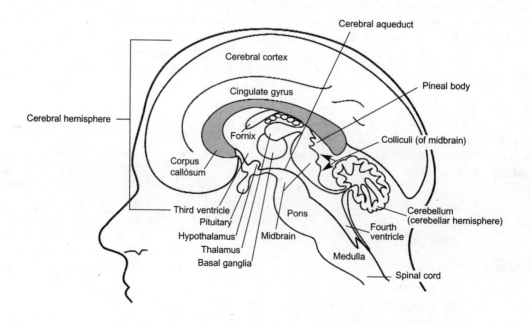

Fig. 3.18 Human Brain seen from medial plane (split down the middle).

brain. Thus, the thalamus can collect information from multiple senses and determine the extent to which information is converging on something important that may require more detailed processing. The thalamus also receives input from the reticular formation, which "highlights" some neural messages.

The limbic system

The *limbic system* is a set of structures with diverse functions, including emotion, motivation, learning and memory. The limbic system includes the septal area, the amygdala and the hippocampus.

The role of the *septal area* is only gradually becoming clear. Early research linked it to, the experience of pleasure: Stimulating a section of the septal area proved to be a powerful reinforcer for rats, which would walk across an electrified grid to receive the stimulation (*Milner, 1991*). More recent research suggests that, like most brain structures, different sections of the septal area appears to be involved in relief from pain and other unpleasant emotional states (*Yadin and Thomas, 1996*). Another part seems to help the animals learn to avoid situations that *lead to*

aversive experiences, since injection of chemicals that temporarily block its functioning makes rats less able to learn to avoid stimuli associated with pain. These regions receive projections from midbrain and thalamic nuclei involved in learning.

The *amygdala* is an almond-shaped structure (amygdala is Latin for "almond") involved in many emotional processes, especially learning and remembering emotionally significant events. One of its primary roles is to attach emotional significance to events. The amygdala appears to be particularly important in fear responses. The amygdala is also involved in recognizing emotion, particularly fearful emotion, in other people.

The *hippocampus* is particularly important in memory. This was demonstrated dramatically in a famous case study by *Brenda Milner* and her colleagues. A man identified as H.M. underwent surgery to control life-threatening epileptic seizures. The surgeon removed sections of his cortex and some underlying structures. Unfortunately, one of those structures was the hippocampus and although H.M. was now free of seizures, he was also "free" of the capacity to remember new information.

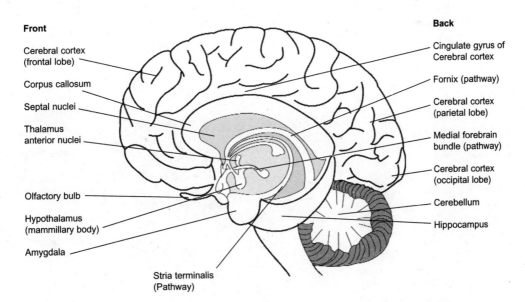

Fig. 3.19 The limbic system; underlined labels indicate limbic system structures

The basal ganglia

The term *basal ganglia* is generally applied to five structures on each side of the brain: the caudate nucleus, putamen and globus pallidus, three large nuclear masses underlying the cortical mantle, and functionally related subthalamic nucleus and substantia nigra. The globus pallidus is divided into an external and an internal segment. The substantia nigra is divided into pars compacta and a pars reticulata. Parts of the thalamus are intimately related to the basal ganglia. The caudate nucleus and the putamen are frequently called the striatum; the putamen and the globus pallidus

are sometimes called the lenticular nucleus.

Studies have made it clear that neurons in the basal ganglia, like those in the lateral portions of the cerebellar hemispheres, discharge before movements begin. These observations, plus careful analysis of the effects of diseases of the basal ganglion in humans and the effects of drugs that destroy dopaminergic neurons in animals, have led to the concept that the basal ganglia are involved in the planning and programming of movement or, more broadly, in the processes by which an abstract thought is converted into voluntary action.

The neurons in the basal ganglia discharge via

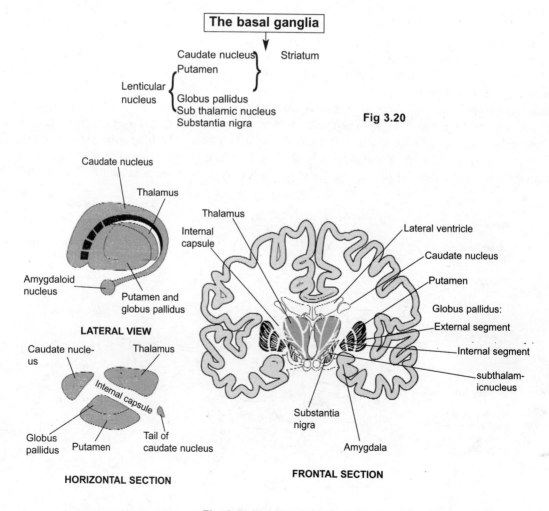

Fig. 3.21 The Basal Ganglia

the thalamus to areas related to the motor cortex, and the descending tracts provide the final common pathway to the spinal motor neurons. The basal ganglia is involved in the planning and programming of movements by preventing oscillation and after discharge in the motor system, i.e. in the processes by which an idea of voluntary movement is converted into the precise action. The activity of the basal ganglia increases during slow, steady damp movement and is silent during rapid, saccadic movement. The basal ganglia inhibits the stretch reflex (muscle tone) throughout the body. This is why damage to the basal ganglia produces rigidity. It regulates the subconscious gross movements occurring in groups of the muscles. It provides appropriate muscle tone for performance of skilled movements and is centre for co-ordination of those impulses which are essential for skilled movements. The basal ganglia is responsible for control of normal automatic and associated movements such as swinging of arms during walking.

Damage to the basal ganglia can also lead to mood and memory disorders, as higher regions of brain fail to receive necessary activation.

The cerebral cortex

Although many components of normal behaviours are produced below the cortex—in the spinal cord and medulla up through the limbic system and basal ganglia—the cerebral cortex coordinates and integrates these components. The cortex consists of a three millimeter thick layer of densely packed interneurons; it is grayish in colour and highly convoluted. The convolution appear to serve a purpose: Just as crumpling a piece of paper into a tight wad reduces its size, the folds and wrinkles of the cortex allow a relatively large area of cortical cells to fit into a compact region within the skull. The hills of these convolution are known as **gyri** (plural of *gyrus*) and the valleys as **sulci** (plural of *sulcus*).

In humans, the cortex performs three functions:
- It allows the flexible construction of sequences of voluntary movements

involved in activities such as changing a tire or playing a piano concerto.
- It permits subtle discrimination among complex sensory patterns; without a cerebral cortex, the words gene and gem would be indistinguishable.
- The cortex makes possible symbolic thinking—the ability to use symbols such as words or pictorial signs to represent an object or concept with a complex meaning.

The capacity to think symbolically enables people to have conversations about things that do not exist or are not presently in view; it is the foundation of human thought and language.

Primary and association areas

The cortex consists of regions specialized for different functions, such as vision, hearing, and body sensation. Each of these areas can be divided roughly into two zones, called primary and association cortex. The *primary areas* process raw sensory information or initiate movement. The *association areas* are involved in complex mental processes such as forming perceptions, ideas, and plans. They were given this name in the nineteenth century because of the belief that higher mental functioning revolves around the association of one idea with another.

The primary areas are responsible for the initial cortical processing of sensory information. Neurons in these zones receive sensory information, usually via the thalamus, from sensory receptors in ears, eyes, skin and muscles. When a person sees a safety pin lying on her dresser, the primary or sensory areas receive the simple visual sensations that make up the contours of the safety pin. Activation of circuits in the visual association cortex enables the person to recognize the object as a safety pin rather than a needle or a formless shiny object.

Neurons in the primary areas tend to have more specific functions than neurons in association cortex. For example, some neurons in the primary visual cortex respond to horizontal lines but not to vertical lines; other neurons

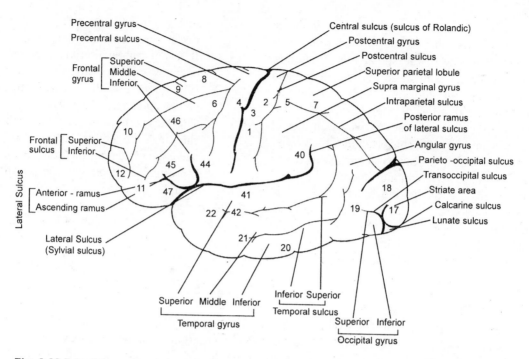

Fig. 3.22 Principle gyri and sulci and cortical Brodmann's areas of left cerebral hemisphere

respond only to vertical lines. Some neurons in the association cortex are equally specific in their functions, but many develop their functions through experience. The brain may be wired from birth to detect the contours of objects like safety pins, but a person must learn what a safety pin is and does. From an evolutionary perspective, this combination of "hard-wired" and "flexible" neurons guarantees that we have the capacity to detect features of any environment that are likely to be relevant to adaptation but can also learn the features of the *specific* environment in which we find ourselves.

Lobes of the cortex

The cerebrum is divided into two roughly symmetrical halves, or *cerebral hemispheres,* which are separated by the *longitudinal fissure.* A band of neural fibers called the *corpus callosum* connects the *right* and *left hemispheres.* Each hemisphere consist of four regions, or *lobes:* occipital, parietal, frontal and temporal. Thus, a person has a right and left occipital lobe, a right

and left parietal lobe and so forth.

It is important to bear in mind that nature did not create clearly bounded cortical regions and rope them off from one another; the functions of adjacent cortical regions tend to be related even if some cells are called "occipital" and others "temporal".

The occipital lobes

The *occipital lobes,* located in the rear portion of the cortex, are specialized for vision. Primary areas of the occipital lobes receive visual input from the thalamus. The thalamus, in turn, receives information from the receptors in the retina via the optic nerve. The primary areas respond to relatively simple features of a visual stimulus, and the association areas organize these simple characteristics into more complex maps of features of objects and their position in space. Damage to the primary areas leads to partial or complete blindness.

The visual association cortex, which actually extends into neighbouring lobes, projects (that is,

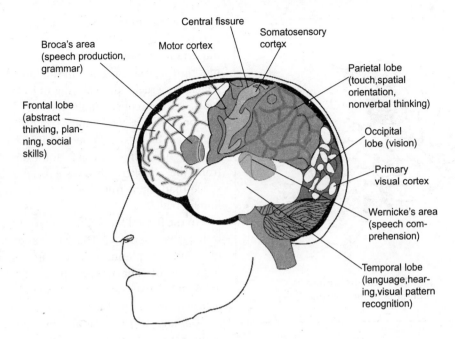

Fig. 3.23 The lobes of the cerebral cortex

sends axons carrying messages) to several regions throughout the cortex that receive other types of sensory information from more than one sensory system are called polysensory areas. The existence of **polysensory areas** at various levels of the brain (including subcortical levels) help us, for example, to associate the sight of a car stopping suddenly with the sound of squealing tires.

The parietal lobes

The *parietal lobes* are located in front of the occipital lobes. They are involved in several functions, including the sense of touch, detection of movement in the environment, located objects in space, and the experience of one's own body as it moves through space. A person with damage to the primary area of the parietal lobes may be unable to feel a thimble on her finger, whereas damage to the association areas could render her unable to recognize the object she was feeling as a thimble or to understand what the object does.

The primary area of the parietal lobe, called the *somatosensory cortex,* lies directly behind the *central fissure,* which divides the parietal lobe from the frontal lobe. Different sections of the somatosensory cortex receive information from different parts of the body. Thus, one section registers sensations from the hand, another from the foot, and so forth. The parietal lobes are also involved in complex visual processing, particularly the posterior regions nearest to the occipital lobes.

The frontal lobes

The *frontal lobes* are involved in a number of functions, including movement, attention, planning, social skills, abstract thinking, memory, and some aspects of personality. The *motor cortex,* through its projections to the basal ganglia, cerebellum and spinal cord, initiates voluntary movement. The motor cortex and adjacent somatosensory cortex send and receive information from the same parts of the body.

As the figures indicate, the amount of space devoted to different parts of the body in the motor

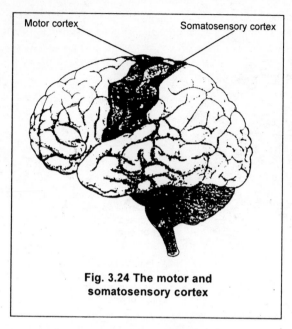

Fig. 3.24 The motor and somatosensory cortex

more space in the motor and somatosensory cortexes. These body parts tend to serve important or complex functions and thus require more processing capacity. In humans, the hands, which are crucial to exploring objects and using tools, occupy considerable territory, whereas a section of the back of similar size occupies only a fraction of that space. Other species have different cortical "priorities"; in cats for example, input from the whiskers receives considerably more space than input from "whiskers" on the face of human males.

In the frontal lobes, the primary area is motor rather than sensory. The association cortex is involved in planning and putting together sequences of behaviour. Neurons in the primary areas then issue specific commands to motor neurons throughout the body.

Damage to the frontal lobes can lead to a wide array of problems, from paralysis to difficulty in thinking abstractly, focusing attention efficiently, coordinating complex sequences of behaviour, and adjusting socially.

In most individuals, the left frontal lobe is also

and somatosensory cortexes is not directly proportional to their size. Parts of the body that produce fine motor movements or have particularly dense and sensitive receptors take up

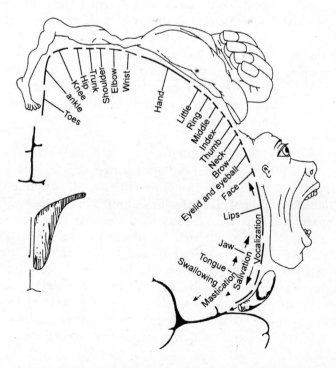

Fig. 3.25 Representation of the body in the motor cortex

involved in language. Broca's area, located in the left frontal lobe at the base of the motor cortex, is specialized for movements of the mouth and tongue necessary for speech production. It also plays a pivotal role in the use and understanding of grammar. Damage to Broca's area causes Broca's aphasia, in which a person may have difficulty in speaking, putting together grammatical sentences, and articulating words, even though he may remain able to comprehend language. Individuals with lesions to this area occasionally have difficulty in comprehending complex sentences if subjects and objects cannot be easily recognized from context. For example, they might have difficulty decoding the sentence, "The cat, which was under the hammock, chased the bird, which was flying over the dog."

Temporal lobes

The *temporal lobes,* located in the lower side portions of the cortex, are particularly important in audition (hearing) and language. The connection between hearing and language makes evolutionary sense because language, until relatively recently, was always spoken (rather than written). The primary cortex receives sensory information from the ears, and the association cortex breaks the flow of sound into meaningful units (such as words). Cells in the primary cortex respond to particular frequencies of sound and are arranged anatomically from low (toward the front of brain) to high frequencies (toward the back).

For most people the left hemisphere of the temporal lobe is specialized for language, although some linguistic functions are shared by the right hemisphere. *Wernicke's area,* located in the left temporal lobe, is important in language comprehension. Damage to Wernicke's area may produce *Wernicke's aphasia,* characterized by difficulty in understanding what words and sentences mean. Patients with Wernicke's aphasia often produce "word salad": They may speak fluently and expressively, as if their speech were meaningful, but the words are tossed together so that they make little sense. In contrast, right temporal damage typically results in nonverbal deficits, such as difficulty in recognizing songs, faces or paintings.

Although psychologists once believed that

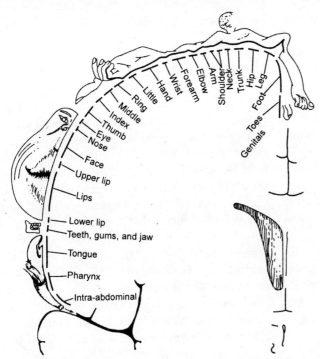

Fig. 3.26 Location of path way termination of different parts of the body in the somatosensory cortex

hearing and language were the primary functions of the temporal lobes, more recent research suggests that the temporal lobes have more than one region and that these different regions serve different functions. For example, one region is comprised of visual association cortex involved in identifying objects. As demonstrated in lesion studies with monkeys and humans, neurons toward the back (posterior regions) of the brain adjacent to the occipital lobes are involved in discriminating qualities of objects such as their shape and size. Toward the front of the brain (anterior), temporal neurons are more involved in memory for objects seen previously.

Cerebral lateralization

The left frontal and temporal lobes tend to play a more important role in speech and language than their right-hemisphere counterparts. This raises the question of whether other cortical functions are *lateralized,* that is localized on one or the other side of the brain, and if so, how extensively.

In general, at least for right-handed people, the left hemisphere tends to be dominant for language, logic, complex motor behaviour, and aspects of consciousness (particularly verbal aspects). Many of these left-hemisphere functions are analytical, breaking down thought and perceptions into component parts and analyzing the relations among them. The left (verbal) brain is said to be the analytical, logical, mathematical hemisphere, concerned with cause-and-effect scientific thinking.

The right hemisphere tends to be dominant for nonlinguistic functions such as forming visual maps of the environment. Studies indicate that it is involved in the recognition of faces, places, and nonlinguistic sounds such as music. The right hemisphere's specialization for nonlinguistic sounds also seem to hold in non-human animals: Japanese macaque monkeys, for example, process vocalizations from other macaques on the left but other sounds in their environment on the right.

MIND, BRAIN AND GENE

Environment and genes interact in staggeringly complex ways that psychologists are just beginning to understand. Psychologists interested in genetics study the influence of genetic blueprints (genotypes) on observable psychological attributes or qualities (phenotypes). Studies in behavioural genetics suggest that a substantial portion of the variation among individuals on many psychological attributes such as intelligence and personality are heritable. Heritability refers to the proportion of variability among individuals on an observed trait (phenotypic variance) that can be accounted for by variability in their genes (genotypic variance).

Several studies of the personality characteristics of twins have produced heritability estimates on a broad spectrum of traits, including conservatism, neuroticism, nurturance, assertiveness, and aggressiveness. Some findings have been very surprising and counterintuitive. For example, identical twins reared apart, who may never have been met each other, tend to have very similar vocational interests and levels of job satisfaction. Researchers have even found a genetic influence on religious attitudes, beliefs, and values.

Species-typical behaviour patterns

For a behaviour pattern to be classed as *species-typical,* all normal members of the species must display the behaviour under certain circumstances. Species-typical behaviours arise from the genetic heritage of the species as it has evolved over time; these behaviours are, in other words, part of the species *"nature"*. But this does not mean that the environment does not play a role in the development of species-typical behaviours. In many cases, the perfection of species-typical behaviours is dependent on the environmental factors present when the young animals are growing up. Since these environmental factors are roughly the same for all members of a species because they all live in a similar habitat, and since species-typical behaviours are based on common genetic heritage, the result is that all normal members of the species display the behaviours.

The concept of *species-typical behaviour,* in case of human beings is greatly complicated by the tremendous flexibility of their behaviour. One of the main results of human evolution is that we have become a species in which behaviour is strongly influenced by learning. In other words, human behaviour is influenced by learning and by the unique events of each individual's life.

Some behaviours of infants and the facial expressions of certain emotions may be considered to be species-typical behaviours.

Within the general framework provided by the species heritage, or *"human nature,"* particular behaviours are learned. For example, our human nature gives us the ability to produce and understand language, but whether we communicate in english, french, german or chinese is a matter of learning.

There are other examples of built-in, programmed behavioural predispositions which human beings have. It is claimed, for example, that tendencies toward competition and aggression, especially among males, are innate. Territoriality, the need for a social organization with leaders, certain things we do in child rearing, male-female roles, and self-sacrifice (or altruism) are all thought to be innate behavioural potentialities which may have a basis in the evolution of our species.

Psychologists tend to emphasize the importance of the unique circumstances of an individual's life in determining behaviour and to give less weight to the role of human nature. One reason for this is that psychology is concerned with understanding, explaining, and predicting differences in behaviour among individuals, and such individual differences are strongly influenced by learning and by the events in a person's life. ■ ■

Sensation and Perception

Sensation and Perception

Sensation and perception are the gateway from the world to the mind. Memory involves the mental reconstruction of past experience—but what would we remember if we could not sense, perceive, and store images or sounds to re-create in our minds? Without our senses, we are literally senseless—without the capacity to know or feel. And without knowledge or feeling, there is little left to being human. It is through our senses that we know about the world.

Sensation refers to the process by which the sense organs gather information about the environment and transmit this information to the brain for initial processing. **Perception** is the process by which the brain organizes and interprets these sensations. Sensations are immediate experiences of qualities—red, hot, bright and so forth—whereas perceptions are experiences of objects or events that appear to have form, order, or meaning. The distinction between sensation and perception is useful though somewhat artificial, since sensory and perceptual processes form an integrated whole, translating physical reality into psychological reality.

BASIC PRINCIPLES

Three basic principles apply across all the senses:

- *There is no one-to-one correspondence between physical and psychological reality*.

  What is "out there" is not directly reproduced "in here". Of course, the relation between physical stimuli and our psychological experience of them is not random; as we will see, it is actually so orderly that it can be expressed as an equation. Yet the inner world is not simply a photograph of the outer. The degree of pressure or pain experienced when a pin presses against the skin—even in those of us *without* painful neuropathy—does not precisely match the actual pressure exerted. Up to a certain point, light pressure is not experienced at all, and pressure only feels like pain when it crosses a certain threshold. The exact correspondence between physical and psychological reality is one of the fundamental findings of psychophysics, the branch of psychology that studies the relation between attributes of the physical world and our psychological experience of them.

- *Sensations and perceptions are active:* Sensation may seem passive—images cast on the retina at the back of the eye; pressure is imposed on the skin. Yet sensation is first and foremost on act of translation, converting external energy into on internal version or *representation* of it. People also orient themselves to stimuli to capture sights, sounds and smell that are relevant to them. We turn our ears toward potentially threatening sounds to magnify their impact on our senses, just as we turn our noses toward the smell of cooking food.

  Like sensation, perception is an active process, which organizes and interprets sensations. The world as subjectively experienced by an individual—the *phenomenological world*—is a joint product of external reality and the person's creative efforts to understand and depict it mentally. People often assume that perception is like photographing a scene or tape recording a sound and that they only need to open their eyes and ears to capture what is "really" there. In fact, perception is probably more like stitching a quilt than taking a photograph. The phenomenological world must be constructed from sensory experience, just as the quilt maker creates something whole from threads and patches.

- *Sensation and perception are adaptive:* From an evolutionary perspective, the ability to see, hear, or touch is the product of millions of adaptations that left our senses exquisitely crafted to serve functions that facilitate survival and reproduction. Humans have neural regions specialized for the perception of faces and facial expressions. Human infants have an innate tendency to pay attention to forms that resemble the human face, and over the course of their first year they become remarkably expert at reading emotions from other people's faces.

SENSING THE ENVIRONMENT

Although each sensory system is attuned to particular forms of energy, all the senses share certain common features:

- They must translate physical stimulation into sensory signals.
- They all have thresholds below which a person does not sense anything despite external stimulation.
- Sensation requires constant decision making, as the individual tries to distinguish meaningful from irrelevant stimulation.

- Sensing the world requires the ability to detect changes in stimulation, to notice when a bag of groceries has gotten heavier or a light has dimmed.
- Efficient sensory processing means "turning down the volume" on information that is redundant; the nervous system tunes out messages that continue without change.

We will examine each of these processes now.

Transduction

Sensation requires converting energy in the world into internal signals that are psychologically meaningful. The more brain processes these signals—from sensation to perception to cognition—the more meaningful they become. Sensation typically begin with an environmental stimulus, a form of energy capable of exciting the nervous system.

Creating a neural code

Specialized cells in the nervous system, called **receptors**, transforms energy in the environment into neural impulses that can be interpreted by the brain. Receptors respond to different forms of energy and generate action potentials in sensory neurons adjacent to them. In the eye, receptors respond to particles of light; in the ear, to the movement of molecules of air. The process of converting physical energy or stimulus information into neural impulses is called transduction. The brain then interprets the impulses generated by sensory receptors as light, sound, smell, taste, touch or motion. It essentially reads a neural code—a pattern of neural firing—and translates it into a psychologically meaningful "language."

Coding for intensity and quality of the stimulus

For each sense, the brain codes sensory stimulation for intensity and quality. The neural code for **intensity**, or strength, of a sensation varies by sensory modality but usually involves the number of sensory neurons that fire, the frequency with which they fire, or some combination of the two. The neural code for **quality**, or nature, of the sensation (such as colour, pitch, taste, or temperature) is often more complicated, relying on both the specific type of receptors involved and the pattern of neural impulses generated. For example, some receptors respond to warmth and others to cold, but a combination of both leads to the sensation of extreme heat.

Thresholds

A **threshold** is a limiting (minimum or maximum) energy change measured in terms of physiological recordings of receptors or nerve cells or in terms of reported sensation (in humans). There are three types of thresholds, each a measurement of physical energy as it affects sensation or receptor response. In visual intensity. For example, the absolute threshold for brightness is the dimmest light the subject can detect. The difference threshold is the smallest difference in brightness the subject can detect. The terminal threshold is the brightest light and the most intense sensation that subject can experience; further increases in intensity do not make the light appear brighter to the subject. All three of these receptor and sensation responses have absolute and fixed values at a given moment. However, the sensitivity of the visual receptors varies from moment to moment. This will cause the absolute, difference and terminal threshold values to vary from one measurement to the next. In addition, the subject makes *errors* in reporting his sensations, the experimenter makes errors in varying the stimulus and recording the results, and the stimulus light is not perfect. Fluctuations in receptor sensitivity and measurement errors are involved. Some kind of average measurement is needed for the absolute, difference, and terminal thresholds. This means that any threshold is a derived from *statistical* value rather than an absolute value for receptor sensitivity.

Absolute threshold

The **absolute threshold** is most precisely defined as the minimum energy that results in a sensation (that stimulates a receptor) 50% of the time. As noted above, the 50% "average" value is used because the sensitivity of the receptor, the attention of the subject, and measurement errors fluctuate. Obviously, the more intense the energy, the greater will be the percentage of occasions that it will stimulate the subject—a more intense light will be detected more often, for example.

Difference threshold

The **difference** threshold is defined as the least difference between two stimuli in a given direction that can be detected 50% of the time. The same considerations requiring an average value for the absolute threshold are doubly involved for the difference threshold, since two stimuli, rather than one, are used.

Terminal threshold

At the other end of the scale from the absolute threshold is the **terminal threshold.** It is applied most readily to differences in the intensity and quality of stimuli. In terms of intensity it would be the stimulus whose increase in intensity leads to, no increase in sensation intensity half the time. As an example from quality thresholds, when increases in the frequency of a sound pass the range where the subject can hear them 50% of the time, the terminal threshold for pitch has been reached. However, there are two difficulties with the terminal threshold:

1. As the terminal threshold for intensity is approached, pain is sensed, and damage to the receptors may result; thus for practical reasons the terminal intensity threshold is often measured in terms of the onset of pain.

2. The terminal intensity threshold is also measured in terms of quality and intensity of stimuli. For example, the sensory range for pitch increases with increased intensity, so that both the absolute and terminal threshold values change—the subject can hear both lower and higher pitches at increased intensity.

Sensory adaptation

A final process shared by all sensory systems is adaptation. You walk into a crowded restaurant, and the noise level is overwhelming, yet within a few minutes, you do not even notice it. Driving into an industrial city, you notice an unpleasant odour that smells like sulphur and wonder how anyone tolerates it; a short time later, you are no longer aware of it. These are examples of **sensory adaptation**—the tendency of sensory receptors to respond less to stimuli that continue without change.

Sensory adaptation makes sense from an evolutionary perspective. Constant sensory inputs provide no new information about the environment, so the nervous system essentially ignores them.

Sensory adaptation also performs the function of "turning down the volume" on information that would overwhelm the brain, by reducing its perceived intensity to a manageable level.

Although sensory adaptation generally applies across senses, the nervous system is wired to circumvent it in some important instances. For example, the visual system has ways to keep its receptors from adapting; otherwise, stationary objects would disappear from sight. The eyes are constantly making tiny quivering motions, which guarantees that the receptors affected by a given stimulus are constantly changing. The result is a steady flow of a graded potentials on the sensory neurons that synapse with those receptors. Similarly, although we may adapt to mild pain, we generally do not adapt to severe pain, again an evolutionarily sensible design feature of a sensory system that responds to body damage.

VISION

The topic of vision can be considered from three points of view:

1. The anatomy and physiology of the eye and its nervous connections.
2. The physical energy that provides the stimulus.

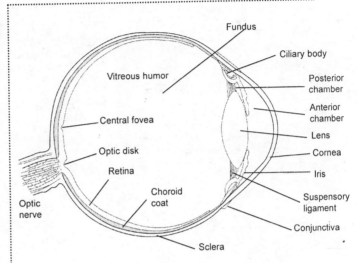

Fig. 4.1 The structure of the eye

3. The physiology of interaction between the stimulus and the visual mechanism that provides a sensation.

Anatomy of the eye

The eye is a sense organ and therefore an organization of different kinds of tissue has a role to play in the eye's response to light.

The eyeball consists of three layers—the **sclerotic coat**, the **choroid coat**, and the **retina**. The **sclerotic coat**, or **sclera** is the tough opaque outer fibrous tissue that forms the "white" of the eye.

It serves a protective and binding function and to some extent prevents light from entering the eye except by way of the pupil. The sclera is continuous with the **cornea** at the front of the eye. Light first enters the interior of the eye through the transparent cornea. The cornea begins the focusing job that the **lens** completes by bringing light rays into focus on the retina.

The **choroid coat** is the middle layer of the

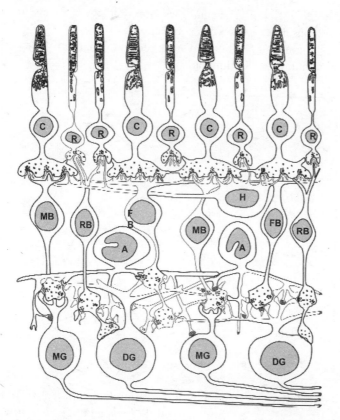

Fig. 4.2 Diagram of receptors and connecting nerve cells of retina. R rod; C cone; MB, midget bipolar; RB, rod bipolar; FB, flat bipolar; H, horizontal cell; A, amacrine cell; MG, midget ganglion cell; DG, diffuse ganglion cell. Light reaches the retina from the bottom of the diagram.

eyeball. It contains many blood vessels that nourish the other tissues of the eye. It is pigmented, or dark coloured, on its inner surface to minimize the scattering of light by reflection inside the eyeball. The choroid coat is continuous with the **ciliary body**, or **ciliary ring**, a ring of smooth muscle that is attached to the lens by the **suspensory ligament**. The ciliary body is also continuous with the **iris**, another smooth muscle structure. It contains circular muscle fibers that contract to constrict the **pupil** and radial muscles that contract to open the pupil.

The **retina** covers only a part of the interior surface of the eyeball—the back portion. The retina contains the light sensitive receptor cells as well as several kinds of nerve cells. The retina is arranged "inside out"; that is, the receptors lie nearest to the choroid coat, and light must pass through several layers of connecting nerve cells to reach the receptors. The receptors, called **rods** and **cones**, form a distinct layer in the retina. The most distinct of the other layers of the retina are the **bipolar cell layer** and the **ganglion cell layer**. The rods and cones pass excitation to the bipolar cells when stimulated by light. The bipolar cells, in turn, pass excitation to the ganglion cells. The axons of the ganglion cells form the optic nerve, the nerve that carries excitation from the eye to visual centers in the brain. In the retina itself there are interconnection between the receptors via **horizontal cells**; **amacrine cells** interconnect the bipolar cells. Excitation and inhibition can thereby spread from one point to surrounding areas of the retina.

Finally, there are efferent fibers reaching the retina from the brain. These fibers probably synapse with amacrine and ganglion cells; their function appears to be inhibitory. The efferent fibers may act to sharpen vision by blocking off extraneous input from other parts of the retina, or they may reduce visual input generally, but this is still speculation.

The fovea is a pit, or depression, in the retina that is in line with the pupil of the eye when the eye is directed toward an object. The **fovea** is the point of clearest vision and is densely packed with receptors. The receptors are arranged radially around the pit, with connecting bipolar and ganglion cells radially connected to them. Therefore, light does not have to pass through the ganglion and bipolar cells to reach the receptors in the fovea. Only cones are found in the fovea, but they are packed so densely together that they take on the elongated shape of rods. Since light reaches foveal cones directly and since they are numerous, foveal vision is clearer than peripheral vision from other parts of the retina. Light rays from objects are focused by the lens on the fovea in visual accommodation.

The cones are the hue-sensitive receptor cells of the retina. Stimulation of cones results in sensations of hue as well as brightness. Light stimulates the cones by breaking down a chemical pigment called **iodopsin**, as well as related chemicals, into intermediate compounds; light further causes the intermediate compounds to break down into vitamin A and coneopsin.

The rods are sensitive only to brightness and give sensations of varied shades of gray. Thus one does not have sensations of hue under conditions of night vision, when rod response predominates. At night there is often not enough light to stimulate cones. Instead of iodopsin the rods contain **rhodopsin.** Light breaks down rhodopsin into intermediate compounds, which stimulate rods; the intermediate compounds may further break down into rod opsin and vitamin A.

Rods and cones excite bipolar cells, which in turn stimulate ganglion cells. It is the ganglion cell axons that leave the eye to form the optic nerve. At the point where the axons leave the eye there are no receptors; this point (the optic disc) is called the blind spot because it is insensitive to light.

Cavities and fluids of the eye

The **anterior chamber** of the eye lies between the cornea and the iris of the eye and communicates with the **posterior chamber** of the eye via the pupil. The posterior chamber lies between the iris on one hand and the ciliary ring, suspensory ligament, and lens on the other. Both anterior and posterior chambers are filled with **aqueous humor** a watery fluid resembling the extracellular and lymph fluids of other parts of the body. Neither chamber communicates with the **fundus**, large interior cavity of the eye, at least not directly. The fundus contains a jelly-like substance, the **vitreous humor**, that is much more viscous than the aqueous humor. Both fluids absorb some light rays and scatter others, as do the lens and cornea. Despite its pigment coating, the interior of the eyeball scatters some light, and still more light leaks through the opaque outer covering (sclera) of the eye ball.

Nervous connections of the eye

The axons of ganglion cells of the innermost layer of the retina converge on the optic disc, or blind spot, and emerge from the eyeball as the **optic nerve**. The optic nerves from the two eyeballs are really *tracts,* since they are part of the central rather than the peripheral nervous system. However, for convenience the ganglion cell axons are called the optic nerve before they reach the **optic chiasma** are called the **optic tract** after they leave it.

When the ganglion cell axons reach the optic chiasma, a hemidecussation, or "half crossing," occurs in the ganglion cells. Fibers from the *nasal,* or medical, halves of each retina cross, whereas fibers from the *temporal* halves of each retina do not cross. As a result the crossing fibres from the nasal halves of the retina of each eye send excitation to the opposite cerebral hemispheres, whereas fibers from the temporal half of each retina, which do not cross, send excitation to the cerebral hemisphere of the

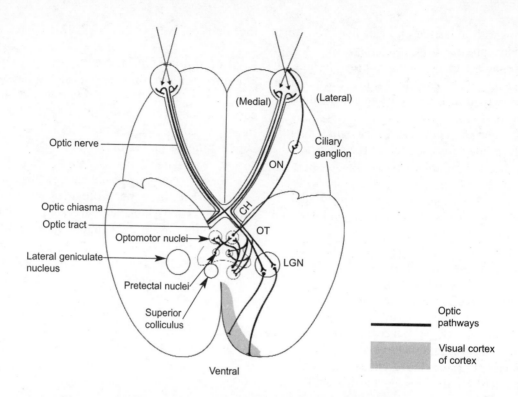

Fig. 4.3 Optic pathway as viewed from beneath brain

same side. The right optic *tract,* for example, would contain fibers from the nasal half of the left retina and the temporal half of the right retina. Thus the nasal half of the left retina and the temporal half of the right retina "see" the *left* half of the visual *field*. Damage to the right optic tract would therefore impair vision in the left visual field.

In contrast, cutting the right optic nerve would mearly blind the right eye. Damage to the crossing fibers of the chiasma would destroy fibers from the nasal halves of both retinas, impairing peripheral vision from the temporal halves of both visual fields.

The optic tract of each side terminates in the *lateral geniculate body,* or lateral geniculate nucleus (LGN). The lateral geniculate nucleus serves mainly as a relay station for the cortex, like thalamus, and is topographically organized. The optic tract also sends fibers to the superior colliculi and pretectal nuclei. The superior colliculi mediate reflex movements of the eyeball in convergence and in other eye movements. These responses are handled by connections with the nuclei of the third, fourth and sixth cranial nerves. The pretectal nuclei, on the other hand, are concerned with the intrinsic muscles of the eye, the ciliary muscles of lens accommodation, and the reflex regulation of the pupil by the iris.

The major function of the lateral geniculate nucleus is to supply the striate cortex, the primary visual projection area in occipital lobes. It corresponds with Brodmann's area 17.

The nature of light

Light is a complex form of energy that is part of the *electromagnetic spectrum* of energy. Light consists of individual particles of matter, each of which demonstrates the property of wavelike

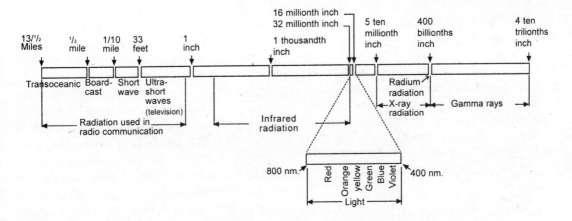

Fig. 4.4 Electromagnetic spectrum, showing range of wave-lengths that stimulate visual receptors (light)

motion at a specific frequency. The wavelengths form a spectrum of wavelengths that are part of the more extensive electromagnetic spectrum. The electromagnetic spectrum includes radio waves, infra-red waves, light, and x-rays and gamma rays. One can see that visible light forms a small part of the electromagnetic spectrum and that its wave lengths are very short. The wavelengths are measured in nanometers (nm, millionth of a millimeter, billionths of a meter, or 10^{-9} meters). The receptors in the human eye are tuned to detect only a very restricted portion of the electromagnetic spectrum, from roughly 400 to 700 nm.

Light is a useful from of energy to sense for a number of reasons. Like other forms of electromagnetic radiation, light travels very quickly, so sighted organisms can see things almost immediately after they happen. Light also travels in straight lines, which means that it preserves the geometric organization of the objects it illuminates; the image an object casts on the retina resembles its actual structure. Perhaps most importantly, light interacts with the molecules on the surface of many objects and is either absorbed or reflected. The light that is reflected reaches the eyes and creates a visual pattern. Objects that reflect a lot of light appear brighter, whereas those that absorb much of the light that hits them appear dark.

Transduction in vision

The rods and the cones contain what are known as photosensitive pigments. When electromagnetic energy in the visible spectrum—light—strikes these pigments, some of the light energy is absorbed by the pigments, and chemical changes occur which initiate the chain of events involved in seeing. Absorption of light energy causes the pigment molecules to change their configuration, or shape, and this process creates electrical energy. Through a series of further electrical steps, involving the horizontal, bipolar and amacrine cells of the retina electrical activity is passed from the rods and cones to the ganglion cells of the retina. The electrical events that have travelled across the retina trigger or generate nerve impulse travels through the optic nerve to the lateral geniculate body and from there it reaches the primary visual sensory area of the cortex.

Accommodation

Light rays that reach the eye from objects more than 15 to 20 feet away are parallel, as compared to light rays from nearby objects that *diverge* noticeably in reaching the eye. If the object is closer than 15 to 20 feet away, light rays from it *diverge* noticeably on their way to the eye. Such diverging rays must be bent more than parallel rays to be focused on the retina. This is accomplished by *thickening* the lens, a process called **accommodation**. The ciliary muscle contracts to constrict the ciliary ring, drawing it forward and decreasing its diameter. This relieves tension on the suspensory ligament holding the lens. Under decreased tension the lens, because of its own elasticity, bulges to become thicker, causing increased bending of diverging light rays as an object is brought closer to the eye. The correction of accommodation problems, is the most common reason for wearing glasses.

The duplicity theory of vision

The initial assumption made about the way in which rod and cone systems work assigns them different intensity ranges and reactions to hue. The rod system is supposed to be **achromatic**, or **scotopic**; that is, it has inputs that do not give sensations of hue and has very low thresholds for functioning in low illumination. The cone system is supposed to be **chromatic** or **photopic**; it has a relatively high threshold and functions under conditions of daylight vision. The evidence behind these statements can be summarized as follows:

1. Two different visual pigments in the eye, iodopsin and rhodopsin, have been discovered.
2. Relative sensitivity to individual wavelengths differs under high illumination as compared to low illumination; the cones seem most sensitive in the yellow-green region of the spectrum (555 nm), whereas the rods seem most sensitive in the green region of the spectrum (511 nm).
3. The curves for spectral sensitivity, or sensitivity to different wavelengths of light for rods and cones, look like curves measuring the amount of light of the same wavelengths that is absorbed by rhodopsin and iodopsin, respectively. Presumably, the more a given wavelength is absorbed to break down rhodopsin, for example, the more sensitive the rhodopsin—containing rod would be to that wavelength.
4. The central part of the retina—the fovea, which contains only cones—provides the most

acute vision in high illumination; the periphery of the retina (peripheral vision), contains nearly all rods and is most sensitive in the dark-adapted eye.

5. When one is looking at a gray field, hues are seen only in the central part of the visual field, where the cones respond; spots of color in the periphery, where the rods respond, are seen as gray.
6. Adaptation to darkness from daylight seems to occur in two stages. For approximately the first five minutes the eyes become more sensitive at a diminishing rate as more iodopsin is built up in the cones, but there is not enough light to break it all down. Later, enough rhodopsin begins to be built up in the rods so that they begin responding. Since rod input is more sensitive than cone input, the eyes again start increasing in sensitivity at a rapid rate, reaching maximum sensitivity after a half or so.

Newton's laws of colour

Many years ago Sir Isaac Newton produced a visible spectrum of hues by separating the wavelengths of light coming from the sun. Using a narrow beam of sunlight coming through a pinhole, he interposed a prism that bent, or refracted, the beam of light. Light refraction depends on wavelength; the shorter wavelengths were bent more than the longer wavelengths, producing an array of wavelengths—the visible spectrum. Different wavelengths are perceived by the eye as different hues, so that bands of different hues were seen from violet through blue, green, yellow, orange and red, with shorter to longer wavelengths over the 400 to 750 nm visible spectrum. Any single wavelength is fairly saturated, that is, distinct in hue, and the spectrum produced in this manner is of intermediate brightness. Having separated the wavelengths to produce the hues of the spectrum, Newton recombined individual hues, a process often called "colour mixing". His experiments led to Newton's three laws of colours, which can be rephrased as follows:

1. Law of complements
For each hue there is another hue that will mix with it in some proportion to cancel both hues and gives a gray or white colour.

2. Law of supplements
Noncomplementary hues will mix to give a hue that lies between them on the spectrum. For example, a yellow-green and or orange will mix to give a yellow. Hues from the ends of the spectrum—violets and reds—mix to give purples, which are not spectral hues.

3. Law of resultants
The same hue may be produced by several mixtures. Mixing two similar hues produced in different ways alters nothing; mixtures that match one another mix without change in hue. For example, a green could be obtained with a single wavelength or by mixing yellow-green and orange-red. If the two greens matched, their apparent hue would not change when they were combined.

Visual response
The eye perceives changes in the physical amplitude—the rate of flow (flux) of light—as a change in brightness, from black to gray to white, for example. Changes in the wavelength of light are perceived as changes in hue—reds, greens, blues and yellows, for instance. But colours that are of the same hue and brightness may differ in saturation—a green may appear as green as it can be or it may be a grayish green—equally bright, of the same basic hue, but "not as coloured." The last statement is a bit misleading since gray, black and white are colours, although they lack hue or saturation. *Saturation is the amount by which a hue differs from the total lack of hue perceived in a gray of equal brightness.* A further complication arises because brightness and saturation interact. The hue,

saturation, and brightness interactions of human visual response are diagrammed in the double pyramid.

The vertical dimension of the figure represents brightness differences and the horizontal dimensions represent saturation differences, with the outside surfaces at all vertical levels representing the maximum saturation response at a given brightness. The figure tells us that maximum saturation of any hue is possible only at intermediate levels of brightness. Thus a sky blue can never be as saturated as a blue or an indigo, but a blue can be desaturated until it is no more saturated than the brighter sky blue of maximum saturation. The corners of the figure are labeled blue, red, yellow, green, white, and black, with gray at the center, since these seem to be unique colours. This is why hues seem more saturated near sunset—in "bright" daylight, they seem "washed out," and as dusk approaches they seem "too dark" to be appreciated. Although black represents absence of stimulation, it is not a true sensation. The retina never ceases signaling the

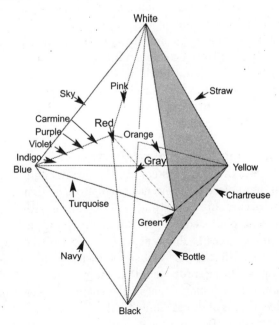

Fig. 4.5 Colour pyramid

brain and a kind of "brain gray" results—the dark gray sensation you have when you close your eyes.

Perceiving in colour

"Roses are red, violets are blue." Well not exactly. Colour is a psychological property, not a quality of the stimulus. Grass is not green to a cow because cows lack—colour receptors; in contrast, most insects, reptiles, fish, and birds have excellent colour vision. As Sir Isaac Newton demonstrated in research with prisms in the sixteenth century, white light is composed of all the wavelengths that constitute the colours in the visual spectrum. A rose appears red because it absorbs certain wavelengths and reflects others, and humans have receptors that detect electromagnetic radiation in that range of the spectrum.

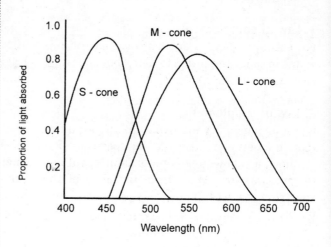

Fig. 4.6 Cone response curves. All three kinds of cones respond to a range of frequencies but they are maximally sensitive at particular frequencies and thus produce different colour sensations

Actually, colour has three psychological dimensions: hue, saturation, and lightness. **Hue** is what people commonly mean by colours, that is, whether an object appears blue, red, violet, and so on. **Saturation** is a colour's purity (the extent to which it is diluted with white or black or "saturated" with its own wavelength, like a sponge in water). **Lightness** is the extent to which a colour is light or dark.

Retinal transduction of colour

How does the visual system translate wavelength into the subjective experience of colour? The first step occurs in the retina, where cones with different photosensitive pigments respond to varying degrees to different wavelengths of the spectrum. In 1802, a British physician named Thomas Young proposed that human colour vision is *trichromatic,* that is, the colours we see reflect blends of three colours to which our retinas are sensitive. Developed independently 50 years later by Hermann von Helmholtz, the **Young—Helmholtz (or trichromatic) theory of the**

colour holds that eye contains three types of receptors, each maximally sensitive to wavelengths of light that produce sensations of blue, green, or red.

Another century later, nobel prize winner George Wald and others confirmed the existence of three different types of cones in the retina. Each cone responds to a range of wavelengths but responds most persistently to waves of light at a particular point on the spectrum. Short-wavelength cones (*S-cones*) are most sensitive to wavelengths of about 420 nm, which are perceived as blue. Middle-wavelength cones (*M-cones*), which produced the sensation of green, are most sensitive to wavelengths of about 535 nm. Long wavelengths cones (*L-cones*), which produce red sensations are most sensitive to wavelength of about 560 nm. Mixing these three primary colours of light—red, green, and blue—produces the thousands of colour shades humans can discriminate and identify.

This list of primary colours differ from the list of primary colours children learn in elementary school from mixing points (blue, red, and yellow). The reason is that mixing point and mixing light alter the wavelengths perceived in different ways, one subtracting and the other adding parts of the spectrum. Mixing points is called **subtractive colour mixture** because each new point added actually blocks out, or subtracts, wavelengths reflected onto the retina. For example, yellow point appears yellow because its pigment absorbs most wavelengths and reflects only those perceived as yellow; the same is true of blue point.

Subtractive colour mixture, then, mixes wavelengths of light before they reach the eye. In contrast, **additive colour mixture** takes place in the eye itself, as light of differing wavelengths simultaneously strikes the retina and thus expands (add to) the perceived section of the spectrum.

Processing colour in the brain

The trichromatic theory accurately predicted the nature of retinal receptors, but it was not a complete theory of colour perception. For example, the physiologist Ewald Hering noted that trichromatic theory could not alone explain a phenomenon that occurs with afterimages, visual images that persist after a stimulus has been removed. Hering wondered why the colours of the afterimages were different in predictable ways from those of the original image. He proposed theory, modified substantially by later researchers, known as **opponent-process theory**. Opponent—process theory argues that all colours are derived from three antagonistic colour systems: black-white, blue-yellow, and red-green. The black-white system contributes to brightness and saturation; the other two systems are responsible for hue.

Hering proposed his theory in opposition to trichromatic theory, but subsequent research suggests that the two theories are actually complementary. Trichromatic theory applies to the retina, where cones are, infact, particularly responsive to red, blue, or green. Opponent-process theory applies at higher visual centers in the brain.

Opponent-process and trichromatic theory together explain another phenomenon that interested Hering: *colour blindness* (or, more accurately, *colour deficiency*). Few people are entirely blind to colour; those who are, can only detect brightness, not colour. Most colour-deficient people confuse red and green. Red-green colour blindness is sex linked, over ten times more prevalent in males than females. It generally reflects a deficiency of either M-cones or L-cones, which makes red-green distinctions impossible at higher levels of nervous system.

How the world becomes represented in the mind

The process by which objects in the external world become translated into an "internal" portrait of them in the mind should now be growing clear. At the lowest level of the nervous system, neurons collect highly specific information from receptor cells that would, by itself, be meaningless. At each subsequent stage, through the thalamus to the most complex modules in the cortex, information is combined to provide a progressively richer, more integrated picture of the bits and pieces of knowledge collected at the prior stage. Through this process, isolated units of stimulus energy gradually undergo a remarkable metamorphosis, in which the brain weaves sensory threads into complex and meaningful perceptual tapestries. As we will see, however, perceptions are not woven *exclusively* from sensory input, that is, from the simple threads. Our beliefs, expectations, and needs also exert an influence on what we perceive, so that knowledge is, from the very start, an interaction between an active perceiver and an environment that never stands still.

HEARING

If a tree falls in a forest, does it make a sound if no one hears it? To answer this question requires an understanding of hearing, or *audition*, and the physical properties it reflects.

The nature of sound

When a tree falls in the forest, the crash produces vibrations in adjacent air molecules, which in turn collide with one another. A guitar string being plucked, a piece of paper rustling, or a tree falling to the ground all produce sound because they create vibrations in the air. Like ripples on a pond, these rhythmic pulsations of acoustic energy (sound) spread outward from the vibrating object as **sound waves**. Sound waves grow weaker with distance, but they travel at a constant speed, roughly 1130 feet (or 340 meters) per second.

Like light, sound waves can be reflected off or absorbed by objects in the environment, but the impact on hearing is different from the impact on vision. When sound is reflected off an object, it produces an echo; when it is absorbed by an object, such as carpet, it is muffled.

Any solid body will vibrate when struck, however brief its motion. The vibrations of some solid objects are regular, consistent, or periodic. This is true of a tuning fork, for example. The regular movements of the tuning fork have a characteristic frequency or rate as well as a characteristic amplitude or extent. The motions of the tines of the tuning fork cause it to strike molecules of air. The air molecules collide with one another to transmit energy from molecule to molecule as the molecules vibrate back and forth. The energy radiates in all directions from the vibrating source. Since the vibrating source has a consistent frequency and amplitude of vibration, so do the air molecules. Air pressure is determined by how close together the molecules are. Since the air molecules are colliding with one another and then moving apart in a regular fashion, waves of air pressure *change* constitute sound.

Frequency

Acoustic energy has three important properties: frequency, complexity, and amplitude. When a person hits a tuning fork, the prongs of the fork move rapidly inward and outward, putting pressure on the air molecules around them, which collide with the molecules next to them. Each sound of expansion and contraction of the distance between molecules of air is known as a **cycle**.

The number of cycles per second determines the sound wave's frequency. **Frequency** is just

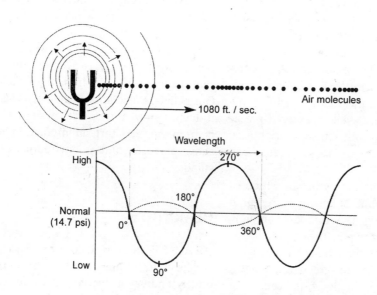

Fig. 4.7 Characteristics of sound energy

what it sounds like—a measure of how often (that is, how *frequently*) a wave cycles. Frequency is expressed in *hertz, or Hz*. One hertz equals one cycle per second, so a 1500-Hz tone has 1500 cycles per second. The frequency of a simple sound wave corresponds to the psychological property of *pitch* (the quality of a tone, from low to high). Generally, the higher the frequency, the higher the pitch. When frequency is doubled—that is, when the number of cycles per second is twice as frequent—the pitch perceived is an octave higher.

The human auditory system is sensitive to a wide range of frequencies. Young adults can hear frequencies from about 15 to 20,000 Hz, but as with most senses, capacity diminishes with aging. Frequencies used in music range from the lowest note on an organ (16 Hz) to the highest note on a grand piano (over 4000 Hz). Human voices range from about 100 Hz to about 3500 Hz, and our ears are most sensitive to sounds in that frequency range.

Complexity

Sounds rarely consist of waves of uniform frequency. Rather, most sounds are a combination of sound waves, each with a different frequency. The **complexity** of a sound wave—the extent to which it is composed of multiple frequencies—corresponds to the psychological property of **timbre**, or texture of the sound. People recognize each other's voices as well as the sounds of different musical instruments, from their characteristic timbre.

The sounds instruments produce, whether in a rock band or a symphony, are music to our ears because we learn to interpret particular temporal patterns and combinations of sound waves as music. What people hear as music and as random auditory noise depends on their culture. The scales and harmonic structures that are standard in contempory jazz would have been musically incomprehensible to Mozart.

Amplitude

In addition to frequency and complexity sound waves have amplitude. Amplitude refers to the height and depth of a wave, that is, the difference between its maximum and minimum pressure level. The amplitude of a sound wave corresponds to the psychological property of **loudness**; the greater the amplitude, the louder the sound. Amplitude is measured in *decibels (dB)*. Zero decibels is the absolute threshold above which most people can hear a 1000-Hz tone.

A loud scream is 100,000 times more intense than a sound at the absolute threshold, but it is only 100 dB different. Conversation is usually held at 50 to 60 dB. Most people experience sounds over 130 dB as painful, and prolonged exposure to sounds over about 90 dB, such as subway cars rolling into the station or amplifiers at a rock concert, can produce permanent hearing loss or ringing in the ears.

The ear

Transduction of sound occurs in the ear, which consists of an outer, middle, and inner ear. The outer ear collects and magnifies sounds in the air; the middle ear converts waves of air pressure into movements of tiny bones; and the inner ear transforms these movements into waves in fluid that generate neural signals.

Transduction

The hearing process begins in the outer ear, which consists of the pinna and the auditory canal. Sound waves are funneled into the ear by the pinna, the skin-covered cartilage that protrudes from the sides of the head. The pinna is not essential for hearing, but its irregular shape is useful for locating sounds in space, which bounce off its folds differently when they come from various locations. Just inside the skull is the auditory canal, a passage way about an inch long. As sound waves resonate in the auditory canal, they are amplified by up to a factor of 2.

The middle ear

At the end of the auditory canal is a thin, flexible

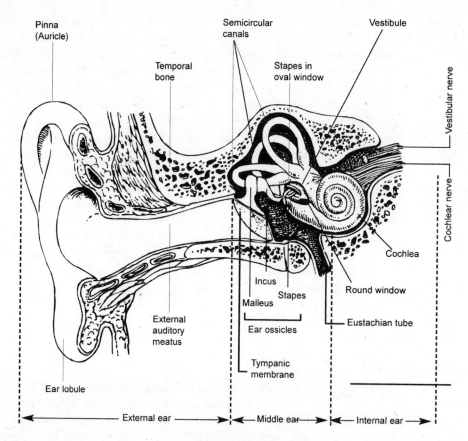

Fig. 4.8 Structure of the ear

membrane known as the **eardrum**, or **tympanic membrane**. The eardrum marks the outer boundary of the middle ear. When sound waves reached the eardrum, they set it in motion. The movements of the eardrum are extremely small—0.00000001 centimeter, or about the width of a hydrogen molecule, in response to a whisper. The eardrum essentially reproduces the cyclical vibration of the object that created the noise, on a microcosmic scale. It is only able to do so, however, if air pressure on both sides of it (in the outer and middle ear) is roughly the same.

When the eardrum vibrates, it sets in motion three tiny bones, named for their distinctive shapes, are called the malleus, incus, and stapes, which translate from the Latin into hammer, anvil and stirrup, respectively. The

ossicles further amplify the sound two or three times before transmitting vibrations to the inner ear. The stirrup vibrates against a membrane called the **oval window**, which forms the beginning of the inner ear.

The inner ear

The inner ear consists of two sets of fluid-filled cavities hollowed out of the temporal bone of the skull; the semicircular canals (involved in balance) and the cochlea (involved in hearing). The temporal bone is the hardest bone in the body and serves as natural sound proofing for its vibration—sensitive cavities. Chewing during a meeting sounds louder to the person doing the chewing than to those nearby because it rattles the temporal bone and thus augments the sounds from the ears.

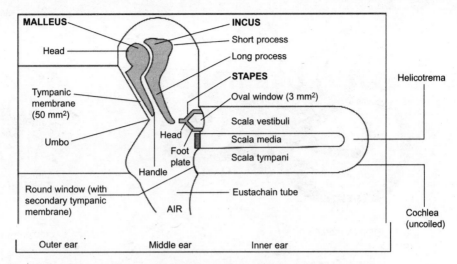

Fig. 4.9 Arrangement of ear (auditory) ossicles in the middle ear and scalae in the cochlea (inner ear)

The **cochlea** is a three-chambered tube shaped like a snail. When the stirrup vibrates against the oval window, the oval window vibrates, causing pressure waves in the cochlear fluid. These waves disturb the **basilar membrane**, which separates two of the cochlea's chambers. Attached to the basilar membrane are the ear's 15,000 receptors for sound, called **hair cells** (because they terminate in tiny bristles, or **cilia**). Above the hair cells is another membrane, the **tectorial membrane**, which also moves as waves of pressure travel through the cochlear fluid. The cilia bend as the basilar and tectorial membranes move in different directions. This triggers action potentials in sensory neurons forming the **auditory nerve**, which transmits auditory information to the brain. Thus, mechanical energy—the movement of cilia and membranes—is transduced into neural energy.

Sensory deficits in hearing, as in other senses, can arise from problems either with parts of the sense organ that channel stimulus energy or with the receptors and neural circuits that convert this energy into psychological experience. Failure of the outer or middle ear to conduct sound to the receptors in the hair cells is called conduction loss; failure of receptors in the inner ear or of neurons in

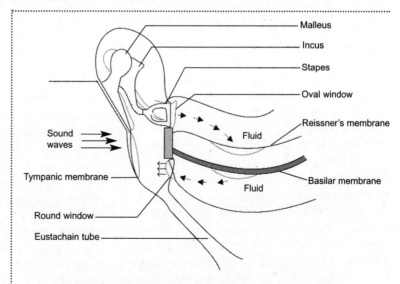

Fig. 4.10 Schematic representation of the way ear (auditory) ossicles movements are transmitted into a wave in the fluid of the inner ear.

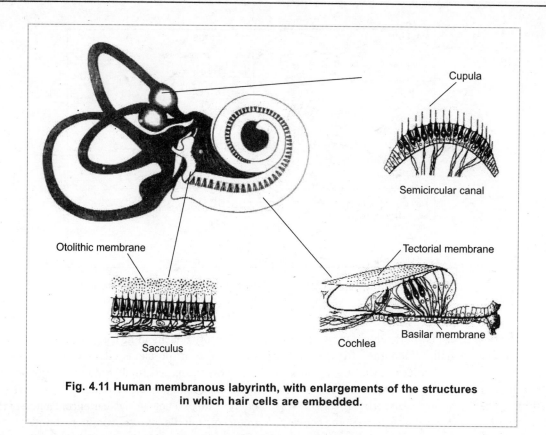

Fig. 4.11 Human membranous labyrinth, with enlargements of the structures in which hair cells are embedded.

any auditory pathway in the brain is referred to as sensorineural loss. The most common problems with hearing result from exposure to noise or reflect changes in the receptors with aging. A single exposure to an extremely loud noise, such as a firecracker, an explosion, or a gun firing at close range, can permanently damage the hair cell receptors in the inner ear.

Sensing pitch

Precisely how does auditory transduction transform the physical properties of sound frequency and amplitude into the psychological experiences of pitch and loudness? Two theories, both proposed in the nineteenth century and once considered opposing explanations, together appear to explain the available data. The first, called **place theory**, holds that different areas of the basilar membrane are maximally sensitive to different frequencies. Place theory was initially proposed

by Herman von Helmholtz, who had the wrong mechanism but the right idea. A Hungarian scientist named Georg von Beksey discovered the mechanism a century after Helmholtz by recognizing that when the stapes hits the oval window, a wave travels down the basilar membrane like a carpet being shaken at one end. Shaking a carpet rapidly (i.e., at high frequency) produces an early peak in the wave of the carpet, whereas shaking it slowly produces a peak in the wave toward the other end of the carpet. Similarly, high-frequency tones, which produce rapid strokes of the stapes, produce the largest displacement of the basilar membrane close to the oval window, whereas low-frequency tones cause a peak in basilar movement towards the far end of the membrane. Peak vibration leads to peak firing of hair cells at a particular location. Hair cells at different points on the basilar membrane thus transmit information about different frequencies

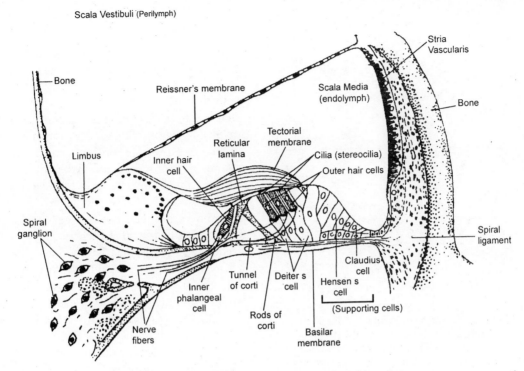

4.12 Structure of organ of corti: the receptor of hearing

to the brain, just as rods and cones transduce electromagnetic energy at different frequencies.

Place theory has one major problem. At *very* low frequencies the entire basilar membrane vibrates fairly uniformly; thus, for very low tones, location of maximal vibration cannot account for pitch. The second theory of pitch, **frequency theory,** overcomes this problem, proposing that the more frequently a sound wave cycles, the more frequently the basilar membrane vibrates and its hair cells fire. Thus, pitch perception is probably mediated by two neural mechanisms: a place code at high frequencies and a frequency code at low frequencies. Both mechanisms likely operate at intermediate frequencies.

Neural pathways

Neurons in the auditory system are similar in many respects to those in the visual system. Firing depends on input from several hair cells, just as firing in ganglion cells reflects the total activity of many photoreceptors. Neurons comprising the auditory nerve also carry information specifying stimulus quality (pitch), as do fibers in the optic nerve (colour). Thus, a neuron will respond to a range of frequencies if the sound is intense enough, but it will most readily respond to a characteristic frequency to which it is tuned. Neurons activated by hair cells near the oval window respond to high frequencies, whereas those activated by hair cells on the other end of the basilar membrane fire more readily for low tones. At each pitch, some neurons respond to relatively low intensities of sound, whereas others fire more at high sound levels. As with light, more intense sounds also cause more neurons to fire.

Information transmitted by the ears along the two auditory nerves ultimately find its way to the auditory cortex in the temporal lobes, but it makes several stops along the way. The auditory nerve from each ear projects to the medulla, where the majority of its fibers cross

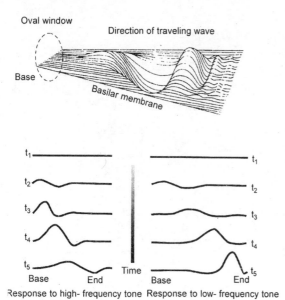

Fig. 4.13 Place Theory. The frequency with which the stapes strikes the oval window affects the location of peak vibration on the basilar membrane. The lower the tone, the farther the maximum displacement on the membrane is from the oval window.

over to the other hemisphere. Some information from each ear, however, does not cross over; thus, information from both ears is represented on both sides of the brain.

From the medulla, bundles of axons project to the midbrain (to the *inferior colliculus,* just below the superior colliculus, which is involved in vision) and on to the thalamus (to the *medial geniculate nucleus,* just toward the center of the brain from its visual counterpart, the lateral geniculate nucleus). The thalamus transmits information to the auditory cortex in the temporal lobes, which has sections devoted to different frequencies. Some neurons in the auditory cortex also respond to the "movement" of sounds—whether frequency changes, moving up or down. Just as the cortical region corresponding to the fovea is disproportionately large, so, too, is the region of primary auditory cortex tuned to sound frequencies in the middle of the spectrum—the same frequencies involved in speech. Indeed, in humans and other

animals, some cortical neurons in the left temporal lobe respond exclusively to particular sounds characteristic of the "language of the species, whether monkey calls or human speech.

Sound localization

Neurons in the thalamus and primary cortex are involved in identifying the location of a sound in space, or **sound localization**. In humans, sound localization requires the integration of information from both ears because the brain uses two main cues for localizing sound: differences between the two ears in loudness, and timing of the sound. Particularly for high-frequency sounds, relative loudness in the ear closer to the source provides information about its location because the head blocks some of the sound from hitting the other ear.

Loudness is less useful for localizing lower frequency sounds because their waves are so long that the head does not effectively block them. For example, a 900-Hz sound (a relatively low tone) cycles about every 40 centimeters, which is twice the diameter of the average head, so it curves right around the head. Localization of sounds at low frequencies relies more on the difference in the arrival time of the sound at the two ears. A sound coming from the left reaches the left ear a split second before reaching the right, particularly if it is moving slowly (that is, at a low frequency). Timing differences are less useful for localizing sounds at high frequencies because they travel so quickly between the two ears. The ability to move the head toward sounds is also crucial for localizing sounds.

Neurologically, the basis for sound localization lies in neurons that respond to relative differences in the signals from the two ears. These *biaural neurons* (i.e., neurons that respond to information from both ears) exist at nearly all levels of the auditory system in the brain, from the brainstem up through the cortex. At higher levels of the brain, this information is connected with visual information about the location and distance of objects, which allows a

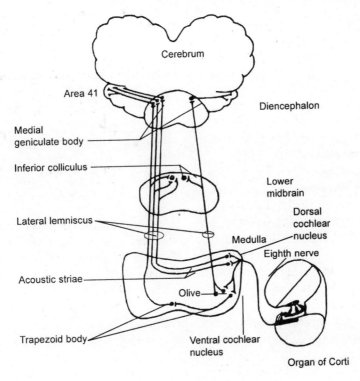

Fig. 4.14 Auditory Nervous Pathways

joint mapping of auditory and visual information.

OTHER SENSES

Vision and audition are the most highly specialized senses in humans, occupying the greatest amount of brain space and showing the most cortical evolution. Our other senses, however, serve important adaptive functions as well. These include smell, taste, the skin senses (pressure, temperature, and pain), and the proprioceptive senses (body position and motion).

Smell

Smell (**olfaction**) serves a

number of functions in humans. It enables us to detect danger (e.g., the smell of something

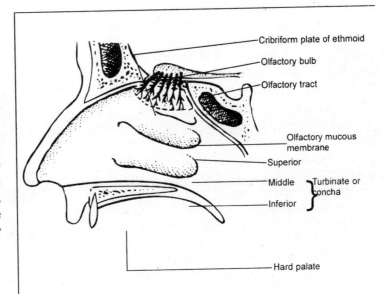

Fig. 4.15 Location of olfactory mucous membrane

burning), discriminate palatable and unpalatable or spoiled foods, and recognize familiar others. Smell plays a less important role in humans than in most other animals, who rely heavily on olfaction to mark territory and track other animals. Many species communicate through **pheromones**, scent messages that regulate the sexual behaviour of many animals and direct a variety of behaviours in insects.

We humans, in contrast, often try to "cover our tracks" in the olfactory domain using perfumes and deodorants to mask odours that our mammalian ancestors might have found informative or appealing. Nevertheless, vestiges of this ancient reproductive mechanism remain. Humans appear both to secrete and sense olfactory cues related to reproduction. Experiments using sweaty hands or articles of clothing have shown that people can identify the gender of another person by smell alone with remarkable accuracy.

Transduction

The environmental stimuli for olfaction are invisible molecules of gas emitted by substances and suspended in the air. Although the nose is the sense organ for smell, the vapours that give rise to olfactory sensations can enter the *nasal cavities*—the region hollowed out of the bone in the skull that contains smell receptors through either the nose or the mouth. When food is chewed, vapours travel up the back of the mouth into the nasal cavity; this process actually accounts for much of the taste.

Transduction of smell occurs in the **olfactory epithelium**, a thin pair of structures (one on each side) less than a square inch in diameter at the top of the nasal cavities. Chemical molecules in the air become trapped in the mucus of the epithelium, where they make contact with olfactory receptors cells that transduce the stimulus into olfactory sensations. Humans have approximately 10 million olfactory receptors, in comparison with dogs, whose 200 million receptors enable them to track humans and other animals with their noses. Psychologist

have long debated whether a small number of receptors coding different qualities combine to produce complex smells or whether the olfactory epithelium contains hundreds or thousands of receptors that bind only with very specific molecules. Recent research on the genes that produce proteins involved in smell transduction suggest that many receptors are responsive to chemicals with very specific molecular structures.

Neural pathways

The axons of olfactory receptors cells form the **olfactory nerve**, which transmits information to the **olfactory bulbs**, multilayered structures that combine information from receptor cells. Olfactory information then travels to the primary olfactory cortex, a primitive region of the cortex deep in the frontal lobes. Unlike other senses, smell is not relayed through the thalamus on its way to the cortex; however, the olfactory cortex has projections to both the thalamus and the limbic system, so that

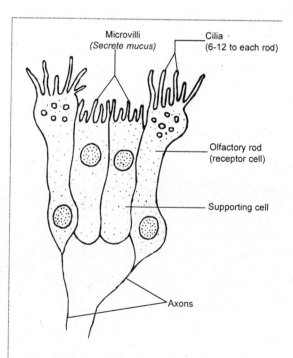

Microvilli
(Secrete mucus)

Cilia
(6-12 to each rod)

Olfactory rod
(receptor cell)

Supporting cell

Axons

Fig. 4.16 Structure of an olfactory receptor

smell is connected to both taste and emotion.

Taste

The sense of smell is sensitive to molecules in the air, whereas taste (**gustation**) is sensitive to molecules soluble in saliva. At the dinner table, the contributions of the nose and mouth to taste are indistinguishable except when the nasal passages are blocked so that food loses much of its taste. From an evolutionary perspective, taste serves two functions: to protect the organism from ingesting toxic substances and to regulate intake of nutrients such as sugars and salt. For example, toxic substances often taste bitter, and foods high in sugar (which provides the body with energy) are usually sweet. The tendency to reject bitter substances and to ingest sweet ones is present even in newborns, despite their lack of experience with taste.

Transduction of taste occurs in the **taste buds**. Roughly 10,000 taste buds are distributed throughout the mouth and throat, although most are located in the bumps on the surface of the tongue called **papillae**. Soluble chemicals that enter the mouth penetrate tiny pores in the papillae and stimulate the taste receptors. Each taste bud contains between 50 to 150 receptor cells. Taste receptors, unlike sensory receptors in the eye or ear, wear out and are replaced every 10 or 11 days. Regeneration is essential, or a burn to the tongue would result in permanent loss of taste.

Taste receptors stimulate neurons that carry information to the medulla and pons in the hindbrain. From there, gustatory information travels along one of two pathways. One leads to the thalamus and on to the primary gustatory cortex deep within a region between the temporal and parietal lobes. This pathway allows the identification of tastes. The second pathway, which has no access to consciousness, leads to the limbic system. This pathway allows immediate emotional and behavioural responses to tastes, such as spitting out bitter substances. It also appears to be involved in learned aversions to tastes that become associated through experience with nausea. As in blindsight, people with damage to the first (cortical) pathway cannot identify substances by taste, but they react with appropriate facial expressions to bitter and sour substances if this second, more primitive pathway, is intact.

The gustatory system responds to four basic tastes: sweet, sour, salty and bitter. Different

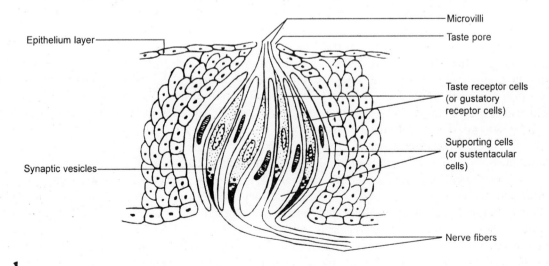

Fig. 4.17 Taste receptor (or taste bud)

Microvilli

Taste pore

Epithelium layer

Taste receptor cells (or gustatory receptor cells)

Supporting cells (or sustentacular cells)

Synaptic vesicles

Nerve fibers

receptors are most sensitive to one of these tastes, at least at low levels of stimulation. This appears to be cross—culturally universal. People of different cultures diverge in their taste preferences and beliefs about basic flavours but they vary little in identifying substances as sweet, sour, salty or bitter. More than one receptor, however, can produce the same sensation, at least for bitterness.

Skin senses

The approximately 18 square feet of skin covering the human body constitutes a complex, multilayered organ. The skin senses help protect the body from injury, aid in identifying objects, help maintain body temperature, and facilitate social interaction through hugs and handshakes. What we colloquially call the sense of touch is actually a mix of atleast three qualities: pressure, temperature, and pain. Receptors in the skin respond to different aspects of these qualities, such as warm or cold or light or deep pressure. The human body contains approximately 5 million touch receptors of various types. Although receptors are specialized for different qualities, most skin sensations are complex, reflecting stimulation across many receptors.

As with other sensory systems, several receptors in the skin typically transmit information to a single sensory neuron, which in turn synapses with other neurons in the spinal cord. The qualities that sensory neurons convey to the nervous system (such as soft pressure, warmth, and cold) depend on the receptors to which they are connected. Like neurons in other sensory systems, those involved in touch also have receptive fields, which distinguish both where and how long the stimulation occured on the skin.

Sensory neurons synapse with spinal interneurons that stimulate motor neurons, allowing animals to respond with rapid reflex actions. Sensory neurons also synapse with neurons that carry information up the spinal cord to the medulla, where neural tracts cross over. From there, sensory information travels to the thalamus and is subsequently routed to the primary touch center in the brain, the somatosensory cortex. The somatosensory cortex contains a map of the body (chapter 3); neurons in the somatosensory cortex have receptive fields corresponding to different parts of the body.

Each of the skin senses transduces a distinct form of stimulation. Pressure receptors transduce mechanical energy (like the receptors in the ear). Temperature receptors respond to thermal energy (heat). Pain receptors do not directly transform external stimulation into psychological experience; rather, they respond to a range of internal and external bodily states, from strained muscles to damaged skin.

Pressure

People experience pressure when the skin is mechanically displaced, or moved. Sensitivity to pressure varies considerably over the surface of the body. The most sensitive regions are the face and fingers; the least sensitive are back and legs. These disparities in sensitivity are reflected in the amount of space taken by neurons representing these areas in the somatosensory cortex. The hands provide tremendous acuity; they have small receptive fields that allow fine discrimination, and the primary cortex devotes substantial space to them. The hands turn what could be a passive sensory process—responding to indentations produced in the skin by external stimulation—into an active process. As the hands move over objects, pressure receptors register the indentations created in the skin and hence allow perception of texture. Just as finger movements allow blind people to read the raised dots that constitute Braille.

Temperature

When people sense the temperature of an object, they are actually sensing the difference between the temperature of the skin and the object, which is why a pool of 80-degree water feels warm to someone who has been standing in the cold rain but chilly to someone lying on a hot beach. Temperature sensation rely on two sets of receptors, one for cold and one for warmth. Cold receptors, however, not only detect coolness but are also involved in the experience of extreme temperatures both hot and cold. Subjects who grasp two pipes twisted together, one containing warm water and the other cold, experience intense heat. As with pressure, the pattern of stimulation, rather than the activation of specific receptors alone, creates the sensation.

Pain

Pain is a skin sense, but of course pain is felt from the interior of the body too. This sense has great significance in human life. It motivates a multitude of behaviours. Pain has immense biological importance because it may signal that something is wrong with the body.

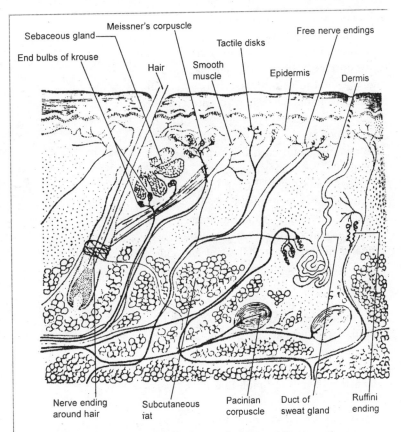

Fig. 4.18 Composite diagram of skin and its receptors.

In contrast to other senses, pain has no specific physical stimulus; the skin does not transduce "pain waves". Sounds that are too loud, lights that are too bright, pressure that is too intense, temperatures that are too extreme, and other stimuli can all elicit pain. Although pain transduction is not well understood, the most important receptors for pain in the skin appear to be the *free nerve ending*. According to one prominent theory, when cells are damaged, they release chemicals that stimulate the free nerve endings, which in turn transmit pain messages to the brain. These chemicals can also activate pain receptors elsewhere in the body, such as in the muscles and teeth and in the spinal nerves that receive input from pain receptors throughout the body. One such chemical is a neuropeptide (a string of amino acids that

serves as a neurotransmitter) called **substance** *P* (for pain).

Of all the senses, pain is probably the most affected by beliefs, expectations, and emotional state and the least reducible to level of stimulation. Anxiety can increase pain, whereas intense fear, stress, or concentration on other things can inhibit it.

Gate control theory

The phenomenological experience of pain is not always initiated by peripheral sensory stimulation. A striking example is phantom limb pain, experienced by a substantial number of amputees. **Phantom limb pain** is the pain felt in a limb that no longer exists. The pain does not originate from severed nerves in the stump. Even if the stump is completely anaesthetized, the pain persists, and medications that should ease it often fail to do so.

One theory designed to account for phenomena such as phantom limb pain is **gate-control theory**, which emphasizes the role of the central nervous system in regulating pain. According to gate control theory, when sensory neurons transmit information to the back of the spinal cord, they do not automatically produce pain sensations because their actions can be inhibited or amplified by input from other nearby sensory neurons as well as from messages descending from the brain.

Gate control theory distinguishes two kinds of neural fibers that open and close spinal "gateways" for pain. Large-diameter fibers (called L-fibers), which transmit neural information very quickly, carry information about many forms of tactile stimulation as well as sharp pain. Once they transmit a message, they close the pain gate by inhibiting the firing of the neurons with which they synapse. Small-diameter fibers (5-fibers) synapse with the same neurons, carrying information about dull pain and burning to the brain.

Because their small axons transmit neural information more slowly, however, their messages may arrive at a closed gate (or, more accurately partially closed gate, since pain does not usually completely disappear) if competing sensory input from L-fibers has inhibited pain transmission. This may explain why rubbing the area around a burn or cut, or even pinching a nearby region of skin, can alleviate pain. These actions stimulate L-fibers, which close the gates to incoming signals from S-fibers. According to gate-control theory, messages from the brain to the spinal cord can also close or open the gates, so that calm or anxious mental states can increase or decrease pain sensations arising from the peripheral nervous system.

Gate-control theory offers one explanation of phantom limb pain. If L-fibers are destroyed by amputation, the gates remain open, allowing

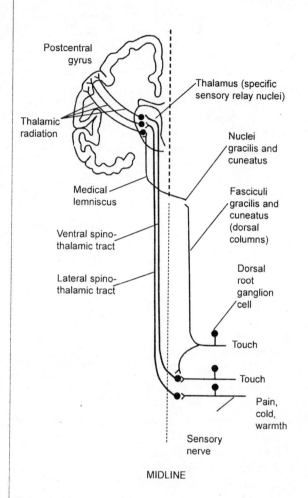

Fig. 4.19 Touch, pain, and temperature pathways from the trunk limbs.

random firing of neurons at the amputation site to trigger action potentials, leading to the experience of pain in the missing limb.

Pain control

Because mental as well as physiological processes contribute to pain, treatment may require attention to both mind and matter—to both the psychology and neurophysiology of pain.

Some techniques target the cognitive and emotional aspects of pain. Though not a panacea, distraction is generally a useful strategy for increasing pain tolerance. Health care professionals often chatter away while giving patients injections in order to distract and relax them. Something as simple as a pleasant view can affect pain tolerance in hospitalized patients. Hypnosis can also be useful in controlling pain. Research suggests that hypnotic procedures can help burn victims tolerate debriding (removing dead tissue and changing dressings on wounds), which can be so painful that patients writhe in agony even on the maximum dosage of medications such as morphine.

Proprioceptive senses

Aside from the five traditional senses—vision, hearing, smell, taste and touch—two additional senses, called **proprioceptive senses**, register body position and movement.

Vestibular sense

This provides information about the position of the body in space by gravity and movement. The vestibular sense organs are in the inner ear, above the cochlea. Two organs transduce vestibular information: the semicircular canals and the vestibular sacs. The **semicircular canals** sense acceleration or deceleration in any direction as the head moves. The *vestibular sacs* sense gravity and the position of the head in space. Vestibular receptors are hair cells that register movement, much as hair cells in the ear transduce air movements. The neural pathways for vestibular sense are not well understood, although impulses from the vestibular system travel to several regions of the hindbrain, notably the cerebellum, which is involved in smooth movement, and to a region deep in the temporal cortex.

Kinesthesia

This provides information about the movement and position of the limbs and other parts of the body *relative* to one another. Kinesthesia is essential in guiding every complex movement, from walking, which requires instantaneous adjustments of the two legs, to drinking a cup of tea. Some of the receptors for kinesthesia are in the joints; these cells transduce information about the position of the bones.

Other receptors present in the tendons and muscles, transmit messages about muscle tension that signal body position.

The vestibular and kinesthetic senses work in tandem, sensing different aspects of movement and position.

PERCEPTION

Perception refers to the way the world looks, sounds, feels, tastes, or smells. In other words, *perception* can be defined as whatever is experienced by a person. Perception *organizes* a continuous array of sensations into meaningful units. Thus *perception*—our experience of the world, arises from sensory input plus the ways we process the sensory information. Many years ago, the famous American psychologist

Fig. 4.20 An ambiguous figure. Whether the perceiver forms a global image of a young or an old woman determines the meaning of each part of the picture; that looks like a young woman's nose from one perspective looks like a wart on an old woman's nose from an other. The perception of the whole even leads to different inferences about the coat the woman is wearing: In one case, it appears to be a stylish fur, whereas in other, it is more likely to be interpreted as an old overcoat.

William James put it this way: "Part of what we perceive comes through the senses from the object before us; another part. . . always comes . . . out of our own head." The "out of our own head" part of this quotation refers to the active processing of sensory input that makes our experience of the world what it is.

Perceptual organization integrates sensations into **percepts** (meaningful perceptual units, such as images of particular objects), locates them in space, and preserves their meaning as the perceiver examines them from different vantage points. Here we explore four aspects of perceptual organization:

Form perception, Depth or distance perception, Motion perception, Perceptual constancy.

Form perception

Form perception refers to the organization of sensations into meaningful shapes and patterns. When you look at this book, you do not perceive it as a patternless collection of molecules. Nor do you perceive it as part of your leg even though it may be resting on it or think a piece of it has disappeared simply because your hand or pen is blocking your vision of it.

Gestalt principles

The first psychologists to study *Form Perception* systematically were the *Gestalt psychologists* of the early twentieth century. **Gestalt** is a german word that translates loosely to "whole" or "form". Proponents of the Gestalt approach argued that in perception the whole (the percept) is greater than the sum of its sensory parts. Consider the ambiguous picture in Fig (4.20), which some people see as an old woman with a scarf over her head and others see as a young woman with a feather coming out of a stylish hat. Depending on the perceiver's gestalt, or whole view of the picture, the short black line in the middle could be either the old women's mouth or the young woman's necklace.

Based on experiments conducted in the 1920s and 1930s, the gestalt psychologists proposed a small number of basic perceptual rules which the brain automatically and unconsciously follows as it organizes sensory input into meaningful wholes.

Figure—ground perception refers to the fact that people inherently distinguish between figure (the object they are viewing) and ground (or background), such as words in black ink against a white page. The second gestalt principle is **similarity**: The brain tends to group similar elements together, such as the circles that form the letter R in fig (4.21a). Another principle, **proximity** (nearness), means that the brain tends to group together objects that are close to one another. In fig (4.21b), the first six lines have no particular organization, whereas the same six lines arranged somewhat differently in the second part of the panel are perceived as three pairs. The gestalt rule of **good continuation** states that, if possible, the brain organizes stimuli into continuous lines or patterns rather than discontinuous elements. For example, in fig (4.21 c), the figure appears to show an X superimposed on a circle, rather than pieces of a

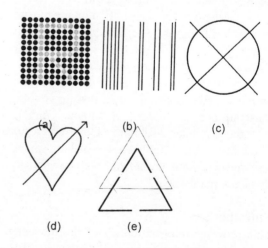

(a)   (b)   (c)

(d)   (e)

Fig. 4.21 Gestalt principles of form perception. The Gestalt psychologists discovered a set of laws of perceptual organization, including (a) similarity, (b) proximity (c) good continuation, (d) simplicity, and (e) closure

pie with lines extending beyond the pie's perimeter.

According to the principle of **simplicity** people tend to perceive the simplest pattern possible. Most people perceive fig (4.21 d) as a heart with an arrow through it because that is the simplest interpretation. Finally, the rule of **closure** states that, where possible, people tend to perceive incomplete figures as complete. If part of a familiar pattern or shape is missing, perceptual processes complete the pattern, as in the triangle shown in fig (4.21e).

Although the gestalt principles are most obvious with visual perception, they apply to other senses as well. For example, the figure-ground principle applies when people attend to the voice of a waitress in a noisy restaurant; her voice becomes figure and all other sounds, ground. In music perception, good continuation allows people to hear a series of notes as a melody; similarity allows them to recognize a melody played on a violin while other instruments are playing; and proximity groups notes played together as a chord.

From an evolutionary perspective, the gestalt principles exemplify the way the brain organizes perceptual experience to reflect the regularities of nature. In nature, the parts of objects tend to be near one another and attached. Thus, the principles of proximity and good continuation are useful perceptual rules of thumb. Similarly, objects often partially block, or occlude, other objects, as when a squirrel crawls up the bark of a tree. The principle of closure leads humans and other animals to assume the existence of the part of the tree that is covered by the squirrel's body.

Combining features

More recent research has focused on the question of how brain combines the simple features detected in primary areas of the cortex (particularly primary visual cortex) into larger units that can be used to identify objects. **Object identification** requires matching the current stimulus array against past percepts stored in memory to determine the identity of the object.

One prominent theory of how the brain forms and recognizes images, was developed by Irvin Biederman. Consider the following common scenario. It is late at night, and you are "channel surfing" on the television—rapidly pressing the remote control in search of something to watch. From less than a second's glance, you can readily perceive what most shows are about and whether they might be interesting. How does the brain, in less than a second, recognize a complex visual array on a television screen in order to make such a rapid decision?

Biederman and his colleagues have shown that we do not even need a *half* of a second to recognize most scenes; 100 milliseconds—a tenth of a second—will typically do. To explain phenomena such as this, Biederman developed a theory called **recognition by-components**, which asserts that we perceive and categorize objects in our environment by breaking them down into component parts and then matching the components and the way they are arranged against similar "sketches"

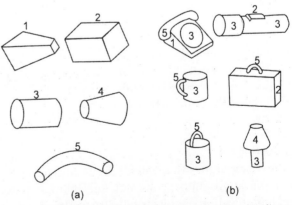

(a)   (b)

Fig. 4.22 Recognition by components. The simple geons in (a) can be used to create thousands of different objects (b) simply by altering the relations among them, such as their relative size and placement

Fig. 4.23 Identifiable and unidentifiable images

other words, the brain fills in gaps in a segment of a geon, such as a blocked piece of a circle.

The theory predicts that failures in identifying objects should occur if the lines where separate geons connections are missing or ambiguous, so that the brain can no longer tell where one component ends and another begins. Experiments have supported this hypothesis: people can identify objects with parts missing, only if the parts do not obscure the relations among the geons.

Perceptual illusions

Sometimes the brain's efforts to organize sensations into coherent and accurate percepts fail. This is the case with **perceptual illusions** in which normal perceptual processes produce perceptual misinterpretations. An *illusion* is *not* a trick or a misperception; it *is* a perception. We call it an *illusion* simply because it does not agree with our other perceptions. For instance, our perception of the line lengths in the **Müller Lyer illusion** of fig (4.24) does not agree with the perception we would have if there were no arrows. The presence of the arrows in the figure causes us to process the sensory input in such a way that we perceive the lines as unequal in length.

Depth perception

A second aspect of perceptual organization is **depth** or **distance perception**, the organization of perception in three dimensions. You perceive this book as having height, width, and breadth and being at a particular distance. A skilled athlete can throw a ball 15 yards into a tiny hoop not much bigger than the ball. These three dimensional judgements arise from a two-dimensional retinal image and it happens with such rapidity that we have no awareness of the computations our nervous system must be making. Although we focus again on the visual system, other sensory systems provide cues for depth perception as well. Auditory cues are particularly important, so are kinesthetic sensations about the extension of the body while

stored in memory. In other words, the brain combines the simple features extracted by the primary cortex (such as lines of particular orientations) into a small number of elementary geometrical forms (called *geons,* for "geometric ions"). From this geometrical "alphabet" of 20 to 30 geons, Biederman argues, the outlines of virtually any object can be constructed, just as millions of words can be constructed from 26 alphabets in various combinations and orders.

Biderman argues that combining primitive visual sensations into geons not only allows rapid identification of objects but also explains why we can recognize objects even when part of them are blocked or missing. The reason is that the gestalt principles, such as good continuation, apply to perception of geons. In

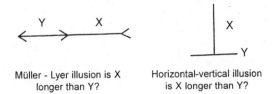

Müller - Lyer illusion is X longer than Y?

Horizontal-vertical illusion is X longer than Y?

Fig. 4.24 Does the X appear longer than the Y? Measurements will give an answer

touching an object and other kinesthetic sensations that occur as a person lifts an object (such as a pencil) held by the hands. Two kinds of visual information provide particularly important information about depth and distance: **binocular cues** (visual input integrated from the two eyes) and **monocular cues** (visual input from one eye).

Binocular cues

Because the eyes are in slightly different locations, all but the most distant objects produce a different image on each retina, or a **retinal disparity**. To see this in action, hold your finger about six inches from your nose and alternately close your left and right eye. You will note that each eye sees your finger in a slightly different position. Now, do the same for a distant object; you will note only minimal differences between the views. Retinal disparity is greatest for close objects and diminishes with distance.

How does the brain translate retinal disparity into depth perception? Most cells in the primary visual cortex are *binocular cells;* that is, they receive information from both eyes. Some of these cells respond most vigorously when the same input arrives from each eye, whether the input is a vertical line, a horizontal line, or a line moving in one direction. Other binocular cells respond to different sorts of disparities between the eyes. Like many cells receptive to particular orientations, binocular cells require environmental input early in life to assume their normal functions. Researchers have learned about binocular cells by allowing kittens to see with only one eye at a time, covering one eye or the other on

alternate days. As adults, these cats are unable to use binocular cues for depth.

Another binocular cue, **convergence**, is actually more kinesthetic than visual. When looking at a close object (such as your finger six inches in front of your face), the eyes converge, whereas distant objects require ocular divergence. **Convergence** of the eyes towards each other thus creates a distance cue produced by muscle movements in the eyes.

Monocular cues

Although binocular cues are extremely important for depth perception, people do not crash their cars whenever an eyelash momentarily gets into one eye because they can still rely on monocular cues. **Interposition** occurs when one object blocks part of another; as a result, the obstructed object is perceived as more distant. **Elevation** refers to the fact that objects farther away are higher on a person's plane of view and thus appear higher up toward the horizon. Another monocular cue is **texture gradient**: When looking at textured surfaces, such as cobblestones or grained wood, the pattern or texture appears coarser at close range and finer and more densely packed at greater distances.

A similar mechanism is **linear perspective**: parallel lines appear to converge at the distance. **Shading** also provides monocular depth cues, since two-dimensional objects do not cast shadows. The brain assumes that light comes from above and hence interprets shading differently toward the top or the bottom of an object. Another cue is **aerial perspective**: since light scatters as it passes through spaces, and especially through moist or polluted air, objects at greater distances appear fuzzier than those nearby. Two other cues rely on the individual's knowledge of the size of familiar objects. **Familiar size** refers to the tendency to assume an object in its usual size, thus, people perceive familiar objects appearing small at some distance. Closely related is **relative size**: when looking at two objects known to be of similar size, people perceive the smaller object as farther away.

A final monocular depth cue arises from movement. When people move, images of nearby objects sweep across their field of vision faster than objects farther away. This disparity in apparent velocity produces a depth cue called **motion parallax**. The relative motion of nearby versus distant objects is particularly striking when looking out of the window of a moving car or train. Nearby trees appear to speed by, whereas distant objects barely seem to move.

Motion perception

From an evolutionary perspective, just as important as identifying objects and their distance is identifying motion. A moving object is potentially a dangerous object—or, alternatively, a meal, a mate, or a friend or relative in distress. Thus, it is no surprise that humans, like other animals, developed the capacity for **motion perception**—the perception of movement in objects. Motion perception occurs in multiple sensory modes. People can perceive the movement of a fly on the skin through touch, just as they can perceive the fly's trajectory through space by the sounds it makes.

Neural pathways

The visual perception of movement begins in the retina itself, with ganglion cells called motion detectors that are particularly sensitive to movement. These cells tend to be concentrated outside the fovea, to respond (and stop responding) very quickly, and have large receptive fields. These characteristics make adaptive sense. An object in the fovea is one we are already "keeping a close eye on" through attention to it; motion detectors in the periphery of our vision, in contrast, provide an early warning system to turn the head or the eyes toward something potentially relevant. Relatively quick onset and offset of neurons that detect motion is also a useful characteristic; otherwise, many objects could escape detection by moving faster than these neurons could fire. In fact, the eyes cannot detect objects that move either too quickly (which appear blurry or cannot be seen at all) or too slowly (which do not "trip" the motion detectors). Large receptive fields are useful for motion detection because each cell receives input from many bipolar cells; the greater the number of bipolar cells that synapse with the ganglion cell, the greater the potential activation. A wider receptive field also covers more visual terrain in which motion might occur, maximizing the likelihood of detecting it.

With each new "stop" along the processing stream in the brain, the receptive fields of neurons that detect motion grow larger. Several ganglion cells project to each motion-detecting neuron in the thalamus (in the lateral geniculate nucleus); thus, these neurons are likely to respond to movement in a slightly larger area of space. Several of these thalamic neurons may then synapse with motion-sensitive neurons in the primary visual cortex. From there, information about the movement of objects travels along the pathway through the upper temporal lobes and into the parietal lobes.

Two systems for processing movement

Tracking an object's movement is a tricky business because the perceiver may be moving as well; thus perception requires distinguishing the motion of the perceiver from the motion of the perceived. Consider the perceptual task of a tennis player awaiting a serve. Most tennis players bob, fidget, or move from side to side as they await a serve, which means that the image on their retina is changing every second, even before the ball is in the air. Once the ball is served, its retinal image becomes larger and larger as it approaches, and somehow the brain must compute its distance and velocity as it moves through space. Making matters more complex, the perceiver is likely to be running, all the while trying to keep the ball's image on the fovea. And the brain must integrate these cues—the size of the image on the retina, its precise location on the retina, the movement of the eyes, and the movement of the body—all in a split second.

Two systems appear to be involved in motion perception. The first computes motion from the changing image projected by the object on the retina; the second makes use of commands from the brain to the muscles in the eye that signal eye movements. A third system, less well understood, likely integrates proprioceptive and other cues to offset the impact of body movements on the retinal image. The first system operates when the eyes are relatively stable, as when an insect darts across the floor in the person's view so quickly that the eyes cannot move fast enough to track it. In this case, the image of the insect moves across the retina. Motion detectors then fire as adjacent receptors in the retina bleach one after another in rapid succession.

The second system operates when people move their head and eyes to follow an object, as when fans watch a runner sprinting towards the finish line. In this case, the image of the object remains at roughly the same place on the retina; what moves is the position of the eyes. This second system computes movement from a combination of the image on the retina and the movement of eye muscles. If the eyes are moving but the object continues to cast the same retinal image, the object must be moving. Essentially, the brain substracts out muscle movements before computing movement from the retinal image. Interestingly, the movements of the eye must be intentional for this mechanism to work (although we are not typically conscious of the directives from the brain to the eye muscles). This is readily apparent by performing a simple experiment: close one eye and then lightly push the other eye ball with your finger. You will perceive— movement in the opposite direction in any object in front of you because the brain does not compensate for involuntary shifts in the position of the eye that do not occur through movement of the eye muscles.

Perceptual constancy

A fourth form of perceptual organization, **perceptual constancy**, refers to the perception of objects as relatively stable despite changes in the stimulation of sensory receptors. As your grandmother walks away from you, you do not perceive her as shrinking, even though the image she casts on your retina is steadily decreasing in size (although you may notice that she has shrunk a little since you last saw her). You similarly recognize that a song on the radio is still the same even though the volume has been turned down. Here we examine three types of perceptual constancy, again focusing on vision: colour, shape, and size constancy.

Colour constancy

Colour constancy refers to the tendency to perceive the colour of objects as stable despite changing illumination. An apple appears of the same colour in the kitchen as it does in the sunlight, even though the light illuminating it is very different. A similar phenomenon occurs with achromatic colour (black and white): Snow in moonlight appears whiter than coal appears in sunlight, even though the amount of light reflected off the coal may be greater. In perceiving the brightness of an object, neural mechanisms essentially adjust for the amount of light illuminating it. For chromatic colours, the mechanism is more complicated, but colour constancy does not work if the light contains only a narrow band of wavelengths. Being in a room with only red light-bulbs causes even familiar objects to appear red.

Shape constancy

A remarkable feat of the engineering of the brain is that we can maintain constant perception of the shape of objects despite the fact that the same object typically produces a new and different impression on the retina (or on the receptors in our skin) every time we encounter it. The brain has to overcome several substantial sources of noise to recognize, for example, that the unkempt beast in the mirror whose hair is pointing in every direction is the same person you happily called "me" the night before. When people see an object for the second time, they are likely to see it from a different position, with different lighting, in a different setting (e.g., against a different background), with different parts of it blocked from view (such as different locks of hair covering the face), and even in an altered shape (such as a body standing up versus on the couch).

Recognition—by—components (geon) theory offers one possible explanation: As long as enough of the geons that define the form of the object remain the same, the object ought to be identifiable. Thus, if a person views a bee from one perspective and then from another as it flies around her face, she will still recognize the insect as a bee as long as it still looks like a tube with a little cone at the back and thin waferlike wings flapping at its sides.

Other theorists, however, have argued that this is not likely to be the whole story. Some have proposed that each time we view an object from a different perspective, we form a mental image of it from that point of view. Each new viewpoint provides a new image stored in memory. The next time we see a similar object, we rotate it in our minds so that we can "see" it from a previously seen perspective to determine if it looks like the same object or match it against a generalized image derived from our multiple "snapshots" of it. Recent research suggests, in fact, that the more a scene diverges the perspective from which a person has seen it before, the longer the person will take to recognize it. This suggests that shape constancy does, to some extent, rely on the rotation of mental images and their comparison against perceptual experiences stored in memory.

Size constancy
A third type of perceptual constancy is **size constancy**: Objects do not appear to change in size when viewed from different distances. The closer an object is, the larger an image it casts on the retina; a car ten feet away will cast a retinal image five times as large as the same car 50 feet away. Yet people do not wonder how the car 50 feet away can possibly carry full-sized passengers. The reason is that the brain essentially corrects for the size of the retinal image based on cues such

as the size of objects in the background.

Helmholtz was the first to recognize that the brain adjusts for distance when assessing the size of objects, just as it adjusts for colour and brightness. He called this process "unconscious inference" because people have no consciousness of the computations involved. Although these computations generally lead to accurate inferences, they can also give rise to perceptual illusions.

Attention

At any given moment, our sense organs are bombarded by a multitude of stimuli, yet we perceive only a few of them clearly. *Attention* is the term given to the perceptual processes that select certain inputs for inclusion in our conscious experience, or awareness, at any given time.

Characteristics of attention
The processes of attention divide our field of experience into a focus and a margin. Events that we perceive clearly are at the focus of experience. Other items are perceived dimly; we may be aware of their presence, but only vaguely so. These items are in the margin of attention.

To illustrate the nature of attention, consider your perceptions at a football game. While you are dimly aware of the tangle of players at the scrimmage line and of the activity of the blockers, it is the ball carrier and his movements that stand out. Your attention is focused on him. At the same time, sensory inputs are coming in from your cold feet, from your stomach as a result of the last hot meal you ate, and from the fellow behind you who is smoking a cigarette. The crowd is also cheering. While the play is going on, you are probably not aware of any of these sensory inputs that are in the margin of your attention. Only when the play is finished or time is called you do perceive how cold your feet are, how queasy your stomach feels, what strong smell the cigarette has, and how noisy the crowd is.

The fact that you do at some point become aware of the marginal inputs illustrates another characteristic of attention, that it is constantly shifting. What is at the focus one moment may be in the margin the next; and what is in the margin may become the focus.

Attention and the processing of information

How have psychologists tried to account for the fact that perception has a focus and that this focus switches from time to time? One set of explanations uses the concept of *filtering*. Since we cannot process all the information in our sensory channels, we *filter*, or partially block out, some inputs while letting other through.

Imagine yourself at a party standing between two groups of people who are simultaneously carrying on two different conversations. You may be able to pick up some of both conversations at the same time—*parallel processing*, as it is called. But you will probably find that one or the other conversation is at the focus of your attention at any given moment; it is hard to pay attention to more than one set of inputs at a time. Thus, you will most likely do what is called *serial processing*—attending to one set of inputs and then another. Or you may even stop switching back and forth, preferring instead to keep only one conversation at the focus of your attention. Whether you process the conversations serially or listen to only one of them, you are filtering out the unattended conversation; you have related these inputs to the margin of your attention.

In the filter models of attention, inputs in the margin shift to the focus when various attention-getting features of the environment are present in the filtered input. Such attention seekers include intense stimuli and novel stimuli. For instance, if you are still between the two conversations of the last paragraph, you will probably switch your attention to the filtered-out conversation if voices are raised in this conversation.

Filter models of attention differ with respect to where the blocking occurs in the sensory channels. Some theorists say that the filter or information bottleneck, is at the sense organs, or at least in the very early stages of the input processing. Others argue that the filtering takes place at later stages of the information flow—for example, at the stages where the input is interpreted as meaningful.

Other information-processing theories of attention are based on the idea of processing capacity. These theories are based on the assumption that we have a limited mental capacity for processing incoming information and therefore we cannot deal with all the sensory input at once. Instead, we must allocate our limited resource—our processing capacity—to one set of inputs or another. Proponents of these theories say that inputs which take up most of our processing capacity are at the focus of our attention. Thus, as you read this, you are devoting a large proportion of your processing capacity to the cognitive processes involved in understanding "what all this stuff about information processing and attention is about," and the text material is at the focus of your attention. If the radio is on, you are not aware of what is playing. But your professor who reads this section probably needs to devote less processing capacity to it; it is "old stuff," your professor can therefore allocate more of his or her processing capacity to what is on the radio and will probably hear more of this input than you. According to the processing-capacity theorists, your attention shifts when your processing capacity must be used to deal with the new input.

Plasticity

The term *plasticity* refers to the modifiability, or moldability, of perception. Special situations, such as prolonged changes in sensory input can modify the ways information is processed in generating perceptions of the world around us.

Visual deprivation

Visual deprivation—restriction of the visual input in some fashion—is especially potent during what is known as the sensitive period for visual development. A sensitive period is the time in the early development of a person or animal during which the environment has its greatest effect on behaviour or on the brain processes underlying behaviour.

In a number of experiments, animals have been raised from birth thus including the sensitive period, translucent contact lenses over their eyes. These animals were thus deprived of from vision because the lenses prevented light from being focused on their retinas.

When the special lenses were removed after the animal's sensitive periods had passed, they had great difficulty in perceiving form. Special training and visual experience after the lenses had been removed improved their form perception somewhat, but judging from the animal's behavioural responses to visual stimuli, it almost never became "normal".

Few unfortunate people are born with congenital cataract, a condition in which the lenses of the eyes are clouded over; others are born with, or developed soon after birth, cloudy corneas. Like the milk-white glass contact lenses used in the animal experiments, either of these conditions makes form vision impossible because light cannot be focused on the retina. These people can perceive large areas of brightness, but they are blind in the sense that they have no useful detail vision. They can be helped by special training; and in some cases, operations can correct the problem. For instance, in cases of cataract, the lenses can be removed and glasses or contact lenses substituted for them; corneal transplants can sometimes be done to replace cloudy corneas. After the operation, light can be focused on the retina and the eyes are ready for normal sight.

When the bandages come off after the operation, these patients can visually recognize objects that were familiar to them through their other senses. They can, for instance, visually recognize objects such as telephones, chairs or spoons that they had learned to recognize through touch when blind. However, they have great difficulty with the visual recognition of "new" objects. For example, faces and letters are hard for them to recognize, and their perception may never be normal for these "new" objects. But as these patients visually experience the environment, their perception gradually becomes more normal, and this recovery is another example of plasticity of perception.

Nature and nurture

Nature refers to innate, or inborn processes that influence behaviour and perception, while *nurture* refers to learning and, in general, the effects of the environment on behaviour and perception. Theorists who argue for the importance of nature in perception are called *nativists;* those who argue for nurture are known as *empiricists.*

Answer to the 'nature—nurture', question

Fig. 4.25 A Kitten in an apparatus designed so that its only visual experience is of vertical lines.

have become more sophisticated as psychologists have come to recognize that the nervous system has certain innate potentials—such as seeing in depth or inferring distance from sound—but these potentials require environmental input to develop. In one set of studies, researchers reared kittens in darkness of their first five months except for five hours each day, during which time they placed the kittens in a cylinder with either horizontal or vertical stripes. The kittens saw only the stripes, since they wore a big collar that kept them from seeing even their own bodies. As adults, kittens reared in horizontal environments were unable to perceive vertical lines, and they lacked cortical feature detectors responsive to vertical lines; the opposite was true of kittens reared in a vertical environment.

Although these cats were genetically programmed to have both vertical and horizontal feature detectors, their brains adapted to a world without certain features to detect.

Other studies have outfitted infant kittens and monkeys with translucent goggles that allow light to pass through but only in blurry, diffuse, unpatterned form. When the animals became adults and the goggles were removed, they were able to perform simple perceptual tasks without difficulty, such as distinguishing colours, brightness, and size. However, they had difficulty with other tasks; for example, they were unable to distinguish objects from one another or to track moving objects. Similar findings have emerged in studies of humans who were born blind but subsequently obtained sight in adulthood through surgery. Most of these individuals can tell figure from ground, sense colours, and follow moving objects, but many never learn to recognize objects they previously knew by touch and hence remain functionally blind. What these studies suggest, is that the brain has evolved to "expect" certain experiences, without which it will not develop normally.

Early experiences are not the only ones that shape the neural systems underlying sensation and perception. In one study, monkeys who were taught to make fine pitch discrimination showed increases in the size of the cortical regions responsive to pitch. Intriguing research with humans finds that practice at discriminating letters manually in Braille produces changes in the brain. A larger region of the cortex of Braille readers is devoted to the fingertips, with which they read. Thus, experience can alter the structure of the brain, making it more or less responsive to subsequent sensory input.

Perceptual processes: individual differences

We know that people differ in the ways they process sensory inputs to give rise to what they experience. Two people may have very different perceptions of the same television drama, lecture, meeting, or interpersonal encounter. Individual differences in learning, sets (expectations), motives, and perceptual styles are at work to make one person's perceptions different from those of another.

Perceptual learning

Eleanor Gibson has defined **perceptual learning** as "an increase in the ability to extract information from the environment as a result of experience or practice with the stimulation coming from it." Perceptual learning can be considered as a variety of the cognitive learning. Gibson gives many examples that show how perception can be molded by learning. She cites the competence of people trained in various occupations to make perceptual distinctions that untrained people cannot make. Skill, or artistry, in many professions is based upon the ability to make these subtle distinctions. Experience is the best teacher for these perceptual skills; usually, they cannot be learned from books.

As Gibson also points out, the remarkable feats of blind people are often matters of perceptual learning. It is not that their sensitivity to nonvisual stimulation is greater than that of sighted people. Instead, blind people learn to extract from the environment information not ordinarily used by sighted people. For instance, many blind people move around in the world, avoiding obstacles with surprising ease. Blind people learn to perceive the sound echoes of their footfalls and cane tappings that bounce back from objects in their paths. Some blind people even learn to distinguish among various shapes and textures of surfaces by perceiving the differences in their sound echoes. It is obvious that learning to extract certain kinds of information from the environment—*perceptual learning*—is of enormous practical and adaptive value.

Perceptual set

Experience with the environment shapes perception by creating perceptual expectations. These expectations, called perceptual set (i.e., the setting, or context, for a given perceptual "decision"), make certain interpretations more likely.

Set refers to the idea that we may be "ready" and "primed for" certain kinds of sensory input. Such expectations, or *sets,* vary from person to person and are a factor in both the selection of sensory inputs for inclusion in the focus of attention and in the organization of inputs.

To illustrate the role of set in attention, consider the husband who is expecting an important phone call. He will hear the telephone ring in the night while his wife does not. The wife, on the other hand, may be more likely to hear the baby crying than the telephone ringing, of course, if the wife is expecting an important call, the situation may be reversed.

Another example of set in perceptual organization: Is it the letter B or the number 13 in fig (4.26)?

Fig. 4.26 The effect of expectancy, or set, on perception. The drawing can be perceived either as a B or the number 13, depending on what a person is set to perceive.

If this drawing is included in a series of two-digit numbers, people will tend to report that they perceive the number 13. But other people, who have seen the figure in the context of letters, will report that it looks like a B to them. In one case,

an expectancy or set, has been acquired for numbers; in the other, for letters.

Motivation and perception

As we have seen, expectations can lead people to see what they expect to hear. But people also frequently hear the words they *want* to hear as well.

There was the argument of a school of perceptual thought in the late 1940s called the *New Look* in perception, which focused on the impact of emotion, motivation, and personality, on perception.

One classic experiment examined the effects of food and water deprivation on identification of words. The experimenters placed participants in one of three groups. Some went without food for 24 hours prior to the experiment; some ate nothing for ten hours; and others ate just before hand. The researchers then flashed two kinds of words on a screen so rapidly that they were barely perceptible: neutral words (e.g., serenade and hunch) and words related to food (e.g., lemonade and munch). The three groups did not differ in their responses to the neutral words. However, both of the deprived groups perceived the need-related words more readily (i.e., when flashed more briefly) than nondeprived controls. A similar phenomenon occurs outside the laboratory: People are often intensely aware of the aroma of food outside a restaurant when they are hungry but oblivious to it when their stomachs are full.

New Look researchers were also interested in applying psychodynamic ideas to perception. The idea is that people's motives will, to some extent, affect the ways in which they organize and perceive the test stimuli. A psychologist may be able to infer from the perceptions what motives are dominant in a particular person. ■ ■

Learning

Learning

In humans, as in other animals, learning is central to adaptation because the environment does not stand still; it varies from place to place and from moment to moment. Knowing how to distinguish edible from inedible foods or to distinguish friends from enemies or predators is essential for survival.

Even though learning has received more attention in terms of experiments than any other object of psychology, there is no one accepted definition of the term. Nevertheless, the various attempts to define it may (without too great a degree of misrepresentation) be formulated as follows: **Learning** consists of relatively persistent changes in possible behaviour in so far as they derive from experience. This restriction of the term excludes short-term changes (adaptation, fatigue, etc.) and those which derive from certain structural alterations of the central nervous system (maturation, ageing, injuries).

Many authors replace the reference to "experience" with terms such as "repetition", "practice," "training," etc., in order to avoid terminology reminiscent of the psychology of *consciousness;* nevertheless, the information theory model would seem to make it possible to interpret experience (without recourse to the psychology of consciousness) as the *reception and processing of information.* The limitation of the term "learning" to *adaptive* changes of behaviour is usually rejected, since the derivation of (at least objectively) unadapted behaviour patterns (e.g., neuroses) from learning processes should not be excluded. The restriction of the definition to *behaviour* is

primarily one of the method; a disadvantage is that the definition is then too far removed from everyday usage, which employs "learning" primarily in the sense of the acquisition and alternation of cognitive structures (learning in school, etc.).

Western tradition attributes learning to the establishment of associations between elements. Twenty-five hundred years ago, *Aristotle* proposed a set of **laws of association**— conditions under which one thought becomes connected, or associated, with another—to account for learning and memory. The most important was the **law of contiguity**, which proposed that two events will become connected in the mind if they are experienced close together in time (such as thunder and lighting). Another was the **law of similarity**, which states that objects that resemble each other (such as two people with similar faces) are likely to become associated. The philosophical school of thought called **associationism** built upon the work of Aristotle, asserting that the most complex thoughts—which allow humans to create airplanes, understand laws of physics, or write symphonies—are ultimately nothing but elementary perceptions that become associated and then recombined in the mind. Principles of association are fundamental to behaviourist theories of learning as well as to cognitive theories of memory, and neuroscientists have now begun to understand their neural basis—all the way down to changes at the synapse.

With the rise of experimental psychology, the association between the contents of consciousness (mental elements such as ideas and images) was replaced by association between signals (stimuli) and responses. Instead of the word "association", *conditioning* is now used, in the sense of conditioned responses and signals. The resulting connection is interpreted physiologically —though diversely.

The **theories of learning** tend to share three assumptions:

- The first is that *experience shapes behaviour*. In complex organisms such as humans, the vast majority of responses are learned rather than innate. The migration patterns of pacific salmon may be instinctive, but the migration of college students to the hills during summer-break is not.
- Second, learning is adaptive. Just as nature eliminates organisms that are not well suited to their environments, the environment naturally selects those behaviours in an individual that are adaptive and weeds out those that are not. Behaviours useful to the organism (such as avoiding fights with large member of its species) will be reproduced because of their consequences (safety from bodily harm).
- A third assumption is that *careful experimentation can uncover laws of learning,* many of which apply to human and nonhuman animals alike.

CLASSICAL CONDITIONING

This theory was originally conceived by **Pavlov** (1928) in order to explain the laws of movement of nervous processes which enable the conditional—reflexive activity of the brain to occur; despite its many neurophysiological references, this is essentially a learning theory. The adaptation of behaviour to the environment occurs (according to pavlov) on the basis of the acquisition of conditioned reflexes. **Classical conditioning** (sometimes called *Pavlovian* or *respondent conditioning*) was the first type of

learning to be studied systematically.

In the late nineteenth century, the Russian physiologist *Ivan Pavlov* was studying the digestive systems of dogs. During the course of his work, he noticed a peculiar phenomenon. Like humans and other animals, dogs normally salivate when presented with food, which is a simple reflex. Pavlov noticed that if a stimulus, such as a bell or tuning fork ringing, repeatedly occurred just as a dog was about to be fed, the dog would start to salivate when it heard the bell, even if food were not presented. As pavlov understood it, the dog has learned to associate the bell with food, and because food produced the reflex of salivation, the bell also came to produce the reflex.

Pavlov's model

An innate reflex such as salivation to food is an unconditioned reflex. *Conditioning* is a form of learning; hence an **unconditioned reflex** is a reflex that occurs naturally, without any prior learning. The stimulus that produces the response in an unconditioned reflex—in this case, food—is called an **unconditioned stimulus (UCS)**. An unconditioned stimulus activates a reflexive response without any learning having taken place; thus, the reflex is unlearned, or unconditioned. An **unconditioned response (UCR)** is a response that does not have to be learned. In pavlov's experiment, the UCR was salivation.

Shortly before presenting the UCS (the food), Pavlov presented a *neutral stimulus*—a stimulus (in this case, ringing a bell) that normally does not elicit the response in question. After the bell had been paired with the unconditioned stimulus (the food) several times, the sound of the bell alone came to evoke a conditioned response, salivation. A **conditioned response (CR)** is a response that has been learned. By pairing the UCS (the food) with the sound of a bell, the bell became a conditioned stimulus (CS)—a stimulus that, through learning, has come to evoke a conditioned response.

Fig. 5.1 Pavlov's apparatus for studying the conditioned salivary (drooling) response

Classical conditioning can explain a wide array of learned responses outside the laboratory as well. For example, a house cat that was repeatedly sprayed with flea repellent squinted reflexively as the repellent got in its eyes. Eventually it came to squint and meow piteously (CR) whenever its owner used an aerosol spray (CS). The same cat, like many house hold felines, also came to associate the sound of an electric can opener with the opening of its favourite delicacies and would dash to the kitchen counter and meow whenever its owner opened any can, whether cat food or green beans.

Another example is that, most of us have probably had the experience of needing to go to the bathroom but deciding to wait until they get home. Upon arriving at the front door—and worse still upon entering the bathroom—the intensity of the urge seems to intensify a thousand—fold, requiring considerable self—control. This phenomenon, too, is a straight forward example of classical conditioning: Stimuli associated with entering the house and especially the bathroom, are CSs that signal an impending eliminatory response.

Conditioned responses

Pavlov also saw how learning could produce maladaptive patterns as well. Three cases in which classical conditioning generally fosters adaptation but can also lead to maladaptive responses are: conditioned taste aversions, conditioned emotional responses, and conditioned immune responses.

Conditioned taste aversions

A **conditioned taste aversion** is a learned aversion to a taste associated with an unpleasant feeling, usually nausea. From an evolutionary perspective, the ability to connect tastes with nausea or other unpleasant visceral ("gut") experiences is crucial to survival; learning to avoid toxic foods can mean the difference between life and death for an animal that forages (that is, scrounges or hunts) for its meals.

Although conditioned taste aversions normally protect the organism from ingesting toxic substances, anyone who has ever developed an aversion to a food eaten shortly before getting the flu knows how irrational these aversions can sometimes be. Cancer patients undergoing chemotherapy often develop aversions to virtually all food—and may lose

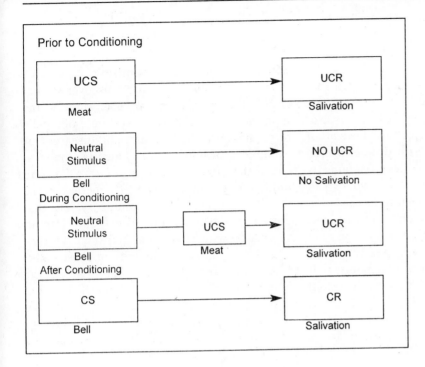

Fig. 5.2 Classical conditioning. In classical conditioning, an initially neutral stimulus comes to elicit a conditioned response

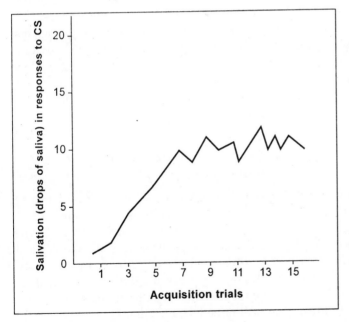

dangerous amounts of weight—because a common side effect of chemotherapy is nausea. To put this in the language of classical conditioning, chemotherapy is a UCS that leads to nausea, a UCR; the result is an inadvertent association of any food eaten (CS) with nausea (the CR). This conditioned response can develop rapidly, with only one or two exposures to the food paired with nausea. Some patients even begin to feel nauseous at the sound of a nurse's voice, the sight of the clinic, or the thought of treatment, although acquisition of these CRs generally requires repeated exposure.

Fig. 5.13 A learning or acquisition curve of a classically conditioned response. Initially the dog did not salivate in response to the sound of the bell. By the third conditioning trial, however, the conditioned stimulus (the bell) had begun to elicit a conditioned response (salivation), which was firmly established by the fifth or sixth trial.

Conditioned emotional responses

One of the most important ways classical conditioning affects behaviour is in the conditioning of emotional responses. Consider the automatic smile that comes to a person's face when hearing a special song or the fear of horses a person may develop after falling off of one. **Conditioned emotional responses** occur when a formerly neutral stimulus is paired with a stimulus that evokes an emotional response (either naturally, as when bitten by an animal, or through prior learning). Conditioned emotional responses are common in everyday life, such as the sweaty palms, pounding heart, and feeling of anxiety that arise after an instructor walks into a classroom and begins handing out a few printed pages of questions.

One of the most famous examples of classical conditioning was the case of little Albert. The study was performed by *John Watson* and his colleague, *Rosalie Rayner* (1920). When Albert was nine months old, Watson and Rayner presented him with a variety of objects, including a dog, a rabbit, a white rat, masks (including a Santa Claus mask), and a fur coat. Albert showed no fear in response to any of these objects; in fact, he played regularly with them. A few days later, Watson and Rayner tested the little Albert's response to a loud noise (the UCS) by banging on a steel bar directly behind his head. Albert reacted by jumping, falling forward, and whimpering.

About two months later, Watson and Rayner selected the white rat to be the CS in their experiment and proceeded to condition a fear response in Albert. Each time Albert reached out to touch the rat, they struck the steel bar, creating the same loud noise that had initially startled him. After only a few pairings of the noise and the rat, Albert learned to fear the rat.

Studies since Watson and Rayner's time have proposed classical conditioning as an explanation for some human **phobias**, that is, irrational fears of specific objects or situations.

Conditioned immune responses

Psychologists have recently discovered that classical conditioning can even impact the immune system, the system of cells throughout the body that fight disease. For example, beside from causing nausea, chemotherapy for cancer has a second unfortunate consequence: It decreases the activity of cells in the immune system that normally fight off infection. Can stimuli associated with chemotherapy, then, become CRs that suppress the activity of these cells? One study tested this by comparing the functioning of immune cells from the blood of cancer patients at two different times. The first time was a few days prior to chemotherapy. The second time was the morning of the day the patient would be receiving chemotherapy, after checking into the hospital. The investigators hypothesized that exposure to hospital stimuli associated with prior chemotherapy experiences (CS) would suppress immune functioning (CR), just as chemotherapy (UCS) reduces the activity of immune cells (UCR). They were right: Blood taken the morning of hospitalization showed weakened immune functioning when exposed to germs.

Stimulus generalization and discrimination

Once an organism has learned to associate a CS with a UCS, it may respond to stimuli that resemble the CS with a similar response. This phenomenon, predicted by Aristotle's principle of similarity, is called **stimulus generalization**. For example, you are at a sporting event and you stand for the national anthem. You suddenly well up with pride in your country (which you realize now, of course, is nothing but a classically conditioned emotional response).

Similarly, in Watson and Rayner's experiment, the pairing of the rat and the loud noise led little Albert to fear not only the rat but also other furry or hairy objects, including the rabbit, the dog, the fur coat, and even Santa's face. In other words, Albert's fear of the rat had *generalized* to other furry objects.

A major component of adaptive learning is, knowing when to generalize and when to be more specific or discriminating. Maladaptive patterns in humans often involve inappropriate generalization from one set of circumstances to others, as when a person who has been frequently criticized by a parent responds negatively to all authority figures. Much of the time, however, people are able to discriminate among stimuli in ways that foster adaptation. **Stimulus discrimination** is the learned tendency to respond to a restricted range of stimuli or only to the stimulus used during training. In many ways, stimulus discrimination is the opposite of stimulus generalization. Pavlov's dogs did not salivate in response to just *any* sound. Organisms learn to discriminate between two similar stimuli when these stimuli are not consistently associated with the same UCS.

Extinction and spontaneous recovery

In the **acquisition**, or initial learning of a conditioned response, each pairing of the CS and UCS is known as a **conditioning trial**. But what happens later if the CS repeatedly occurs *without* the UCS? What would have happened if Watson and Rayner had, on the second, third, and all subsequent trials, exposed little Albert to the white rat without the loud noise?

Albert's learned fear response would eventually have been *extinguished,* or eliminated, from his behavioural repertoire. **Extinction** in classical conditioning refers to the process by which a CR is weakened by presentation of the CS without the UCS. If a dog has come to associate the sound of a bell with food, it will eventually stop salivating at the bell tone if the bell rings enough times without the presentation of food. The association is weakened—but not obliterated. If days later the

dog once more hears the bell, it is likely to salivate again. This is known as **spontaneous recovery**—the reemergence of a previously extinguished conditioned response. The spontaneous recovery of a CR is typically short-lived, however, and will rapidly extinguish again without renewed pairings of the CS and UCS.

Factors affecting classical conditioning

Classical conditioning does not occur everytime a bell rings or a baby startles. Several factors influence the extent to which classical conditioning will occur. These include the interstimulus interval, the individual's learning history, and the organism's preparedness to learn.

Interstimulus interval

The **interstimulus interval** is the time between presentation of the CS and the UCS. Presumably, if too much time passes between the presentation of these two stimuli, the animal is unlikely to associate them, and conditioning is less likely to occur. For most responses, the optimal interval between the CS and UCS is very brief, usually a few seconds or less. The optimal interval depends, however, on the stimulus. A CS that occurs about a half a second before a puff of air blows on the eye will have the maximum power to elicit a conditioned eyeblink response in humans. This makes evolutionary sense because we usually have very little warning between the time we see or hear something and the time, debris reaches our eyes. At the other extreme conditioned taste aversions do not occur when the interstimulus interval is *less than* ten seconds, and learning often occurs with intervals up to several hours. Given that nausea or stomach pain can develop hours after ingestion of a toxic substance, the capacity to associate tastes with feelings in the gut minutes or hours later clearly fosters survival.

The temporal order of the CS and the UCS—that is, which one comes first—is also crucial. Maximal conditioning occurs when the onset of the CS precedes the UCS—called **forward** ▶

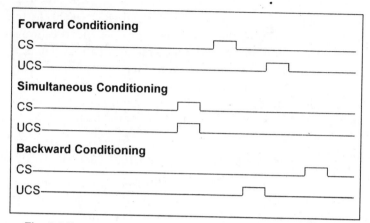

Fig. 5.4 Forward, simultaneous, and backward conditioning

conditioning. Less effective is **simultaneous conditioning**, in which the CS and UCS are presented at the same time. A third pattern, **backward conditioning**, is the least effective of all. Here, the CS is presented after the UCS has occurred. These principles, too, make evolutionary sense, since a CS that consistently occurs after a UCS offers little additional information, whereas a CS that precedes a UCS allows the organism to prepare.

The individual's learning history

Another factor that influences classical conditioning is the individual's learning history. An extinguished response is usually easier to learn the second time around, presumably because the stimulus was once associated with the response. This suggests that neuronal connections established through learning may diminish in their strength when the environment no longer supports them but do not entirely disappear; later learning can build on old "tracks" that have been covered up but not obliterated.

In other circumstances, prior learning can actually *hinder* learning. Suppose a dog has learned to salivate at the sound of a bell (conditioned stimulus A, or CSA). The researcher now wants to teach the dog to associate food with a flash of light as well (conditioned stimulus B, or CSB). If the bell continues to sound even occasionally in learning trials pairing the light (CSB) with food (the UCS), the dog is unlikely to produce a conditioned response to the flash of light. This phenomenon is known as blocking. **Blocking** refers to the failure of a stimulus (such as a flash of light) to elicit a CR when it is combined with another stimulus that already elicits the response. If a bell is already associated with food, a flashing light is of little consequence unless it provides additional, nonredundant information. Interestingly, if the CR to the bell (CSA) is subsequently extinguished, the animal will more quickly develop a CR to the CSB (the light) than control animals who have not undergone blocking trials. What this suggests is that the organism was in fact forming associations between the blocked CS (CSB) and the CR but that these were never expressed in *behaviour* because they were blocked by prior associations.

A similar phenomenon occurs in latent inhibition, in which repeated exposure to a neutral stimulus without a UCS makes it less likely than a noval stimulus to become a CS; in other words, the familiar stimulus is less likely to produce a CR.

For instance, a person who has drunk from water fountains 999 times and become sick two hours after the thousandth time is unlikely to associate water with nausea. If, however, she *repeatedly* gets sick after drinking from that fountain, she may start to associate water with nausea. Alternatively, she may learn to discriminate this fountain from others or may develop a more complex, compound association: The CSA (water) is associated with nausea only if the CSB (the fountain) precedes presentation of the water (CSA). Complex associations of this sort are extremely important in daily life. For example, a child may normally feel happy (a conditioned emotional response) in the presence of her father (CSA) but learn over time to feel afraid (a different conditioned emotional response) if she hears her father slam the door when he enters the house (CSB).

Preparedness to learn

A third influence on classical conditioning is the organism's readiness to learn certain associations. Research has shown that some responses can be conditioned much more readily to certain stimuli than to others.

The phenomenon of **prepared learning**—the biologically wired *preparedness* to learn some associations—is not limited to some conditions. This suggests an evolutionary explanation: Natural selection has favoured organisms that more readily associate stimuli that tend to be associated in nature are lucky enough to survive after eating a poisonous caterpillar is more likely to survive if it can associate nausea with the right stimulus.

Humans show some evidence of biological preparedness as well. Readers of this book, for example, are much likely to have snake or spider phobias than automobile phobias, despite the fact that they are more than 10,000 times more likely to die at the wheel of a car than at the mouth of a spider—and to have experienced a car accident rather than a snakebite. Experimental data suggest that humans may also be biologically predisposed to associate aversive experiences more readily with angry faces than smiling ones.

Biological preparedness, of course, has its limits, especially in humans, whose associative capacities are *almost* limitless. One study, for example, found people equally likely to develop a fear of handguns as of snakes (*Honeybourne* 1993). Where biological predispositions leave off, learning begins as a way of naturally selecting adaptive responses.

What organisms learn in classical conditioning

Precisely what organisms learn when they are classically conditioned, however, has been a topic of considerable debate. Some behavioural theorist have argued that in classical conditioning the organism learns to associate the CS with the UCS—a *stimulus-stimulus,* or S-S, associated. Others have argued that what is learned is an association between the CS and the CR—a *stimulus-response,* or S-R, association. Both explanations are consistent with Aristotle's proposition that humans learn by associating events that tend to co-occur, and both probably occur in classical conditioning. For example, the S-S association may occur first, through repeated co-occurrences (contiguity) of the two stimuli; shortly thereafter, an S-R association forms as the CS begins to co-occur with the CR.

Pavlov was influenced by associationism and hypothesized that in classical conditioning the CS essentially becomes a *signal* to an organism that the UCS is about to occur. As a result, the organism responds to the CS as if it *were* the UCS. Pavlov proposed a neurological mechanism for this, hypothesizing that repeated pairings of the UCS and the CS lead to connections between them in the brain, as a result, the two stimuli eventually trigger the same response. Although Pavlov was probably right in broad strokes, subsequent research suggests that the CR and the UCR, though usually similar, are rarely identical. Dogs typically do not salivate as much in response to a bell as to the actual presentation of food, which means that the CS is not triggering the exact same response as the UCS.

Sometimes the CR is even the opposite of the UCR as in **paradoxical conditioning**, where the CR is actually the body's attempt to *counteract* the effects of a stimulus that is about to occur. For example, the sight of drug paraphernalia in heroin addicts can activate physiological reactions that reduce the effect of the heroin they are about to inject. This produces a *conditioned tolerance* or decreased sensitivity, to the drug with repeated use, as the body counteracts dosages that were previously effective. This conditioned response may be involved in the processes that force addicts to take progressively higher doses of a drug to achieve the same effect.

Significance of classical conditioning

In human life emotional responses become conditioned to certain stimuli. Many of our subjective feelings—from our violent emotions to the subtle nuances of our moods—are probably conditioned responses.

Since some emotional responses to stimuli are learned, perhaps they can be *unlearned.* Or perhaps other, less disturbing responses can be associated with the stimuli that produce unpleasant emotional responses. The extinction and alteration of disturbing emotional responses by classical conditioning is one form of *behaviour therapy,* or it is also called *behaviour modification.*

OPERANT CONDITIONING

According to **E.L. Thorndike** if an organism is placed in a problem situation, it will react to that situation (because of its instinctive equipment or previously acquired behaviour patterns) in the way possible to it, until one of its responses happens (i.e. by chance) to have a successful outcome (trial-and-error behaviour).

In 1898, Edward Thorndike placed a hungry cat in a box with a mechanical latch and then placed food in full view just outside the box. The cat meowed, paced back and forth, and rubbed against the walls of the box. In doing so, it happened to trip the latch. Immediately, the door to the box opened, and the cat gained access to the food. Thorndike repeated the experiment, and with continued repetitions the cat became more adept at tripping the latch. Eventually, it was able to leave its cage almost as soon as food appeared.

Thorndike proposed a law of learning to account for this phenomenon, which he called the **law of effect**: An animal's tendency to reproduce a behaviour depends on that behaviour's effect on the environment and the consequent effect on the animal. If tripping the latch had not helped the cat reach the food, the cat would not have learned to keep brushing up

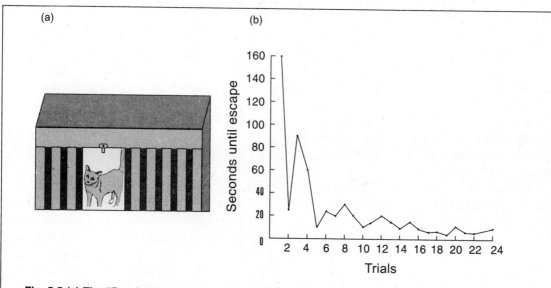

Fig. 5.5 (a) The "Puzzle-box" used by thorndike in his experiments on instrumental conditioning. (b) The learning or acquisition curve in Thorndike's "Puzzle-box" experiment

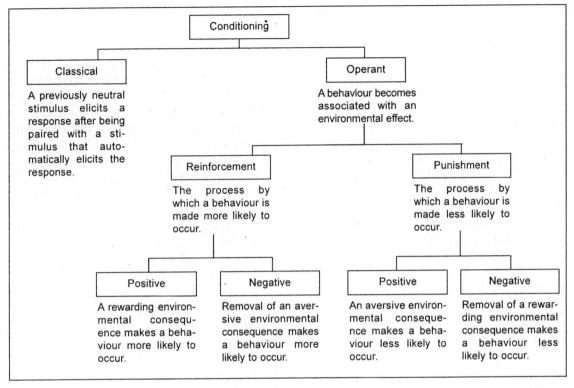

Fig. 5.6 Conditioning Processes

against the latch. More simply, the law of effect states that *behaviour is controlled by its consequences.*

New (behavioural) habbits are formed on the basis of the connection of *situation* (situational characteristics) and *response(s)* if this association is directly followed by a "satisfying state of affairs" which causes its intensity to increase and hence the probability that on the next similar occasion the appropriate behaviour will occur again.

The behaviour of Thorndike's cats exemplifies a second form of conditioning, known as instrumental or operant conditioning. Thorndike used the term **instrumental conditioning** because the behaviour is instrumental to achieving a more satisfying state of affairs. **B.F. Skinner**, who spent years experimenting with and systematizing the ways in which behaviour is controlled by the environment, called it **operant conditioning,** which means learning to operate on the environment-to produce a consequence.

The major distinction between operant and classical conditioning is that in classical conditioning an environmental stimulus initiates a response, whereas in operant conditioning a *behaviour* (or operant) produces an environmental response. **Operants** are behaviours that are emitted (spontaneously produced) rather than elicited by the environment. Thorndike's cat spontaneously emitted that conditioned future behaviour.

In operant conditioning the behaviour *precedes* the environmental event that condition future behaviour. By contrast, in classical conditioning, an environmental stimulus (such as a bell) precedes a response.

The basic idea behind operant conditioning, then, is that behaviour is controlled by its consequences. There are two types of environmental consequences that produce operant conditioning: **reinforcement**, which increases the probability that a response will occur, and **punishment**, which diminishes its likelihood.

Reinforcement

Reinforcement means something in the environment fortifies, or supports, a behaviour. A **reinforcer** is an environmental consequence that occurs after an organism has produced a response and makes the response more likely to recur. Psychologists distinguish two kinds of reinforcement, positive and negative.

Positive reinforcement

Positive reinforcement is the process whereby presentation of a stimulus (a reward or payoff) after a behaviour makes the behaviour more likely to occur again.

For example, in experimental procedures pioneered by B.F. Skinner, a pigeon was placed in a cage with a target mounted on one side. The pigeon spontaneously pecked around in the cage. This behaviour was not a response to any particular stimulus; pecking is simply innate avian behaviour. If, by chance, the pigeon pecked at the target, however, a pellet of grain dropped into a bin. If the pigeon happened to peck at the target again, it was once more rewarded with a pellet. The pellet is a **positive reinforcer**—an environmental consequence that, when presented, strengthens the probability that a response will recur. The pigeon associated with the positive reinforcer.

Positive reinforcement is not limited to pigeons. In fact, it controls much of human behaviour as well. For instance, students learn to exert effort studying when they are reinforced with praise and good grades, salespeople learn to appease obnoxious customers and laugh at their jokes because doing so yields them commissions, and people learn to go to work each day because they receive a paycheck.

Negative reinforcement

Eliminating something aversive can itself be a reinforcer or reward. **Negative reinforcers** are aversive or unpleasant stimuli that strengthen a behaviour by their removal. Just as the presentation of a positive reinforcer rewards a response, the removal of an aversive stimulus rewards a response. This is known as **negative reinforcement**—the process whereby termination of an aversive stimulus makes a behaviour more likely to occur. Hitting the snooze button on an alarm clock is negatively reinforced by the termination of the alarm; cleaning the kitchen is negatively reinforced by the elimination of unpleasant sights and smell.

Negative reinforcement occurs in both escape learning and avoidance learning. In **escape learning**, a behaviour is reinforced by the elimination of an aversive situation. For example, a rat presses a lever and terminates an electric shock; or a child cleans his room to stop his parents from nagging. **Avoidance learning** occurs, as an organism prevents an expected aversive event from happening.

In this case, avoidance of a potentially aversive situation reinforces the operant. For example, a rat presses a lever when it hears a tone that signals that shock is about to occur; or the child always keeps his room clean to avoid nagging.

Punishment

Another type of environmental consequence that controls behaviour through operant conditioning is called **punishment**. Whereas reinforcement always *increases* the likelihood of a response, either by the presentation of a reward or the removal of an aversive stimulus, punishment decreases the probability that a response will recur. Thus, if Skinner's pigeon received an electric shock each time it pecked at the target, it would be less likely to peck again because this operant resulted in an aversive outcome. The criminal justice system also operates on a system of punishment, attempting to discourage elicit behaviours by imposing penalties.

Like reinforcement, punishment can be positive or negative. ("Positive" and "negative" here do not refer to the feelings of the participants, who rarely consider punishment a positive experience. Positive simply means something is presented, whereas negative means something is taken away). In positive punishment, such as spanking, exposure to an aversive event following a behaviour reduces the likelihood of the operant recurring. Negative punishment involves losing, or not obtaining, a reinforcer as a consequence of behaviour, as when an employee fails to receive a pay increase because of frequent lateness or absenteeism.

Common problems in using punishment

- Problem in using punishment with animals and young children is that the learner may have difficulty distinguishing which operant is being punished. People who yell at their dog for coming, after it has been called several times are actually punishing good behaviour—coming when called. The dog is more likely to associate the punishment with its action than its inaction—and is likely to adjust its behaviour accordingly, by becoming even less likely to come when called.
- Second and related problem associated with punishment is that the learner may come to fear the person meeting out the punishment (via classical conditioning) rather than the action (via operant conditioning). A child who is harshly punished by his father may become afraid of his father instead of changing his behaviour.
- Third, people who rely heavily on punishment often fail to recognize that punishment may not eliminate existing rewards for a behaviour. In nature, a single action may have multiple consequences, and behaviour can be controlled by any number of them. A teacher who punishes the class clown may not have much success if the behaviour is reinforced by classmates. Sometimes, punishing one behaviour (such as stealing) may inadvertently reinforce another (such as lying).
- Fourth, people typically use punishment when they are angry, which can lead both to poorly designed punishment (from a learning point of view) and to the potential for abuse. An angry parent may punish a child for misdeeds just discovered but that occurred a considerable time earlier. The time interval between the child's action and the consequence may render the punishment ineffective because the child does not adequately connect the two events. Parents also frequently punish depending more on their mood than on the type of behaviour they want to discourage, which can prevent the child from learning what behaviour is being punished, under what circumstances, and how to avoid it.
- Finally, aggression that is used to punish behaviour often leads to further aggression. The child who is beaten typically learns a much deeper lesson: that problems can be solved with violence. In fact, the more physical punishment parents use, the more aggressively their children tend to behave at home and at school. Correlation does not, of course, prove causation; aggressive children may provoke punitive parenting. Nevertheless, the weight of evidence suggests that violent parents tend to create violent children. Since beating children tends to make them more likely as adults to have *less* self-control, lower self-esteem, more troubled relationships, and more depression and to be more likely to abuse their own children and spouses.

Punishment tends to be most effective when it is accompanied by reasoning—even in 2 and 3 year old (*Larzelere, 1996*)—and when the person being punished is also reinforced for an alternative, acceptable behaviour. Explaining helps a child correctly connect an action with a punishment. Having other positively reinforced behaviours to draw on allows the child to generate alternative responses.

Extinction

As in classical conditioning, learned operant responses can be extinguished. *Extinction* occurs if enough conditioning trials pass in which the operant is not followed by the consequence previously associated with it. A child may reduce effort in school if hard work no longer leads to reinforces (such as "good work!" written on homework), just as a corporate executive may choose to stop producing a product that is no longer bringing in profits.

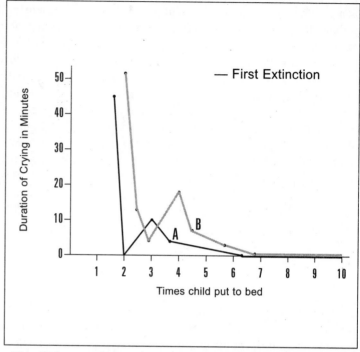

Fig. 5.7 Extinction of tantrum behaviour in a 21-month old child

Knowing how to extinguish behaviour is important in everyday life, particularly for parents. Consider the case of a 21-month-old boy who had a serious illness requiring around-the-clock attention. After recovering, the child continued to demand this level of attention, which was no longer necessary. His demands were especially troublesome at bedtime, when he screamed and cried unless a parent sat with him until he fell asleep, which could take up to two hours.

Relying on the principle that unreinforced behaviour will be extinguished, the parents, with some help from a psychologist, began following a new bedtime regimen. In the first trial of the extinction series, they spent a relaxed and warm good-night session with their son, closed the door when they left the room, and refused to respond to the wails and screams that followed. After 45 minutes, the boy fell asleep, and he fell asleep immediately on the second trial. The next several bedtimes were accompanied by tantrums that steadily decreased in duration, so that by the tenth trial the parents fully enjoyed the sounds of silence.

As in classical conditioning, spontaneous recovery (in which a previously learned behaviour recurs without renewed reinforcement) sometimes occurs. In fact, the boy cried and screamed again one night when his aunt attempted to put him to bed. She inadvertently reinforced this behaviour by returning to his room; as a result, his parents had to repeat their extinction procedure.

Behaviour shaping

Behaviour shaping is a special form of instrumental learning; in this case each approximation to the desired behaviour is rewarded, so that the behaviour to be acquired is formed gradually.

For example, circus animals (and gymnasts) learn to do backflips and perform other behaviours not usually seen in their natural habits. How does this occur? A procedure used by animal trainers, called **shaping**, produces novel behaviour by reinforcing closer and closer approximations to the desired response. Skinner (1951) described a shaping procedure that can be used to teach a dog to touch its nose to a cupboard door handle. The first step is to bring a hungry dog (in behavioural terms, a dog that has been deprived of food for a certain number of hours or until its body weight is a certain percent below normal) into the kitchen and immediately reward him with food any time he happens to face the cupboard; the dog will soon face the cupboard most of the time. The next step is to reward the dog whenever it moves toward the cupboard, then to reward it when it moves its head so that its nose comes closer to the cupboard, and finally to reward the dog only for touching its nose to the cupboard handle. This shaping procedure should take no more than five minutes, even for a beginner.

The same shaping techniques can be used to teach more complex behaviour. The key, as a trainer, is to begin by reinforcing a response the animal can readily produce. Gradually, the trainer reinforces only certain ways of performing the desired behaviour, so that the animal eventually produces a very specific operant. With humans, shaping is common in all kinds of teaching. A tennis instructor may at first praise a student any time he holds the racquet in a way that resembles a good grip and gets the ball over the net. Gradually, however, the instructor compliments only proper form and well-placed shots, progressively shaping the student's behaviour. Shaping does not require instruction and often occurs naturally as well. A tennis player may evolve a particular grip on the racket as his behaviour is progressively reinforced toward a grip that originally would have felt completely unnatural and would never have been spontaneously produced.

Shaping is a classic concept in instrumental and operant conditioning: Reinforce the steps leading to the desired response and that response will eventually occur. But classical conditioning also seems to make an important contribution to the shaping process.

The subjects of this experiment were hungry pigeons who learned to peck a key in an operant chamber. Pigeons can be shaped to peck a key just as rats can be shaped to press a lever—by the use of contingent positive reinforcement and the method of successive approximations. In this experiment, however, classical—not instrumental—conditioning principles were used to train the birds to peck a key. The key was dark most of the time, but it was lighted just before food was presented. Neither the lighting of the key nor the presenting of the food depended upon any particular response by the pigeons. Thus, as in classical conditioning, two stimuli were paired independently of the learner's responses. Key illumination was the CS and presentation of food was the US. After a number of CS-US pairings, the pigeons approached the key and began to peck it. This classical conditioning method of shaping animals in an operant chamber has come to be called **auto-shaping**.

Operant conditioning of complex behaviours

So far we have discussed relatively simple behaviours controlled by their environmental consequences—pigeons pecking, rats pressing, and people showing up at work for a paycheck. In fact, operant conditioning offers one of the most comprehensive explanatory accounts of the range of human and animal behaviour ever produced. We will now explore four phenomena that substantially increase the breadth of the behaviourists account of learning: schedules of reinforcement, stimulus discrimination, stimulus generalization and characteristics of learner.

Schedules of reinforcement

In the examples described so far, an animal is rewarded or punished every time it performs a behaviour. This situation, in which the consequence is the same each time the animal emits a behaviour, is called a **continuous reinforcement schedule** (because the behaviour is *continuously* reinforced). Just as a rat might receive a pellet of food each time it presses a lever. Such consistent reinforcement, however, rarely occurs in nature or in human life. More typically, an action sometimes leads to reinforcement but other times does not. Such reinforcement schedules are known as **partial** or **intermittent schedules of reinforcement** because the behaviour is reinforced only part of the time, or intermittently. (These are called schedules of *reinforcement,* but the same principles apply with *punishment*).

Intuitively, one would think that continuous schedules would be more effective. Although this tends to be true during the initial learning (acquisition) of a response (presumably because continuous reinforcement renders the connection between the behaviour and its consequence clear and predictable), partial reinforcement is usually superior for maintaining learned behaviour. For example, suppose you have a relatively new car, and everytime you turn the key the engine starts. If one day, however, you try to start the car ten times and the engine will not turn over, you will probably give up and call a mechanic. In contrast, if you are the proud owner of rusted-out old car and are accustomed to ten turns of the ignition before the car finally cranks up, you may try 20 or 30 times before enlisting the help of a mechanic. Thus, behaviours maintained under partial schedules are usually more resistant to extinction.

Behaviourist researchers, notably Skinner and his colleagues, have categorized intermittent reinforcement schedules as either ratio schedules or interval schedules. In **ratio schedules**, payoffs are tied to the number of responses emitted; only a fraction of "correct" behaviours receive reinforcement (such as one out of every five, for a ratio of 1:5). In **interval schedules**, rewards are delivered only after some interval of time. The organism can produce a response as often as it wants, but the response will only be reinforced (or punished) after a certain amount of time has elapsed.

Reinforcement schedules are often studied with a **cumulative response recorder**, an instrument that tallies the number of times a subject produces a response, such as pressing a bar or pecking a target. Fig (5.9) illustrates typical cumulative response recordings for the four reinforcement schedules: fixed ratio, variable ratio, fixed interval, and variable interval.

Fixed-ratio schedule

In a **fixed-ratio (FR) schedule**, of reinforcement, an organism receives reinforcement for a fixed proportion of the responses it emits. Piecework employment uses a fixed-ratio schedule of reinforcement: A person receives payment for every box of apples packed (an FR-1 schedule) or for every ten scarves woven (an FR-10 schedule). Workers weave the first nine scarves without reinforcement; the payoff occurs when the tenth scarf is completed. FR schedules are characterized by rapid responding, with a brief pause after each reinforcement.

Variable-ratio schedule

In **variable-ratio (VR) schedules**, the individual receives a reward for some percentage of responses, but the number of responses required before reinforcement is unpredictable (that is, variable). Variable-ratio schedules specify an *average* number of responses that will be rewarded. Thus, a pigeon on a VR-5 schedule may be rewarded on its fourth, seventh, 13th, and 20th responses, averaging one reward for every five responses. Variable-ratio schedules generally produce rapid, constant responding and are probably the most common in daily life. People cannot predict that they will be rewarded or praised for every fifth good deed, but they do receive occasional, irregular social reinforcement, which is enough to reinforce altruistic behaviour in most people.

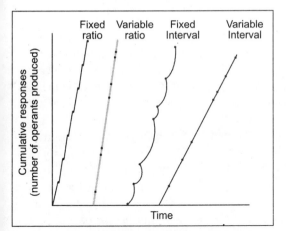

Fig. 5.8 Schedules of Reinforcement.
A cumulative response record graphs the total
number of responses that have been emitted at
any point of time. Different schedules of
reinforcement produce different patterns of
responding

Fixed-interval ratio

In a **fixed-interval (FI) schedule** an animal
receives reinforcement for its responses only
after a fixed amount of time. For example, a rat
that presses a bar is reinforcement with a pellet
of food every ten minutes. The rat may press the
bar 100 times or one time during that ten
minutes; doing so does not make a difference in
the delivery of the pellet, just as long as the rat
presses the bar at some point during each ten-
minute interval.

An animal on an FI schedule of reinforcement
will ultimately learn to stop responding except
toward the end of each interval, producing the
scalloped cumulative response pattern shown in
Fig. (5.9). Fixed-interval schedules affect human
performance in the same way. For example,
workers whose boss comes only by two o'clock are
likely to relax the rest of the day.

Variable-interval schedule

A **variable interval (VI) schedule**, like a
fixed-interval schedule, ties reinforcement to an
interval of time after which the individual's
response leads to reinforcement. In a VI
schedule, however, the animal cannot predict

how long that time interval will be. Thus, a rat
might receive reinforcement for bar pressing,
but only at five, six, twenty and forty minutes (1-
10 and I-VI schedule).

Variable-interval schedules are more
effective then fixed-interval schedules in
maintaining consistent performance. Random,
unannounced governmental inspections of
working conditions in a plant are much more
effective in getting management to maintain
safety standards than inspections at fixed
intervals.

Stimulus discrimination

In everyday life, rarely does a response receive
continuous reinforcement in a given situation,
such as work or school. Making matters even
more complicated for learners is that a single
behaviour can lead to different effects in different
situations. Professors receive a pay-check for
lecturing in their classes, but if they lecture new
acquaintances at a cocktail party, the
environmental consequences will not be the same.

In some situations, then, a connection
might exist between a behaviour and a
consequence (called a response *contingency*,
because the consequence is dependent, or
contingent, on the behaviour). In other
situations, however, the contingencies might be
different, so the organism needs to be able to
discriminate circumstances under which
different contingencies apply. A stimulus that
signals the presence of a particular
contingencies of reinforcement is called a
discriminative stimulus *(S^D)*. In other
words, a person learns to produce certain
actions only in the presence of the
discriminative signals that lecturing behaviour
will be reinforced. In an experimental
demonstration, rats were rewarded for turning
clockwise when they were placed in one
chamber and turning anticlockwise when placed
in another, the chamber was the discriminative
stimulus signaling different contingencies of
reinforcement (*Richards, 1990*).

Stimulus discrimination is one of the keys to

the complexity and flexibility of human and animal behaviour. Behaviour therapists, who apply behaviourist principles to maladaptive behaviours, use the concept of stimulus discrimination to help people recognize and alter some very subtle triggers for maladaptive responses, particularly in relationships. For example, one couple was on the verge of divorce because the husband complained that his wife was too passive and indecisive and the wife complained that her husband was too rigid and controlling. A careful analysis of their interactions suggested some complex contingencies controlling their behaviour. The couple often engaged in mutually enjoyable conversation, in which each felt comfortable and relatively spontaneous. At times, however, the woman would detect a particular "tone" in her husbands voice (an S^D) that she had associated with his getting angry; upon hearing this tone, she would "shut down" and become more passive and quiet. Her husband, however, found her passivity (an S^D for him) infuriating and would then begin to push her for answers and decisions, which only intensified her "passivity" and his "controlling" behaviour. She was not, in fact, always passive, and he was not always controlling. Easing the tension in the marriage thus required isolating the discriminative stimuli that controlled each of their responses.

Stimulus generalization

Like in classical conditioning stimulus generalization also occurs in instrumental conditioning. The response in instrumental conditioning is made in a particular stimulus situation—in an operant chamber with a certain type of light, for example. If the stimulus situation is changed, the response still occurs but less readily than it did in the original stimulus situation. Furthermore, the tendency to respond depends upon the degree of similarity between the original training situation and the changed one. The following experiment illustrates **stimulus generalization in instrumental conditioning**. (Olson and King, 1962).

Pigeons were shaped and trained with positive reinforcement to peck a disk, or "key" in an operant chamber. During the original learning, a moderately bright light illuminated the key. After the pecking response to this stimulus had been well learned and the rate of response was high and steady, the animals were tested with six other intensities on the key. These test stimuli were spaced in steps of equal intensity from low to high. In the graph of fig (5.10), the original stimulus is called 8; the more intense stimuli are 2, 4, and 6; and the less intense stimuli are 10, 12, and 14. The graph shows that the pigeons had a tendency to respond to these new stimuli and that the degree to which they responded depended on the size of the brightness difference between the original and test stimuli.

Figure (5.10) also illustrates what is known as a gradient of generalization. This simply means that the amount of generalization is graded—great or small—depending on how similar the test stimuli are to the original, or training, stimulus.

Enduring characteristics of the learner

Not only to prior learning experiences influence operant conditioning, but so, too, do enduring characteristics of the learner. The role of the learner was especially clear in an experiment that attempted to teach three octopi (named *Albert, Bertram,* and *Charles*) to pull a lever in their saltwater tanks to obtain food (*Dews*, 1959). The usual shaping procedures worked successfully on Albert and Bertram, who were first rewarded for approaching the lever, then for touching it with a tentacle, and finally for tugging at it. With Charles, however, things were diferent. Instead of *pulling* the lever to obtain food, charles tugged at it with such force that he broke it. Charles was generally a surly subject, spending much of his time "with eyes above the surface of the water, directing a jet of water at any individual who approached the tank."

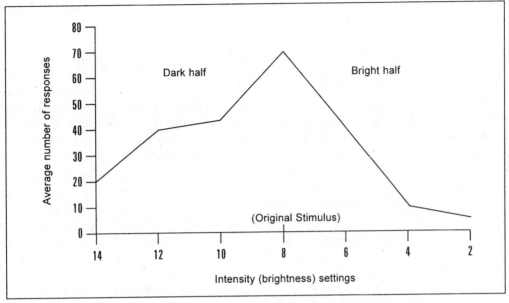

Fig. 5.9 A gradient of generation for an instrumentally conditioned response—key pecking by a pigeon

Humans differ in their "conditionability" as well. Many individuals with antisocial personality disorder, who show a striking disregard for society's standards, tend to be relatively unresponsive to punishment. Their lack of anxiety when confronted with potential punishment renders them less likely to learn to control selfish, aggressive, or impulsive behaviours that other people learn to inhibit. Similarly, genetic and environmental factors lead to differences among individuals in the ability to solve problems quickly and efficiently.

Significance of instrumental conditioning

Instrumental conditioning is more than just a game played between experimental psychologists and rats or pigeons. Animal experiments have demonstrated some principles that can be extended to human life. Some of our beliefs, customs, and goals may be learned through the mechanisms of instrumental conditioning. Such learning is most evident when young children are being taught the ways of their group—that is, when they are being *socialized*. Parents and other agents of society usually do not deliberately shape behaviour, but society is arranged so that reinforcements are contingent upon behaviour.

For instance, in *programmed learning:*

1. The final complex task is broken up into small steps.
2. Reinforcement is contingent upon the performance of each step, and
3. The learner makes responses at his or her own pace.

Programmed learning is thought to be an effective way of learning facts, rules, formulas, and the like. It has the further advantage of giving teachers who use it more time to devote to enriching the learning experience with other types of material.

The personalized system of instruction (PSI) is another educational application of instrumental, or operant, conditioning principles. In this system the basic idea is that the material in the course is divided into small units, each of which must be mastered at a high level of proficiency before the next unit is attempted. For instance, students might be required to pass an examination at the end of each unit with a score of 90 percent or better; if they do not, they must study the material again until they can pass at this level.

In business operations, applications of reinforcement principles can often increase employee productivity and company profits.

Instrumental, or operant, conditioning is also applied in some forms of *behaviour therapy,* or *behaviour modification.* The instrumental—conditioning forms of behaviour therapy treat psychological disorders by contingently reinforcing socially adaptive behaviours and by extinguishing maladaptive ones. For instance, it may help people eliminate bad habits, such as smoking or eating too much; it may help mild—mannered individuals become more assertive. In general, we might say that instrumental, or operant, conditioning—often combined with other learning techniques—can help people reach goals they have set for themselves. In other words, applied instrumental conditioning can be

important in changing behaviour in the direction of greater self-control.

COGNITIVE—SOCIAL THEORY

By the 1960's, many researchers and theorists had begun to wonder whether a psychological science could be built strictly on observable behaviours without reference to thoughts. Most agreed that learning is the basis of much of human behaviour, but some were not convinced that classical and operant conditioning could explain *everything* people do. From behaviourist learning principles thus emerged **cognitive—social theory** (sometimes called *cognitive social learning* or *cognitive—behavioural theory*), which incorporated concepts of conditioning but added two new features: a focus on cognition and a focus on social learning.

Learning and cognition

According to cognitive-social theory, the way an

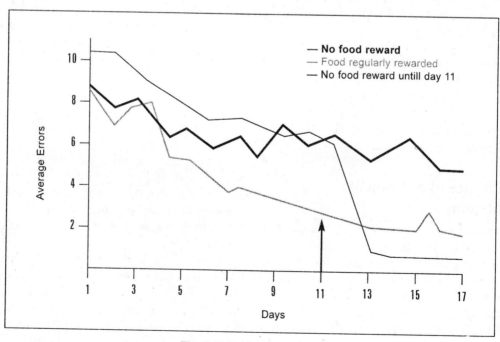

Fig. 5.10 Latent Learning

animal construes the environment is as important to learning as actual environmental contingencies. That is, humans and other animals are always developing mental images of, and expectations about, the environment that influence their behaviour.

Latent learning

Some of the first research to question whether a science of behaviour could completely dispense with thought was conducted by the behaviourist *Edward Tolman*.

In a paper, entitled "Cognitive maps in rats and men" (1948). Tolman described learning that occurred when rats were placed in a maze without any reinforcement, similar to the kind of learning that occurs when people learn their way around a city while looking out the window of a bus. In one experiment, Tolman let rats wander through a maze in ten trials on ten consecutive days without any reinforcement. A control group spent the same amount of time in the maze, but these rats received a food reinforcement on each trial.

The rats that were reinforced learned quite rapidly to travel to the end of the maze with few errors; not surprisingly, the behaviour of the unreinforced rats was less predictable. On the 11th day, however, Tolman made food available for the first time to the previously unreinforced rats and recorded the number of errors they made. As fig (5.11) shows, his findings were striking: These rats immediately took advantage of their familiarity with the maze and were able to obtain food just as efficiently as the rats who had previously received reinforcement. A third group of rats who still received no reinforcement continued to wander aimlessly through the maze.

To explain what had happened, Tolman suggested that the rats who were familiar with the maze had formed **cognitive maps**—mental representations or images—of the maze, even though they had received no reinforcement. Once the rats were reinforced, their learning became observable. Tolman called learning that has occurred but is not currently manifest in behaviour as **latent learning**. To cognitive–social theorists, latent learning was evidence that knowledge or beliefs about the environment are crucial to the way animals behave. And so began the effort to look inside the black box that lies between behaviours and environmental events while still maintaining a scientific, experimental approach to behaviour.

Conditioning and cognition

Many learning phenomena have been reinterpreted from a cognitive perspective. For example, in classical conditioning, why does an organism respond to a previously neutral stimulus (such as a particular taste) with a conditioned response (such as nausea)? A cognitive explanation suggests that the presence of the CS alerts the animal to prepare for a UCS, that is likely to follow. In other words, the CS predicts the presence of the UCS. If a CS does not routinely predict a UCS, it will not likely draw a CR. In fact, experimental data show that when a UCS (such as electric shock) frequently occurs in the absence of a CS (a tone), rats are unlikely to develop a conditioned fear response to the CS, regardless of the number of times the CS has been paired with the UCS. In cognitive language, rats will not become afraid of a stimulus unless it is highly predictive of an aversive event. This does not imply that rats are *conscious* of these predictions; it simply means that their nervous systems are making them. This was, in fact, an argument offered by Pavlov himself, who described these predictions as "unconscious". From a cognitive point of view, stimulus discrimination and generalization similarly reflect an animal's formation of a concept of what "counts" as a particular type of stimulus, which may be relatively general (any furry object) or relatively specific (a white rat).

Expectancies

Cognitive–social theory proposes that the *expectations*, or **expectancies** an individual forms about the consequences of a behaviour are

I more strongly believe that		
1. Promotions are earned through hard work and persistence.	**OR**	Making a lot of money is largely a matter of getting right breaks.
2. In my experience I have noticed that there is usually a direct connection between how hard I study and the grades I get.	**OR**	Many times the reactions of teachers seem haphazard to me.
3. I am the master of my fate.	**OR**	A great deal that happens to me is probably a matter of chance.

Fig. 5.11 Items from Rotter's locus of—control questionnaire; called the Internal—External scale.

what render the behaviour more or less likely to occur. If a person expects a behaviour to produce a reinforcing consequence, she is likely to perform it as long as she has the competence or skill to do so. Julian Rotter (1954), one of the earliest cognitive—social theorists, distinguished expectancies that are specific to concrete situations ("If I ask this professor for an extension, he will refuse") from those that are more generalized ("you can't ask people for anything in life—they'll always turn you down"). Rotter was particularly interested in **generalized expectancies** that influence a broad spectrum of behaviour. He used the term **locus of control of reinforcement** (or simply **locus of control**) to refer to the generalized expectancies people hold about whether or not their own behaviour can bring about the outcomes they seek. Individuals with an **internal locus of control** believe they are the masters of their own fate; people with an **external locus of control** believe their lives are determined by forces outside (external to) themselves.

Fig (5.12) shows some of the items included in Rotter's questionnaire for assessing locus of control. People who believe they control their own destiny are more likely to learn to do so, in part simply because they are more inclined to make the effort.

Learned helplessness and explanatory style

In a series of studies by *Martin Seligman* (1975), Seligman harnessed dogs so that they could not escape electric shocks. At first the dogs howled, whimpered, and tried to escape the shocks, but eventually they gave up; they would lie on the floor without struggle, showing physiological stress responses and behaviours resembling human depression. A day later Seligman placed the dogs in a shuttlebox from which they could easily escape the shocks. Unlike dogs in a control condition who had not been previously exposed to inescapable shocks, the dogs in the experimental condition made no effort to escape and generally failed to learn to do so even when they occasionally *did* escape. The dogs had come to expect that they could not get away; they had learned to be helpless. **Learned helplessness** consists of the expectancy that one cannot escape aversive events and that the motivational and learning deficits result from this belief.

Seligman and his colleagues observed that some people have a positive, active coping attitude in the face of failure or disappointment, whereas others become depressed and helpless. They demonstrated in dozens of studies that **explanatory style**—the way people make sense of bad events—plays a crucial role in whether or not they become, and remain, depressed. Individuals with a depressive or **pessimistic explanatory style** blame themselves for the bad things that happen to them; in the language of helplessness theory, pessimists believe the causes of their misfortune are *internal* rather than external, leading to lowered self-esteem. They also tend to see these causes as *stable* (unlikely to change) and *global* (broad, general, and widespread in their impact).

Social learning

Cognitive—social theory proposes that individuals learn many things from the people around them, with or without reinforcement, through **social learning** mechanisms other than classical and operant conditioning.

A major form of social learning is **observational learning**—learning by observing the behaviour of others. The impact of observational learning in humans is enormous, from learning how to give a speech, to learning how to feel and act when someone tells an inappropriate joke, to learning what kind of clothes, haircuts or foods are fashionable.

Observational learning in which a human or other animal learns to reproduce behaviour exhibited by a model is called **modeling**.

The likelihood that a person will imitate a model depends on a number of factors, such as the model's prestige, likeability, and attractiveness. Whether an individual actually *performs* modeled behaviour also depends on the behaviour's likely outcome. This outcome expectancy is, itself, often learned through an observational learning mechanism known as vicarious conditioning. In **vicarious conditioning**, a person learns the consequences of an action by observing its consequences from someone else. For example, adolescents attitude toward high-risk behaviours such as drinking and having sex without a condom are influenced by their perceptions of the consequences of their older siblings' risk taking behaviour.

Another form of social learning is direct tutelage—teaching concepts or procedures primarily through verbal explanation or instruction. This process is responsible for most formal education—and is occurring at this very moment. At times, conditioning processes, direct tutelage, and observational learning can influence behaviour in contradictory ways. For example, most children receive the direct message that smoking is harmful to their health (tutelage). At the same time, they learn to associate smoking with positive images through advertising (classical conditioning) and may see high-status peers or parents smoking (modeling). In many cases, however, social learning processes, such as learning from a textbook (tutelage) work in tandem with conditioning processes. ▪▪

CHAPTER 6

Memory

MEMORY THEORIES
— A theory of general memory functions
— Information—processing theories
— The levels-of-processing theory

LONG TERM MEMORY
— Varieties of long-term memory
— Encoding and organization of long-term memory

FORGETTING
— Decay theory
— Interference theory
— Retrieval problems
— Motivated forgetting

AMNESIA
— Psychological amnesias
— Biological amnesias

REMEMBERING
— Mnemonic devices

Memory

The memory system is an extremely important system. It makes possible the storage of information that has been gained from life experiences, so that a person may learn from the past and utilize the stored information to create and foresee future occurrences. Without a device for storing the thoughts a person thinks, the experiences one has, and the facts learned, all of the past would be of no consequence. The memory system makes available the information it has stored to other elements of the psyche, facilitating the functioning of the systems of the brain, and the performance of the higher mental processes utilized by individuals in their striving to accomplish their ends.

A **memory** is an organism's unwritten record of some past event. The German psychologist **Ebbinghaus** first developed laboratory methods for studying memory in 1885, and provided the first quantitative law for the rate at which memories fade with time.

Memory is the ability of an organism to store information from earlier learning processes (experience; retention) and reproduce that information in answer to specific stimuli. The information is reproduced in the form of conscious representation, verbal statements or motor activity.

MEMORY THEORIES

In the present state of research, memory theories are bound to remain purely speculative.

A number of psychological, physiological, biochemical, cybernetic and physical models have been proposed to explain the phenomenon of *"memory"* but they remain unsatisfactory so long as they fail to take into account any motivational aspects of memory in the living organism. The classical explanation of memory phenomena assumes as a working hypothesis that learning processes leave traces (*engrams*) which are renewed by repetition and form the physiological correlate for reproduction of information. The traces are considered as changes in the ganglionic cells of the cerebrum or as being *"purely psychological"*.

A theory of general memory functions

One theory, a simple one agreed on by most psychologists; includes three distinct processes of memory that have been identified. These are an *encoding process,* a *storage process,* and a *retrieval process.* **Encoding** is the process of receiving sensory input and transforming it into a form or code, which can be stored; **storage** is the process of actually putting coded information into memory; and **retrieval** is the process of gaining access to stored, coded information when it is needed.

Information—processing theories

Imagine you are like a computer in which the data (information) is feeded; now this computer processes the data (information) in steps, or stages; and then produces output. The models of memory which are based on this idea are called *information-processing theories*.

According to this model, memory consists of three stores: sensory memory (or sensory registers), short-term memory, and long-term memory. Storing and retrieving memories involves passing information from one store to the next and then retrieving the information from long-term memory. This information processing theory was developed by *Richard Atkinson* and *Richard Shiffrin* (1968).

In the Atkinson—Shiffrin theory, memory starts with a sensory input from the environment. This input is held for a very brief time—several seconds at most—in a *sensory register* associated with the sensory channels (vision, hearing, touch, and so forth). Information that is attended to and recognized in the sensory register may be passed on to *short-term memory* (STM), where it is held for perhaps 20 or 30 seconds. Some of the information reaching short-term memory is processed by being *rehearsed*—that is, by having attention focused on it, perhaps by being repeated over and over, or perhaps by being processed in some other way that will link it up with other information already stored in memory. Information that is rehearsed may then be passed along to *long-term memory*

(LTM); information not so processed is lost. When items of information are placed in long-term memory, they are organized into categories, where they may reside for days, months, years, or for a lifetime. When you remember something, a representation of the item is withdrawn, or *retrieved,* from long term memory.

Sensory registers

Suppose you grab a handful of six or seven coins from your pocket and, while looking away, stretch out your hand so that all of the coins are visible. If you then glance for a second at your hand but look away before counting the change, you are still likely to be able to report accurately the number of coins in your hand because the image is held momentarily in your visual sensory register. **Sensory registers** hold information about a perceived stimulus for a split second after the stimulus disappears, allowing a mental representation of it to remain in memory briefly for further processing.

Till date, most research has focused on visual and auditory sensory registration. The term **iconic storage** is used to describe visual sensory registration. For a brief period after an image disappears from vision, people retain a mental image (or "icon") of what they have seen. This visual trace is remarkably accurate and contains considerably more information than

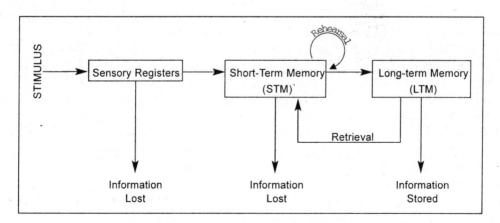

Fig. 6.2 Standard Model of Memory

people can report before it fades. The duration of icons varies from approximately half a second to two records, depending on the individual, the context of the image, and the circumstances.

The sensory register holds information for such a brief time that some psychologists prefer to discuss it in connection with perception rather than memory. However it is part of the information processing model under discussion, and it is a step that information passes through before it reaches short-term memory.

Short-term memory

Many of the stimuli people perceive in the course of a day register for such a short time that they drop out of the memory system without further processing. Other stimuli make a greater impression. Information about them is passed on to **short-term memory (STM)**, a memory store that holds a small amount of information in consciousness—such as a phone number—for roughly 20 to 30 seconds, unless the person makes a deliberate effort to maintain it longer by repeating it over and over.

Short-term memory has limited capacity; that is, it does not hold much information. On the average, people can remember about seven pieces of information at a time, a normal range of from five to nine items.

Hermann Ebbinghaus (1885) was the first to note the seven-item limit to STM. Ebbinghaus pioneered the study of memory using the most convenient and agreeable subject he could find—himself—with a method that involved inventing some 2300 nonsense syllables (such as pir and vup). Ebbinghaus randomly placed these syllables in lists of varying lengths and then attempted to memorize the lists; he used nonsense syllables rather than real words to try to control the possible influence of prior knowledge on memory. Ebbinghaus found that he could memorize up to seven syllables, but no more, in a single trial. The limits of STM seem to be neurologically based, as they are similar in other cultures, including those with very different languages.

Because of STM's limited capacity, psychologists have often likened it to a lunch counter. If only seven stools are available at the counter, some customers will have to get up before new customers can be seated. Similarly, new information "bumps" previous STMs from consciousness.

The storage capacity of short-term memory can be increased, however, by a process known as *chunking*. Most of us have learned to combine several items into a "chunk" as we receive them; then we can retain several (7, plus or minus 2) of these "chunks" of information in our short term memories. Telephone numbers for instance consists of 8 items arranged in 2 (or 3) chunks. With practice, most of us can easily hold 3 telephone numbers in short-term memory-24 items arranged in 6 chunks.

Since the capacity of this memory stage is so small, much information stored here is lost because it is displaced by incoming items of information. Before it is lost, however some of the information can be retrieved and used. Some of the information in short-term memory is neither lost nor retrieved but passed along to the next memory stage—long-term memory—through rehearsal.

Rehearsal

The process of **rehearsal** consists of keeping items of information in the center of attention, perhaps by repeating them silently or aloud. Just going over and over what is to be remembered to prevent it from fading is called **maintenance rehearsal**, since its purpose is to *maintain* information in STM.

Rehearsal is also important in transferring information to long-term memory, which will not surprise anyone who has ever memorized lines of a poem from a play, or a math formula by repeating it over and over. Maintenance rehearsal is not useful for storing information in long-term memory as elaborative rehearsal.

Elaborative rehearsal involves giving the material organization and meaning as it is being rehearsed; it is an active rehearsal process, not just the passive process of repetition. In elaborative rehearsal, people use strategies that give meaning and organization to the material so that it can be fitted in with existing organized long-term memories.

Long term memory

Long-term memories may last for days, months, years, or even a lifetime. Also, the storage capacity of long-term memory has no known limit.

Some theorists believe that there is no true forgetting from long-term memory. According to this view, once information is stored in long-term memory, it is there for good; when we seem to forget, it is because it has not been stored in an organized fashion or because we are not searching for it in the right part of the memory storehouse. Other students of memory maintain that we forget because of the confusion and interference produced by new things which have been learned and put into long-term memory.

Two different but related long-term memory stores said to exist. One, called **semantic memory** (the word *semantic* refers to "meaning"), contains the meanings of words and concepts and the rules for using them in language; it is a vast network of meaningfully organized items of information. The other, containing memories of specific things that have happened to a person (reminiscences) is called **episodic memory**. We shall come back to these details later while discussing long-term memory in detail.

The levels-of-processing theory

Information-processing theories of memory, as we have seen, view the memory process in terms of discrete stages, each with its own characteristics. Information is transferred from stage to stage until some of it is finally lodged in long-term memory. A contrasting model of memory involves what are called *levels of processing,* with, more recently, the idea of elaboration added to the *levels-of-processing* framework.

According to the levels—of—processing idea, incoming information can be worked on at different levels of analysis; the deeper the analysis goes, the better the memory. The first level is simply *perception,* which gives us our immediate awareness of the environment. At a somewhat deeper level, the *structural* features of the input (what it sounds like or looks like, for example) are analyzed; and, finally, at the deepest level of processing, the meaning of the input is analyzed. Analysis to the deep level of meaning gives the best memory.

Thus, good memory results from deeper and, more elaborate processing of perceptual input. Many times, however, it is not important for a person to process information deeply, it is enough to hold the information long enough to act on some structural feature of it and then to discard it. Many of the routine happenings of daily life are not processed deeply. It is enough, for example, to respond appropriately at the moment when driving to work; we usually cannot remember the details of our morning drive because there was no need to process much of the information to the meaning level.

Rehearsal plays a role in the deeper processing of information, as it does in the stage theories of memory. But according to the levels—of—processing view, simply repeating the information—maintenance rehearsal is not enough for good memory. All this does maintain the information at a given level of depth; for deeper levels to be reached, the rehearsal must be elaborative. In other words, rehearsal must process the information to the meaning level if the information is to be well retained. Rehearsal is thus seen as a process which gives meaning to information.

The idea of elaboration has been added to the levels—of—processing theory. Elaboration refers to the degree to which incoming information is processed so that it can be tied to, or integrated with, existing memories. The greater the degree of elaboration given to an

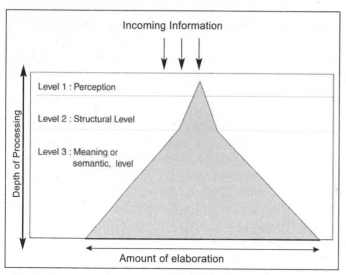

Fig. 6.2 A summary diagram of the relationships among levels of processing. The amount of information retained is shown by the shaded portion of the figure

item of incoming information, the more likely it is that it will be remembered.

Fig (6.2) shows that the amount remembered, indicated by the shading, depends on both the level of processing and the degree to which information is elaborated. The best memory is the result of processing to the meaning level, where the amount of elaboration is also greatest.

LONG TERM MEMORY

More important information goes from STM to **long-term memory (LTM)**, where representations of facts, images, thoughts, feelings, skills, and experiences may reside for as long as a lifetime. According to the standard model, the longer information remains in STM, the more likely it is to make a permanent impression in LTM. Human long-term memory is not an untidy jumble of unrelated information; we keep our memory store in order. We recognize, categorize, and classify information in a number of ways. Long-term memory is a bit like library with a good cross-indexing system.

Varieties of long-term memory

The major types of memory distinguished by researchers are:

Declarative and procedural memory

In general, people store two kinds of information, declarative and procedural. **Declarative memory** refers to memory for facts and events, much of which can be consciously stated or "declared". **Procedural memory** refers to "how to" knowledge of procedures or skills.

Declarative memory

When we think of memory, we usually mean declarative memory: knowledge of facts and events. Remembering a happy memory from the past or retrieving the name and location of the store where we found a particular brand of tea requires access to declarative memory.

Declarative memory can be semantic or episodic. **Semantic memory** (or **generic memory**) refers to general world knowledge or facts, such as the knowledge that summers are hot in katmandu or that NaCl is the chemical formula for table salt. The term is somewhat misleading because semantic implies that general knowledge is stored in words, whereas people know many things about objects, such as their colour or smell, that are encoded as sensory representations.

Episodic memory consists of memories of particular events, rather than general knowledge. Episodic memory allows people to travel mentally through time, to remember thoughts and feelings (or in memory experiments, word lists) from the recent or distant past or to imagine the future. In everyday life, episodic memory is often *autobiographical,* as when people remember what they did on their 18th birthday or what they ate yesterday. It is also closely linked to semantic memory, since when people experience similar episodes over time (such as 180 days a year in school or hundreds of thousands of interactions with their father), they gradually developed generic memories of what those situations were like (e.g., "I used to love weekends with my father").

Procedural memory

Declarative memory is the most obvious kind of memory, but another kind of memory is equally important in daily life: procedural memory, or memory for skills. People are often astonished to find that even though they have not skated or drived for 5 years, the skills are reactivated easily, almost as if their use had never been interrupted. When people tie their shoes, speak grammatically, or drive car, they are drawing on procedural memory. Other procedural skills are less obvious, such as reading, which involves a set of complex procedures for decoding strings of letters and words.

Explicit and implicit memory

For much of the last century psychologists studied memory by asking subjects to memorize word lists, nonsense syllables, or connections between pairs of words and then asking them to recall them. These tasks all tap **explicit memory,** or conscious recollection. Recently, however, psychologists have recognized another kind of memory: implicit memory. **Implicit memory** refers to memory that is expressed in behaviour but does not require conscious recollection, such as tying a shoe, which people do effortlessly without consciously retrieving the steps involved.

Explicit memory

Explicit memory involves the conscious retrieval of information. Researchers distinguish between two kinds of explicit retrieval: recall and recognition. **Recall** is the spontaneous conscious recollection of material from LTM, as when a person brings to mind memories of her wedding day or the name of the capital of Egypt.

Recognition refers to the explicit feeling or remembrance that something currently perceived has been previously encountered or learned (as when a researcher asks a subject to identify a word on a list that was on a different list the previous day).

Recent PET data suggest that recall and recognition rely on similar networks in the frontal lobes. However, recall requires more "effort" from neural circuits below the cortex, presumably because it involves actually *generating* the memory rather than simply matching currently perceived information against information stored in memory. The greater difficulty of recall over recognition is illustrated by the **tip-of-the-tongue** phenomenon, the experience of trying to remember a piece of information and knowing that "it's in there" but not being quite able to call it to mind.

Implicit memory

Implicit memory is evident in skills, conditioned learning, and associative memory (that is, associations between one representation and another). It can be seen in skills such as turning the wheel in the right direction when the car starts to skid in the snow, which skilled drivers in cold regions do before they have even formed the thought "I am skidding," as well as in response learned through classical and operant conditioning, such as avoiding, a food that was once associated with nausea even when the person has no explicit recollection of the event.

Implicit associative memory emerges in experiments on **priming effects,** in which prior exposure to a stimulus (the *prime*) facilitates or inhibits the processing of new information. Participants in memory experiments show priming effects even when they do not consciously remember being exposed to the prime. For example, they might be exposed to a list of words that are relatively rarely used in everyday conversation, such as *assassin*. A week later, they may have no idea whether "*assassin*" was on the list, but if asked to fill in the missing letters of a word fragment such as A—A—IN, they are more likely to complete it with the word *"assassin"* than control subjects who studied a different list the week earlier. Priming effects appear to rely on activation of information stored in LTM, even though the person is unaware of what has been activated.

Encoding and organization of long-term memory

We have now completed our tour of the varieties of memory. But how does information find its way into LTM in the first place? And how is information organized in the mind so that it can be readily retrieved? In this section we explore these two questions.

Encoding

For information to be retrievable from memory, it must be **encoded**, or cast into a representational form, or "code", that can be readily accessed. The manner of encoding—how, how much, and when the person tries to learn new information—has a substantial influence on its *accessibility* (ability to be retrieved, or *accessed*).

Levels of processing

Anyone who has ever crammed for a test rehearsal is important for storing information in LTM. As noted earlier, however, the simple, repetitive rehearsal that maintains information momentarily in working memory is not optimal for LTM. A more effective strategy is usually to attend to the *meaning* of the stimulus and form mental connections between it and previously stored information. Some encoding is deliberate, such as studying for an exam, learning lines for a play, or trying to remember a joke. However, much of the time encoding simply occurs as a byproduct of thought and perception, which is why people can remember incidents that happened to them ten years ago even though they were not trying to commit them to memory.

Deep and shallow processing: The degree to which information is elaborated, reflected upon, and processed in a meaningful way during memory storage is referred to as the depth or **level of processing**. Information may be processed at a shallow, structural level (focusing on physical characteristics of the stimulus); at a somewhat deeper, phonemic level (focusing on simple characteristics of the language used to describe it); or at the deepest semantic level (focusing on the meaning of the stimulus). For example, at a shallow, structural level, a person may walk by a restaurant and notice the typeface and colours of its sign. At a phonemic level, she may read the sign to herself and notice that it sounds Spanish. Processing material deeply in contrast, means paying attention to its meaning or significance noticing for instance, that this was the restaurant a friend has been recommending for months.

Different levels of processing activate different neural circuits. As one might guess, encoding that occurs as people make judgements about the meaning of words (such as whether they are concrete or abstract) leads to greater activation of the left temporal cortex, which is involved in language comprehension, than attending to qualities such as whether they are printed in upper-or-lower case letters. *Deliberate* use of strategies to remember, activates regions of the prefrontal cortex involved in other executive functions such as manipulating information in working memory.

Encoding specificity: Advocates of depth-of-processing theory originally thought that deeper processing is always better. Although this is generally true, subsequent research has shown that the best encoding strategy depends on what the person later needs to retrieve. If a person is asked to recall shallow information (such as whether a word was originally presented in capital letters), shallow encoding actually tends to be more useful. The fact that ease of retrieval depends on the match between the way information is encoded and later retrieved is known as the **encoding specificity principle**.

For example, a student who studies for a multiple-choice test by memorizing definitions and details without trying to understand the underlying concepts may be in much more trouble if the professor decides to include an essay question, since the student has encoded the information at too shallow a level.

Context and retrieval: According to the encoding specificity principle, the *contexts* in which people encode and retrieve information can also affect the ease of retrieval. One study presented scuba divers with different lists of words, some while the divers were under water and others while they were above. The divers had better recall for lists they had encoded under water when they were under water at retrieval; conversely, lists encoded above water were better recalled above water. Similarly, recalling material from lectures is easier if students are sitting in the same lecture room when they take the examination. The same may

also be true of the emotional state at encoding and retrieval, a phenomenon called **state-dependent memory**: Being in a similar mood at encoding and retrieval (e.g., angry while learning a word list and angry while trying to remember it) can facilitate memory, as long as the emotional state is not so intense that it inhibits memory in general. Having the same context during encoding and retrieval facilitates recall because the context provides **retrieval cues**, stimuli or thoughts that can be used to facilitate recollection.

Spacing: Another encoding variable that influences memory is of particular importance in educational settings: the interval between study sessions. Students intuitively know that if they cram the night before a test, the information is likely to be available to them when they need it the next day. They also tend to believe that *massed* rehearsal (that is, studying in one long session or several times over a short interval, such as a day)

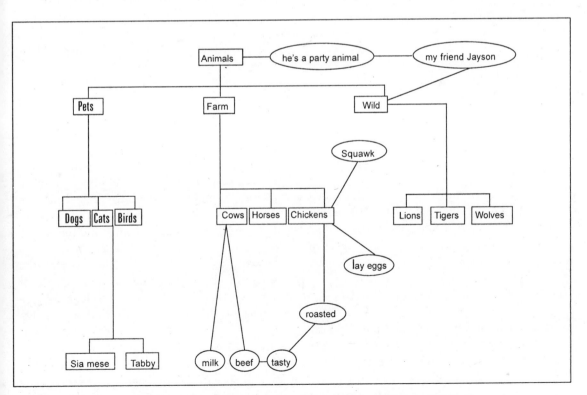

Fig. 6.3 Hierarchical organization of information in LTM

is more effective than *spaced,* or *distributed,* rehearsal over longer intervals. But is this strategy really optimal for long-term retention of the information?

In fact, it is not. Massed rehearsal *seems* superior because it makes initial acquisition of memory slightly easier, since the material is at a heightened state of activation in a massed practice session. Over the long run, however, research on the **spacing effect**—the superiority of memory for information rehearsed over longer intervals—demonstrates that spacing study sessions over long intervals tends to double long-term retention of information.

Students who wants to remember information for more than a day or two after an exam should space their studying over time and avoid cramming.

Representational modes and encoding: The ability to retrieve information from LTM also depends on the modes used to encode it. In general, the more ways a memory can be encoded, the greater the likelihood that it will be accessible for later retrieval. Storing a memory in multiple representational modes— such as words, images, and sounds—provides more retrieval cues to bring it back to mind. For instance, many people remember phone numbers not only by memorizing the digits but also by forming a mental map of the buttons they need to push and a motoric (procedural) representation of the pattern of buttons to push that becomes automatic and is expressed implicitly. When pushing the buttons, they may even be alerted that they have dialed the wrong number by hearing a sound pattern that does not match the expected pattern. Suggesting auditory storage as well.

Hierarchical organization of information

Efficient retrieval requires some degree of organization of information so that the mind can find its way through dense networks of neural trails. Some researchers have compared LTM to a filing cabinet, in which important information is kept toward the front of the files and less important information is relegated to the back of our mental archives, or a box in the attic.

The filling cabinet metaphor also suggests that some information is filed hierarchically: Broad categories are composed of narrower subcategories, which in turn consist of even more specific categories. For example, a person could store information about animals under the subcategories pets, farm animals, and wild animals.

Under farm animals are cows, horses, and chickens. At each level of the hierarchy, each node will have features associated with it (such as knowledge that chickens squawk and lay eggs) as well as other associations to it (such as roasted chicken, which is associated with being tasty).

Hierarchical storage is generally quite efficient, but it can occasionally lead to errors. For instance, when asked, "Which is farther north, Seattle or Montreal?" Most people say Montreal. In fact, Seattle is farther north. People mistakenly assume that Montreal is north of Seattle because they go to their general level of knowledge about Canada and the United States. In reality, some parts of the United States are farther north than many parts of Canada. A better strategy in this case would be to visualize a map of North America and scan it for Seattle.

Schemas

Psychologists have argued for a century about the adequacy of principles of association in explaining memory. Some have argued that we do not associate isolated bits of information with each other but instead store and remember the gist of facts and events.

According to this view, when confronted with a novel event, people match is against *schemas* stored in memory. **Schemas** are patterns of thought, or organized knowledge structures, that render the environment relatively predictable. When students walk into a classroom on the first day of class and a person resembling a professor begins to lecture, they listen and take notes in a routine fashion. They are not surprised that one person has assumed control of the situation and begun talking because they have a schema for events that normally transpire in a classroom.

Proponents of schema theories argue that memory is an active process of *reconstruction* of the past. Remembering means combining bits and pieces of what we once perceived with general knowledge that helps us fill in the gaps. In this view, memory is not like taking snapshots of an event; it is more like *taking notes*.

Consider the following passage (*Rumelhart, 1980*)

- "Business had been slow since the oil crisis. Nobody seemed to want anything really elegant anymore. Suddenly the door opened and a well-dressed man entered the showroom floor. John put on his friendliest and most sincere expression and walked toward the man."

- Most readers gradually realize that this paragraph is about selling cars through a process of generating and rejecting or confirming hypotheses. The first sentence suggests that the passage is somehow related to the economy and that it probably has something to do with the auto or gas industry. The second sentence narrows the choices: The word "elegant" relates to cars but not generally to gas stations. The phrase "showroom floor" in the third sentence supports the hypothesis that the passage relates to the auto industry.

- Finally, John's reaction on the fourth sentence confirms this interpretation because our general knowledge structures, that is, schemas, about car salesmen often include "insincere."

- Schemas affect the way people remember in two ways: by influencing the information they encode and by shaping the way they reconstruct data that they have already stored.

Schemas and encoding

Schemas influence the way people initially understand the meaning of an event and thus the manner in which they encode it in LTM. Harry Triandis (1994) relates an account of two Englishmen engaged in a friendly game of tennis in nineteenth century China. The two were sweating and panting under hot August sun. As they finished their final set, a chinese friend sympathetically asked, "could you not get two servants to do this for you?" operating from a different set of schemas, their chinese friend encoded this event rather differently than would an audience at Wimbledon.

A brief experiment illustrates the influence of schemas on encoding (*Bransford & Johnson, 1977*):

The procedure is actually quite simple. First you arrange things into different groups. Of course, one pile may be sufficient depending on how much there is to do. If you have to go somewhere else due to lack of facilities, that is the next step, otherwise you are pretty well set. It is important not to overdo things. That is, it is better to do too few things at once than too many. After the procedure is completed, one arranges the materials into different groups again. Then they can be put into their appropriate places. Eventually they will be used once more and the whole cycle will then have to be repeated.

Most readers have difficulty comprehending this paragraph, let alone remembering its component parts five minutes later. But try rereading the passage with the title, "Washing clothes." The title activates a schema that organizes the information and allows it to be stored efficiently, so that its parts can later be more readily retrieved.

Schemas and retrieval

Titling, a paragraph also aids memory because of the influence of schemas on retrieval. Schemas not only provide hooks on which to hang information during encoding, but they also provide hooks for fishing information out of LTM. Many schemas have "slots" for particular kinds of information. A person shopping for stereo equipment who is trying to recall the various compact disk players she saw that day is likely to remember the names Sony and Pioneer but not Vijay Kumar (the salesman at one of the stores). Unlike Sony, Vijay Kumar does not fit into the slot "brand names of compact disk players." The slots in schemas often have **default values**, or standard answers, that fill in missing information the person did not initially notice or bother to store. When asked if the cover of this book gives the author's name, you are likely to report that it does (default value=*yes*) even if you never really noticed because the author's name normally appears on a book cover. In fact, people are generally unable to tell which pieces of information in a memory are truly remembered and which reflect the operation of default values.

Without schemas, life would seem like one random event after another, and efficient memory would be impossible. Yet as the research shows, schemas can lead people to misclassify information, to believe they have seen what they really have not seen, and to fail to notice things that might be important.

FORGETTING

The flipside of memory is **forgetting**, the inability to remember. Ebbinghaus (1885) documented over a century ago a typical pattern of forgetting that occurs with many kinds of declarative knowledge, beginning with rapid initial loss of information after initial learning and only gradual decline thereafter (fig 6.4). Researchers have recently refined Ebbinghaus's

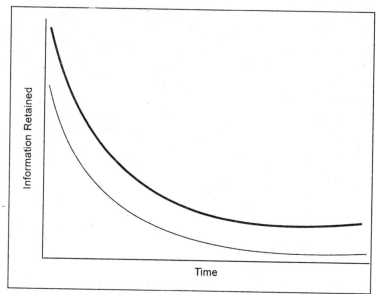

Fig. 6.4 Forgetting follows a standard pattern, with rapid initial loss of information followed by more gradual later decline. Increasing initial study-time (the dark line) increases retention, but forgetting occurs at the same rate. In other words, increased study shifts the curve upward but does not change the rate of forgetting or eliminate it.

forgetting curve, finding that the relation between memory decline and length of time between learning and retrieval is logarithmic, which essentially means that the rate of forgetting is initially very high but eventually becomes very low (*Wixted & Ebbesen*, 1991). Interestingly, this forgetting curve seems to apply whether the period of time is hours or years. The same curve emerged when researchers studied people's ability to remember the names of old television shows: They rapidly forgot the names of shows canceled within the last seven years, but the rate of forgetting trailed off after that (*Squire*, 1989).

Why do people sometimes forget things entirely? Psychologists have proposed several explanations, including decay, interference, retrieval and motivated forgetting.

Decay theory

The **decay theory** explains forgetting as a result

of a fading memory trace. Having a thought or perception produces changes in synaptic connections, which in turn creates the potential for remembering if the neural circuits that were initially activated are later reactivated. According to decay theory, these neurophysiological changes fade with disuse, much as a wilderness path grows over unless repeatedly trodden. The decay theory is difficult to corroborate or disprove empirically, but some studies show a similar pattern of rapid and then more gradual deactivation of neural pathways in the hippocampus, which is involved in memory consolidation, suggesting a possible physiological basis for decay.

Interference theory

Memories of similar information or events tend to interfere with one another, as when students confuse two theories they learned about around the same time or two similar-sounding words in a foreign language. Finding the right path in the neural wilderness is difficult if two paths are close together and look alike. Or to use the filing cabinet metaphor, storing too many documents under the same heading makes finding the right one difficult.

Cognitive psychologists distinguish two kinds of interference. **Proactive interference** refers to the interference of previously stored memories with the retrieval of new information, as when a person calls a new romantic partner by the name of an old one. In **retroactive interference**, new information with retrieval of old information, as when people have difficulty recalling their home phone numbers from past residences. One reason children take years to memorize multiplication tables, even though they can learn the names of cartoon characters or classmates with astonishing speed, is the tremendous interference involved, because every number is paired with so many others (*Anderson*, 1995).

Although retroactive and proactive interference have been shown to be important causes of forgetting, the ways in which they work on memory are still, after years of study, the subject of some debate.

If interference produces confusions in what is associated with what or, as some experiments indicate, actually produces "unlearning" of the associations, forgetting will be the result. Another idea is that interference somehow has its greatest effect on the memory of retrieval cues. We have seen that memory depends on retrieval cues, so if interference results in problems with the use of these cues, forgetting will result.

Retrieval problems

Retrieval is facilitated by organization of the stored material and the presence of retrieval cues that can guide our search through our long-term memory for stored information. Without appropriate retrieval cues, the sought-for items stored in long-term memory may not be found— one *forgets*. But while we often cannot recall something while actively searching for it, we may later recall the sought-for information when we have given up the search and are doing something else. The new activity in which we are engaged, or the new context, gives us another set of appropriate reminders, or retrieval cues. And perhaps the new situation leads us to search through portions of our long-term memory store not examined before. The result may be that we suddenly remember what we could not previously retrieve—"Aha! He is Steven Spielberg who made a movie on dinosaurs." Thus when we think we have forgotten something, it is often a good idea to give up and do something else in order to generate new retrieval cues.

The reconstructive process present at the time of retrieval can act to distort our recall of what is stored in our longterm memory. We may remember something that did not happen and forget what did happen.

Emotional factors can also play a role in the retrieval failure that is the cause of so much forgetting. State-dependent memory is an example. If we encode information while in one emotional state and try to retrieve it while in another, our recall may suffer. Another more common and powerful hindering influence of emotions on retrieval is found in the phenomenon of *motivated forgetting*—difficulties with the retrieval of unpleasant, anxiety-provoking information stored in long-term memory.

Motivated forgetting

Another cause of forgetting is **motivated forgetting**, or forgetting for a reason. People often explicitly instruct themselves or others to forget, as when a person stops in the middle of a sentence and says, "oops—forget that. That's the wrong address. The right one is . . ." (*Bjork & Bjork*, 1996). At other times, the "intention" to forget is implicit, as when a person who parks in the same place everyday implicitly *remembers to forget* where she parked today. Experimental evidence suggests that this kind of goal-directed forgetting requires active inhibition of the forgotten information, which remains active but inaccessible. Researchers have demonstrated this using *directed forgetting* procedures, in which participants learn a list of words but are told midway through to forget the words they just learned and just remember last part of the list. This procedure reduces recall for the words in the first part of the list and decreases proactive interference from them, so that words in the last half of the list are more easily remembered. This suggests that the procedure is in fact inhibiting retrieval of the to-be-forgotten words. On the other hand, this procedure does *not* decrease recognition of, or implicit memory for, the to-be-forgotten words, suggesting that they remain in an activated state.

Other studies show that instructing a person not to think about something can effectively keep the information from consciousness but that doing so creates an automatic, unconscious process that "watches out" for the information and hence keeps it active (*Wegner*, 1992).

In a sense, goal-directed forgetting is like a form of prospective memory, in which the intention is to forget something in the future rather than to remember it.

In real life, people often try to inhibit unpleasant or anxiety-provoking thoughts or feelings. When they do this consciously, as when they tell themselves not to worry about a medical procedure they are about to undergo, it is called suppression. When they do this unconsciously, it is called repression. People often forget things they do not want to remember, such as "over looking" a dentist appointment. If dentists were handing out heavy bills instead of filling teeth, few people would forget their appointments.

AMNESIA

Strictly speaking, the term refers to a complete loss of memory for past events. In practice it is used to refer to a general impairment of memories previously acquired, due to some temporary or permanent pathological process which may be organic or functional. It is not used to refer to an inability to recall past events, the memory for which has faded with time.

The term is also used for cases in which encoding and storage are impaired so that new memories cannot be formed. Thus *amnesia* is a profound memory deficit due either to the loss of what has been stored or to the inability to form new memories.

Some amnesias have a biological basis; the memory machine—the brain—is disturbed in some way. These may be called *biological amnesias*. Other amnesias may be called *psychological amnesias*. Without any known brain malfunction, these amnesias result from major disturbances in the process of information encoding, storage, and retrieval.

Psychological amnesias

When we think of amnesia, we often have in mind the person who forgets almost everything, including his or her identity. But in a sense, everyone is an amnesia victim; we remember very little of our early childhoods and our dreams.

Infantile amnesia

The observation that infancy is not remembered was noted with interest by students of the mind, and probably by others as well throughout the ages (*Augustine* 400; *Rousseau 1798; Freud 1901*). The experimental data confirm folk psychology: adults do not remember autobiographical episodes that had occurred prior to the age of about 3 or 4 years, and report that their inner personal narratives begin to make sense (if they ever do) only about the age of 6 to 7 years (*Dudycha* and *Dudycha* 1941; *Nelson* 1992).

Over the years, several types of explanations for infantile amnesia have been proposed. They involve different conceptual frameworks (biological, cognitive, psychosocial), and some of them refer to different phases of memory (acquisition, consolidation, retention, retrieval).

One class of explanations suggests that the problem lies already at the acquisition phase: early personal memories are not retained to begin with, because the brain systems that are required for autobiographical, episodic memory simply do not mature before the age of 3-4 years (*Nadel* and *Zola-Morgan* 1984; *Nelson* 1998). A related suggestion implicates both acquisition and retention rests on cognitive rather than neurological arguments. It claims that the infant's mind cannot form the appropriate mental structures that serve as inner frameworks for organizing new information in a sensible manner. The generic term for such abstract mental structures is '*schemata*'. In the absence of mature schemata, autobiographical experiences cannot be stored in an effective, retrievable form. A version of this argument considers the intense episodes of infantile memory inconsistent with the categories of the adult schemata, hence incapable of being assimilated into the adult memory (*Schachtel*, 1947). Similar suggestions invoke the lack in infancy of linguistic competence, which is assumed to be required in encoding autobiographical episodes (*Nelson* 1992); immaturity of a 'me' system, postulated to be necessary for integrations of episodic information into the internal personal narrative (*Howe* and *Courage* 1997); or, similarly, immaturity of a 'self-memory system', postulated to hold the autobiographical memory base together with the current goals of the self (*Conway* and *Pleydell Pearce* 2000).

Deficiencies in retrieval comprise another class of explanations for infantile amnesia. Here the most famous argument is that early memories are formed but later suppressed to become non-retrievable, because of their damaging emotional load; furthermore, those early memories that are recalled are actually 'screens', which hide the real, difficult experience (*Freud* 1901). No experimental evidence has been reported so far to support this psychoanalytical account. Similarly, there is no firm experimental evidence to support the popular view that special methods, such as hypnosis, can retrieve repressed or forgotten infantile memories.

And there are also psychosocial explanations, which search for the roots of infantile amnesia within the framework of the interaction of the individual with society. Autobiographical episodes, so it is suggested, become encoded properly only after the infants becomes aware of the social function of autobiographical memory, which is postulated to be, according to this view, the development of a life history that can be shared with others (*Nelson* 1993).

Immature brain circuits in infancy, such as frontal cortex and cortico limbic circuits, may be yet unable to subserve the cognitive and the psychosocial faculties of categorization, 'inner language', self-comprehension, or social understanding. All this does not imply that very young infants do not have the ability to acquire ad-hoc declarative knowledge, or that their brain is incapable of amazing feats of learning and memory. Even fetuses may have learning and memory capabilities that parents-to-be commonly disregard. In estimating the mental capacity of infants, it took a lot of grant money to reach the conclusion reached by every normal parent: these babies outperform us in many ways.

So, regardless of the exact mechanism, what could be the phylogenetic and ontogenetic rationales for preventing adults from remembering their adventures in the crib? It might be related to a mix of biological constraints and selective pressures. First, evolution did not come up (yet?) with the ability to construct instantly a perfect brain; it takes years to develop. Second, slow brain maturation may have an advantage in coping with a changing environment, as it reduces the chance of fast and robust encoding of erroneous outcomes of certain types of learning in early infancy. Third, autobiographical memory could lack significant phylogenetic advantage early in life. All the above combined, it probably pays better to dedicate first the brain power of the newborn to the acquisition of critical, basic skills, rather than to the long-term declarative memory of the pains and the joys of the first months of life.

Dream amnesia

We dream several times each night, but we remember few of these experiences. Freud considered dreams to be expressions of forbidden or aggressive sexual urges. These forbidden sexual urges can produce strong guilt or anxiety if we become aware of them in ourselves. So their expression in dreams is hidden behind a disguise—the actual content of the dream. But even the disguised urges—dreams—have the capacity to generate some guilt or anxiety feelings. Hence they are forgotten.

Other interpretations stress the differences in the symbol systems used in dreaming and waking (*Hall*, 1953), a situation similar to that in one of the interpretations of childhood amnesia described above. If memory-symbol networks of waking life are different from those of dreaming, we may have difficulty retrieving dreams in the waking state.

The dreaming brain seems to be in a special state different from that of the waking brain. As we have seen when discussing state-dependent memory, information stored in one state is difficult to retrieve when in another state. Thus dream amnesia may be just another example of state-dependent memory.

Defensive amnesia

This is the well-publicized, but relatively rare, type of psychological amnesia that has captured the popular imaginations. People with this form of amnesia may forget their names, where they have come from, who their spouses are, and many other important details of their past lives. It is called defensive because this type of amnesia is usually considered to be a way of protecting oneself from the guilt or anxiety that can result from intense, intolerable life situations and conflicts. We often wish we could forget a nagging problem. The defensive amnesiac does what we might wish to do and, because the problem has so many ramifications in his or her life, forgets much more than the specific problem itself. Defensive amnesia is thus an extreme form of repression.

Amnesic episodes can last for weeks, months, or years. When they are over, the amnesiac regains, often suddenly, memories of his or her earlier life, but information stored during the episode itself is usually not retrievable—there is a memory gap.

While repression may be the basis for amnesic episodes themselves, why is there a memory gap for amnesic for information stored during the episode? Perhaps the gap occurs because memories formed during the episode are themselves repressed. Alternatively, after the stream of memory has returned to normal, perhaps retrieval cues are lacking for the information stored during the episode.

Biological amnesias

Blows on the head, or other damages to the

brain, temporary disturbances in the brain's blood supply, certain drugs, and brain diseases are some of the major biological causes of amnesia.

Transient global amnesia

This is a profound memory problem with no loss of consciousness. It comes on suddenly without any obvious cause, and it typically lasts for only a few hours or days before memory becomes normal again. Fortunately, most people who experience such amnesia have it only once. This type of amnesia is called global because so much of what has already been stored in memory is forgotten and because, even though the victim is conscious and can go about the routine business of daily life, no new memories are formed while the attack is in progress. In other words, both retrograde amnesia (forgetting events one was exposed to in the past) and antegrade amnesia (the inability to encode and store new information) characterize transient global amnesia. The cause of transient global amnesia is not known, but a currently favoured hypothesis is that it is due to temporary alterations in the normal pattern of blood flows to the brain.

Substance—induced amnesia

This results from the intake of poisons, drugs of abuse, or medications with amnestic side-effects (for example certain anxiolytics). Chronic excessive consumption of alcohol could result in vitamin deficiency and encephalopathy (brain inflammation), which is manifested in **Korsakoff's amnesia**, at which stage it is also categorized as organic amnesia. Antegrade amnesia (the inability to form new memories) is one of the prominent symptoms of Korsakoff's amnesia. Patients with this kind of amnesia also have some loss of what are called remote memories—remembrances of events that occurred early in their lives (*Squire & Cohen*, 1982). Memory is not the only information—processing problem of korsakoff patients; they have difficulties with attention and perception

that may impair their performance on some remote—memory tests.

Diseases of the brain

The disease that can result in amnesia are syphilis of the brain and other brain infections, strokes and other permanent disorders of brain blood flow, brain tumours, disorders of brain metabolism, multiple sclerosis, various conditions caused by toxic chemicals, senile dementia, and primary degenerative dementia.

Senile dementia (the word *senile* refers to old age) is characterized by deficits in many intellectual abilities—memory, attention, judgement, and abstract thought, for example—that can occur in aged people. The amnesia in senile dementia is at first largely anterograde. Thus the old person with this disorder has trouble learning and cannot recall well what happened last month, yesterday, or even a few hours ago. Memories of the years before the disease are largely intact until the brain damage becomes widespread and severe.

Senile dementia is usually the result of a reduction in blood flow to the brain. Arteriosclerosis deprives brain cells of adequate supplies of oxygen and nutrients so that some cells die and others malfunction. The brain is said to atrophy.

Primary degenerative dementia has many of the same characteristics as senile dementia. A major difference is that the symptoms often begin in middle age. **Alzheimer's disease** is a form of primary degenerative dementia in which there is a cluster of specific degenerative brain changes of unknown origin. Some evidence indicates that the amnesia in Alzheimer's disease is related to deficiencies in the brain neurotransmitter chemical acetylcholine.

Alzheimer's disease begins relatively early in life and, unlike senile dementia, where death quickly ends the suffering, life continues with progressive mental deterioration. The amnesia, for instance, often goes from a relatively mild anterograde memory problem to a profound anterograde and retrograde deficit—both the recent and remote past are largely gone.

REMEMBERING

The general memory principles described in this chapter have suggested ways in which you can improve your memory, but more specific aids to remember are available; and some of those are as follows:

Mnemonic devices

The principles of encoding help explain the utility of many **mnemonic devices**—systematic strategies for remembering information (named after the Greek word *mneme,* which means "memory"). People can use external aids (such as note taking or asking someone else) to enhance their memory, or they can rely on internal aids, such as rehearsal and various mnemonic devices (*Intons-Peterson* & *Fournier*, 1986). Most mnemonic devices draw on the principle that the more retrieval cues that can be created, and the more vivid these cues are, the better memory is likely to be.

Method of loci

One mnemonic strategy is the method of loci, which uses visual imagery as a memory aid. *Cicero* attributed this technique to the ancient Greek poet *Simonides,* who was attending a banquet when he was reportedly summoned by the gods from the banquet hall to receive a message. In his absence, the roof collapsed, killing everyone. The bodies were mangled beyond recognition, but Simonides was able to identify the guests by their physical placement around the banquet table. He thus realized that images could be remembered by fitting them into an orderly arrangement of locations (*Bower,* 1970).

To use the method of loci, you must first decide on a series of "snapshot" mental images of locations with which you are very familiar. For instance, locations in your bedroom might

be your pillow, your closet, the top of your dresser, and under the bed. Now, suppose that you need to do the following errands: pick up vitamin C pills, buy milk, return a book to the library, and make plans with one of your friends for the weekened. You can remember these items by visualizing each in one of your loci, making the image as vivid as possible to maximize the likelihood of retrieving it. Thus, you might picture the vitamin C pills spilled all over your pillow, a bottle of milk poured over the best outfit in your bed until friday night. Often, the more ridiculous the image, the easier it is to remember. While you are out doing your errands, you can mentally flip through your imagined loci to bring back the mental images.

Peg method

A second mnemonic technique, called the peg method, uses imagery as well as a auditory cue, rhyming. Here, people "hang" information to be remembered on mental pegs such as numbers. For example, you might create a number rhyme that you cannot possibly forget such as, "One is a bun, two is a shoe, three is a tree, four is a door," and so forth. Note that each number in this rhyme is associated with an object that can easily be visualized.

Like the various locations in the method-of-loci approach, these images then act as mental pegs with which you can associate the items that you need to remember. To return to the list of errands, you might hang the first item, vitamin C, on the "one is bun" image by visualizing a hamburger bun full of vitamin C pills. You might likewise visualize a shoe full of milk, your library book caught in the branches of a tree, and your friend coming to the door on the way out for the evening.

SQ$_3$R method

The method of loci and the peg method can lead to dramatic increases in memory performance, but people who learn them in memory improvement courses tend to stop using them after a few months, in part because the most effective mnemonic strategies tend to apply to a specific task or situation (*Herramann,* 1988). A task-specific strategy developed to help students remember the information they read in textbooks is called the **SQ3R method**, for the five steps involved in the method: survey, question, read, recite, and review (*Martin,* 1985; *Robinson,* 1961). The SQ3R method fosters active rather than passive learning while reading. The first step is to *survey,* or glance through the organization of the chapter, looking at headings and the summary, so that you know the gist of it and therefore organize the material more efficiently as you encode. *Questioning* refers to turning the headings into questions; this orients you to the content of each section and makes reading more interesting. For example, for the subheading long-term memory systems, you might ask yourself, "What evidence could demonstrate the existence of separate memory systems? Could patients with different brain lesions have one kind of LTM intact and another disrupted? The third step is to *read,* trying to find answers to the questions that you posed. Fourth, *recite* the answers to these questions as well as other relevant information in each section before going on to the next section. Finally, when you have finished the chapter, *review* the material by recalling your questions and answers and actively thinking about the material, relating the new material you have learned, to things that you know about and that interest you. (The only catch is that you may need a mnemonic to help you remember the acronym SQ3R).

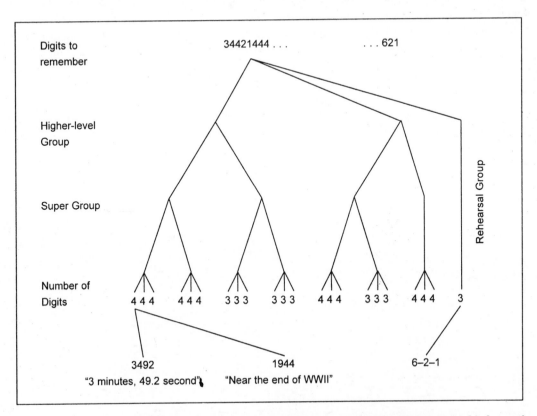

Fig. 6.5 Chunking. An ordinary subject (SF) demonstrates extraordinary control of information in STM. SF grouped sequences of digits into hierarchically organized groups. Except for the group of three digits at the end that he rehearsed mentally.

Chunking

Perhaps the best example of the interaction between working memory and long-term memory in daily life is a strategy people use to expand the capacity of their working memory in particular situations (*Erickson & Kintch*, 1995).

Consider the working memory capacity of a skilled waiter or waitress. How can a person take the order of eight people without the aid of a notepad, armed only with a *mental* sketchpad and a limited-capacity verbal store? One way people increase their mental workspace in situations such as this is to use knowledge stored in LTM to group information in larger units than single words or digits, a process known as **chunking**.

The value of chunking as a memory aid was demonstrated in a remarkable study done with an undergraduate student of average intelligence called SF (*Ericsson & Chase*, 1982). The goal was to increase SF's capacity to memorize strings of digits. SF was a long-distance runner, and early in the study he noticed that he could group some of the digits to resemble running times for races. For instance, SF remembered the number 3492 as "3 minutes and 49.2 seconds," close to the world record at that time for running a mile. Not all of the numbers he was asked to memorize lent themselves to running times, however so he also incorporated ages and dates into his system. Thus, the number "893 became" 89.3 years old, a very old person," and "1944 became" near the end of world war II." The next step was to group the running times, ages, and dates into larger "supergroups," consisting of three groups of three-or-four-digit numbers (Fig. 6.5). Any number SF could not organize meaningfully he remembered by simple rehearsal.

SF began the study with unexceptional memory abilities; after about 20 months of practice (one hour a day, three to five days a week), he had increased the number of digits he could remember in one presentation from seven to 80. By calling upon information in LTM, SF was able to increase his temporary memory for digits more than ten times the widely believed upper limit for STM. ■ ■

Thinking and Language

Thinking and Language

Thinking is important to all of us in our daily lives. The way we think affects the way we plan our lives, the personal goals we choose, and the decisions we make. Good thinking is therefore not something that is forced upon us in school: It is something that we all want to do, and want others to do, to achieve our goals and theirs.

In many ways, thought is simply an extension of perception and memory. When we perceive, we form a mental representation. When we remember, we try to bring that representation to mind. When we think, we use representations to try to solve a problem or answer a question. Thinking means manipulating mental representations for a purpose.

THE THINKING PROCESS

The symbols that we use in thinking are often words and language, and therefore thinking and language are closely related. A language makes available hundreds of thousands of potential symbols and gives us rules for using them. To a large degree, the availability of language symbols is what makes human thinking so much more sophisticated than the thinking of other animals.

Manipulating mental representations

People can manipulate virtually any kind of representation in their minds. You may not have realized it, but the last time you sniffed the milk and decided it was spoiled, you were thinking with your nose (actually, with olfactory representations). Or consider what happens when people harmonize while singing along with the radio. Although their companions in the car may not appreciate it, they are engaged in an impressive act of musical thinking, unconsciously manipulating auditory representations and using sophisticated rules of harmonic structure, probably with no awareness what-so-ever.

Thinking in words and images

Much of the time people think using words and images. When people try to figure out whether they have enough money with them to buy an extra bag of pretzels, how to tell an unwanted suitor they are not interested, or how to reorganize their department at the office to increase efficiency, they usually think in words. At other times they rely on **mental images**, visual representations such as the image of a street or a circle.

Psychologists once disagreed about whether people actually think in images or whether they convert visual questions into verbal questions in order to solve them. For example, to figure out how to carry a large desk through a narrow doorway, people do somehow rotate a visual image of the desk in their minds, or do they convert the problem into statements (e.g., "the desk won't fit if it isn't turned sideways")?

One study addressed this question by showing subjects pictures of a stimulus such as a capital R, rotated between 0 and 360 degrees. The subject had to decide whether the letter was shown normally or in mirror image.

The results were clear: The amount of time subjects took to answer varied directly with the degree of rotation from upright. In other words, the more the rotation, the longer the reaction time. This indicated that subjects were actually mentally rotating an image of the letter to come to a conclusion (*Cooper & Shepard*, 1973). Supporting these findings, PET studies show that perceiving, remembering, and mentally manipulating visual scenes all involve activation of the visual cortex and that people typically solve problems of this sort without activating left-hemisphere language centers (*Kosslyn*, 1993).

Mental models

People also frequently think using **mental models**, representations that describe, explain, or predict the way things work (*Johnson-Laird*, 1995). Mental models may be quite simple like most people's understanding of automobile ("If the car doesn't start, there's a problem somewhere under the hood") or a child's understanding of what a "cavity" is (a bad thing in the mouth that requires a trip to the dentist). On the other hand, they can be quite complex, such as the mental models used by mechanics to troubleshoot a car or a dentist's conception of the processes that produce cavities.

Although mental models often include visual elements (such as the dentist's visual representations of different kinds of teeth and what erosion in a tooth looks like), they always include descriptions of the relations among elements. For example, the dentist may have a casual model of how buildup of food

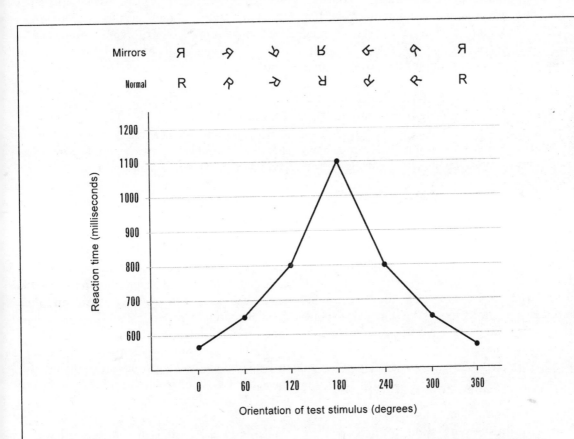

Fig. 7.1 **The manipulation of visual representations. The investigators asked participants to determine whether the "R" they saw at different degrees of rotation was forward or backward. As can be seen, the more subjects had to rotate the letter mentally, the longer they took to complete the task. Peak reaction time was at 180 degrees, which requires the furthest rotation**

residues leads to bacterial action that eats away at a tooth.

CONCEPTS AND CATEGORIES

Before people can think about an object, they usually first have to classify it so that they know what it is and what it does. An approaching person is a friend or a stranger; a piece of fruit on the table is an apple or an orange; a political commentator on television is a conservative or a liberal.

People and things fall into groupings based on common properties called categories. A concept is a mental representation of a category, that is, an internal portrait of a class of objects, ideas, or events that share common properties (*Murphy & Medin*, 1985). Some concepts can be visualized, but a concept is broader than its visual image. For example, the concept car stands for a class of vehicles with four wheels, seating space for at least two people, and a generally predictable shape. Other concepts, like honest, defy visualization or representation in any other sensory mode, although they may have visual associations (such as an image of an honest face).

The process of identifying an object as an instance of a category—recognizing its similarity to some objects and dissimilarity to others—is called categorization. Categorization is essential to thinking because it allows people to make inferences about objects. For example, if I classify the drink in my glass as an alcoholic beverage, I am likely to make assumptions about how much I can drink, what I will feel like after drinking it, and so forth.

Defining features and prototypes

For years, philosophers and psychologists have wrestled with the question of how people categorize objects or situations (*Huttenlocher & Hedges*, 1994). How do they decide that a crab is an animal rather than an insect, even though crabs look like big spiders?

Defining features

One possibility is that they compare the features of the objects with a list of **defining features**— qualities that are essential, or necessarily present in order to classify the object as a member of the category. For some concepts this strategy could work. Concepts like salt, water, or triangle are **well-defined concepts** which have properties that clearly set them apart from other concepts. A triangle can be defined as a two-dimensional geometric figure with three sides and three angles, and anything that does not fit this definition is not a triangle.

Most of the concepts used in daily life, however, are not easily defined by a precise set of features; rather, they are **fuzzy concepts** (*Holland*, 1986). Consider the concept *good*. This concept takes on different meanings when applied to a meal or a person: Few of us look for tastiness in a person or honesty and sensitivity in a meal.

Prototypes

Even when concepts are well defined, consulting a list of defining features is, in psychological time (that is, milliseconds), a rather slow procedure. People typically classify objects rapidly by judging their *similarity* to concept stored in memory (*Tversky*, 1977).

Researchers have learned how people use similarity in classification by using both visual and verbal categorization tasks. In visual categorization tasks, the experimenter states the name of a target category (e.g., bird) and then presents a picture and asks whether it is a member of the category. In verbal categorization tasks, the target category is followed by a word instead of a picture (e.g., *sparrow*); the task for the subject is to judge whether the second word is an instance of the category.

Psychologists have learned about the role of similarity in classification by measuring the time subjects take to respond in tasks such as these. For example, people rapidly recognize that a sparrow is a bird but take 100 to 200 milliseconds longer to classify a penguin. The reason is that a sparrow is a

Sparrow

enguins

Fig. 7.2 People readily recognize sparrows as birds. Categorizing penguins takes a little more thought—and hence measurably more time

more *prototypical* bird, that is, it shares more of the characteristic features of the concept (Rosh; 1978). A **prototype** is an abstraction across many instances of a category (such as sparrows, bluebirds, and robins). When people construct a prototype in their minds, they essentially abstract out the most important common features of the objects in a category. Thus, the prototype of a bird does not look exactly like any particular bird the person has ever seen; it is more like an airbrushed photograph that smoothes out idiosyncratic features.

When people judge similarity in visual tasks, they rely primarily on shape. When they judge similarity verbally, they tend to rely on **characteristic** or **prototypical features**, that is, qualities typically found in members of a category. For example, most birds fly, and lay eggs. People classify sparrows quickly because they do all this. Penguins take longer to classify because they lay eggs but do not share many other features of birds, except for having wings.

Most concepts include both visual information and information about characteristic features, so that in everyday categorization, people often use some combination of the two. In judging similarity, people may also compare an object to an exemplar, or a prototypic example of the category, rather than an abstract prototype (*Lamberta*, 1996).

Implicit and explicit categorization

There are two views of categorization—one based on defining features and the other on similarity. In everyday life, concepts probably represent information in multiple ways that are used flexibly in different categorization tasks. Rapid, implicit categorization usually relies primarily on similarity. If a person has difficulty in implicitly classifying a novel object based on similarity or if the classification task is complex, she may switch to explicit categorization based

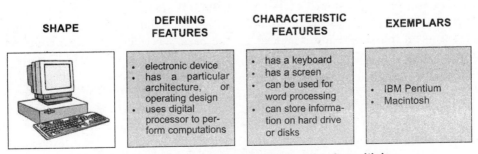

Fig. 7.3 Concepts can represent information in multiple ways that aid categorization

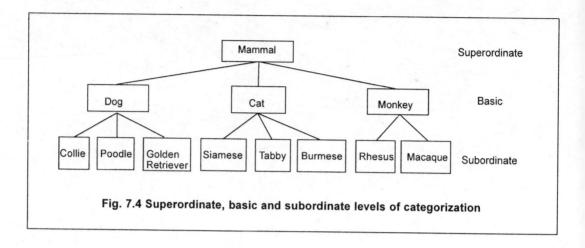

Fig. 7.4 Superordinate, basic and subordinate levels of categorization

on defining features (or on features that may not be defining but are nevertheless *definitive* or *diagnostic*. Complex classification tasks generally require careful, explicit evaluation of the data. A doctor will not diagnose appendicitis in a patient whose symptoms appear similar to a textbook case of appendicitis (a prototype) or cases she has seen before (exemplars) unless a laboratory test shows an abnormal white blood cell count, particularly since the symptoms of appendicitis are similar to those of food poisoning and the flu.

Hierarchies of concepts

Many concepts are hierarchically ordered at multiple levels of abstraction. We categorize all pets that pant, slobber, and bark as dogs, but we can further subdivide the concept *dog* into more specific categories such as *collie* and *poodle*. Similarly, *dog* is itself an instance of larger, more general categories such as *mammal* and vertebrate. Efficient thinking requires choosing the right level of abstraction. A woman walking down the street in a bright purple raincoat belongs to the categories *mammal, vertebrate,* and *human* just as clearly as she belongs to the category *woman*. Yet we are more likely to say "Look at the woman in the purple raincoat" than "Look at the vertebrate in brightly coloured apparel."

The level people naturally tend to use in categorizing objects is known as the **basic level**. This is the broadest, most inclusive level at which objects share common attributes that are distinctive of the concept—that is, that "stand out" (*Rosch*, 1978). It is also the level at which people categorize most quickly; it is thus the "natural" level to which the mind gravitates. Thus, *woman* is a basic-level category; so are *dinner, car,* and *bird*.

At times, however people categorize at a more specific or **subordinate level** as when people on a nature hike distinguish between robins and wrens. Actually, the natural level (sometimes called the *entry level*) at which people tend to classify an unusual instance of a category, such as penguin, is often the subordinate level (*Jolicoeur*, 1984). For these atypical cases, a more subordinate level than the basic level maximizes similarity of objects within the category and minimizes similarity with objects outside the category, which is what the basic level does for most concepts. People also sometimes classify objects at the larger or **superordinate level**, as when a farmer asks, "are the animals in the barn?" rather than running down a list including chickens, horses, and so forth. The superordinate level is one level more abstract than the basic level, and members of this class share fewer common features.

One person's basic may be another's subordinate

The basic level shows surprising similarity across people and cultures, the more a person knows about a particular domain, the more likely she is to use more specific rather than basic-level terms (*Geoghehan*, 1976; *Tanaka & Taylor*, 1991). For example, clinical psychologists and psychiatrists do not use words like "nut" to describe a psychotic patient or say that a person "has problems," as people do in everyday discourse. Instead, they make a more specific diagnosis that identifies precisely what the problem is.

The basic level of categorization also changes according to the situation. During the workday, furniture makers may refer to chairs according to specific types (for instance, an oak ladder-back reproduction), but when the day ends and they are ready to rest their feet, "chair" will suffice (*Holland*, 1986).

REASONING, PROBLEM SOLVING, AND DECISION MAKING

Mental images, mental models, and concepts are the building blocks of thought. Next we will explore how people manipulate these elementary units of thought to reason, solve problems, and make decisions.

Reasoning

Reasoning refers to the process by which people generate and evaluate arguments and beliefs (*Anderson*, 1985). Philosophers have long distinguished two kinds of reasoning: inductive and deductive.

Inductive reasoning

After taking a new medication for three days, a woman finds she has developed a rash on her chest. She cannot think of any new foods she has eaten in the past few days, so she concludes that she is probably allergic to the medication. This type of thinking is called **inductive reasoning**—reasoning from specific observations to more general propositions that seem likely to be true (*Holland*, 1986). The inductive logic that led to the woman's conclusions might be summarized as follows:

- Today I had a rash.
- For the past three days I had been taking a new medication.
- For the past three days I had not eaten any food to which I am allergic.
- Therefore, I must be allergic to the new medication.

Inductive reasoning relies on probabilities. An inductive conclusion is not *necessarily* true because its underlying premises are only probable, not certain. For example, the woman with the rash may have been exposed to chicken pox, so that the symptoms appeared coincidentally with her new medication schedule.

Although inductive reasoning is **fallible**, it is essential in daily life. In fact, everytime we categorize an object, we are using a form of inductive reasoning.

Deductive reasoning

Deductive reasoning is logical reasoning that draws a conclusion from a set of assumptions, or premises. In contrast to inductive reasoning, it starts with an idea rather than an observation. In some ways, deduction is the flipside of induction: Whereas induction starts with specifics and draws general conclusions, deduction starts with general principles and makes inferences about specific instances. For example, if you understand the general premise that all dogs have fur and you know that Barkley is a dog, then you can deduce that Barkley has fur, even though you have never made Barkley's acquaintance. Unlike inductive reasoning, deductive reasoning can lead to *certain* rather than simply *probable* conclusions, as long as the premises are correct and the reasoning is logical.

Reasoning by analogy

When people encounter a novel situation, they

often rely on *analogies* to make inferences about what it is and what to do. Reasoning by analogy, or **analogical reasoning**, is the process by which people understand a novel situation in terms of a familiar one. Thus, to a cognitive psychologist, the mind is like a computer or a network of neurons; to a premedical student primarily studying physics, biology, and organic chemistry; a literature course may be "a breath of fresh air."

People use analogies to categorize novel situations, make inferences, and solve problems. They also try to influence the inferences other people will make and the conclusions they will reach by using analogies that suit their own goals. During the Gulf war, U.S. President George Bush compared Saddam Hussein with Hitler. If one accepts this premise, then Iraq's invasion of Kuwait was like Germany's invasion of its neighbours at the start of world war II, which implied that Saddam must be stopped immediately before becoming a danger to the world. Similarly, Saddam compared Bush and the United States to Satan, which implied that fighting the enemy was a holy war.

A key aspect of analogies of this sort is that the familiar situation and the novel situation must each contain a system of elements that can be mapped onto one another. For an analogy to take hold, the two situations need not *literally* resemble each other; Saddam did not look much like Hitler, and Iraq was not a mighty power like Germany. However, the *elements* of the familiar situation must relate to one another in a way that explains how the elements of the novel situation are related. Thus, it did not matter that Hitler was European and Saddam was Middle Eastern. If one accepted the analogy that Saddam was like Hitler, then his behaviour could be understood as the actions of a ruthless, powerhungry megalomaniac who must be stopped before he took over any more of his neighbours.

To reason from analogies, the person must first activate one or more relevant *analogs—* mental models of familiar situations—from long-term memory. Selecting the best-fitting analogy

involves meeting three sets of constraints. First, the current situation must, at some level, be similar enough to the familiar situation to activate the analog. Second, the elements of the novel situation and the analog must be readily mapped onto one another in a way that seems to make sense. Third, the choice of an analog depends on the reasoner's goals.

Problem solving

Life is a series of problems to solve. How much should you tip the waiter? How are you going to afford a new car? What can you do to get your boyfriend to be more responsive? Problem solving refers to the process of transforming one situation into another to meet a goal. The aim is to move from a current, unsatisfactory state (initial state) to a state in which the problem is resolved (the goal state). To get from the initial state to the goal state, the person used operators, mental and behavioural processes aimed at transforming the initial state until it eventually approximates the goal (*Anderson*, 1993).

Let us look at one classic toy puzzle: The Towers of Hanoi. The puzzle consists of three round pegs with a number of disks, in graduated sizes, on each peg.

The problem is to move all of the disks from peg A to peg C. You must pick up only one disk at a time, and you can never put a disk on top of a smaller disk (for example, you cannot put disk 2 on top of disk 1).

Consider what would happen if you approached the Towers of Hanoi problem using a means-ends analysis without subgoals. On the first move, you might notice that disk 1 was on peg A rather than peg C. You could reduce this difference by moving disk 1 to peg C. On the next move, transferring disk 2 to peg C would be illegal, because disk 2 is larger than disk 1, which is already on the peg. So, you might move disk 2 to peg B. You will find that if you continue this way, you will reach a blind alley.

A more sophisticated version of such an analysis is "thinking ahead." The idea here is to develop a general plan for moving a *pair* of disks. For example, in the first—move group, one could move *both* disks 1 and 2 to peg C by moving disk 1 to B, disk 2 to C, then disk 1 to C. This method, however, leads to a blind alley again.

At this point, I am going to reveal the elegant solution. The solution involves subgoals. Think of your goal: to move the whole stack. If you could move disk 4, the largest disk, which has to be on the bottom, then you would have the simpler problem of moving only the three smaller disks, so moving disk 4 is your first subgoal. What must you do to accomplish that? Move disks 1 through 3 out of the way-specifically, to peg B. You wind up with the following list of moves:

Goal : disks 1-4 to C
Subgoal : disk 4 to C
Sub-subgoal : disks 1-3 to B
Sub-sub-subgoal: disk 3 to B
Sub-sub-sub-subgoal : disks 1-2 to C
Sub-sub-sub-sub-subgoal : disk 1 to B

Now you know the solution. Begin by moving disk 1 to B, then disk 2 to C, disk 1 to C, disk 3 to B, disk 1 to A, disk 2 to B, disk 1 to B, disk 4 to C, and so on. The problem of moving four disks to C reduces to the problem of moving three disks to B, which reduces to moving one disk to B. Each time that you solve a simpler problem, you return to the goal or subgoal that gave rise to it. Once you try this a few times, so that you see how it works, you will be able to solve a problem with any number of disks, although the number of moves required may become rather large.

Some problems are *well-defined;* the initial state, goal state and operators are easily determined. The mathematics problems that students confront countless times in their school careers are examples of well-defined problems (*Kintsch & Greeno*, 1985). In real life,

however, few problems are so straightforward; rather, most are **ill-defined**, since both the information needed to solve them and the criteria for determining whether the goals have been met are vague. For example, a manager trying to raise moral among his employees faces an ill-defined problem, since he may not know the extent of the problem, or how to be sure whether his efforts to solve it have really worked.

Solving a problem, once it has been clarified, can be viewed as a four-step process. The first step is to compare the initial state with the goal state to identify precise differences between the two. The second step is to identify possible operators and select the one that seems most likely to reduce the differences. The third step is to apply the operator or operators, responding to challenges or roadblocks by establishing subgoals—minigoals on the way to achieving the broader goal. This subgoal then creates a search for operators (and flight attendants) that might help you attain it. The final step is to continue using operators until all differences between the initial state and goal state are eliminated.

Problem-solving strategies

Problem solving would be impossible if people had to try every potential operator in every situation until they found one that worked. Instead, they employ **problem-solving strategies**, techniques that serve as guides for solving a problem.

Algorithm

A procedure for solving a problem or achieving a goal in a finite number of steps.

The term 'algorithm' is derived from Latinization of the name of one of the most creative mathematician in medieval Islam, Al-Kwarizmi (*Colish*, 1997). In modern times algorithmic is a field fundamental to the science of computing (Harel, 1987). Computers use algorithms in memory searches, as when a spellcheck command compares every word in a

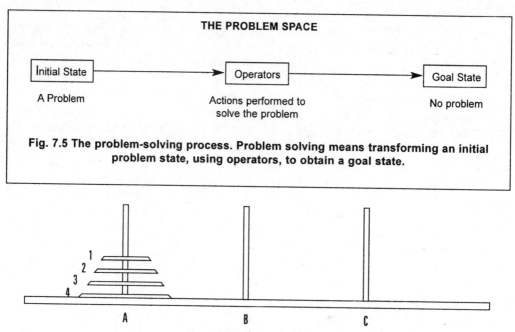

THE PROBLEM SPACE

Initial State → Operators → Goal State

A Problem

Actions performed to
solve the problem

No problem

**Fig. 7.5 The problem-solving process. Problem solving means transforming an initial
problem state, using operators, to obtain a goal state.**

Fig. 7.6 The tower of Hanoi

file against an internal dictionary. Humans also use algorithms to solve problems, such as counting the number of guests coming to a party and multiplying by 2 to determine how many pizzas to buy. Algorithms are guaranteed to find a solution as long as one exists, but they are generally only practical for solving relatively simple problems. Imagine solving for the square root of 16, 129 by methodically squaring 1, then 2, then 3, and so forth, each time checking to see if the answer is 16, 129. (You would eventually arrive at the right answer, but only on your 127th try).

Hypothesis testing

Another common problem-solving strategy is **hypothesis testing**, or formulating an educated guess about what might solve the problem and then testing it. One study examined the relationship between medical student's hypothesis-testing skills and their cost-effectiveness in ordering diagnostic tests (Durand, 1991). Researchers presented third-year medical students with case studies and asked them to generate hypotheses about

possible diagnoses and list the tests they would order. Students whose hypotheses were logically organized suggested fewer and less expensive tests than their peers who did not systematically rule in and rule out possible disorders.

Mental simulation

One of the most important problem-solving strategies is **mental simulation**—imagining the steps involved in solving a problem mentally before actually undertaking them. People conduct mental simulations of this sort every day, such as imagining precisely how they will tell their boss about the vacation they want to take during the busy season or picturing alternative routes they could take to make it to three different stores after work before the stores close.

Although many self-help books encourage people to visualize desired outcomes (the "power of positive thinking"), mentally simulating the steps to achieve that outcome, which is usually more beneficial (Taylor, 1998). One study demonstrated this with introductory psychology students facing a midterm examination. Students

	CONDITION		
Outcome	Mental Simulation	Positive Thinking	Control
Number of hours studying	16.07	11.57	14.50
Grade (% of questions correct)	80.60	72.57	77.68

Fig. 7.7 Effects of mental simulation on exam performance. Students who mentally simulated the steps involved in solving the problem of getting a good grade studied harder and were more successful than other students.

in one condition were told to visualize in detail the things they needed to do to get a good grade—picturing themselves on their beds reviewing lecture notes, and so forth. Students in the "positive-thinking" condition were instructed, instead, to visualize themselves receiving the grade they wanted and how good they would feel.

Students who imagined the steps to achieve a good grade studied harder and scored better in the exam than students in the positive thinking group, who actually did worse than students in a control condition who did not visualize anything.

Problem solving gone awry

Most of us muddle through our lives solving problems relatively well. However, human problem solving is far from perfect. One common problem is **functional fixedness**, the tendency for people to ignore other possible functions of an object when they have a fixed function in mind. In one experiment, *Duncker* (1945) gave subjects a problem in which they were asked to attach three small candles to a wall. "On the table lie, among many other objects, a few tacks and the crucial objects: three little pasteboard boxes." The solution is to attach the boxes to the wall with the tacks, so that the boxes can serve as platforms for the candles. In one condition (that is, one version of the procedure), the boxes contained candles, tacks, and matches, respectively. In the other condition, the boxes were empty, and the candles, tacks, and matches were on the table. Subjects solved the problem more quickly in the condition in which the boxes were empty.

Duncker interpreted this result (and several others like it) as an indication of "**functional fixedness**." When the boxes were used as containers, he theorized, this inhibited the subject from perceiving their possible function as platforms. Duncker suggested that this inhibition occurs only when the problem is solved by suggestion from below—that is, when the box itself suggests the idea of a platform. The box was less likely to suggest the idea of a

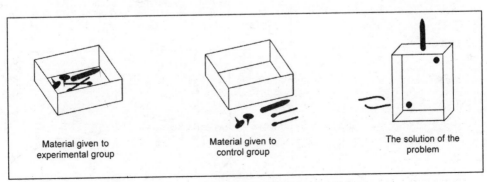

Material given to experimental group

Material given to control group

The solution of the problem

Fig. 7.8 The arrangement of materials and the problem solution in an experiment on functional fixedness

platform when it was already serving the function of a container. If the subject was already looking for a platform, the box would be found equally easily, whether it was full or empty.

Another common error in problem solving is confirmation bais, the tendency for people to search for confirmation of what they already believe (Oakhill & Garnham, 1993). In one study, the experimenters presented participants with three numbers (2, 4 and 6) and asked them to discover the rule used to construct this sequence of numbers by generating their own sets of numbers (Wason, 1960). Each time, the experimenters told participants whether or not their response. Correctly illustrated the rule. In fact, the rule was quite simple: any three numbers, arranged from smallest to largest. However, the way most people tried to solve the problem kept finding the rule. Instead of testing a variety of sequences—such as 3, 12, 428, or 7, 4, 46—until only one rule remained plausible, most participants did just the opposite. Early on, they formed a hypothesis such as "add 2 to each number to form the next number" and repeatedly generated one sequence after another that confirmed this rule until they were satisfied they were right. Confirmation bias can be a particular problem for experts in a field; for example, scientists studying a topic may only

test hypotheses and use methods that fit with current thinking (Sternberg, 1996).

Decision making

Just as life is a series of problems to solve, it is also a series of decisions to make, from the mundane. ("Should I buy the cheaper brand or the one that tastes better?") to the consequential ("What career should I choose?") **Decision making** is the process by which an individual weighs the pros and cons of different alternatives in order to make a choice.

Calculating expected utilities

According to one of the information-processing model, when people make decisions, they consider two things : the *utility,* or value to them, of the outcomes of different options and the *probability,* or estimated likelihood, of each outcome. For example, if you have found three apartments near campus and must choose one, you are likely to consider rent, proximity to campus, attractiveness, availability of parking and so on. According to this model, a rational decision maker would begin by assigning a weight to each attribute according to its importance (Edwards, 1977). Thus, if budget is the most important factor, rent would receive

		ALTERNATIVE APARTMENTS						
		Street A		Street B		Street C		
Attributes (In Order of Importance)	Importance (Numerical Weight)	Utility Value	Weighted Utility Value	Utility Value	Weighted Utility Value	Utility Value	Weighted Utility Value	
Rent	5	+ 10	x 5= 50	+ 8	x 5 = 40	+ 5	x 5 = 25	
Location	4	0	x 4= 0	+ 3	x 4 = 12	+ 10	x 4 = 40	
Livability	3	+ 8	x 3 = 24	+ 3	x 3 = 9	+ 1	x 3 = 3	
Parking	2	+ 10	x 2 = 20	+ 10	x 2 = 20	− 2	x 2 = −4	
Pets	1	+ 10	x 1 = 10	− 10	x 1 = −10	+ 10	x 1 = 10	
			104		71		74	

Fig. 7.9 Calculating weighted utility value

	ALTERNATIVE APARTMENTS		
	Street A	Street B	Street C
Weighted Utility Value	104	71	74
Probability of getting apartment	x .10	x .50	x .90
Expected Utility =	**10.4**	**35.5**	**66.6**

Fig. 7.10 Calculating Expected Utility

the highest weight. Then, for each apartment, you would assign a **utility value** to each attribute, which represents the extent to which the potential choice (the apartment) meets each criterion (such as affordable price).

The next is to multiply the weight of the attribute (how important it is) by its utility value (how well the option fulfills the criterion) for each option (apartment). This yields to a **weighted utility value**, a combined measure of the importance of an attribute and the extent to which a given option satisfies it.

In reality, of course, as the noted psychologist Mick Jagger pointed out, "you can't always get what you want," and shooting for an unattainable goal may carry heavy costs. For example, a particular apartment may have place to live by a certain date. Making a rational decision, then, involves integrating information about both the value and probability of different options; this combined assessment is called **expected utility**. The expected utility of an alternative is obtained by multiplying the weighted utility by the expected probability of that outcome.

If you have a 10 percent chance of getting the Street A apartment, the expected utility of that choice is .10 x 104, or 10.4. By comparison, if you have a 50 percent chance of getting the Street B apartment and a 90 percent chance of getting the Street C apartment, the expected utilities of those alternatives are 35.5 and 66.6, respectively. If you need to make a decision quickly, the then one to choose is Street C.

Most decisions are risky in the sense that we can not be sure of the outcome. A tossed coin, for example, normally has a 50/50 chance of coming up heads or tails. We are not sure which it will be and must take knowledge about the probability of the outcome into account when making a decision about whether the coin will come up heads or tails. In tossing a coin we know what the head/tail probabilities of the coin are; but in making complex "real life" decisions, we do not know the precise likelihood of various outcomes; we can only make our own estimates of the probabilities. Such guessed-at, or perceived, probability estimates are known as **subjective probabilities**.

Heuristics

The assault on human rationality in psychology began when researchers started to notice the extent to which people rely on cognitive shortcuts, or heuristics, that allow them to make rapid, but sometimes irrational, judgements (Dawes, 1997). One example is the **representativeness heuristic**, in which people categorize by matching the similarity of an object or incident to a prototype but ignore information about its probability of occurring. Consider the following personality description (Tversky & Kahneman, 1974):

"Steve is very shy and withdrawn, invariably helpful, but with little interest in people or in the world of reality. A meek and tidy soul, he has a need for order and structure and a passion for detail."

Is Steve most likely a farmer, a salesman, an airline pilot, a librarian, or a physician? Most people think he is probably a librarian, even if they are told that librarians are much less common in the population from which Steve has been drawn than the other occupations. Although Steve's attributes seem typical or representative of a librarian, if the population has 50 salesmen for every librarian, the chances are high that Steve is a salesman, even though he fits the prototype of a librarian.

Using the **availability heuristic**, people infer the frequency of a class of events or the likelihood of something happening on the basis of its availability in memory (that is, how readily it comes to mind) (Tversky & Kahneman, 1973). The availability heuristic is generally adaptive because things that "stick in our minds" tend to be important, familiar or vivid occurrences came to mind more readily than less familiar or less striking events. Availability can, however, lead to biased judgements when striking or memorable events are in fact infrequent.

Bounded rationality

Researchers studying heuristics challenged the rational models described earlier by suggesting that human thought is highly susceptible to error. An alternative and emerging perspective takes this critique of pure reason one step further, arguing that because people rarely have complete information and limitless time, they are often better off using strategies for making inferences and decisions that might seem less than optimal to a philosopher (Gigerenzer & Goldstein, 1996).

Underlying this view is the notion of *bounded rationality:* People are rational *within bounds,* and those bounds depend on the environment, their goals, and their abilities. In this view, instead of making *optimal* judgements, people typically make *good-enough* judgements. Herbert Simon (1956) called this *satisficing,* a combination of *satisfying* and *sufficing.* When we choose a place to have dinner, we do not go through every restaurant in the phone book; rather, we go through a list of the restaurants that come to our minds and choose the one that seems most satisfying at that moment.

According to one theory, when people are called upon to make rapid inferences or decisions, they often use the strategy "take the best, ignore the rest" (Gigerenzer & Goldstein, 1996). Thus, instead of weighing all the information possible, they begin with a quick yes/no judgement; if that works, they stop and assume their inference is good enough. If it does not work, they go on to the next quickest judgement, and down the list until they get a "satisficing" answer.

LANGUAGE

So much thinking is done with words that understanding thought is impossible without understanding language. Beyond its role in thinking, language is fundamental to one of the most basic activities of people in literate societies: reading. Without the ability to manipulate and comprehend the written word, we would be unable to carry out the simplest activities, from selecting items from a menu to filling out a form.

Language is the system of symbols, sounds, meanings and rules for their combination that constitutes the primary mode of communication among humans.

Language and thought

The Hanunoo people of the Philippines have 92 names for rice (Anderson, 1985). Does this mean that the Hanunoo can think about rice in more complex ways than North Americans who are hard pressed to do much better than "white rice" and "brown rice"? This line of reasoning led Bejamin Whorf (1956) and others to formulate what came to be called the **Whorfian hypothesis of linguistic relativity**, the idea that language shapes thought (Hardin, 1997). According to the *Whorfian hypothesis,* what people can even think is constrained by the words in their language. Subsequent research has not generally supported the hypothesis—people often seem to have ideas about things that can only inadequately be expressed in words—although language is central to some abstract categories and some forms of reasoning. Thought also shapes language, and language evolves to express new concepts.

Transforming sounds and symbols into meaning

One of the defining features of language is that its symbols are arbitrary. In this next section, we examine how sounds and symbols are transformed into meaningful sentences, beginning with the elements of language: Phonemes, morphemes, phrases, and sentences. We then explore the grammatical rules people implicitly follow as they manipulate these elements to produce meaningful utterances.

Elements of language

Language is processed hierarchically, from small units of sound people produce through their mouths and noses to the complex combinations of words and sentences that are produced to convey meaning. The smallest units of sound that constitute speech (as opposed to grunts or sniffles) called **phonemes,** are strung together to create meaningful utterances. In the English language, phonemes include not only vowels and consonants but also the different ways of pronouncing them (such as the two pronunciation of the letter 'a' in at and ate).

A string of randomly connected phonemes, however, does not convey any message. To be meaningful, strings of phonemes must be combined into **morphemes,** the smallest units of meaning in language. Words, suffixes and prefixes are all morphemes, such as *pillow, horse, the, pre-,* and *-ing.* The word cognition, for example, consists of two morphemes: *Cognit—,* from the Latin *Cogito* ("to know") and *-ion,* meaning "the act of."

Morphemes are combined into phrases, groups of words that act as a unit and convey a meaning. In the sentence, *'when people speak, they make many sounds',* the words *when people speak* and *many sounds* are phrases. Morphemes and phrases are combined into **sentences,** organized sequences of words that express a thought or intention. Some sentences are intended as statements of fact or propositions; others ask questions or make requests (e.g., "Sam, come here!").

ELEMENT	DEFINITION	EXAMPLES
Phonemes	Smallest units of sound that constitute speech	th, s, ē, ĕ
Morphemes	Smallest units of meaning	anti-, house, the, -ing
Phrases	Group of words that act as a unit and convey a meaning	in the den, the rain in Spain, ate the candy
Sentences	Organized sequences of words that express a thought or intention	The house is old. Did you get milk?

Fig. 7.11 Elements of Language.

Syntax: the rules for organizing words and phrases

Speakers of a language intuitively know that they cannot place words of phrases wherever they want in a sentence. An English speaker would never ask, "Why you did come here today?" because it violates implicit rules of word placement. Consider, in contrast, the pseudo-sentence *"The sten befted down the flotway."* Although the individual words have no meaning, readers will intuitively recognize it as grammatical: *Sten* is clearly a noun and the subject of the sentence: *befted* is a verb in the past tense (as indicated by the morpheme-*ed*), and *flotway* is the direct object. This pseudo sentence "feels" grammatical to an English speaker because it conforms to the **syntax** of the language, that is, to the rules that govern the placement of words and phrases in a sentence.

Linguists (people who study languages) and *psycholinguists* (psychologists who study the way people use and acquire language) map the structure of sentences using diagrams such as the one presented in Fig. (7.12), which maps the simple sentence. *The young woman kissed her anxious date.* Two aspects of this mapping are worth noting. The first is the extent to which rules of syntax determine the way people create and comprehend linguistic utterances. Much of the way psychologists think about syntax in sentences like this reflects the pioneering work of the linguist Noam Chomsky (1957, 1965). Chomsky views **grammar** (which includes syntax) as a system for generating acceptable language utterances and identifying unacceptable ones. According to Chomsky, the remarkable thing about language is that by acquiring the grammar of their linguistic community, people can generate an infinite number of sentences they have never heard before; that is, grammar is *generative*. People can also readily transform one sentence into another with the same *underlying meaning* despite a very different apparent syntactic construction, or *surface structure,* of the sentence. For example, instead of stating. "The young woman kissed her anxious date," a speaker could just as easily say, "The anxious date was kissed by the young woman."

A second aspect of this mapping worth noting is the interaction of syntax and semantics (the rules that govern the *meanings,* rather than

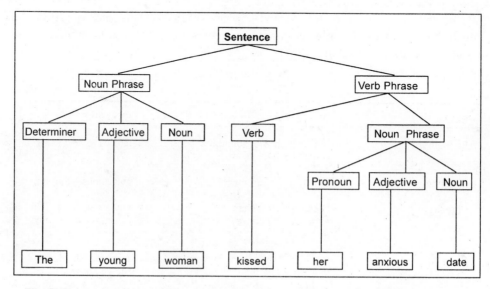

Fig. 7.12 A syntactic analysis of sentence and phrase structure. Sentences can be broken down through treelike diagrams, indicating noun phrases and verb phrases and their component parts

the order, of morphemes, words, phrases, and sentences) in understanding what people say. For example, the word *date* has multiple meanings; perhaps the woman who kissed the date could really love fruit. The presence of *anxious* as a modifier, however, constrains the possible interpretations of *date* and thus makes the fruity interpretation unlikely. But to recognize this semantic constraint, the reader or listener has to recognize a syntactic rule, namely that an adjective preceding a noun typically modifies the noun.

The interaction between syntax and semantics—between grammatical information processed heavily in Broca's area in the prefrontal cortex and Wernicke's area of the temporal lobes—is particularly useful in resolving the meaning of ambiguous sentences.

The remarkable thing about this interaction of semantic and syntactical knowledge is how quickly and unconsciously it takes place. People do not consciously break sentences down into their syntactic structures and then scan memory for the meanings of each word.

The use of language in everyday life

Two people catch each other's eyes at a party. Eventually, one casually walks over to the other and asks, "Enjoying the party?" A linguist could easily map the syntax of the question: It is a variant of the proposition *you are enjoying the party,* constructed by using a syntactic rule that specifies how to switch words around to make a question (and dropping the *you,* which is the understood subject). But that would completely miss the point. The sentence is not a question at all, and its meaning has nothing to do with the party. The real message is, "We have caught each other's eyes several times and I would like to meet you." Psychologists interested in the **pragmatics** of language—the way language is used and understood in everyday life—are interested in how people decode linguistic messages of this sort (*Fussel & Krauss, 1992*).

More recently, some researchers have begun to focus on levels of linguistic processing broader than the isolated sentence. Rather than studying the elements of language from the bottom up, they have turned to the analysis of **discourse**—the way people ordinarily speak, hear, read, and write in interconnected sentences (Graesser, 1997). Much of our time is spent, in fact, telling and hearing stories—new stories, gossip, events in our lives. Discourse analysts point out that the meaning (and even the syntactic structure) of every sentence reflects the larger discourse in which it is embedded. The question *Enjoying the party?* Made sense to both people involved in the conversation because it come in the context of a party and some significant nonverbal communication. The move away from an exclusive focus on processing at the level of individual sentences reflects a growing sense that language is about conveying *meaning,* not just about constructing and interpreting grammatically correct sentences.

Multiple levels of discourse

According to many discourse analysts, people mentally represent discourse at multiple levels. At the lowest level is the *surface code,* which refers to the exact wording of the phrases and sentences written or spoken. When people read or hear a sentence, they generally retain a surface code—a memory for precisely what was said—only briefly, while they process the rest of the sentence or the next few phrases. When later called upon to remember a sentence such as *Sam took the car into the shop,* people generally remember the gist but cannot recall the exact wording (e.g., they are just as likely to remember the sentence as *Sam took the car into the* auto *shop*). This gist is called the *textbase,* which includes the general meaning of the sentence along with some inferences about it (e.g., that the "shop" was an auto shop). These inferences, which are largely automatic and implicit, influence both what people "hear" and what they remember (*Bransford,* 1972).

Above the level of the gist or textbase is the *situation model,* the miniworld into which the speaker or narrator wants the reader or listener to enter. Consider for example, a chapter opening with the words, "you are sitting in a cafe" with your closest friend, and she tells you tearfully, 'I think my relationship with my husband has hit a deadend". The aim is to bring readers into the scene, to paint an evocative picture that allows them to suspend reality and enter into a different time and place.

One step above the situation model is the *communication* level, which reflects what the communicator is trying to do, such as impart ideas in a textbook or tell a story. At an even broader level of discourse is the *text genre*—the type of communication the text is, whether a story, a news report, a textbook, a joke, or a comment at a party intended to start a conversation. From a cognitive perspective, the simple act of "getting" a joke is an extraordinary feat that requires parallel processing at multiple levels, from distinguishing phonemes and morphemes up through using knowledge of the genre (that is, what jokes are) to figure out that a punch line is coming and recognizing it when it hits.

Principles of communication

When people converse or write, communications are guided not only by syntactic rules that shape the way they put words together but also by a set of shared rules of conversation that are implicit in the minds of both participants (Grice, 1975). For example, people keep track of what their listener knows, and when they introduce a new term or idea, they typically signal it with a change in syntax and embellish it with examples or evocative language. They also use various cues to signal important information. In writing, people usually put the topic sentence of a paragraph first so that readers know what the main point is. In public speaking, people often use *intonation* (tone of voice) to make particular points forcefully or use phrases such as "the point to remember here is. ......"

These "literary devices" of everyday life may seem obvious, but what is remarkable is how effortlessly people use them and how individuals who share a culture pick up on these cues automatically. Consider again the above example: "you are sitting in a cafe with your closest friend, and she tells you tearfully, 'I think my relationship with my husband has hit a dead-end.'" By switching to a narrative mode more characteristic of fiction, the author was signaling to the reader that something different was happening—namely that he was "setting the stage" for a chapter and a new set of ideas.

Nonverbal communication

People communicate verbally through language, but they also communicate nonverbally, and aspects of speech other than nouns and verbs often speak louder than words. When a parent calls a child by her whole name, it may be to chastise or to praise, depending on the inflection and intonation.

Nonverbal communication includes a variety of signals: intonation, body language, gestures, physical distance, nonverbal vocalization (such as sighs or throat clearnings), facial expressions, and touch (Feldman & Rime, 1991). Being conversant in the grammar of nonverbal communication can be just as important in interpersonal relations as understanding the grammar of verbal language. When a person sits too close to you on a bus or stands too close when talking, the effect can be very unsettling. Like other grammar, this one is largely unconscious, encoded as procedural knowledge. ■ ■

CHAPTER 8

Intelligence

THE NATURE OF INTELLIGENCE
— Intelligence is multifaceted and functional

APPROACHES TO INTELLIGENCE
— The psychometric approach
— The information-processing approach
— A theory of multiple intelligences

INTELLIGENCE TESTING
— Binet's scale
— The wechsler intelligence scales
— Frequency distribution of IQ scores

HEREDITY AND INTELLIGENCE
— Individual differences in IQ
— Group differences race and intelligence

THE EXTREMES OF INTELLIGENCE
— Mental retardation
— Giftedness
— Creativity and intelligence

APTITUDES
— An aptitude test
— Value of aptitude testing
— Uses of aptitude test results
— How to improve aptitude?

Intelligence

We may seem to understand what is meant by intelligence, e.g., in connection with an intelligence test, there is as yet no generally recognized definition of the term. Admittedly intelligence denotes an "ability," i.e., a condition or a complex of conditions for specific performances or achievements. But the specific types of performance which require intelligence have not yet been unambiguously defined, except to the extent that the term covers cognitive problems.

The definition of intelligence as the ability to overcome difficulties in new situations (proposed almost simultaneously by *E. Claparede* and *W. Stern*) is most widely accepted today.

THE NATURE OF INTELLIGENCE

The concept of intelligence has so successfully eluded definition that long ago one psychologist somewhat sarcastically defined intelligence as "what intelligence tests measure" (*Boring*, 1923). When asked what intelligence means, most people emphasize problem—solving abilities and knowledge about the world; they also sometimes distinguish between academic intelligence and social intelligence or interpersonal skill. In recent years, psychologists have come to recognize that intelligence is many-faceted, functional, and culturally defined.

Intelligence refers to the application of cognitive skills and knowledge to learn, solve problems, and obtain ends that are valued by an individual or culture. Intelligence is multifaceted and functional, directed at problems of adaptation.

Intelligence is multifaceted and functional

Intelligence is multifaceted; that is, aspects of it can be expressed in many domains. For example, one psychologist with a national reputation in his field is equally well known among his friends and students as the prototypical absent-minded professor. He once drove to a colleague. As we will see, speaking of "intelligence" may be less useful than speaking of "intelligences."

Intelligence is also functional. Intelligent behaviour is always directed toward accomplishing a task or solving a problem. According to one definition, intelligence is "the capacity for goal-directed adaptive behaviour" (*Sternberg & Salter*, 1982). From an evolutionary perspective, intelligent behaviour solves problems of adaptation and hence facilitates survival and reproduction. From a psychodynamic perspective, people use their intelligence to satisfy wishes and avoid things they fear. From a cognitive perspective, intelligence is applied cognition, that is, the use of cognitive skills to solve problems or obtain desired ends.

APPROACHES TO INTELLIGENCE

There are three approaches to understand the nature of intelligence, the psychometric approach, the information—processing approach, and a theory of multiple intelligences.

The psychometric approach

The **psychometric approach** tries to identify

	Sprint	Weights	Pullups	Sit-Ups
Sprint	—	.35	.45	.41
Weights		—	.70	.52
Pullups			—	.57
Pulse				—

Fig. 8.1 Identifying or common factor.

groups of items in a test that correlate highly with one another in order to identify underlying skills or abilities. If subjects perform multiple tasks, strong performance on some of tasks is likely to predict strong performance on others. Subjects who have good vocabularies, for example, usually have strong verbal reasoning skills (such as figuring out the meaning of unfamiliar proverbs) as well. Because vocabulary and verbal reasoning are highly correlated, usually a person's score on one will predict her's score on the other.

The primary tool of the psychometric approach is *factor analysis,* a statistical procedure for identifying common elements, or *factors* (in this case, primary mental abilities), that underlie performance across a set of tasks. Using factor analysis, researchers set up a table, or matrix, that shows how scores on tests of different abilities correlate with one another. Their aim is to reduce ten, 50, or 100 scores to a few combined variables. Once they identify a factor empirically, they examine the various items that comprise it to try to discover the underlying attribute it is measuring, such as verbal intelligence or arithmetical ability.

For example, of a diverse sample were tested on four kinds of athletic ability and the scores for each measure were correlated, the result might look something like the matrix presented in Fig. (8.1). The correlations between each pair are moderate to strong. People who are good sprinters tend to be good at weightlifting, and so forth. A common factor shared by all these variables that accounts for the positive correlations may be physical conditioning or athletic ability. The extremely high correlation

between weight-lifting ability and number of pullups probably reflects a more specific factor, muscle strength.

Spearman's two-factor theory

The English psychologist *Charles Spearman* was the first to apply factor analysis to intelligence tests. Spearman (1904, 1927) set up a matrix of correlations to see how children's test scores on various measures were related to their academic ranking at a village school in England. His analysis formed the basis for his **two-factor theory**, so named because Spearman believed the correlations he found were the result of two types of factors or abilities.

Spearman called the first factor the **g-factor**, or **general intelligence**. Children with the highest academic ranking tended to score well on such measures as arithmetic ability, general knowledge, and vocabulary, suggesting a general intelligence factor. Spearman believed the g-factor explained why almost any two sets of items assessing intellectual functioning will tend to correlate with one another.

Yet Spearman also noted that subjects who performed well or poorly in mathematics tests did not necessarily score equally well or poorly in other measures, such as vocabulary or general knowledge. The correlations among different subtests on a correlation matrix were far from uniform, just as the correlation between weightlifting and number of pullups was far higher than the correlation between weightlifting and sprinting speed in fig. (8.1). Spearman therefore proposed another type of factor, called as **s-factor** ("s" for *specific*), to explain the differences in correlations between different pairs

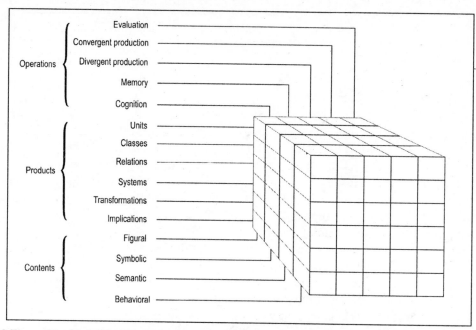

Fig. 8.2 The cubical models of intelligence. Each of the 120 small cubes represents a primary ability that is some combination of operations, products, and contents.

of measures. According to Spearman, s-factors reveal specific abilities unique to certain tests or shared only by a subset of tests. Individuals vary in overall intellectual ability (g-factor), but some people are adept at some kinds of reasoning (such as mathematical, spatial, or verbal) while mediocre at others.

Other factor theories

Factor analysis has proven useful in identifying common factors among the mountains of statistical data produced by intelligence tests. However, both the number of factors and types of mental abilities reveal through factor analysis can vary depending on who is doing the analysis.

Factor analysis can yield many varying interpretations of the same findings, and it cannot rule out the possibility that different factors might have emerged if other tasks had been included.

Different interpretations

In fact, when other psychologists applied Spearman's factor analytic technique, they arrived at different interpretations. For example, L.L. *Thurstone* (1938, 1962) argued against the existence of an overriding g-factor, finding instead seven primary factors in intelligence: word fluency, comprehension, numerical computation, spatial skills, associative memory, reasoning, and perceptual speed. The most comprehensive re-analysis of data from over 400 data sets collected from 1927 to 1987 (*Carroll*, 1993) produced a hierarchical, three-level solution that in some ways resembles a compromise between Spearman's and Thurstone's models. At the highest level is a g-factor shared by all lower level abilities. At the middle level are more specific factors similar to those Thurstone discovered. At the bottom level of the hierarchy are simple processes, such as speed of recognizing objects, that are ultimately necessary for producing any intelligent action.

Gf-Gc Theory

Another major approach, called **Gf-Gc theory**, also proposes a hierarchical model (*Horn & Noll*, 1997). Instead of encompassing all lower order factors under a *single* g-factor, however, this model distinguishes two general intelligence factors, rather than one, at the highest level: fluid and crystallized intelligence. **Fluid intelligence** refers to intellectual capacities that have no specific content but are used in processing information and approaching novel problems, such as the ability to draw inferences recognize patterns. **Crystallized intelligence** refers to people's store of knowledge, much of it learned from their culture, such as vocabulary and general world knowledge. At a lower hierarchical level are seven more specific factors: short-term memory, long-term memory, visual processing, auditory processing, processing speed on simple tasks, correct decision speed (processing speed on tasks that are much more difficult, such as solving problems), and quantitative knowledge (mathematical reasoning). Gf-Gc theory has two advantages:

- First, many of its dimensions make theoretical sense in light of research in cognitive science on the components of information processing, such as the distinctions between long-term and short-term (working) memory.
- Second, the theory can distinguish components of intelligence that change independently over the life span.

In general, crystallized intelligence—general knowledge— continues to increase through at least age 60, whereas fluid intelligence declines gradually but steadily in adulthood. The capacity to consolidate and retrieve long-term memories increases until age 30 and then levels off; processing speed and visual processing ability decline steadily after about age 25. By way of comparison what happens to a measure of "g" over time—namely, nothing. Proponents of Gf-Gc theory suggests that relying solely on "g" thus considerably understates the complexity of cognitive changes through the life span and fails to distinguish components of intelligence that have different developmental trajectories.

The information-processing approach

The information-processing approach tries to understand the processes that underlie intelligent behaviour (*Sternberg*, 1997). In other words, the information-processing approach looks at the "how" of intelligence and not just the "how much". It defines intelligence as a process rather than a measurable quantity, and it posits that individual differences in intelligence reflect differences in the cognitive operations people use in thinking (*Brody*, 1992; *Ceci*, 1990).

In principle, a cognitive psychologist interested in intelligence would test the abilities of subjects on various information—processing abilities, such as working memory capacity, efficiency of various longterm memory systems, and ability to apply strategies for manipulating mental representations to solve problems and make decisions. He would present subjects with tasks such as repeating digits to measure aspects of working memory or memorizing word lists to test explicit memory. For each process, a subject's score would be plotted on a frequency distribution (Fig 8.3). The cognitive psychologist might then try to see which of the many bell curves best predicted some criterion of achievement, such as academic performance or success at engineering, and whether some combination of these abilities is necessary for success in particular endeavours.

Researchers from this perspective have found that three variables are particularly important in explaining individual differences as assessed by intelligence tests. Speed of processing, knowledge base, and ability to acquire and apply mental strategies.

Speed of processing

In fact, processing speed appears to be an important aspect of intelligence and a strong correlate of IQ (*McGeorge*, 1996). One experimental design presents participants with pairs of letters and measures the amount of time they take to decide whether the letters are identical physically (as are the letters AA in Fig. 8.4) or identical in name (as in the pair Aa). Identifying

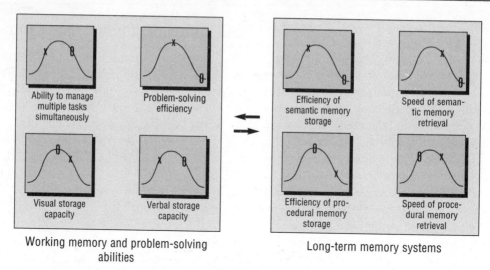

x = subject 1
O = subject 2

Fig. 8.3 Multiple components of information processing. People have different degrees of ability hence fall on different points of a bell-shaped curve on various components of information processing. Subject 2 is generally superior to subject 1 in problem-solving ability and verbal information processing

letter with the same name but different physical appearance is the more complicated of the two tasks; to judge whether two letters have the same name even though they do not look alike, the subject must perform an additional step, searching long-term memory for the name of each letter form before comparing the two symbols. The difference in response times between these two types of task reflects the speed of memory search (*Posner*, 1969).

Research shows children with above-average scholastic abilities tend to perform this kind of task more rapidly than average-ability children, as do college students with higher IQs than their peers (*Lindley & Smith*, 1992).

Knowledge base

Variation among individuals in intellectual functioning also reflects variation in their **knowledge base**—the information stored in long-term memory. Differences in knowledge base that affect performance include not only the amount of knowledge a person has but the way it is organized and its accessibility for retrieval.

Florists, for example, can generally recognize and classify flowers more quickly than people with less exposure to (and interest in) flowers.

Ability to acquire and apply cognitive strategies

A third variable that correlates with many measures of intelligence is the ability to acquire mental strategies (such as mnemonic devices and formulas for solving math problems) and apply them to new situations. Cognitive strategies are essential for many everyday tasks, from remembering grocery lists to calculating a server's tip. Their efficient use distinguishes children from adults and individuals with differing IQ levels from their peers. Children are less likely than adults to apply mnemonic strategies such as rehearsal in memorizing information, although their performance improves considerably when they are taught and encouraged to use them.

A theory of multiple intelligences

Intelligence tests may measure the kinds of

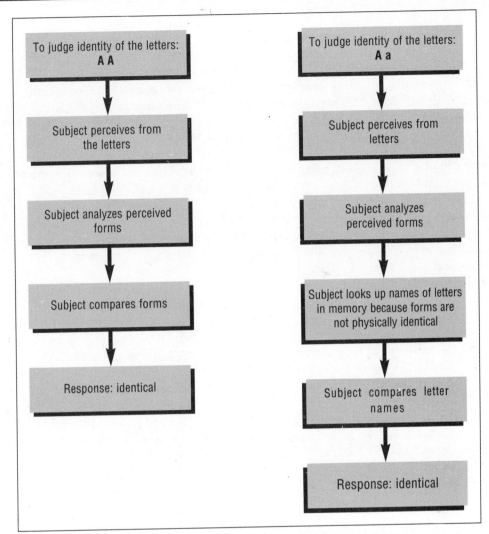

Fig. 8.4 Speed of processing. In this study of speed of processing, investigators measured the time subjects took to decide whether pairs of letters were physically identical (AA) or identical in name (Aa)

intellectual abilities that foster success in school, but what about practical intelligence (the ability to put plans into action in real life), emotional intelligence (the ability to read people's emotions and use one's own emotional responses adaptively), or creativity?

A third view of intelligence that addresses questions such as there is Howard Gardner's **theory of multiple intelligences** (Gardner, 1983). Gardner views intelligence as "an ability or set of abilities that is used to solve problems or fashion products that are of consequence in a particular cultural setting." He identifies seven intelligences: musical, bodily/ kinesthetic (such as control over the body and movement that distinguishes great athletes and dancers), spatial (the use of mental maps), linguistic or verbal, logical/mathematical, intrapersonal (self-understanding), and interpersonal (social skills). Gardner would map a person's intelligence on seven different bell curves, one for each type of intelligence, rather than on a single

IQ curve. Someone could be a brilliant mathematician but inhabit the lowest percentile of musical or interpersonal intelligence.

Gardner argues that defining intelligence only by the abilities assessed on IQ tests is problematic for several reasons. Although conventional IQ tests have some capacity to predict later occupational success, they are much better at predicting grades in school. A person with high interpersonal intelligence may become a superb salesperson despite having only average logical/mathematical abilities, or a brilliant composer may have poor linguistic skills. Furthermore the emphasis on verbal and logical/mathematical intelligence in IQ measures reflects a bias toward skills valued in technologically advanced societies.

Selecting intelligences

To recognize the existence of multiple forms of intelligence, Gardner recommends a simple exercise: Instead of asking "How smart are you?" try asking, "How are you smart?" (Chen & Gardner, 1997). The answer is likely to be a list of intellectual strengths and weaknesses, such as "I am a really good writer, but I am terrible at mathematics," that will include some of the intelligences he has isolated.

Gardner acknowledges that one can never develop "a single irrefutable and universally acceptable list of human intelligences." On what basis, then, did he choose each of his seven intelligences? One criterion was whether an intelligence could be isolated neuropsychologically. According to Gardner's view, people have multiple intelligences because they have multiple neural modules. Each module has its own modes of representation, its own rules or procedures and its own memory systems.

As intellectual skill that can be specifically affected or spared by brain damage qualifies as an independent intelligence. The modularity of intelligence means that a person's ability in one area does not predict ability in another (Gardner, 1983).

Another criterion emerged from savant and prodigy studies. **Savants** are individuals with extraordinary ability in one area but comparatively low functioning in others. For example, young man with an IQ in the mentally retarded range was able to memorize lengthy and complex piano pieces in only a few hearings (Sloboda, 1985).

The existence of **prodigies**—individuals with extraordinary and generally early-developing genius in one area but normal abilities in others—also supports the notion of separate, modular intelligence systems. Indeed, creative geniuses in fields such as music generally require strikingly little time to master their fields.

A third criterion for selecting an intelligence is its distinctive developmental course from childhood to adulthood. The fact that one domain may develop more quickly or slowly than others supports the notion of multiple intelligences. Children learn language and mathematics at very different paces. The existence of prodigies is again instructive. If a Mozart could write music before he could even read, then the neural systems involved in musical intelligence must be separate from those involved in processing language.

INTELLIGENCE TESTING

Psychologists use **psychometric instruments**—psychological tests that compare individuals in a population—to determine how people differ on dimensions such as personality attributes or intellectual abilities. **Intelligence tests** are measures designed to assess an individual's level of cognitive capabilities compared to other people in a population.

Galton believed that the building blocks of intelligence are simple perceptual, sensory and motor abilities. The earliest attempts at a psychological diagnosis of intelligence were made in the nineteenth century. Sir Francis Galton of England was the first to organize relatively large-scale systematic experiments to detect interindividual differences in the sphere of intelligence. He postulated the standard distribution of intelligence generally accepted today.

Binet's scale

Pioneering work was done by Alfred Binet, in France; he published (with T. Simon) in 1905 the first procedure to justify the use of the term "intelligence test" in its present sense.

Unlike Galton, Binet believed that a true measure of intelligence is an individual's performance on *complex* tasks of memory, judgement, and comprehension (*Berg*, 1992). Binet was also less interested in comparing intellectual functioning in adults than in measuring intellectual potential in children.

Binet's purpose was in fact quite practical. In 1904, an education commission in France recommended the establishment of special schools for retarded children. This project required some objective way of distinguishing these children from their intellectually normal peers. Binet and his associate, *Theodore Simon*, noted that problem—solving abilities increase with age, so they constructed a series of tasks ranging in difficulty from simple to complex to capture the ability of children at different ages. A seven-year old could explain the difference between paper and cardboard, for instance, whereas a typical five-year old could not (Peterson, 1925).

To express a child's level of intellectual development, Binet and Simon (1908) introduced the concept of mental age. **Mental age (MA)** is the average age at which children achieve a particular score. A child with a chronological (or actual) age of 5 who can answer questions at a seven-year-old level has a mental age of 7. A five-year old who can answer the questions expected for her own age but not for higher ages has a mental age of 5. Thus, for the average child, mental age and chronological age coincide. From this standpoint, a mentally retarded child is just what the term implies: retarded, or slowed, in cognitive development. A mentally retarded seven-year-old might miss questions at the seven - and six-year-old levels and be able to answer only some of the five-year-old items. Fig (8.5).

Binet's scale was translated and extensively revised by Lewis Terman of Standford University, whose revision was known as the **Standford-Binet Scale** (1916). Perhaps the most important modification was the **intelligence quotient**, or **IQ**, a score meant to quantify intellectual functioning to allow comparison among individuals. To arrive at an IQ score, Terman relied on a formula for expressing the relation between an individual's mental age and chronological age developed a few years earlier in Germany. The formula derives a child's IQ by dividing mental age by chronological age (CA) and multiplying by 100:

$$IQ = (MA/CA) \times 100$$

Thus, if an eight-year-old performs at the level of a 12-year-old (that is, displays a mental age of 12), the child's IQ is 12/8 x 100, or 150. Similarly, a 12-year-old child whose test score is equivalent to that expected of an eight-year-old has an IQ of 66; and a 12-year-old who performs at the expected level of a 12-year-old has an IQ of 100. By definition, then, a person of average intelligence has an IQ of 100.

Group tests

At the time of Terman's 1916 revision of his test, the United States was involved in world war I, and the army needed to recruit hundreds of thousands of soldiers from among millions of men, many of them recent immigrants. Testing IQ promised a way of determining quickly which men were mentally fit for military service and, of those, which were likely to make good officers (*Weinberg*, 1989).

The army appointed a committee that included Terman to adapt mental testing to these needs. The result was two tests, the army Alpha for literate adults and the army Beta for men who were either illiterate or did not speak english. Unlike the Standford-Binet, which required one-to-one administration by trained personnel, the army tests were **group tests**, paper-and-pencil measures that can be administered to a roomful of people at a time. Between september 1917 and january 1919, over 1.7 million men took the army Alpha test. Group tests are widely used today to assess IQ and related attributes.

The wechsler intelligence scales

Although the army Beta tried to circumvent the problem of language, the intelligence tests used early in this century were linguistically and culturally biased toward native-born English speakers. *David Wechsler* attempted to minimize these biases by creating a new instrument, the Wechsler-Bellevue tests (Wechsler, 1939). The latest renditions of these tests are the **Wechsler Adult Intelligence Scale—Third Edition**, or **WAIS-III** (1997), and the child version (appropriate through age 16), the **Wechsler Intelligence Scale for children**, or **WISC-III** (1991). As measured by the WAIS-III, IQ is a composite score derived from 11 of 14 subtests; six of these subtests depend on verbal ability and other five do

AGE	TYPE OF ITEM	DESCRIPTION
2	3-hole from board	Places forms (circle, triangle, square in correct holes after demonstration.
	Block building : tower	Builds a 4-block tower from model after demonstration
3	Block building : bridge	Builds a bridge consisting of 2 side blocks and 1 top block from-model after demonstration.
	Pure vocabulary	Names10 of 18 line drawings.
4	Naming objects from memory	One of 3 objects (for example, car, dog, or shoe) is covered after child has seen them; child then names object from memory.
	Picture identification	Points to correct pictures of objects on a card in response to "Show me what we cook on" or "What do we carry when it is raining?"
7	Similarities	Answers such questions as "In what way are coal and wood alike? Ship and automobile?"
	Copying a diamond	Draws 3 diamonds following a printed sample.
8	Vocabulary	Defines 8 words from a list.
	Memory for stories	Listens to a story, then answer questions about it.
9	Verbal absurdities	Says what is foolish about stories similar to "I walking down the street with his hands in his pockets and twirling a brand new cane."
	Digit reversal	Repeats 4 digits backward.
Afterage adult	Vocabulary	Defines 20 words from a list (same list as at age 8, above).
	Proverbs	Explains in own words the meaning of two or more common proverbs.
	Orientation	Answer questions similar to "Which direction would you have to face so your left hand would be toward the south?"

Fig. 8.5 Some items from the Stanford-Binet Intelligence scale. On the average, these items should be passed at about the ages indicated

Verbal Subtests		Performance Subtests	
Comprehension:	"What does this saying means: 'A rolling stone gathers no moss?"	Picture arrangement	Putting a set of pictures in order so that they tell a coherent story.
		Picture completion	Finding incomplete or missing parts of pictures that are otherwise complete.
Arithmetic:	"A boy ran 50 yards in 10 seconds. How many yards did he run per second?"	Block design	Arranging coloured blocks into a design that matches one that is pictured on a card.
Similarities:	"How are fast and slow alike?"	Object assembly	Putting pieces of a jig sawlike puzzle together correctly.
Digit Span:	"Repeat the following numbers backward: 8–4–2–1–9."	Digit symbol	Learning to use a coding system in which nonsense symbols (for example, and represent numbers.

Fig. 8.6 Sample items similar to those on selected WAIS-III verbal and performance subtests

not. The verbal subtests require facility at symbolic thought and language, such as knowledge of general information, arithmetic skills, ability to hold and manipulate numbers in working memory, and vocabulary. The non-verbal subtests present tasks such as picture arrangement (arranging a series of out-of-order cartoon frames into their correct order to make a story) and picture completion (finding missing elements in a picture) that do not depend as heavily on verbal thinking.

In addition to a single, overall IQ score, the WAIS-III yields separate scores for each of the 14 subtests and overall scores for verbal and performance (nonverbal) IQ. It also yields more specific subscales of verbal comprehension (how well the person thinks using language, a predominantly left-hemisphere function), perceptual organization (how well the person thinks using visual images, a predominantly right-hemisphere function), working memory (which relies substantially on functioning of the frontal lobes), and processing speed (which probably is not localized to any particular region of the brain). This allows psychologists to identify specific problem areas or strengths.

Frequency distribution of IQ scores

Wechsler was responsible for another important innovation in IQ testing. The formula originally devised for deriving IQ (MA/CA x 100) was useful in assessing children's test performance, but it was logically inconsistent when applied to adult test scores. As people grew older, the denominator (chronological age) in the formula grew larger, while the numerator (mental age) remained relatively constant. Thus, subjects seemed to become less intelligent with age. Although this supports the intuitive theories held by many teenagers about their parents; it is not really true. Further, the differences between a 26-year-old and a 22-year-old are not comparable to the differences between a 5 year old and a 10-year-old, whose abilities are developing at a rapid pace. Wechsler remedied these problems by abandoning the concept of mental age and calculating IQ as an individual's position relative to peers of the same age on a frequency distribution.

A frequency distribution describes the frequency of various scores in the population. Like the distributions for weight, height, and many other human traits, the distribution for IQ takes

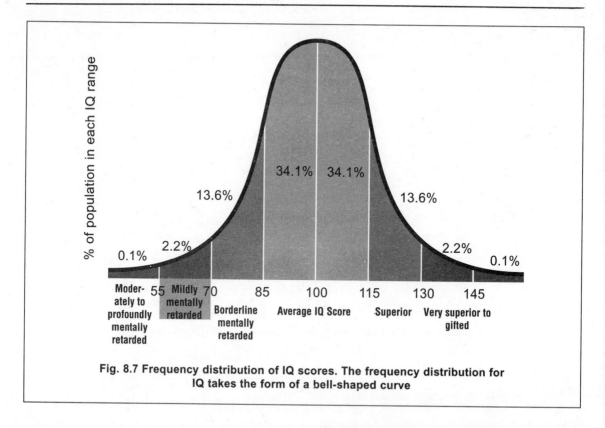

Fig. 8.7 Frequency distribution of IQ scores. The frequency distribution for
IQ takes the form of a bell-shaped curve

the form of a normal, bell-shaped curve (Fig 8.7). A normal curve is a frequency distribution in which the vast majority of subjects receive scores close to the mean, resulting in the bell-shaped curve. Extremely high IQ scores, such as 150, are relatively rare, as are extremely low scores, such as 50. Most people's scores fall within the average range (between about 85 and 115), while a progressively smaller percentage fall within ranges that deviate farther from the norm.

HEREDITY AND INTELLIGENCE

Having, some concept of what intelligence is and how to measure it, we have now come to address the most controversial issue surrounding the concept of intelligence: its origins. We begin by examining research on the roots of differences among individuals in IQ and then turn to the thorny issue of differences among groups.

Individual differences in IQ

The influence of both nature and nurture on the individual differences in intelligence is well established. In humans, an enriched home environment, positive mother-child interactions that fosterer interest and exploration, and maternal knowledge about child rearing and child development are among the best predictors of a child's performance on tests of IQ and language in the toddler and preschool years.

Environmental effects such as these persist into adolescence. In one *longitudinal study* (a study following individual overtime), the investigators examined the relation between the number of risk factors to which the child was exposed in early childhood and the child's IQ at age four and 13. Among these risk factors were maternal lack of education, maternal mental illness, minority status (associated with, among other things, low standard of living and inferior schools), and family size. The child's IQ varied inversely with the number of risk factors: the more risk factors, the lower the child's IQ. Furthermore, low maternal IQ and multiple risks at age four were highly predictive of IQ at age 13.

The results of this study are striking, but they cannot definitively tease apart the relative contributions of heredity and environment. Maternal IQ could influence the child's IQ genetically or environmentally, and it could indirectly influence some environmental risk factors, such as low maternal education level. Other methods—notably twin, family, and adoption studies—can, however, more clearly distinguish some of the influences of nature and nurture.

Results of twin, family and adoption studies

The data across dozens of studies suggest that IQ, like nearly every psychological trait on which individuals differ, reflects a combination of heredity and environment. On the other hand, the data clearly suggest an environmental impact: Being born at the same time (and presumably being treated more alike than siblings who are not twins) produces a higher correlation between dizygotic twins than between siblings, even though both are related.

On the other hand, the data on monozygotic twins suggest a strong genetic effect. The higher correlation between monozygotic and dizygotic twins reared together does not in itself prove a genetic effect; parents tend to treat identical twins more similarly than fraternal twins, which could also influence the size of the correlations between their IQs (Beckwith, 1991). However, most data suggest that the genetic effect is more powerful (Kendler, 1993).

Adoption studies provide a particularly important source of information on the relative impact of heredity and environment. Most of these studies compare the IQs of adopted children with those of other members of their adoptive family, their biological family, and a control group matched for the child's age, sex, socioeconomic status, and ethnic background. Beginning with the earliest adoption studies conducted in the first half of this century (Skodak & Skeels, 1949), the results have identified genetic influences as the primary determinant of differences between individuals on IQ, with environmental circumstances substantially limiting or augmenting the effects of native ability.

The impact of the family environment decreases with age as the impact of genetics increases. Similarities among the IQs of family members are apparently a greater reflection of their shared genes than their shared environment (*Brody*, 1992).

Group differences: Race and intelligence

Arthur Jensen created a storm of controversy over two decades ago when he concluded, based on the available data, that "between one-half and three-fourth of the average IQ difference between American Negroes and Whites is attributable to genetic factors." Many denounced Jensen's interpretation of the data as blatantly racist, questioning both his science and his politics. The potential implications of Jensen's hypothesis made it among the most passionately debated in the history of psychology.

Other research suggests that the average difference in standardized achievement test scores between blacks and whites in the United States has diminished in recent decades as educational opportunities have expanded and African Americans have climbed up the socioeconomic ladder (*Williams & Ceci*, 1997). Further, across all the industrialized countries, IQ appears to be rising, so that a person who is of only average IQ today would have been above average in comparison to other people 50 years ago. Although the reasons for this are unclear, this steady increase probably reflects the greater complexity of the occupational and technical tasks required of people today than in their grandparent's day. In any case, these data suggest that social and environmental conditions can lead to changes in IQ as large as the average difference between blacks and whites. As a leading researcher in the area concludes, "it is highly unlikely that genetic differences between the races could account for the major portion of the usually observed differences in the performance levels of [blacks and whites]" (*Scarr & Carter-Saltzmann, 1982*).

THE EXTREMES OF INTELLIGENCE

Having explored the nature of intelligence and the factors that contribute to it, we now turn to the extremes of intelligence—mental retardation and giftedness—and to the relationship between creativity and intelligence.

Mental retardation

A **mentally retarded** person is significantly below average in general intellect functioning (IQ less than 70), with deficits in adaptive functioning that appear in more than one realm (such as communicating with others, living autonomously, interacting socially, functioning in school or work, and maintaining safety and health) and are first evident in childhood (American Association on Mental Retardation, 1992; American Psychiatric Association, 1994). IQ is easier to quantify than adaptive functioning, which includes a broad range of skills such as social judgement and self-care abilities, but IQ scores alone are not enough to diagnose retardation (*Wechsler, 1997*).

This definition encompasses a wide spectrum of disabilities, ranging from mild to moderate retardation (IQ between 50 and 70) to more severe conditions (IQ below 50). By far the largest number (about 75 to 90 percent) of people classified as retarded fall into the mild to moderate category. Individuals in this range can learn academic skills at an elementary school level, and as adults they are capable of self-supporting activities, although often in special, supervised environments. Their retardation is frequently not diagnosed until they reach school age, when teachers notice not only their difficul-

ty with academic demands but also troubles they may experience on the playground, at lunch, and in extracurricular activities. Only about 10 percent of retarded individuals are classified as severely to profoundly retarded; in these cases, retardation is often accompanied by physiological handicaps and a mortality rate three or more times the norm.

Causes of mental retardation

Mental retardation can stem from any of a number of catastrophe might be a genetic or a chromosomal defect. **Down syndrome**, for example, is usually caused by a failure of the mother's twenty-first chromosome pair to separate. The two chromosomes join with the single twenty-first chromosome from the father, forming an abnormal condition known as **trisomy 21**. The result is a distinctive physical appearance (Fig. 8.8) and mental retardation. Individuals with down syndrome have wide-set eyes, flattened facial features, and stunted body shape. Doctors can now diagnose Down Syndrome during pregnancy through genetic testing of the amniotic fluid that surrounds the fetus.

Severe forms of retardation are often related to a genetic abnormality, as with down syndrome and **phenylketonuria (PKU)**. Phenylketonuria reflects the presence of a recessive gene that caus-

Fig. 8.8 Down Syndrome

es the body to produce insufficient quantities of an enzyme that normally converts the amino acid phenylalanine into another amino acid. Without the appropriate enzyme, phenylalanine is converted instead into a toxin that damages the infant's developing central nervous system, resulting in severe mental retardation. If detected early, PKU is treatable by minimizing phenylalanine in the child's diet.

Other physiological causes of retardation are environmental, not genetic. For example, pregnant women who contract rubella (German measles), scarlet fever, syphilis, or even mumps may give birth to infants who have suffered brain damage as a result. Also, insult or injury to the brain or nervous system before or after birth may result in retardation. Such damage may be done by x-rays, by inappropriate drugs, by severe pressure on the infant's head during birth, by oxygen shortages during or after birth, and even by severe maternal malnutrition.

Testing mental retardation

Some forms of retardation, such as those caused by nutritional or other environmental deficits, may be prevented or treated if diagnosed in time. However, most forms are not curable in the sense of restoring the person to normality. Unfortunately, though, once serious retardation has been identified, there is usually no way to undo it. However, special training can sometimes produce modest changes in IQ and adaptive behaviour. Training can also enhance the retarded person's all-important social skills. A friendly style and an endearing smile can be major assests for a down-syndrome child like the one shown in fig. (8.8); such simple social skills may go a long way toward ensuring that people outside the family meet the child's legitimate needs for help and affection and that peers will accept the child. Later in life, the retarded person's ability to live in community settings such as neighbourhood group homes will depend partly on the social and self-help skills the individual has developed. In short, education and training are not likely to cure

mental retardation, but they can make a big difference in the personal, social and occupational adjustment of the retarded person.

Giftedness

Mental retardation occupies the extreme left-hand side of the bell-shaped IQ distribution. People whose IQs fall on the extreme right-hand side are generally classified as gifted. Like definitions of intelligence, definitions of giftedness depend on whatever skills or talents a society labels as gifts.

Definitions of giftedness depend on definitions of intelligence. In accord with Gardner's theory of multiple intelligences, many psychologists consider giftedness at least partially domain specific or limited to particular abilities. The prodigy who can mentally multiply two three-digit numbers in 30 seconds may be gifted in mathematics but have only normal abilities in other areas. A broader definition of giftedness, proposed by psychologist *Robert Sternberg* identifies domains of special talent, ranging from intellectual skills (such as verbal, mathematical, spatial, and memory skills) to artistic and physical abilities (Sternberg & Davidson, 1985).

Creativity and intelligence

A quality related to both intelligence and giftedness is **creativity**, which can be defined as the ability to produce valued outcomes in a novel way. Creativity is moderately correlated with intelligence, but not all people who are high in "g" are high in creativity. In general, intelligence in a particular area seems necessary but not sufficient for creativity. A person who has little ability in mathematics or architecture would be hard pressed to solve problems in those fields creatively, but many competent mathematicians and architects have no flare for innovation. Individuals with IQs below 120 are less likely to display creative thinking than those with a higher IQ, but above 120, the correlation between intelligence and creativity is essentially zero.

Because people do not express creativity in any uniform way, creativity can be extremely difficult to measure. Thus, some researchers have turned to the study of eminent people, such as Enstein and Darwin, to learn about the nature and origins of creativity (Simonton, 1997). Others have attempted to devise measures of creativity that can be administered in the laboratory. One strategy is to measure **divergent thinking**, the ability to generate multiple possibilities in a given situation, such as describing all the possible uses of a paper clip. At face value, divergent thinking seems to be related to creativity because it involves finding unusual or unconventional ways of solving a problem.

The best-known creativity tests measure either the thought processes involved in creativity or the personality characteristics of creative people. Evaluating creativity by examining attributes of the person instead of the process reflects the view that creativity is as much as personality trait as a cognitive trait or aspect of intelligence. Indeed, research has linked creativity to such personality traits as high energy, intuitiveness, independence, self-acceptance, a willingness to take risks, and an intensely passionate way of engaging in certain tasks for the sheer pleasure of it. Creative activity also depends in part on environmental conditions. Social and economic circumstances, such as exposure to role models and access to financial resources, can also foster or hinder creative activity.

APTITUDES

The terms *intelligence, ability,* and *aptitude* are often used interchangeably to refer to behaviour that is used to predict future learning or performance. However, subtle differences exist between the terms. The tests designed to measure these attributes differ in several significant ways.

An aptitude test

Like intelligence tests, aptitude tests measure a student's overall performance across a broad range of mental capabilities. But aptitude tests also often include items, which measure more specialized abilities—such as verbal and numerical skills—that predict scholastic performance in educational programs.

Compared to achievement tests, aptitude tests cover a broader area and look at a wider range of experiences. Achievement tests tend to measure recent learning and are closely tied to particular school subjects.

Aptitude tests tell us what a student brings to the task regardless of the specific curriculum that the student has already experienced. The difference between aptitude and achievement tests is sometimes a matter of degree. Some aptitude and achievement tests look a lot alike. In fact, the higher a student goes in levels of education, the more the content of aptitude tests resembles achievement tests. This is because the knowledge that a student has already accumulated is a good predictor of success at advanced levels.

Value of aptitude testing

Research data show that individually administered aptitude tests have the following qualities:

- They are excellent predictors of future scholastic achievement.
- They provide ways of comparing a child's performance with that of other children in the same situation.
- They provide a profile of strengths and weaknesses.
- They assess differences among individuals.
- They have uncovered hidden talents in some children, thus improving their educational opportunities.
- They are valuable tools for working with handicapped children.

In addition, group aptitude tests—usually given as part of a group achievement battery of tests—can be given quickly and inexpensively to large numbers of children. Children who obtain extreme scores can be easily identified to receive further specialized attention. Aptitude tests are valuable in making program and curricula decisions. They can also be used for grouping students as long as grouping is flexible.

Uses of aptitude test results

In general, aptitude test results have three major uses:

Instructional
Teachers can use aptitude test results to adapt their curricula to match the level of their students, or to design assignments for students who differ widely. Aptitude test scores can also help teachers form realistic expectations of students. Knowing something about the aptitude level of students in a given class can help a teacher identify which students are not learning as much as could be predicted on the basis of aptitude scores. For instance, if a whole class was performing less well than was predicted from aptitude test results, then curriculum, objectives, teaching methods, or student characteristics might be investigated.

Administrative
Aptitude test scores can identify the general aptitude level of a high school, for example. This can be helpful in determining how much emphasis should be given to college preparatory programs. Aptitude tests can be used as help identify students to be accelerated or given extra attention, for grouping, and in predicting job-training performance.

Guidance
Guidance counselors use aptitude tests to help parents develop realistic expectations for their child's school performance and to help students understand their own strengths and weaknesses.

How to improve aptitude?

Although studies seem to suggest that aptitude test scores cannot be improved, other research show that may not be the case. Tests such as the **Scholastic Aptitude Tests** contain many questions that are content specific, particularly in mathematics areas. Performance on these specific types of items is trainable.

Some experts feel that short-term cramming might not affect aptitude test scores. However, long-term instruction in broad cognitive skills might improve general test performance. Cognitive theory and research suggest that learning ability can be improved by training students in learning strategies. Improving academic aptitude may be possible through a systematic curriculum that complements direct training in learning strategies with both the development of general thinking approaches and the application of those approaches over a variety of different tasks and content areas.

What has been learned about training to improve aptitude can be summarized as follows:

- Attempts to train aptitude must go well beyond practice and feedback. What's needed is intensive training in strategies involved in task performance along with higher level monitoring and control strategies involved in guiding performance and in transferring skills to new areas.
- Educational efforts to improve aptitude need to be long-term.
- Abilities of students and methods of training interact. Attempts to train strategies must fit the tested aptitudes of students.
- Practice and feedback can be effective when students are already proficient in the ability to be trained.
- Intrusive training may be harmful to high aptitude students.
- Training ability works best when treatment utilizes some of the student's other strengths.
- Some aspects of intellectual aptitude may be more easily trained than others.

■ ■

CHAPTER 9

Motivation

THE FUNCTIONS OF MOTIVATION

THEORETICAL CONCEPTS OF MOTIVATION
— Drive theories
— Incentive theories
— Opponent—process theory
— Optimal-level theories

BIOLOGICAL MOTIVATION
— Homeostasis
— Hunger
— Thirst
— Sexual motivation

SOCIAL MOTIVES
— Measurement of social motives
— Need for Achievement
— Need for power or power motivation
— Human aggression
— Need for Affiliation

MOTIVES TO KNOW AND TO BE EFFECTIVE
— Stimulation and exploration needs
— Effectance motivation
— Self-actualization motivation

CONFLICTS AND FRUSTRATIONS
— Definition of conflicts
— Types of conflict
— Frustration

Motivation

The word **motivation** derives from the Latin to *move (movere)* and refers to the moving force that energizes behaviour. Motives cannot be directly observed but are inferred from behaviour. Motivation has two components: what people want to do and how strongly they want to do it. The first component refers to the *direction* in which activity is motivated, namely, which goals the person is pursuing or avoiding. The range of goals humans can be motivated to pursue is truly extraordinary, from going to the library, to murdering a lover in a fit of rage. Motives also vary in their *strength*. People may have dozens of motives available to them at any given point, but they only act on those that currently "move" them.

Motivation is one of the hypothetical processes involved in the determination of behaviour in addition to the effect of a stimulus or perceived situation, the processes of learning and certain other factors, such as abilities. Whereas abilities primarily influence the yield or level of adaptation of a specific pattern of behaviour, motivation determines to level of activation, intensity and consistency as well as general direction. Learning or acquired associations determine (for non-instinctive behaviour) the concrete direction toward a given object. It is however, clear that the effect of stimuli is not always distinctly separate from the effect of motivation. Some categories of excitation, above all those for which internal stimuli are responsible (as well as those caused by external stimuli which lead to a disagreeable condition), are often interpreted as corresponding to primary needs (homeostatic disequilibrium), while other stimuli (e.g., objects) have valences and act as motives or releasors. The state of motivation is then understood as a factor which lowers the stimulus threshold for these stimuli.

THE FUNCTIONS OF MOTIVATION

Motivation as an energizer should explain behaviour. A distinction can be made between the factors which determine the general degree of activation of the organism and its state of excitation and alertness and the question as to why an individual performs specific actions. While the first problem may be considered from the standpoint of energy sources which form the basis of vital activity in general, or from the angle of activity of the nervous system (e.g., the reticular formation), the explanation of the fact that an individual is more interested in one class of objects than another is a matter for motivation studies as such.

This in turn raises the problem of regulative behaviour. The fundamental aspect of motivation lies in the regulative influence. This problem can be solved if two different levels of control are assumed. On the one hand, control may signify the actual path followed by behaviour to reach the given target which it had already achieved before, on an earlier occasion. This concrete form of control in based on learning, except in the case of innate or instinctive behaviour. However, the fact that an individual who is in a state of motivation or need and turns away from certain objects in order to dwell on others, shows that motivated behaviour has a general orientation or control. In this search for a relatively large category of objects or situations we can distinguish the general control of behaviour which E.C. Tolman defined as its *"purposiveness"* and which represents nothing other than its orientation toward a specific aim. The fact that some objects or situations, unlike others, evoke a state of reduced need, satisfaction and adaptation is explained by this fundamental and implied orientation.

The function of motivation in relation to behaviour (in addition to the roles of arousal and control) resides in the fact that it endows a range of behaviour with unity and comprehensive importance. In fact it is motivation which through its orientation toward a target object means that a series of movements which vary widely from the physical angle, represent behaviour in the true sense of the word, i.e., an appropriate reaction to a situation.

THEORETICAL CONCEPTS OF MOTIVATION

The actual nature of the basic needs and their effects on behaviour has been considered in terms of various theoretical concepts.

Drive theories

According to *Freud*, humans, like other animals, are motivated by internal tension states, or **drives**, that build up until they are satisfied. Freud proposed two basic drives: sex and aggression. The sexual drive includes desires for love, lust, and intimacy, whereas the aggressive drive includes not only blatantly aggressive or sadistic impulses but desires to control or master other people and the environment. These drives may express themselves in subtle ways. Aggression, for example, can underlie sarcastic comments or enjoyment of violent movies.

Although few psychologists (or even psychoanalysts) now accept Freud's theory of aggression as an instinct that builds up until discharged.

In general, drive theories say the following: When an internal driving state is aroused, the individual is pushed to engage in behaviour which will lead to a goal that reduces the intensity of the driving state. In human beings, at least, reaching the appropriate goal which reduces the drive state is pleasurable and satisfying. Thus motivation is said to consist of:

1. A driving state
2. The goal-directed behaviour initiated by the driving state
3. The attainment of an appropriate goal
4. The reduction of the driving state and subjective satisfaction and relief when the goal is reached.

After a time, the driving state builds up again to push behaviour toward the appropriate goal. The sequence of events just described is sometimes called the *motivational cycle*.

Some theorists, including Freud conceived of the driving state as being inborn, or instinctive. Other drive theorists have emphasized the role of learning in the origin of driving states. Such **learned drives**, as they called them, originate in the person's or animal's training or past experience and thus differ from one individual to another. Because of previous use of the drugs, a heroin addict, for example, develops a drive to get the substance and is therefore pushed in that direction. And in the realm of human social motives, people are said to have learned drives for power, aggression, or achievement, to name just a few of the social motives, such learned driving states become enduring characteristics of the particular person and push that person toward appropriate goals; another person may learn other social motives and be driven toward different goals.

Incentive theories

Although drive-reduction theories explain a wide range of behaviours, they leave others unexplained. Why, for instance, do people sometimes stay up until 3:00 a.m. to finish a novel, even though they are exhausted? And why are some people unable to refuse dessert, even after a filling meal?

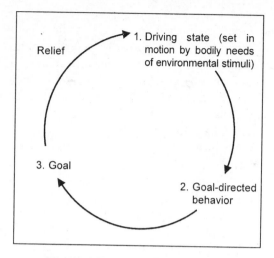

Fig. 9.1 The motivational cycle

Such behaviours seem motivated more by the presence of an external stimulus or reward—called an **incentive**—than by an internal need state. Incentives control much of human behaviour as when a person not previously hungry is enticed by the smells of a bakery or an individual not previously sexually aroused becomes excited by an attractive, scantily clad body on a beach. In these cases, stimuli activate drive states rather than eliminate them. Drive-reduction theories also have difficulty explaining the motivation to create stimulation, encounter novelty, or avoid boredom, which is present to varying degrees in different individuals and even in other animal species (*Zuckermann*, 1994).

Thus, in contrast with the push of drive theories, *incentive theories* are "**pull theories**" of **motivation**; because of certain characteristics they have, the goal objects pull behaviour toward them. The goal objects which motivate behaviour are known as *incentives*. An important part of many incentive theories is that individuals expect pleasure from the attainment of what are called **positive incentives** and from the avoidance of what are known as **negative incentives**. In a work-a-day world, motivation seems to be more a matter of expected incentives—wages, salaries, bonuses, vacations, and the like—than of drives and their reduction.

Opponent—process theory

The neo-hedonic need theory considers to desire for pleasure (or, more accurately, to avoid disagreeable sensations) as the decisive dynamic basis of behaviour. The opponent process theory says we are motivated to seek goals which give us good emotional feelings and avoid goals resulting in displeasure. Furthermore, this theory says that many emotional—motivating states are followed by opposing, or opposite states.

For example, a person using heroin for the first time may feel an initial rush of intense pleasure; followed by a less-intense, good feeling; and then by craving and displeasure before the emotional—motivating state returns to normal—the baseline.

Starting from the baseline, fig. (9.2) shows the general course followed by emotional states. The peak point of the emotional—motivational state (called state A) occurs soon after the emotion—provoking situation is encountered. Note that state A can be a pleasant or an unpleasant emotional state. Next, with the emotion—provoking stimulus still present, the intensity of the emotional—motivational state adapts and declines to a steady state. When the emotion—provoking situation terminates, an after-reaction occurs in which the emotional—motivational state (state B) is the opposite of state A. State B (the *opponent state*) gradually declines until baseline is again reached. Thus, the sequence of emotional—motivational changes goes like this:

Baseline ⟶ Peak of state A ⟶ Decline of state A to a steady state ⟶ State B ⟶ Decline of state B to baseline.

Now, suppose that the same emotion—provoking situation has happened many times. With repeated usage, as drug tolerance develops, the heroin user will experience less pleasure (less state A), while the intensity of the unpleasant after response (state B) will increase. At first, the heroin user was motivated by the expected pleasure of the rush; after becoming a confirmed user, he or she is now motivated to use the drug in order to

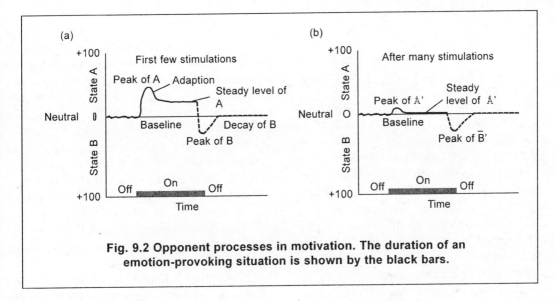

Fig. 9.2 Opponent processes in motivation. The duration of an emotion-provoking situation is shown by the black bars.

reduce the discomfort felt in the drug-free state. Either way, the user is hooked and is motivated to use the drug.

This theory gives us a way of thinking, about the basis of some learned motives. The heroin addict acquires a need for the drug in order to prevent the unpleasant consequences of withdrawal.

Optimal-level theories

In general, these are hedonistic theories which say that there is a certain optimal, or best, level of arousal that is pleasurable. Optimal level theories might be called "just-right theories." The individual is motivated to behave in such a way as to maintain the optimal level of arousal. For instance, if arousal is too low, a person will seek, situations or stimuli to increase arousal; if arousal is too high, behaviour will be directed towards decreasing it. Imagine yourself on an extremely busy day at work; too much is happening, and you are highly aroused. More than likely, you find yourself doing things such as taking the telephone off the hook in order to reduce the overload of arousal to which you are being subjected. In doing so, you are behaving so as to move toward a level of optimal arousal. And low levels of arousal (such as occur when not much is happening and we are bored) may

also motivate behaviour directed at increasing arousal levels to the optimum.

BIOLOGICAL MOTIVATION

The biological motives are, to a large extent, rooted in the physiological state of the body. There are many such motives, including hunger, thirst, a desire for sex, temperature regulation, sleep, pain avoidance, and a need for oxygen.

Homeostasis

Survival involves basic motives such as eating, drinking, and sleeping, which are regulated by a biological process called homeostasis. **Homeostasis** refers to the body's tendency to maintain a relatively constant state that permits cells to live and function; it literally means "same state." Since cells live within a fairly narrow range of conditions, the body monitors such variables as temperature and nutrient levels through specialized receptors. These receptors provide **feedback**, information about a variable in relation to its *set point,* or biologically optimal level (e.g., 98.6 degrees Fahrenheit for temperature). The hypothalamus and other central nervous system structures use this feedback to determine whether the nervous system needs to respond with autonomic responses (such as shivering or sweating) or voluntary responses (putting on or taking off a jacket) to prevent body heat from diverging too far in either direction from its set point.

Thus, the biological motive states are aroused, in large part, by departures from homeostasis; and the motivated behaviour driven by these homeostatic imbalances helps to restore the balanced condition.

Certain hormones, or "chemical messengers" circulating in the blood are also important in the arousal of some biological motive states. For instance, sexual motivation in lower animals is tied to hormone levels. In human beings, however, sensory stimuli, rather than hormone levels, are the most important triggers of sexual drive.

Sensory stimuli and *incentives,* also play a role in the arousal of other drive states; the smell of a savory dish can arouse hunger in a person who is not biologically, very far out of homeostatic balance. Perhaps the best example of a drive state aroused by sensory stimulation is pain. Pain acts as a motive and is aroused almost entirely by sensory stimulation.

Hunger

Hunger is a primary, basic motive necessary for life. There are three theories that explain hunger motivation:

(a) Stomach contractions theory
(b) Glucose or blood sugar level theory
(c) Role of hypothalamus

(a) Stomach contractions theory

Cannon suggested that hunger was caused by stomach contractions after he performed an experiment in which he abstained from food for several days and then swallowed a balloon that was connected by a tube to a pressure-measuring device. When the stomach contracted, it squeezed the balloon, and increased pressure was indicated. Without seeing the pressure measurements, he signaled when he sensed a hunger pang. The sensations corresponded with

stomach contractions. Subsequent studies have cast some doubt on this famous experiment. It has been shown that the presence of the balloon in the stomach stimulates stomach contractions, for example. However, powerful stomach contractions and hunger pangs do occur during starvation, although they are reported to last for only three to five days. None of this tells us whether stomach contractions, as sensitizing stimulus, are necessary and sufficient to arouse and sustain the hunger drive. Other evidence suggests that stomach contractions are unnecessary to the hunger drive, although they may contribute to the aroused and sustained behaviour for a time.

Some of the evidence comes from operations performed on people with stomach ulcers. In some cases nerves leading to the stomach were cut to block parasympathetic facilitation of automatic stomach contractions and stop the stimulation of acid secretion by the stomach. Denervating the stomach also cuts sensory nerves and eliminates sensations caused by stomach contractions. It does not alter the arousal or regulation of eating behaviour in these patients. In other ulcer operations all or part of the stomach except that less can be eaten at one time (until the small intestine enlarges to store food as the stomach once did). Although these patients eat less, they eat more frequently, and food intake is thus regulated as before.

Therefore, stomach contractions as a sensitizing stimulus are neither necessary nor sufficient to arouse or sustain the hunger drive, although they may contribute to the regulation of normal food intake.

(b) Glucose or blood sugar level theory

Glucose or blood sugar level is now believed to be an important substance involved in the initiation of hunger motivation and feeding. It has long been known that injections of the hormone insulin, which lowers levels of circulating blood sugar, will induce hunger and eating. Observations and experiments indicate that the glucose signal for hunger is triggered more by the rate at which the glucose is being used by the body than by its absolute levels in the blood. Low rates of glucose use, such as occur after long periods without food and in diabetics, are correlated with reports of hunger and eating behaviour; high utilization rates such as occur just after meals, relate to satiety, i.e., the absence of hunger motivation. Glucose, of course, is not the only body fuel. Others are free fatty acids from the breakdown of fat stores and ketones from the metabolism of free fatty acids. The role of these fuels in stimulating hunger motivation is just beginning to be appreciated.

(c) Role of hypothalamus

The hypothalamus has long been considered important in the regulation of hunger motivation. The classic work of the 1940s and 1950s emphasized the contributions of two regions of the hypothalamus, namely the lateral hypothalamus (LH) and the ventromedial hypothalamus (VMH). The lateral hypothalamus was considered to be an excitatory region for hunger motivation, while the ventromedial hypothalamus was said to be involved in the cessation of eating—that is satiety. These ideas were either destroyed by lesion or electrically stimulated by means of small wires called as electrodes, placed in the brain. Electrical stimulation of the lateral hypothalamus was found to elicit eating; ventromedial stimulation was found to stop ongoing eating behaviour. The lesions made in the two areas were found to have effects opposite to those of stimulation. Animals with damage to the lateral hypothalamus would not eat and drink and eventually died of starvation unless given special care. When the damage was done to ventromedial area the animals developed voracious appetites, consumed great quantities of food, and gained weight rapidly. It was found that the rats with ventromedial lesions may become two or three times heavier than normal. After initial spurt of weight gain, the animals with VMH lesions reached a new baseline weight at which they maintained themselves. Humans with tumours of the brain or other conditions that have damaged the VMH area overeat and become obese.

The results of these early studies were interpreted as indicating that the LH is a feeding centre while the VMH is a satiety centre. More recent work has confirmed the earlier results of feeding behaviour, but has raised questions about the interpretation of the LH and VMH as centres for the control of hunger drive.

Besides these above three physiological factors, hunger is also influenced by cultural and religious factors (to eat vegetarian or non-vegetarian diet), sight, smell and taste of food. Hunger is also influenced by the time. Through childhood conditioning we have learned when to feel hungry and eat and when not to feel hungry and avoid meal.

Cessation of eating—satiety

Restoration of fuel levels after a meal takes hours. But, of course, we stop eating long before this restoration occurs. So the body must have some way of reducing hunger motivation and stopping eating that is independent of the activating factors. Experiments have shown that the stomach contains nutrient receptors which provide satiety—"stop eating"—signals (*Deutsch, 1978*). Another satiety signal may be provided by hormone called *cholecystokinin* (CCK). This hormone, which is involved in the breakdown of fats, is released when food reaches the part of the intestine immediately below the stomach. Injections of CCK into food-deprived rats who are eating causes them to stop eating and to start grooming and other behaviours which are part of satiety in rats (*Smith & Gibbs, 1976*). But the role of CCK as a satiety hormone has been questioned. One reason is that the amounts of CCK in the injections used to produced satiety in rats exceed those released naturally (*Deutsch, 1978*); another problem is that the relatively large amounts of CCK in the injections may make the experimental animals feel sick and therefore less inclined to eat. (*Deutsch & Hardy, 1977*).

Thirst

Thirst is another important biological motive.

Thirst, besides physiological factors, is also influenced by a wide variety of stimulus factors. We, many a times, drink water or cold drink or other liquid not only to satisfy our thirst, but also for wide variety of other reasons.

The homeostatic mechanisms of the body play an important role in regulating the fluid level of the body and in maintaining its water balance. The body's water level is maintained by physiological events in which several hormones play a vital role. One of these is the antidiuretic hormone (ADH), which regulates the loss of water through the kidneys. But physiological mechanisms, involved in maintaining the body's water level are not directly involved in thirst motivation and drinking.

Thirst motivation and drinking are mainly triggered by two conditions of the body:

(a)   loss of water from cells and

(b)   reduction of blood volume.

When water is lost from body fluids, water leaves the anterior of the cells, thus dehydrating them. In the anterior, or front, of the hypothalamus are nerve cells called osmoreceptors, which generate nerve impulses when they are dehydrated. These nerve impulses act as a signal for thirst and drinking. Thirst triggered by loss of water from the osmoreceptors is called as **cellular-dehydration thirst**.

The idea that cellular dehydration and hypovolemia contribute to thirst and drinking is called the **double deletion hypothesis**.

Drinking is also monitored by certain receptors that are found in the mouth, stomach, intestine etc., which indicates that enough water has been consumed.

Sexual motivation

Sexual behaviour is another very important motive which is classified as a biological motive. But besides its biological base it also has social and psychological base. Sexual motivation is social because it involves other people and provides, according to many, the basis for social groupings in higher animals—baboon troops and the human family, for example; and sexual behaviour is powerfully regulated by social pressures and religious beliefs. Sex is psychological in the sense that it is an important part of our emotional lives; it can provide intense pleasure, but it can also give us agony and involve us in many difficult decisions.

Sexual behaviour though a biological motive, differs from other biological motives as follows:

•   Firstly, sex is not necessary to maintain the life of an individual, although it is necessary for survival of the species.

•   Secondly, sexual behaviour is not aroused by a lack of substances in the body.

•   Thirdly, in higher animals at least, sexual motivation is perhaps more under the influence of sensory information from the environment than are other biological motives.

Organizational role of sex hormones

Estrogens, the female sex hormones, come in large part from the ovaries, but they also come from the adrenal glands. Estradiol is one of the most important estrogens. Androgens, the male sex hormones, are secreted into the blood from both the testes and the adrenal glands. Testosterone is the major androgen. Both male and female sex hormones are present in both men and women; it is the relative amounts which differ.

The organizational role of sex hormones has to do with their effect on the structure of the body and the brain especially the regions of the hypothalamus that regulate hormone release. While a person's sex is inherited (genes on the so-called sex chromosomes provide the basis for the growing baby to develop as either male or female), the organization of the body and brain as either male or female depends on the presence of the appropriate sex hormones during early life in the womb. Genes on the sex chromosomes start sexual development off in one direction or the other; under their influence, a fetus with female sex chromosomes will develop ovaries which secrete estrogen while androgen— secreting testes will develop in a fetus with male sex chromosomes. These hormones then direct further sexual development of the body and brain. Later in life (at puberty), the sex organs grow rapidly, and hormone release increased markedly. Secondary sexual characteristics— breast development, body shape, pitch of voice, and amount and texture of facial hair, for example—develop under the influence of estrogens or androgens at puberty.

Not only the body, but the brain, too, seems to be organized by sex hormones to predispose a person to behave in male or female ways.

Since the cyclical release of hormones involved in the menstrual cycle is controlled by the hypothalamus, it is clear that the brains of females and males, who have no such cyclical fluctuations, are organized differently.

SOCIAL MOTIVES

Social motives are complex motive states, or needs, that are the wellsprings of many human actions. They are called social because they are learned in social groups, especially in the family as children grow up, and because they usually involve other people. Gregariousness is a social motive. These human motives can be looked upon as general states that lead to many particular behaviour. The social motives are given various names by psychologists. Some simply call them acquired or learned motives, others call them as complex or secondary motives; but the word social motives is more appropriate because most of these motives stem from the organised social life which human beings lead. Infact, these motives can give us some insight into an individual's social behaviour.

What sort of social motives will activate an individual is dependent upon an individual's own social experience, which is unique to himself and depends upon his ways of perceiving things, his personality make-up, his learning capacity, his intelligence and his own share of the experiences of life. This is the reason why psychologists have always found it difficult to arrive at a commonly agreed list of social motives, as they have done in the case of biological motives.

Another great hurdle we have to face in the study of social motives is that we have no reliable methods of measuring these motives. This difficulty stems from the fact that we do not know which particular type of behaviour is associated with which particular motive. Actually, human beings may exhibit a wide variety of behaviour, even if they are dominated by one and the same social motive. For instance, a motive for aggression which is a social motive, may be either expressed by a direct act of aggression or withdrawal. Sometimes different motives may be expressed through similar behaviour. Thus, two persons may take up oil painting, one to please his parents (motive for social approval) the other to annoy them (motive for aggression). Sometimes motive may appear in disguised forms. For instance, persons have been shown to steal because of some deep-seated sexual conflict. In such a case, the motive to steal is not a motive to acquire, but a disguised expression of sexual drive. Again, any single act of behaviour may express several motives. For instance, a scientist engaged in research may be motivated by his pursuit of truth, by a desire for fame, and even by a passion to improve his economic prospect.

All these factors make the search for a concise list of human motives often extremely difficult. This is also the reason why it is difficult to arrive at a commonly accepted inventory of human motives.

Measurement of social motives

To measure social motives, or needs, psychologists try to find *themes,* or common threads, which run through samples of action and imagined action. To find these themes, they use:

1. Projective tests

2. Personality questionnaires
3. Situational tests

Projective tests

These tests or techniques, are based on the idea that people will read their own feelings and needs into ambiguous or unstructured material. In other words, their descriptions of the material will express their social motives because they will project their motives into it.

The **Thematic Appreception Test (TAT)** is a projective technique. The TAT consists of the series of ambiguous pictures about which subjects make up a story. Researchers then code the stories for motivational themes: Do these stories describe people seeking success or achievement? Power? Affiliation with other people? Intimacy in a close relationship? The motives a subject attributes to characters in stories are highly predictive of long-term behavioural trends. For example, in samples from both the United States and India, the number of achievement themes a person produces predicts entrepreneurial success over time (*McClelland, 1989*). Similarly, the number of intimacy themes expressed in stories at age 30 predicts the quality of material adjustment almost 20 years later.

Personality questionnaires

Several pencil-and-paper tests, called questionnaires or inventories, have been developed to measure the strength of social motives. These inventories consist of questions for people to answer about their typical behaviour and preferences—what they would do or prefer to do in certain situations, for example.

Situational tests

A third way to assess social motives is to create situations in which a person's actions will reveal his or her dominant motives. For example, the need for affiliation might be measured by giving an individual a choice between waiting in a room with other people or waiting alone. Children's aggressiveness can be measured by letting them play with dolls and observing the number of aggressive responses they make. Or aggression can be studied by insulting people to see whether they reply in an angry way.

Morgan (1986) has classified social motives into three types namely the need for achievement, need for power and human aggression. Murray has classified social motives into 17 different types as shown in the fig. 9.3

A few of the social motives are:
(a)   Need for achievement
(b)   Human aggression, and
(c)   Need for affiliation

(a) Need for Achievement

Need for achievement was one of the first social motive to be studied in detail by *MCClelland, Atkinson, Litwin* and *Feathers*. Research into this motive continues even today. In recent years, *Spence* has done considerable work on this motivation.

Need for achievement can be defined as one which "relates to accomplishment: mastering, manipulating and organising the physical and social environment; overcoming obstacles and maintaining high standards of work; competing through striving to excel one previous performance, as well as rivalling and surpassing others and the like."

Development of need for Achievement

Researchers have found that differences in the early life experiences lead to variations in the amount of achievement motivation (and other social motives, as well). More specifically, children learn by copying the behaviour of their parents and other important people who serve as models.

The expectations parents have for their children are also said to be important in the develop-

MOTIVE	GOAL AND EFFECTS
Abasement	To submit passively to others; to seek and accept injury, blame, and criticism
Achievement	To accomplish difficult tasks; to rival and surpass others
Affiliation	To seek and enjoy cooperation with others; to make friends
Aggression	To overcome opposition forcefully; to fight and revenge injury; to belittle, curse, or ridicule others
Autonomy	To be free of restraints and obligations; to be independent and free to act according to impulse
Counteraction	To master or make up for failure by renewed efforts; to overcome weakness and maintain pride and self-respect on a high level
Defense	To admire and support a superior person; to yield eagerly to other people
Dominance	To control and influence the behaviour of others; to be a leader
Exhibition	To make an impression; to be seen and heard by others; to show off
Harm avoidance	To avoid pain, physical injury, illness, and death
Infavoidance	To avoid humiliation; to refrain from action because of fear of failure
Nurturance	To help and take care of sick of defenseless people; to assist others who are in trouble
Order	To put things in order; to achieve cleanliness, arrangement, and organization
Play	To devote one's free time to sports, games, and parties; to laugh and make a joke of everything; to be lighthearted and gay
Rejection	To remain aloof and indifferent to an inferior person; to jilt or snub others.
Sentience	To seek and enjoy sensuous impressions and sensations; to enjoy the arts genuinely

Fig. 9.3 Some major social motives

ment of achievement motivation. Parents who expect their children to work hard and to strive for success will encourage them to do so and praise them for achievement directed behaviour. Independent training in childhood coupled with parental expectation lead to development of achievement motivation in the children.

Achievement Motivated Behaviour

People who are high in need for achievement, may also have fear of failure which may inhibit the need for achievement in them. Similarly, many women who have high need for achievement, may not manifest this need in behaviour due to their tendency to experience "fear of success". We would now see the characteristics of people who have high need for achievement.

1. Those who have high need for achievement prefer to work on moderately challenging tasks which promises success. They do not like to work on very easy tasks, where there is no challenge and so no satisfaction of their achievement needs; nor do they like very difficult tasks, where the likelihood of their success is low. Thus, people high in need for achievement are likely to be realistic in the tasks, jobs and vocations they select, i.e., they are likely to make good match between

their abilities and what will be demanded of them.

2. High need for achievement people like tasks in which their performance can be compared with that of others; they like feedback on "how they are doing."

3. High need for achievement people tend to be persistent in working on tasks they perceive as career related or as reflecting those personal characteristics (such as intelligence) which are involved in "getting ahead."

4. When high need for achievement people are successful, they tend to raise their levels of aspiration in a realistic way so that they will move on to slightly more challenging and difficult tasks.

5. High need for achievement people like to work in situations in which they have some control over the outcome, they are not gamblers.

These achievements related behaviours tend to be present in many men and some women who are successful in business and in certain professions. But many in high need for achievement women do not show the achievement behaviours characteristic of men. Many women who are high on need for achievement do not, for example, like to work on moderately risky tasks. Thus, a gender difference exist in the expression of the need for achievement.

Horner found that in many women need for achievement is suppressed due to fear of success. Because success in a conventional task does not always bring social success. Success at work, in women, often brings stress and rejection from family and isolation from colleagues. Hence, many women fear of being successful and hence suppress their achievement oriented goals.

One classic study with respect to achievement is what is called as ring toss game carried by Atkinson and Litwin in 1950s. We will not go into the details of this study but some of the salient features or conclusions of this study worth noting are as follows:

1. Persons who score high on measures of need for achievement enjoy exercising and testing their competencies and hence are attracted to tasks that are moderately difficult and that have some risk. They are, in effect, more attracted to success than they are frightened by the possibility of failure. Tasks that are too easy, with no chance for failure, are less attractive, because they offer little challenge. On the other hand, very high-risk tasks in which the elements for success are largely beyond the individual's control are not attractive to them: the costs are much greater than the potential rewards.

2. Persons scoring low in need for achievement measures lack confidence in themselves and are more anxious about failure than they are interested about success. They tend to have a low opinion of their abilities as well. They are therefore, attracted to low-risks, in which there is little chance for failure. Middle risk tasks are avoided, partly because of lack of confidence and partly because of their strong fear of failure. Oddly enough, high risk ventures attract them, because they feel that success beyond the easiest task is just a matter of luck anyhow and if you are lucky you will succeed. It is probably the low need for achievement people who provide the best market for lottery tickets, whereas the high need for achievement individual, if he gambles at all is likely to prefer a game of skill in which he can compete with individuals who are about his own level of competence.

(b) Need for power or power motivation

According to Morgan (1986) power motivation can be defined as the need to "influence, control, cajole, persuade, lead, charm others and to enhance one's own reputation in the eyes of other people." People with strong power motivation derive satisfaction from achieving these goals.

Power motivation can be expressed in many ways; the manner of expression depends greatly on the person's socioeconomic status, sex, level of maturity and the degree to which the individual fears his or her own power motivation. A number of behavioural clusters have been related to high need for power. The following are some of the ways in which people with high power motivation express themselves.

1. By impulsive and aggressive action, especially by men in lower socioeconomic brackets.
2. By participation in competitive sports, such as hockey, football, boxing, swimming etc., especially by men in lower socioeconomic brackets and by college men.
3. By joining organizations and holding office in the organizations.
4. Among men, by drinking and sexually dominating women. Strong power needs in men, but not in women, are related to the stability of dating couples; only 9 percent of the couples in one study married when the man was high in need for power, while 52 percent of other couples in the study did so.
5. By obtaining and collecting possessions, such as fancy for cars, guns, elaborate stereo sets, numerous credit cards, and the like.
6. By associating with people who are not particularly popular with others and who, perhaps, are more easily controlled by the high need for power person because they depend on him or her for friendship.
7. By choosing occupations such as teaching, diplomacy, business, and the clergy, occupations in which, people with high need for power, have a chance to have an impact on others.
8. By building and disciplining their bodies; this seems especially characteristic of women with strong power needs.

Related to power motivation is a concept of Machiavellianism. The term **machiavellianism** has been coined in psychology to describe people who express their power motivation by manipulating and exploiting others in a deceptive and unscrupulous fashion.

Machiavellianism is not the same as power motivation, it refers to the particular strategy that some people, dubbed "Machiavels" use to express their power motivation. In addition to being manipulators, "Machiavels", generally show little warmth in their personal relationships, are only weakly guided by conventional morality in their dealings with others, are reality oriented (interested in practical results), and have little interest in ideologies. Research results have shown that people with high scores on a test of machiavellianism do, indeed, manipulate others, make and break interpersonal relationships in an opportunistic way, deny cheating in laboratory games use lies to manipulate other people, are very persuasive when arguing about subjects in which they are emotionally involved, are perceived to others in their group as leaders, and, tend to be on the winning side in laboratory games.

(c) Human aggression

Baron has defined aggression as "any form of behaviour directed toward the goal of harming or injuring another living being who is motivated to avoid such treatment."

Aggression can be physical or verbal, active or passive, direct or indirect. The physical-verbal distinction is the distinction between bodily harm and attack with words; the active passive difference is the difference between overt action and the failure to act, direct aggression means face to face contact with the person being attacked, while indirect aggression occurs without such contact.

Causes of aggression in humans
While it is true that portions of human and lower animal's brain regulate the expression of aggression and that levels of certain hormones (testosterone, for example) are related to aggression, most psychologist like *Baron, Bandura* and *Berkowitz* reject this biological view of aggression, instead these researchers stress the importance of environmental, social and learning factors in the causation and regulation of aggressive behaviour.

Long ago in 1939, *Dollard* pointed out that frustration is the major cause of aggression. He proposed the frustration—aggression hypothesis, which states that frustration always result in aggressive behaviour and that all aggressive behaviour is a result of frustration. However, later on researchers pointed out that whether frustration results in aggression seems to depend on two factors:

(i)   frustration must be intense and

(ii)   frustration must be perceived as being the result of arbitrary action. Aggression is more likely when the frustration is perceived as unjustified, and aggression may not occur at all if the thwarting of motives is considered justified by the frustrated individual.

The most common, everyday source of aggression is a verbal insult or negative evaluation from another person. The insult may not be intended as such. But if it is perceived as intended and if harmful intent is attributed to the insulter, the insult is interpreted as an aggressive act. This aggressive act arouses aggression in the person being insulted, and this person responds with counteraggression. Especially in public situations in which we are trying to maintain our esteem in the eyes of others, counteraggression to insults is likely to intensify the original aggression, and a vicious circle of escalation results, which can lead, ultimately, to physical aggression.

Aggression in many cases is due to environmental conditions. Researchers have demonstrated that high temperatures, intense noise and under some conditions crowding increases aggression, especially in people who have already been angered in some way.

Aggression is a learned Social Behaviour

Albert Bandura was the first to point out that aggression results due to social learning, especially by initiating those who indulge in aggressive behaviour. Both laboratory experiments and everyday life situations indicate the aggression is contagious.

Modelling is most effective if the aggressive behaviour is seen as being both justified and achieving a reward and if the watcher is already angry. Modeling is said to work because it serves to—

1. direct the observer's attention to one of several possible behaviour sequences.

2. show the observer that certain behaviours are all right, thus decreasing inhibitions to aggression.

3. enhance the emotional arousal of the observer which, under some conditions, can facilitate aggression; and

4. show the observer some specific aggressive actions that may be copied.

Mass media, especially television and films provide us with many aggressive models and the question of their contribution to studies have generally shown moderately enhanced aggression, especially among boys, following the viewing of television or movie violence.

Instrumental and Hostile Aggression

Hostile aggression is any form of behaviour directed toward the goal of harming or injuring another living being who is motivated to avoid such treatment (Baron, 1977). This definition implies that the aggressor intends to harm the victim; although intent is often hard to judge, we should be reasonably sure it is there before we label an act aggressive. In **instrumental aggression,** the individual uses aggression as a way of satisfying some other motive. For example, a person may use threats to force others to comply with his or her wishes; or a child may use aggression as a way of gaining attention from others.

Controlling Human Aggression

It is possible to manage and control human aggression to greater extent. Researchers have found that under some conditions, punishment, catharsis, the presence of non-aggressive models or the induction of responses that are incompatible with aggression may serve to lessen aggressive behaviour.

Punishment for aggression has been one ·

TYPE OF AGGRESSION	EXAMPLES
Physical-active-direct	stabbing, punching, or shooting another person
Physical-active-indirect	setting a booby trap for another person; hiring an assassin to kill an enemy
Physical-passive-direct	physically preventing another person from obtaining a desired goal or performing a desired act (as in a sit-in demonstration)
Physical-passive-indirect	refusing to perform necessary tasks (e.g., refusing to move during a sit-in)
Verbal-active-direct	insulting or derogating another person
Verbal-active-indirect	spreading malicious rumors or gossip about another person
Verbal-passive-direct	refusing to speak to another person, to answer questions, and so on
Verbal-passive-indirect	failing to make specific verbal comments (e.g., failing to speak up in another person's defense when he or she is unfairly criticized)

Fig. 9.4 Some forms of human aggression

of the classic approaches to the control of human aggression. **Punishers** are usually, though not necessarily, unpleasant, events which follow behaviour; chastisements, fines, loss of social acceptance, embarrassment, imprisonment, and the like can serve as punishers. It is widely held in our society that punishment of aggression will reduce it, but punishment may not be so effective as usually thought.

Punishment seems to work best when it is strong, when the aggressor is relatively sure of receiving it, when it immediately follows aggressive behaviour, when the instigation for aggression is relatively weak, when the payoff for aggression is not great, and when the person perceives the punishment as being legitimate and appropriate (*Baron, 1977*). When punishment is used ineffectively, it may actually increase aggressive tendencies. Punishment is a frustrator, and it may therefore further arouse and anger the person being punished.

Another approach to the reduction of anger and aggression is called catharsis. **Catharsis** refers to venting an emotion, or "getting it out of one's system." For example, it is often said that we can get anger and aggression out of our systems by pounding on a table or kicking a dog. While catharsis may help us reduce our anger for a short time, it does not seem to decrease the likelihood that we will aggress in the future against the particular person who made us angry.

Aggressive models can induce aggressive actions and *non-aggressive models* lessen them. For instance, if we know, before an attack on us occurs, that the aggressor was upset for reasons out of his or her control, we will make allowances for the aggressive behaviour and reduce our counteraggression (*Zillmann & Cantor, 1976*).

Another interesting approach to the control of aggression is based on the notion that certain emotions and feelings are incompatible with anger and aggression. Thus anger may disappear when a person is induced to smile, feels concern about the object of his or her attack (empathy), or perhaps is mildly sexually aroused. The results of laboratory studies seem to show that such emotions and responses are incompatible with anger and aggression and thus serve to lessen it (*Baron, 1983*).

(d) Need for Affiliation

It is a common social motive that relates to socialising, interacting with others, particularly with peers; pleasing others and winning their affection, expressing and maintaining attitudes of loyalty to family and to friends.

Need for affiliation tends to be antithetical to need for affiliation and need for power. A person who is high in need for affiliation will sacrifice his achievements in order to preserve his social relations and fulfill his needs for affiliation. He/she may not strive to achieve power or position in life.

Need for affiliation has also been studied to a very great extent by *McClelland* and *Atkinson* using that TAT cards and other related projective techniques.

MOTIVES TO KNOW AND TO BE EFFECTIVE

Besides biological and social motives human beings as well as animals, also has a desire to know their environment, to explore and manipulate the environment and seek sensory stimulation. Individuals as well as animals, indulge in these activities not only to satisfy their biological as well as social motives but also because these motives help us to satisfy our curiosity about the natural surroundings or are satisfying in themselves.

There is no specific term but some call such motives as lucid motives, play motives, nonhomeostatic motives or curiosity motives. *Morgan* (1986) have called such motives as "*motives to know and to be effective*".

Needs to know and to be effective persist throughout life and are difficult, if not impossible, to satisfy. Even when our biological and social needs have been met, we continue to seek contact with the environment and to engage in restless and relentless activity. Because they are so persistent and seem to exist to one degree or another in everyone, these need to know and to be effective are often considered innate, a part of the human species heritage. We would now discuss three such motives, namely—

    (a)   Stimulation and exploration needs
    (b)   Effectance motivation
    (c)   Self - actualization motivation

Stimulation and exploration needs

A wide variety of experiments on human beings as well as animals have clearly demonstrated that human beings have a tendency to seek sensory as well as physical stimulation and are motivated to explore their surrounding and environment in order to know more about their surrounding and satisfy their curiosity.

As early as 1881, *Romain* had reported that monkeys would tirelessly investigate their surroundings and manipulate any new object, although no reward was to be gained. One of his monkeys worked two hours to open a box containing nuts, even though heaps of nuts were within easy reach. During the first day or two of their lives, monkeys show visual curiosity and exploration, starting and trying to reach an object that is kept outside their reach.

Even the lowly rats are no exception to this. The first thing they do after they are put in a new maze or cage is to explore every corner of its. The commonness of such behaviour in many animals have led some psychologists to postulate what is known as the inherited exploratory or curiosity drive.

The curiosity motive is, novel things or situations does not last for a long time. The earlier charm of things gradually wears off, and an animal shows no curiosity about it, once it has become familiar with an object. Children, who might fight or cry to obtain a new toy, may not even look at it once they have played with it for a sufficiently long time.

Closely related to curiosity motive is a need for sensory stimulation as is indicated by wide body of research data collected from human as well as animal experiments. Need for sensory stimulation can be defined as an urge to experience changing stimulation. Some evidence for it comes from research work on animals as well as humans. Any novel and complex situation attracts our attention. People seek novel as well as complex stimuli because such stimuli arouses feelings of pleasure in us and increases our awareness and knowledge.

Effectance motivation

The concept of effectance motivation was given by *White*, (1959). It is a general motive to act competently and effectively when interacting with the environment. We try to be effective not only in mastering the environment but also in our social relationship, work and other activities.

A concept some what like effectance motivation is **intrinsic motivation,** defined as "a person's need for feeling and self determining in dealing with his environment." The concept of intrinsic motivation was put forward by *Deci* (1975). It is called intrinsic because the goals are internal feelings of effectiveness, competence and self determination. In contrast, **extrinsic** motivation is directed towards goals external to the person, such as money or grades in school. Extrinsic motivation have their uses in guiding behaviour in business and in school, but reliance on them can some times stifle intrinsic motivation and impair performance.

Self-actualization motivation

This motive was put forward by Maslow (1954). It is related to effectance and intrinsic motivation. Self-actualization refers to an individual's need to develop his or her potentialities, in other words to do what he or she is capable of doing. "Self-actualizers" then are the people who make the fullest use of their capabilities.

Self-actualization is thought to be the top need in the hierarchy of needs, or motives. For Maslow human needs are its base and others at higher levels. Maslow believed that when the more basic needs are satisfied, other higher needs emerge.

Physiological Needs

These refer to the basic physiological needs like the need for food, clothing and shelter. In human motivation, however, these needs are not very important because they are satisfied most of the time.

Safety and Security Needs

These needs tend to be satisfied in most of the individuals in modern lives. Safety needs are of greater importance in childhood. The failure to satisfy these needs in children can make them fearful, insecure adults who are unable to cope with the ordinary demands of the environment.

Need for love and belongingness

This include need for affection, logical and safety needs are satisfied. The secure individuals will be able to reach out for friends, affiliate with a group, and ultimately take on the responsibility in marriage of being the spouse and parent.

Self-Esteem Needs

These refers to the need for gaining respect, confidence and admiration of others. People strive to achieve and be competent and to win recognition for their accomplishment.

Need for Self-Actualization

This is the highest need in the hierarchy of motives and is called as the *growth need*. It is the need for self fulfillment, the sense that one is capable of becoming everything that he or she is capable of being.

CONFLICTS AND FRUSTRATIONS
Definition of conflicts

Conflict has often been defined as: When in an organism when two drives (e.g., hunger and thirst) are simultaneously present. As *Haner & Brown* (1955) have pointed out, this is illogical, since drive states will conflict only when alternative possibilities of action exist (for instance, water and food are both present, but only one may be chosen). **Conflict** may more logically be defined as "any pattern of stimulation presented to an organism which has the power to elicit two or more incompatible responses, the

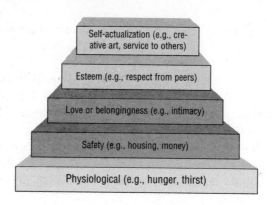

Fig. 9.5 Maslow's hierarchy of needs. Except for self-actualization, all of Maslow's needs are generated by a lack of something, such as food or shelter

strengths of which are functionally equal" (*Maher, 1966*).

Types of conflict

The first serious experimental study of conflict was carried out by *Luria* (1932) who devised many conflict situations, both experimental and real-life. More generally, he devised the "*Luria technique*" of the "combined motor method" in which both voluntary and involuntary motor responses, as well as verbal reaction-time, were measured. He distinguished three major types of conflict, arising respectively from the prevention of excitation from issuing into action ("conflict of the setting"); from lack of preparedness for reacting ("conflicts of defection"); and from the diversion of suppressed activity into central processes.

The contribution of Luria was overshadowed by the simultaneous work of *Lewin* (1935) who defined conflict as "a situation in which oppositely directed, simultaneous acting forces of approximately equal strength work upon the individual (Lewin, 1935). He described three basic types of conflict situation:

Type I : approach-approach
Type II : approach - avoidance
Type III : avoidance-avoidance

Approach-approach conflict

An *approach-approach conflict* is a conflict between two positive goals—goals that are equally attractive at the same time. For instance, a physiological conflict arises when a person is hungry and sleepy at the same time. In the social context, a conflict may arise when a person wants to go to both a political rally and a party scheduled for the same day. Such conflicts are usually resolved either by satisfying first one goal and then the other or by choosing one of the goals and giving up the other. Compared with other conflict situations, approach conflicts are usually easy to resolve and generate little emotional behaviour.

Approach—avoidance Conflict

The second type of conflict, *approach-avoidance,* is often the most difficult to resolve because, in this type of conflict, a person is both attracted and repelled by the same goal object. If, at some point during the approach to the goal, its repellent aspects become stronger than its positive aspects, the person will stop before reaching the goal. Because the goal is not reached, the individual is frustrated.

People in these conflicts approach the goal until negative aspect becomes too strong, and then they back away from it often however, the negative aspect is not repellent enough to stop the approach behaviour. In such cases, people reach the goal, but much more slowly and hesitatingly than they would have without the negative aspect; and, until the goal is reached, there is frustration. Even after the goal is reached, an individual may feel uneasy because of the negative aspect attached to it. Whether a person is frustrated by reaching a goal slowly or by not reaching it at all, emotional reactions such as fear, anger, and resentment commonly accompany approach-avoidance, conflicts.

Avoidance-Avoidance Conflict

A third type of conflict, *avoidance-avoidance,* involves two negative goals and is a fairly common experience. A student must spend the next 2 days studying for an examination or face the possibility of failure. A woman must work at a job she intensely dislikes or take the chance of losing her income. Such conflicts are capsuled in the saying, "Caught between the devil and the deep blue sea." We can all think of things we do not want to but must do or face even less desirable alternatives.

Two kinds of behaviour are likely to be conspicuous in avoidance-avoidance conflicts. One is vacillation of behaviour and thought, meaning that people are inconsistent in what they do and think; they do first one thing and then another. In practice, however, there are often additional negative forces in the periphery of the situation that prevent them from leaving.

Many intense emotions are generated by avoidance-avoidance conflicts. If the two negative goals are fear-producing and threatening, a person caught between them will experience fear. Or the individual may be angry and resentful at being trapped in a situation where the goals are negative.

Multiple Approach-Avoidance Conflicts

Multiple approach-avoidance conflicts, means that several goals with positive and negative aspects are involved. Suppose a woman is engaged to be married; further suppose, that the goal of marriage has a positive aspect for her because of the stability and security it will provide and because she loves the man she will be marrying. Suppose, on the other hand, that marriage is repellent to her because it will mean giving up an attractive offer of a job in another city. With respect to her career, the woman is attracted to the new job but also repelled by the problems it will create for her marriage. What will she do? In part, the answer depends on the relative strengths of the approach and the avoidance tendencies. After a good deal of vacillation, she might break the engagement if the sum total of the positive career aspect minus the negative career aspect is greater than that for positive and negative aspects associated with marriage. Or, if the overall sum of the marriage aspects is greater than that of the career ones, she might hesitate for a while, vacillating back and forth, and then get married. Thus, what a person does in a multiple approach-avoidance conflict will depend on the relative strengths of all the positive and negative aspects involved.

Frustration

The term *frustration* refers to the blocking of behaviour directed toward a goal. Although there are many ways in which motives can be *frustrated*—that is, prevented from being satisfied—conflict among simultaneously aroused motives is perhaps the most important reason why goals are not reached. If motives are *frustrated,* or blocked, emotional feelings and behaviour often result. People who cannot achieve their important goals feel depressed, fearful, anxious, guilty, or angry.

Sources of Frustration

Generally speaking, the causes of frustration are to be found in:

1. Environmental forces that block motive fulfillment.
2. Personal inadequacies that make it impossible to reach goals.
3. Conflicts between and among motives.

Environmental frustration

By making it difficult or impossible for a person to attain a goal, environmental obstacles can frustrate the satisfaction of motives. An obstacle may be something physical, such as a locked door or a lack of money. Or, it may be people—parents, teachers, or police officers, for example—who prevent us from achieving our goals.

Personal frustration

Unattainable goals can be important sources of frustration. These are largely learned goals that cannot be achieved because they are beyond a person's abilities. For instance, a boy may be taught to aspire to high academic achievement but lack the ability to make better than a mediocre record. He may be motivated to join the football team, or act the lead in a play and be frustrated because he does not have the necessary talent. Thus people are often frustrated because they aspire to goals—have a *level of aspiration*—beyond their capacity to perform.

Conflict-produced frustration

A major source of frustration is found in motivational conflict, in which the expression of one motive interferes with the expression of other motives. In expressing aggression, for example, people are often caught in such a conflict. On the one hand, they would like to give vent to their rage; on the other, they fear the social disapproval which will result if they do so. Aggression is thus in conflict with the need for social approval. Other common conflicts are between independence and affiliation needs or career aspirations and economic realities. Life is full of conflicts and the frustrations arising from them. ■■

Emotion, Stress, and Coping

Emotion, Stress, and Coping

What are emotions? This is a question that almost everyone is interested in. There have been many answers, many of them surprisingly unclear and ill-defined (Strongman 1996; Oatley and Jenkins 1996). Emotions are states elicited by rewards and punishments, including changes in rewards and punishments. A reward is anything for which an animal will work. A punisher is anything that an animal will work to escape or avoid.

EMOTION

The term emotion can have many meanings and has been defined in many ways. It is applied to a distinctive category of experience for which a variety of verbal labels is used: fear, anger, love, and so on.

Everyone has an intuitive sense of what an emotion is, but emotion can be exceedingly difficult to define. **Emotion,** or **affect** (a synonym for emotion, pronounced with the accent on the first syllable), is an evaluative response (a positive or negative feeling) that typically includes some combination of physiological arousal, subjective experience, and behavioural or emotional expression.

Physiological components

Over a century ago, *William James* (1884) argued that emotion is rooted in bodily experience. According to James, an emotion-inducing stimulus elicits visceral, or gut reactions and voluntary behaviours such as running or gesturing. The physical experience in turn leads the person to feel aroused, and the arousal stimu-

lates the subjective experience of fear. In this view, confronting a bear on a camping trip causes a person to run, and running produces fear.

James thus offered a counterintuitive proposition: We do not run because we are afraid, rather, we become afraid because we run. Jame's theory is sometimes called the **peripheral theory of emotion** because it sees the origins of emotion in the peripheral nervous system. Recall that the peripheral nervous system controls both muscle movements and autonomic responses such as racing heart and shortness of breath in the face of fear-eliciting stimuli. Because the Danish physiologist Carl Lange (1885) proposed a similar view at about the same time as James, this view of emotion is known as the **James-Lange Theory**.

As the theory would predict, some emotional experiences—particularly sexual arousal, fear, and anger—do appear to be blunted in individuals with spinal cord lesions that prevent them from moving or experiencing gut feelings (Jasmos & Hakmiller, 1975).

Not all evidence on spinal injuries, however, supports the James—Lange theory, and the theory was challenged on other grounds over a half century ago by Cannon (1927) and Bard (1934). Cannon and Bard noted that autonomic responses are typically slow, occurring about one to two seconds after presentation of a stimulus. In contrast, emotional responses are immediate and often precede both autonomic reactions and behaviours such as running. Cannon and Bard argued further that many different emotional states are linked to the same visceral responses, so that arousal is too generalized to translate directly into discrete emo-

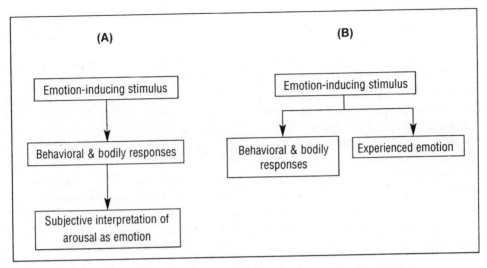

Fig. 10.1 (a) The James-Lange theory. (b) The Cannon-Bard theory

tional experiences. For instance, muscle tension and quickened heart rate accompany sexual arousal, fear, and rage, which people experience as very different emotional states. Cannon and Bard offered the alternative view (known as the **Cannon-Bard theory**) that emotion-inducing stimuli simultaneously elicit both an emotional experience, such as fear, and bodily responses, such as sweaty palms.

Cannon and Bard's first criticism (about the relative speed of autonomic and emotional responses) continues to be valid. However, their second criticism, that visceral arousal is general, has been challenged by more recent research. In fact, different emotions appear to be associated with distinct patterns of autonomic arousal (Ekman, 1992). Different clusters of emotions show modest but consistent differences on variables such as heart rate acceleration, finger temperature, and skin conductance (a measure of sweat on the palms related to arousal or anxiety, also known as galvanic skin response, or GSR). Anger and fear, for example, produce greater heart rate acceleration than happiness. This makes evolutionary sense, because anger and fear are related to fight-or-flight responses, which require the heart to pump more blood to the muscles. Anger and fear are also distin-

guishable from each other autonomically. The language we use to describe anger ("hot under the collar") appears to be physiologically accurate: People who are angry do get "heated" in their surface skin temperatures. Moreover, psychologists have found the same links between emotional experience and physiology among men from the island of Sumatra in Indonesia, as in the West, suggesting that the connection is wired into the brain (Levenson, 1992).

Subjective Experience

The most familiar component of emotion is **subject experience**, or what it feels like to be happy, sad, angry, or elated. Individuals differ tremendously in the intensity of their emotional states (Bryant, 1996), and these differences already begin to be apparent in preschool children (Cole, 1997). At the extreme high end of the bell curve of emotional intensity in adults are people with severe personality disorders, whose emotions spiral out of control. At the other end of the bell curve are people with a psychological disorder called **alexithymia** (Taylor and Taylor 1997), which literally means "no language for emotions." Alexithymics have difficulty telling one emotion from another and often report that seem to be meaningful, painful, or traumatic experiences with bland indifference. One alexithymic patient told his therapist about a "strange event" that had occurred the previous day. He had found himself shaking and felt his eyes tearing and wondered if he had been crying. The patient showed no recognition that his tears could have been related to frightening news he had received that morning about the results of a biopsy on a suspicious growth on his skin. Alexithymics appear to pay a toll for their inability to feel: They are more likely to suffer from stress-related illnesses such as chronic pain and ulcers (Fukunishi, 1997).

Emotional Disclosure

Acknowledging and examining one's feelings can have a positive impact on health. For example, in one study, Holocaust survivors talked for one to two hours about their experiences during world war II. While the investigators measured the extent to which they disclosed emotionally about traumatic events (Pennebaker, 1989). The more the survivors disclosed the better their health for over a year later. Another study assessed the impact of emotional disclosure on an ongoing stressful events in college students, such as an academic or a relationship problem (Taylor, 1998). The experimenters first asked college student participants to identify an ongoing stressful event. In the emotional disclosure condition, they were instructed to visualize what led up to the problem, what happened step by step, what they did to cope with it, and so forth. In a second condition, students were asked to imagine the problem resolving, to experience the satisfaction they would feel when it was over, and so forth ("positive thinking"). A control group did not visualize anything. A week later, participants in the emotional disclosure condition had taken positive steps to resolve the problem and had sought advice from people about it, whereas participants in the "positive thinking" condition were indistinguishable from controls. This suggests that emotional disclosure may not only directly affect feelings and

health but indirectly affect it by helping the person address the ongoing problem directly.

The effects of disclosure are not always immediate. In fact, disclosure can initially be quite difficult but have positive consequences down the road.

Researchers have been tracking down some of the precise mechanisms through which disclosure affects health (Pennebaker, 1997). Writing about stressful unpleasant events has been shown to increase the functioning of specific cells in the immune system (the system of cells in the body that fight off disease) against various viruses. Disclosure also decreases autonomic reactivity that keeps the body on red alert and gradually takes its toll over time. Perhaps most importantly, disclosure permits a change in cognitive functioning that signals a reworking of the traumatic experience in thought and memory: People who benefit from disclosure tend to begin with disorganized, disjointed narratives about the event, suggesting emotional disruption of their thinking, but after writing, their narratives become more coherent. The narratives of people whose health improves also show a higher level of cognitive complexity relative to people who remain less well. It seems likely that people who are either afraid to think about their experiences and put them into words, or those who ruminate on negative events rather than really coming to some kind of resolution, are least affected by disclosure.

Feeling Happy

A growing body of research has examined the subjective experience of happiness (Myers & Diener, 1995). On average, men and women are equally happy, as are the young and old. In contrast, some of the largest differences in self-reported happiness are cultural.

One predictor of happiness is the extent to which a culture is more individualist or collectivist: People in individualistic cultures, which focus on the needs and desires of individuals, tend to be happier than people in collectivist cultures, which emphasize the needs of the group. Another predictor is political. The correlation between life satisfaction and the number of uninterrupted years of democracy in a country is .85, which is one of the largest observed correlations ever produced in psychology between two seemingly dissimilar variables (*Inglehart,* 1990).

Does money buy happiness? The answer appears to be yes and no. Across cultures, the correlation between self-reported happiness and economic prosperity is substantial. Interestingly, however, within cultures, happiness and income are not hightly correlated. Apparently, a decent income is necessary but not sufficient for happiness. Other variables that predict happiness are a large network of close friends and strong religious faith.

Emotional expression

A third component of emotion is *emotional expression,* the overt behavioural signs of emotion. People express feelings in various ways, including facial expressions, posture, gestures, and tone of voice.

Facial Expression and Emotion

In a twist on William James's peripheral hypothesis of emotion, some theorists argue that the face is the primary centre of emotion (*Tomkins,* 1980). Whereas James asserted that we feel afraid because we run, these theorists argue that we feel afraid because our face shows fear. In this view, emotion consists of muscular responses located primarily in the face (and secondarily of muscular and glandular responses throughout the body).

Different facial expressions are, in fact, associated with different emotions. Terror is marked by eyes that are open wide "in a fixed state or moving away from the dreaded object to the side" (Tomkins, 1980).

Facial expressions not only indicate a person's emotional state, but they also influence its physiological and subjective components. In a classic study, researchers gave participants specific directions to contract their facial muscles in particular ways. For instance, they instructed participants to raise their eyebrows and pull

them together, then raise their upper eyelids, and finally stretch their lips horizontally. The result was an expression of fear, even though the participants had not been instructed to show a particular emotion. The experimenters similarly created expressions characteristic of anger, sadness, happiness, surprise, and disgust. Participants held these expressions for 10 seconds, during which their heart rate and finger temperature were measured.

The researchers found a striking causal relation between the simple act of changing facial expression and patterns of autonomic response. Although some research has challenged this finding, other research has found that when people imitate positive and negative expressions in photographs, their own emotions tend to change accordingly (Kleinke, 1998).

Furthermore, true and fake smiles appear to be physiologically different and rely on different sets of muscles. "True" smiles use eye muscles as well as cheek muscles. Interestingly, children have some capacity to detect these differences as early as the preschool years, which allows them to distinguish between "real" and "fake" emotions (Banerjee, 1997).

The flipside of emotional expression is *suppression* of the overt expression of emotion, as when people try to hide their feelings from others or decrease the intensity of an emotion by "keeping a stiff upper lip." Suppressing the behavioral expression of emotion is not, however, without its. costs.

In one study, participants were instructed to inhibit emotional expression while watching sad, amusing, and neutral films showed diminished enjoyment of both the sad and amusing videos (Gross & Levenson, 1997). In addition, emotional suppression had the paradoxical effect of increasing sympathetic nervous system activity, particularly in the cardiovascular system. Thus, trying to shut off emotional expression and heighten arousal, leading to increase heart rate.

Cultural and Emotional Display Rules

Some facial expressions are universally recog-

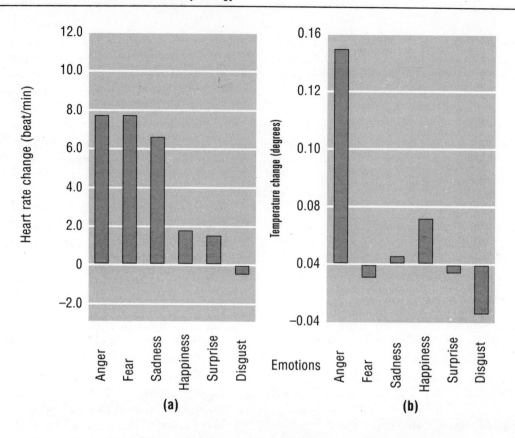

Fig. 10.2 Facial expression and physiological response. The figure shows changes in heart rate and finger temperature associated with certain emotional expressions.

nized. Cross-cultural studies have identified six facial expressions recognized by people of every culture examined: surprise, fear, anger, disgust, happiness, and sadness. Shame and interest also may have universal facial expressions. These findings suggest that some emotions are biologically linked not only to distinct autonomic states but also to certain facial movements which people in all cultures can decode.

People learn to control the way they express many emotions, using patterns of emotional expression considered appropriate within their culture or subculture, called **display rules** (*Ekman*, 1982).

Gender and Emotional Expression

Display rules differ not only by culture but also by gender. Evidence suggests that women probably experience emotion more intensely, are better able to read emotions from other people's faces and nonverbal cues, and express emotion more intensely and openly than men (Brody & Hall, 1993). A recent study found that women and men differed in both emotional expression and autonomic arousal while watching emotional films, suggesting that men and women do, in fact, differ in their experience of emotion (Kring & Gordon, 1998). These distinctions apply to children as well (Strayer and Roberts, 1997). Interestingly, even children as young as 3 years old recognize that females are more likely to express fear, sadness, and happiness, and that males are more likely to express anger (Birnbaum, 1983).

The reasons for gender differences in emotion are a matter of debate. On the one hand, they likely reflect adaptation to the roles that men and women have historically tended to occupy. Women are generally more comfortable with emotions such as love, happiness, warmth, shame, guilt, and sympathy, which foster affiliation and caretaking. Men, on the other hand, are socialized to compete and to fight; hence, they avoid "soft" emotions that display their vulnerabilities to competitors and enemies or discourage them from asserting their dominance when the need arises (Brody & Hall, 1993).

On the other hand, gender differences make sense from an evolutionary perspective. In particular, nurturing children requires attention to feelings. Attention to feelings—particularly empathy and fear—can be dysfunctional for males when they are fighting, defending territory, or competing with other males for mates. This is not, of course, absolute: Men who understand others well, which means being able to read their emotions, are likely to be more socially successful and to compete more successfully than females. Thus, males may have countervailling pressures to feel and not to feel.

THE FUNCTIONS OF EMOTIONS

Understanding the functions of emotions is also important for understanding the nature of emotions, and for understanding the brain systems involved in the different types of response that are produced by emotional states. Emotion appears to have many functions, which are not necessarily mutually exclusive. Some of these functions are:

- The first function proposed for emotion is the elicitation of autonomic responses (e.g. a change in heart rate) and endocrine responses (e.g. the release of adrenaline). It is of clear survival value to prepare the body, for example by increasing the heart rate, so that actions which may be performed as a consequence of the reinforcing stimulus, such as running, can be performed more efficiently.

- The second function proposed is flexibility of behavioural responses to reinforcing stimuli. The thesis here is that when a stimulus in the environment elicits an emotional state, we can perform any appropriate response to obtain the reward, or avoid the punishment. This is more flexible than simply learning a fixed behavioural response to a stimulus. More formally, the first state in learning, for example, avoidance would be classical conditioning of an emotional response such as fear to a tone associated with shock.

| Happy | Depressed | Fear | Anger |
| Disgust | Surprise | Shocked | Worried |

Fig. 10.3 The photographs representing set of primary emotions

- A third function of emotion is that it is motivating. For example, fear learned by stimulus-reinforcer association formation provides the motivation for actions performed to avoid noxious stimuli. Similarly positive reinforcers elicit motivation, so that we will work to obtain the rewards.
- A fourth function of emotion is in communication. For example monkeys may communicate their emotional state to others, by making an open-mouth threat to indicate the extent to which they are willing to compete for resources, and this may influence the behaviour of other animals. Communicating emotional states may have survival value, for example, by reducing fighting.
- A fifth function of emotion is in social bonding. Examples of this are the emotions associated with the attachment of the parents to their young, with the attachment of the young to their parents, and with the attachment of the parents to each other.
- A sixth function of emotion may be generalized from the above. It may be suggested that anything that feels pleasant to the organism, and is positively reinforcing, so that actions made to obtain it are performed, has survival value. One example of this is slight novelty, which may feel good and be positively reinforcing because it may lead to the discovery of better opportunities for survival in the environment (e.g., a new food).
- A seventh effect of emotion is that the current mood state can affect the cognitive evaluation of events or memories, and this may have the function of facilitating continuity in the interpretation of the reinforcing value of events in the environment.
- An eighth function of emotion is that it may facilitate the storage of memories. One way in which this occurs is that episodic memory (i.e., one's memory of particular episodes) is facilitated by emotional states. This may be advantageous in that storage of as many details as possible of the prevailing situation when a strong reinforcer is delivered may be

useful in generating appropriate behaviour in situations with some similarities in the future.

A second way in which emotion may affect the storage of memories is that the current emotional state may be stored with episodic memories, providing a mechanism for the current emotional state to be stored with episodic memories, providing a mechanism for the current emotional state affect which memories are recalled. In this sense emotions acts as a contextual retrieval cue, that as with other contextual effects influences the retrieval of episodic memories.

A third way in which emotion may affect the storage of memories is by guiding the cerebral cortex in the representations of the world which are set up. For example, in the visual system, it may be useful to build perceptual representations or analysers which are different from each other if they are associated with different reinforcers, and to be less likely to build them if they have no association with reinforcement.

A ninth function of emotion is that by enduring for minutes or longer after a reinforcing stimulus has occurred, it may help to produce persistent motivation and direction of behaviour.

A tenth function of emotion is that it may trigger the recall of memories stored in neocortical representations.

A TAXONOMY OF EMOTIONS

Some aspects of emotion, are universal, whereas others vary by culture and gender. How many emotions do humans experience, and how many of these are innate?

Basic emotions

Psychologists have attempted to produce a list of basic emotions, emotions common to the human species, similar to primary colours in perception, from which all other emotions and emotional blends are derived. An emotion is basic if it has characteristic physiological, subjective, and expressive components (Izard & Buechler, 1980).

Although theorists generate slightly different lists, and some even argue against the existence of basic emotions, most classifications include five to nine emotions (Russell, 1991). All theorists of basic emotions list, anger, fear, happiness, sadness, and disgust. Surprise, contempt, interest shame, guilt, joy, trust, and anticipation sometimes make the roster (Russell, 1991).

Positive and negative affect

Perhaps a distinction even more fundamental than differences among the basic emotions is between **positive affect** (pleasant emotions) and **negative affect** (unpleasant emotions). Factor analysis of data from several cultures suggests that these two factors underlie people's self-reported emotions and are in fact distinct in infancy. Within these two factors, emotions are substantially intercorrelated. In other words, people who frequently experience one negative emotion, such as guilt, also tend to experience others, such as anxiety and sadness.

Positive and negative affect are negatively correlated with one another but not very highly;

that is, people who often feel anxious or guilty may also frequently feel happy. Brain imaging studies suggest that positive and negative affect are largely neurologically distinct but share some neural pathways that lead to feelings of emotional arousal regardless of emotional aspect.

Approach and Avoidance

The distinction between positive and negative affect is congruent with behaviourist and neuropsychological data distinguishing a pleasure—seeking, approach oriented system driven by negative affect (Lang, 1995). Approach-oriented feelings and motives are processed to a greater extent in the left frontal lobe, whereas avoidance-oriented feelings and motives are associated with right frontal activation. Discovery of this distinction has allowed researchers to predict mood and other related variables from the difference in activation levels of the two frontal lobes using EEG recordings. For example, among four-year-olds, those with greater relative activation on the left tend to be more socially competent and less isolated interpersonally than those who show little difference between the hemispheres or greater right frontal activation.

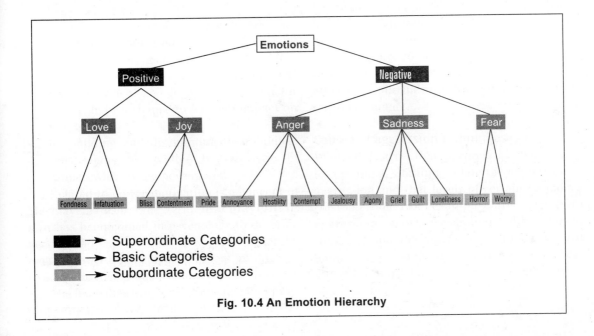

Fig. 10.4 An Emotion Hierarchy

People who are particularly prone to negative affect may organize their lives around preventing potentially aversive events from occurring. In contrast, people who are more driven by positive affect tend to seek novel and exciting events. For most people, positive and negative affect provide an internal set of checks and balances, leading them to pursue things they enjoy but putting on the brakes when they are about to get themselves into trouble. People who are high on one and low on the other, in contrast, are at risk for psychological problems:

They may be vulnerable to depression and anxiety on the one hand, or excessive risk taking and antisocial behaviour on the other.

Positive and negative affect are regulated by different neurotransmitter systems, suggesting that individual differences in the tendency to experience one or the other are related to individual differences in neurotransmitter functioning (Cloninger, 1998). According to one hypothesis, people who are fear-driven have an abundance of, or strong reactivity to, norepinephrine. In contrast, people who are reward- or pleasure-driven are more reactive to dopamine. Part of the tendency to experience positive and negative emotions is heritable.

An emotion hierarchy

How can the various views of emotion be reconciled, with their competing claims about the number of emotions and the relative importance of biology and culture? One solution is to organize emotions hierarchically. The most universal categories are positive and negative affect. All cultures make this distinction, and it is the first drawn by young children, who use words such as *nice, mean, good, bad, like,* and *don't like*. The basic emotions at the next level of the hierarchy also apply across cultures. Below this level, however, most emotion concepts are culturally constructed. Western culture, for example, distinguishes different forms of love, such as infatuation, fondness, sexual love, nonsexual love, and puppy love. Indian culture, in contrast, distinguishes only two forms of love: vatsalya bhava, a mother's love for her child, and madhurya bhava, erotic love (Lynch, 1990). Children recognize these culture-specific distinctions much later than the basic emotions.

THE NEUROPSYCHOLOGY OF EMOTION

Poets often locate emotion in the heart, whereas theorists locate it in the face or the peripheral

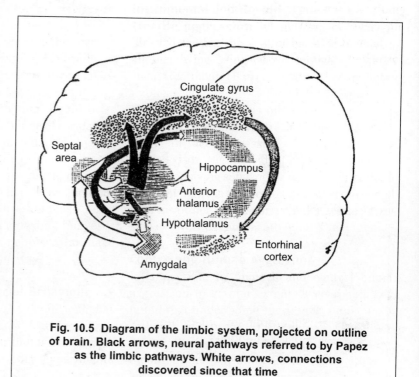

Fig. 10.5 Diagram of the limbic system, projected on outline of brain. Black arrows, neural pathways referred to by Papez as the limbic pathways. White arrows, connections discovered since that time

nervous system. Still other researchers have searched for the neural circuits underlying emotion in the central nervous system. They have found that affects, like cognition, are distributed throughout the nervous system and are not located in any particular region. Three areas of the brain, however, are particularly important: the hypothalamus, the limbic system, and the cortex.

The hypothalamus

Since the 1930s, psychologists have recognized the role of the hypothalamus in emotion. Electrical stimulation of this region can produce attacks, defense, or flight reactions, with corresponding emotions of rage or terror. *Papez* (1937) considered the hypothalamus a crucial component of a circuit or "loop" involved in the generation of emotion.

Papez argued that when the hypothalamus receives emotionally relevant sensory information from the thalamus (which functions as a sensory relay station), it instigates activity in a circuit of neurons higher up in the brain. These neurons, which include what is now referred to as the limbic system as well as the cortex, process the information more deeply to assess its emotional significance. Once the circuit is completed, it feeds back to the hypothalamus, which in turn activates autonomic and endocrine responses.

The limbic system

Many aspects of Papez's theory have turned out to be anatomically correct, although contemporary theories place more emphasis on the limbic system. In some species, motivation is largely controlled by the hypothalamus, and hence by instinct. However, the evolution of the limbic system meant that in other species, especially humans, behaviour is controlled less by instinct than by learning, and particularly by emotional responses to stimuli.

Perhaps the most important limbic structure for emotion is the amygdala. The amygdala is the brain's "emotional computer" for calculating the emotional significance of a stimulus. In 1937, researchers discovered that lesioning a large temporal region (which later turned out primarily to involve the amygdala) produced a peculiar syndrome in monkeys (Kluver & Bucy, 1939). The monkeys are no longer seem to understand the emotional significance of objects in their environments, identifying them. The animals showed no fear of previously feared stimuli and were generally unable to use their emotions to guide behaviour. They would, for example, eat faeces or other inedible objects that normally elicited disgust or indifference.

Researchers have subsequently found that lesioning the neurons connecting the amygdala with a specific sense, such as vision or hearing, makes the monkeys unable to register the emotional significance of objects perceived by that sense (Le Doux, 1989). In other words, the amygdala (together with the hippocampus, which is involved in memory) plays a crucial role in associating sensory and other information with pleasant and unpleasant feelings.

The mechanism through which this occurs appears to involve changes in the way neurons in the amygdala respond to stimuli that have previously been associated with reward or punishment. For example, in one study, the experimenters classically conditioned a fear response in rats by pairing a tone with an aversive stimulus (Rogan, 1997). Following acquisition of a conditioned emotional response (fear when hearing the tone), neurons in the region of the amygdala that receives auditory information showed enduring changes in the way they responded to the conditioned stimulus (the tone) that were not present in control rats that had not learned to associate the tone with electric shocks.

In humans, the amygdala also plays a crucial role in detecting other people's emotions, particularly from observing their facial expressions. Supporting the role of the amygdala specifically in fear responses, PET imaging research has found that the amygdala is more responsive to facial expressions of fear than of happiness (Morris, 1996). In fact, the more fear a face shows, the more activated the amygdala becomes.

Two systems for processing emotion

The amygdala is in many respects the neuronal hub of emotion because of its connections with both the cortex and the hypothalamus. The amygdala also receives some sensory information directly from the thalamus. This information is relatively simple, based on neurons in the thalamus that process primitive sensory patterns, but it can elicit an immediate emotional response (such as to a snake approaching). Conditioning can also occur through this thalamo-limbic circuit even when links between the amygdala and the cortex have been severed, as long as the neural connections between the amygdala and the hippocampus are intact. (The reason is that the hippocampus allows memory of associations between stimuli and emotional reactions). For primitive vertebrates, this simple circuit was probably the role basis of emotional reaction.

In humans, however, the amygdala is also connected to higher processing centers in the cortex. Thus, when the thalamus sends sensory information to the amygdala, it simultaneously routes information to the cortex for more thorough examination. Once the cortex has processed the information, it transmits information down to the amygdala. A second emotional response may then occur, based on this more complex information processing.

The emotional reaction to a stimulus, then, may pass through two stages, reflecting two somewhat independent processes. One is quick response, involving a circuit running from the thalamus to the amygdala. (A dark shadow in water frightens a bather). The second process is slower, based on a more thorough cognitive appraisal, involving a thalamus-to-cortex-to-amygdala circuit. (The bather realizes that the dark shadow is a boy). The initial thalamus-to-amygdala process typically occurs faster because it involves fewer synaptic connections; that is, the circuit is shorter. The endocrine and autonomic responses it triggers will in turn produce sensations that are processed by the cortex, which must interpret their significance.

The existence of two circuits for emotional processing raises fascinating questions about what happens when the affective reactions generated by these two circuits are in conflict. For example, a cancer patient may have an immediate aversive conditioned response to the room in which she receives chemotherapy but also recognize that what happens in this room may be key to her survival. She therefore overrides the avoidance behaviour that would ordinarily be elicited by the conditioned emotional response and keeps appearing for her treatments.

The cortex

The cortex plays several roles with respect to emotion. It allows people to consider the implications of a stimulus for adaptation or well-being. People with damage to the regions of the frontal cortex that receive input from the amygdala have difficulty making choices guided by their emotions and often behave in ways what are socially inappropriate (Damasio, 1994). The cortex is also involved in interpreting the meaning of peripheral responses, as when a person's experience of shaky knees and a dry throat while speaking in front of a group shows her that she is anxious. In addition, the frontal cortex plays an important part in the social regulation of the face, such as the ability to amplify, minimize, or feign an emotion.

Finally, the right and left hemispheres appears to be specialized, with the right hemisphere dominant in processing emotional cues from others and producing facial displays of emotion. Further, approach-related emotions are associated with activation of the left frontal cortex, whereas avoidance-related emotions are associated with activation of the right frontal lobe. People who show strong asymmetries in activation of regions of the left versus the right hemisphere tend to report corresponding asymmetries in their experience of positive and nega-

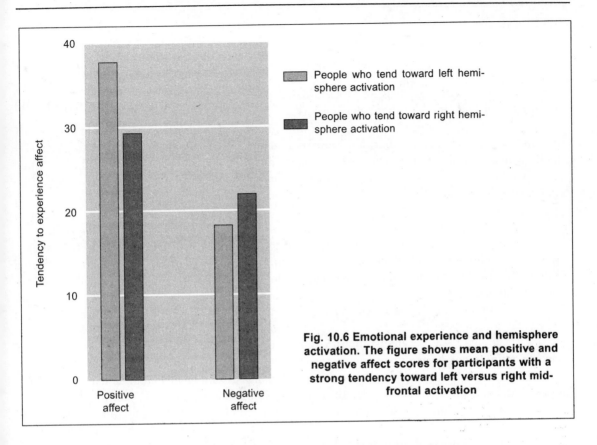

Fig. 10.6 Emotional experience and hemisphere activation. The figure shows mean positive and negative affect scores for participants with a strong tendency toward left versus right mid-frontal activation

tive affect. In other words, participants who tend toward more left than right hemisphere activate report that they experience more positive than negative affect.

EMOTION REGULATION

Because emotions feel good or bad and can draw positive or negative responses from other people, from early in life people learn to regulate their emotions. **Emotion regulation** (or *affect regulation*) refers to efforts to control emotional states. People can regulate emotions before or after they occur. For example, they can avoid placing themselves in distressing situations, or deliberately undertake activities associated with pleasure. Alternatively, once an emotion has occurred, they can try to "reframe" an unpleasant situation ("Losing that job was probably a blessing in disguise") or attempt to escape the emotion directly (e.g., by drinking or distracting themselves).

People use similar strategies to try to regulate **moods**, which are relatively extended emotional states. Unlike emotions, moods typically do not shift attention or disrupt ongoing activities (Oatley & Jenkins, 1992).

Emotion regulation strategies are a form of procedural knowledge; that is, they are strategies people use to try to alter their emotional states in desired directions. Many of these strategies are conscious, as when people exercise when they are angry or depressed to "blow off steam" or "take the mind off" whatever is bothering them.

PERSPECTIVES OF EMOTION

We have now examined the components of emotion and its basis in the nervous system and now turn to perspectives of emotion. The psychodynamic, cognitive and evolutionary perspectives offer additional insights into the nature and function of emotion.

⌐Psychodynamic perspectives

A growing body of evidence supports a central, and somewhat counterintuitive, contention of psychodynamic theory: that people can be unconscious of their own emotional experience and that unconscious emotional processes can influence thought, behaviour, and even health (Westen, 1998).

Psychodynamic theory asserts that people regularly delude themselves about their own abilities and personality attributes as a way of avoiding unpleasant emotion, and a considerable body of experimental data supports this view.

Cognitive Perspective

In the 5th century B.C., emotion has been viewed as a disruptive force in human affairs. Plato asserted that reason must rein in the passions, which otherwise distort rational thinking. Today cognitive theorists empirically study the impact of feelings on cognitive processes such as memory and judgement, as well as the reverse—the influence of cognition on emotion.

Interpretation and Emotion

You have just climbed four flights of stairs to your apartment on a frigid day, to be confronted by a roommate complaining about dirty dishes in the sink. Your heart is racing, and your face feels flushed. Are you angry? Or is your body simply registering the impact of four flights of stairs and a sudden change in temperature? The way you react may well depend on the **attribution** (inferences about causes) you make about these bodily sensations.

In a classic paper, Stanley Schachter and Jerome Singer (1962) argued that a cognitive judgement or attribution is crucial to emotional experience. That is, when people experience a state of nonspecific physiological arousal, which could be anger, happiness, or any other feeling, they try to figure out what the arousal means. If situational cues suggest that they should be afraid, they interpret the arousal as fear; if the cues suggest excitement, they interpret their arousal as excitement. Thus, according to the Schachter-Singer theory, emotion involves two factors: physiological arousal and cognitive interpretation.

To test their hypothesis, Schachter and Singer injected subjects with either adrenaline or an inert placebo and then placed them in a waiting room. Participants were either correctly informed, misinformed, or told nothing about the possible effects of the injection, in order to see whether their emotional state would be influenced by knowing they had been physiologically aroused. Next, participants in each condition were joined by a presumed participant, who either behaved angrily and stormed out of the room or assumed a playful and euphoric attitude, throwing paper wads into the wastebasket, flying paper airplanes, and generally enjoying himself.

Schachter and Singer predicted that participants who knew they had been injected with an arousing drug would have attributed their arousal to the drug, whereas those who became aroused but did not know why, would think they were either angry or euphoric, depending on the condition. The results were as predicted, suggesting that emotional experience is not simply the subjective awareness of arousal. Rather, it is a complex cognitive-affective state that includes inferences about the meaning of the arousal.

Schachter and Singer's conclusions have

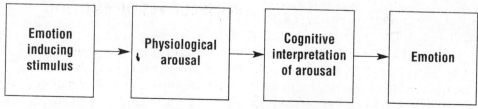

Fig. 10.7 The Schachter-Singer Theory

drawn criticism on a number of grounds. For example, people can experience emotions without arousal. Even when physiological arousal is inhibited pharmacologically, people sometimes report feeling as anxious or angry as control subjects. Thus, while arousal may intensify emotional experience, it may not be necessary for an emotion too occur. Moreover, as the research reviewed earlier suggests, different emotions do, in fact, have distinct physiological correlates; thus, emotion is not simply the interpretation of general arousal.

Finally, studies using experimental designs similar to Schachter and Singer's have often failed to replicate the original findings.

Cognition and Appraisal

According to many cognitive theorists, people's emotions reflect their judgements and appraisals of the situations or stimuli that confront them. Anger results from a judgement that a perceived punishment is caused by another person and is unfair. An event that affects a person's well-being in the present leads to joy or distress, whereas an event that influences the person's potential well-being in the future leads to hope or fear.

Cognitive processes also play a central role interpreting *other* people's emotions. Research from a cognitive perspective has, in fact, recently suggest that facial expressions provide only one source of information about people's emotions and that knowledge about the situation can shape or even override information from the face.

Facial expressions provide a powerful, "hard-wired" set of constraints that influence the interpretation of another person's emotion, but they provide only one of the sets of constraints that

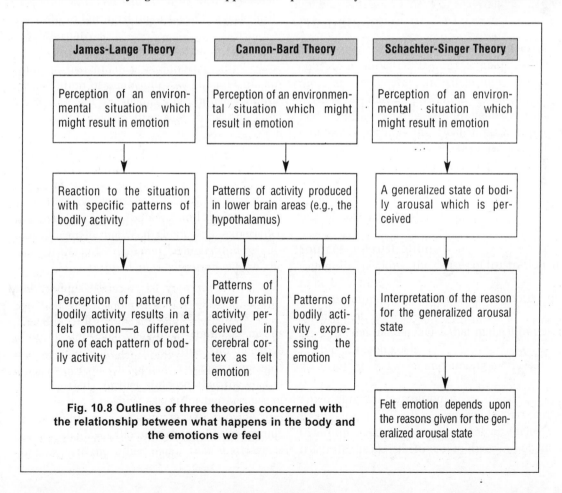

Fig. 10.8 Outlines of three theories concerned with the relationship between what happens in the body and the emotions we feel

influence interpretation of emotion; in everyday life, knowledge may colour the way a person interprets another's facial expression.

Although cognitive appraisals often underlie emotions, they do not always do so. Indeed, emotional responses can sometimes preceded complex cognitive evaluations of a stimulus—or as psychologist Robert Zajonc (1980) has put it, "preferences need no inferences". Zajonc and his colleagues made use of the **mere exposure effect**, which shows that people become more positive about stimuli the more times they are exposed to them. The experimenters briefly exposed participants several times to Japanese ideographs (written characters). When later asked about their preferences for particular characters, as expected from the mere exposure effect, participants preferred characters they had previously seen—even when they did not consciously recognize having seen them. Zajonc concluded that the subjective sense of liking or disliking a stimulus may occur independently of cognition about that stimulus. At the very least, affect may preceded the *conscious* cognitive appraisals proposed by many theorists.

The Influence of Emotion and Mood on Cognition

Just as cognition can influence emotion, so, too, can emotion and mood influence ongoing thought and memory.

Emotion can affect memory and thought in multiple ways. For example, anxiety can reduce working memory capacity and explicit problem solving by distracting the person from focusing on the task at hand. Mood can also influence the way people make judgements, inferences, or predictions. People who are depressed, for example, tend to underestimate the probability of their own success and overestimate the probability of bad events occurring in the future (*Beck*, 1991).

Numerous studies have documented the influence of emotional states on both the encoding and retrieval of information in long-term memory. Individuals in a positive mood tend both to store and to retrieve more positive information.

Positive mood also tends to facilitate memory more generally: Being in a good mood increases overall recall of information, independent of its emotional quality (*Levine & Burgess*, 1997).

Emotional processes can also have a direct physiological effect on memory: stressful emotional experiences can alter the structure of the brain. In one study, monkeys in one condition were exposed to an emotionally threatening encounter—being placed in another monkey's cage, who attacked until the "intruder" cowered in the corner. In comparison to monkeys in a control condition, these traumatized monkeys showed reduced production of neural cells in the hippocampus, a neural structure that plays a crucial role in memory.

Evolutionary perspectives

The evolutionary perspective on emotion derives from Charles Darwin's (1872) view that emotions serve an adaptive purpose. Darwin stressed their communicative function: Animals, including humans, signal their readiness to fight, run, or attend to each other's needs through a variety of postural, facial, and other non-verbal communications. These communications regulate social behaviour and increase the individual's chances of survival. The expression people display when angry—bared teeth and clenched jaws—shares the same evolutionary roots as the expression of other animals prepared to attack and bite an adversary. Darwin's theory explains why basic emotional expressions are wired into the organism and recognized cross-culturally.

Darwin's theory has received support from brain imaging studies demonstrating that existence of hardwired neural circuits whose function is recognition of emotion in other people. As we have seen, the amygdala includes specific regions that allow people to recognize emotions such as fear and anger from other people's faces.

Emotion and Motivation

Evolutionary theorists also view emotion as a powerful source of motivation—an internal communication that something must be done. In fact, the words "motivation" and "emotion" share the same Latin root, *movere*, which means to move. For example, when people are threatened, they feel fear, which in turn leads them to deal with the threatening situation through either fight or flight.

From an evolutionary perspective, different emotions serve different functions. Fear facilitates flight in the face of danger; disgust prevents ingestion of potentially toxic substances such as rottening meat.

INTEGRATING THE PERSPECTIVES ON EMOTION

The various perspectives on emotion clearly focus on different parts of the fabled elephant, and one would hope that ultimately a more fully elephantine portrait might emerge. As a step in that direction, we briefly explore a model of emotion that attempts to integrate aspects of the evolutionary, behavioural, psychodynamic, and cognitive perspectives. According to this model, feelings—including both emotions and sensory experiences of pleasure and pain caused by tactile stimulation—are mechanisms for selecting behavioural and mental responses. In other words, feelings regulate thought and behaviour.

From an evolutionary perspective, the model suggests that emotions perform a central function in animals whose behaviour is not rigidly controlled by instinct: They select behaviour that enhances survival and reproduction by associating specific responses and stimuli to pleasant and unpleasant feelings. This evolved function can also provide the basis for dysfunctional behaviour.

From a behaviourist perspective, the model proposes that the consequences of an action determine whether or not it is maintained or produced again. Those consequences typically involve feelings. When a baby discovers that crying brings its caretaker and alleviates physical or emotional discomfort, crying behaviour is reinforced; that is, crying behaviour is selected for continued use out of all the baby's other past and potential behaviours.

Behaviour is also influenced by expectancies about the likely positive or negative impact of an action or event.

From a psychodynamic perspective, mental processes, like behaviours, can also be conditioned—that is, selectively retained—by their association with emotion. *Dollard* and *Miller* (1950) argued many years ago that repression is essentially an internal flight mechanism - flight from a thought that would bring on an unpleasant feeling. In real life, avoiding consciousness of thoughts associated with unpleasant emotions is reinforced by the elimination of the aversive emotion.

From a cognitive perspective, emotions often reflect a person's judgement about the extent to which current or potential realities match representations of desired states (wishes) or feared states (fears). For example, an individual may worry that his lover is going to leave. Discrepancies between cognition about reality (his lover's presence is comforting) and desired or

STIMULUS EVENT	EMOTION	BEHAVIOUR
Threat	Fear, Terror, anxiety	Fight, flight
Obstacle	Anger, rage	Biting, hitting
Potential mate	Joy, ecstasy, excitement	Courtship, mating
Loss of valued person	Sadness, grief	Crying for help
Group member	Acceptance, trust	Grooming, sharing
New territory	Anticipation	Examining, mapping
Sudden novel object	Surprise	Stopping, attending

Fig. 10.9 Evolutionary links between emotion and behaviour in humans and other animals

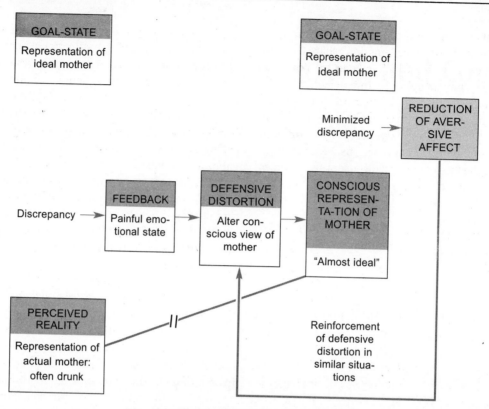

Fig. 10.10 An integrated model of emotion

feared states (his lover might leave) produce emotional feedback (anxiety, sadness, guilt, shame, and so forth. These emotional signals in turn activate behavioural and mental responses (such as pleading, or convincing himself that the relationship really does not matter) designed to minimize negative feelings and maximize positive ones.

Any number of goal—states can energize human thought and behaviour, such as desired closeness to a loved one, values and ideals (e.g., fighting poverty), ideals for oneself such as behaving morally or competently in some domain.

Over the long run, the goal-states people pursue tend to promote survival and reproduction, and they are influenced by innate preferences (such as worries about infidelity). Violation of goal-states produces unpleasant emotions and can initiate either mental or behavioural responses. A student who arrives at college and feels lonely (violation of goal-states regarding affiliation or

intimacy) may respond behaviourally (joining organizations) or mentally (telling herself that things will get better). If these responses reduce the loneliness, they will be reinforced; that is, they will be maintained and more likely used in similar situations in the future.

Fig. (10.10) illustrates how this integrated model might account for the behaviour of a teenage boy with an alcoholic mother. The mother had often been grossly negligent in her caretaking, yet the son claimed he did not resent her "little drinking problem" and described model, confronted with the painful discrepancy between his wished-for or ideal mother and the mother he really had, the boy distorted his view of his mother in a positive direction. His conscious view (mother as "almost ideal") then became cognitively cut-off from more realistic memories of her.

STRESS

Emotion and stress are closely related concepts. *Stress* refers to a challenge to a person's capacity to adapt to inner and outer demands, which may be physiologically arousing and emotionally taxing and call for cognitive or behavioural responses. This definition points to two important aspects of stress: that stress is a psychobiological process, and that stress entails a transaction between people and their environments.

Stress as a psychobiological process

Stress is a psychobiological process, with physiological and psychological components and consequences. An early contribution to the understanding of stress was the physiologist Walter Cannon's (1932) description of the fight-or-flight responses, in which the organism prepares for danger with sympathetic and endocrine activation. If the danger does not abate, however, the organism remains perpetually aroused, which leads to deteriorating health as the body continues to divert its resources away from everyday maintenance and toward emergency readiness.

Another major contribution to the study of stress occurred several decades ago when a young Canadian scientist made an accidental discovery (*Selye*, 1936, 1976). Hoping to discover a new sex hormone, Hans Selye injected rats with extracts of ovarian tissue. At first he thought he had discovered a new substance because the injections consistently produced specific effect: bleeding ulcers, an enlarged adrenal cortex, and a shrinking thymus gland (which contains white blood cells responsible for fighting disease). However, when he injected tissue from other parts of the body, it produced exactly the same syndrome, suggesting that the effects were not caused by a sex hormone.

At first, the reaction baffled Selye, but eventually he realized he had uncovered something very important about the physiology of stress. Experiments with a wide range of stressful events, from injections to fatigue to extreme cold, revealed that the body responds to stressful conditions with a **general adaptation syndrome** consisting of three stages; alarm, resistance, and exhaustion. The first state, *alarm,* involves the release of adrenaline and other hormones such as cortisol and activation of the sympathetic nervous system. This is what occurs biologically in fight-or-flight responses. Blood pressure, heart rate, respiration, and blood sugar rise as blood is diverted from the gastrointestinal tract to muscles and other parts of the body that may be called upon for an emergency response.

The alarm stage cannot last indefinitely however, and the parasympathetic nervous system soon comes into play, returning levels of respiration and heart rate to normal. This second stage is what Selye calls the *resistance* state. At this stage, all systems may appear to have returned to normal. However, the blood still has elevated levels of glucose (for energy) and some hormones (including adrenaline and the pituitary hormone ACTH), and the body continues to use its resources at an accelarated state. Essentially, the organism remains on red alert with heightened energy and arousal, but it has begun to adapt to a higher level of stress. Remaining on red alert, however, is not without its costs. During this stage the organism is especially vulnerable to illness, which is why Selye's rats developed many of their symptoms. It is also why overworked college students become susceptible to influenza, mononucleosis, and whatever garden-variety colds happen to be making the rounds. The situation is analogous to a country that deploys all its military troops to one border to protect against an invasion, leaving its other borders unprotected.

If the resistance phase lasts long enough, the body eventually wears down, and the organism enters a third stage, *exhaustion.* In this stage, physiological defenses break down, resulting in greatly increased vulnerability to serious or even life-threatening disease. Organs such as the heart that are vulnerable genetically or environmentally (from smoking, too much lifelong cholesterol intake, etc.) are the first to go during the exhaustion stage.

Stress as a transactional process

Richard Lazarus, who developed the most widely used model of stress, views normally occurring stress as a *transaction* between the individual and the environment rather than a property of either the person or the environment alone. Just as the amount of stress on a rope is jointly determined by the quality of the rope and the amount of weight pulling on it, so too, is the amount of stress a person experiences a joint function of the individual's internal resources and the external situations "tugging" at the person.

Stress entails an individual's perception that demand of the environment tax or exceed her available psychosocial resources. Thus, in this view, stress depends on the meaning of an event to the individual: An event that fills one person with excitement, such as a new business opportunity, can make another feel overwhelmed and anxious. The extent to which an event is experienced as stressful therefore depends on the person's appraisal of both the situation and her ability to cope with it.

Lazarus's model identifies two stages in the process of stress and coping, neither of which is entirely conscious. In a **primary appraisal** of the situation, the person decides whether the situation is benign, stressful, or irrelevant. If the situation is appraised as stressful, she must determine what to do about it. This second stage, during which the person evaluates the options and decides how to respond, is called **secondary appraisal**.

Lazarus distinguishes three types of stress: *harm* or *loss,* when a person loses a loved one or something greatly valued, such as a job; *threat,* which refers to perceived anticipated harm; and *challenge,* which refers to opportunities for growth that may nonetheless be fraught with disruption and uncertainty. Stress, then, is not always negative. Positive forms of stress, or challenges, include events such as getting married or entering college. These events can be exceedingly stressful—that is, psychologically and physiologically taxing—because of all the changes and

adjustments they entail. Thus, while stress is often associated with anxiety, sadness, and anger, it can also entail pleasure, excitement, and interest.

Sources of stress

Stress is an unavoidable part of life. Events that often lead to stress are called stressors, and they range from the infrequent, such as the death of a parent, to the commonplace, such as a demanding job or a noisy neighbour. Research on stressors has focused on life events, catastrophes, and daily hassles.

Life events

One of the most significant sources of stress is change. Virtually any event that requires someone to make a readjustment can be a stressor. Years ago, researchers devised a scale to measure stress of various *life events* that require change and adaptation (*Holmes & Rahe,* 1967). Although this scale offers a good rough estimate of the amount of stress a person is encountering, it does not take into account the different meanings of various experiences for different individuals. Consequently, some researchers have turned, instead, to measures of *perceived stress*—that is, the extent to which participants *consider* the experiences they have undergone stressful.

Major stressors

One of the most stressful events any individual can experience is the death of the spouse or child. Some early studies suggested that the effects of such a loss were relatively transitory and that the grieving process could take as little as four to six months. However, the weight of research now points toward longer-lasting effects. A study of people who had lost a spouse or child in a car accident indicated that, for many bereaved persons, distress lasts as long as four to seven years after a sudden loss. Symptoms of prolonged distress included depression, sleep disturbances, fatigue, panic attacks, loneliness, and higher mortality rate.

RANK	LIFE EVENT	MEAN VALUE
1.	Death of spouse	100
2.	Divorce	73
3.	Marital separation	65
4.	Jail term	63
5.	Death of a close family member	63
6.	Personal injury or illness	53
7.	Marriage	50
8.	Fired at work	47
9.	Marital reconciliation	45
10.	Retirement	45
11.	Change in health in family member	44
12.	Pregnancy	40
13.	Sex difficulties	39
14.	Gain of new family member	39
15.	Business readjustment	39
16.	Change in financial state	38
17.	Death of close friend	37
18.	Change to different line of work	36
19.	Change in number of arguments with spouse	35
20.	Mortgage over $10,000 (1964 dollars)	31
21.	Foreclosure of mortgage or loan	30
22.	Change in responsibilities at work	29
23.	Son or daughter leaving home	29
24.	Trouble with in-laws	29
25.	Outstanding personal achievement	28

Fig. 10.11 Top 25 stressors on the Holmes-Rahe life events

Another major stressor, unemployment, can also lead to impairments in both physical and mental health, although the effects are generally not as dramatic.

Major stressors such as loss or unemployment actually include many specific sources of stress, and the effect of these life events on a given person depends on the individual's vulnerabilities to these specific stressors. For example, unemployment can be devastating because of the financial strain on an individual or family. It can also produce other forms of stress, including marital strain, forced relocation, and loss of social contact with friends from work. Even a person who has other sources of income, such as unemployment compensation or savings, may nevertheless experience lowered self-esteem, loneliness, or anxiety.

Acculturative stress
A severe form of life stress that is increasingly confronting people throughout the world is **acculturative stress**. Acculturative means coming into contact with a new, typically dominant culture. Thus, acculturative stress refers to the stress people experience in trying to adapt to a new culture, whether they willingly emigrate for better opportunities or flee as refugees from persecution. Acculturative stress is associated with anxiety, depression, uncertainty and conflict about ethnic identity, and alcohol abuse, although individual responses vary widely.

Like other major life stresses, acculturative stress includes many specific stresses. People entering new cultures frequently encounter difficulty communicating (because of language differences), racial or ethnic prejudice, lower socioeconomic status than they enjoyed at home, separation from loved ones, total disruption of familiar routines, loss of familiar surroundings, and new values and beliefs.

Catastrophes

Catastrophes are stressors of massive proportions—rare, unexpected disasters such as earthquakes, floods, or other traumatic, events that affect many people. Catastrophes may be caused by nature, but they may also be caused by humans, as were the Holocaust, the bombing of London during world war II.

Catastrophes sometimes lead to post-traumatic stress disorder (PTSD), which includes symptoms such as nightmares, flashbacks to the traumatic event, depression, anxiety, and intrusive thoughts about the experience. Most severe life events, including losses, do not elicit PTSD. The major exception is rape, which leads to PTSD 80 percent of the time (*Breslau*, 1991).

A man-made (and seldom woman-made) stress of catastrophic proportions, practiced by dozens of countries, is torture.

The most common psychological effects of torture include emotional symptoms such as anxiety and depression, social withdrawal, problems with memory and attention, sexual dysfunction, nightmares, insomnia, and personality changes.

Daily Hassles

Although the concept of stressors tends to bring to mind major events such as death, unemployment, and catastrophes, more mundane but nonetheless potent sources of stress are **daily hassles** "the irritating, frustrating, distressing demands that to some degree characterize everyday transactions with the environment." Daily hassles range from interpersonal conflicts to commuting during rush hour.

Daily hassles are correlated with self-reports of distress and stress-related illnesses, although it is not entirely clear whether hassles cause stress-related problems or whether people who are distressed notice daily hassles more and find minor complaints more upsetting.

Stress and health

Stress has a considerable impact not only on psychological well-being but also on health and mortality. People under stress often suffer from headaches, depression, and other health problems such as influenza, sore throat, and backache. Several studies have also linked stress to vulnerability to cancer, and studies have shown that psychotherapy can substantially increase life expectancies in some cancer patients.

Stress can have a direct effect on health by decreasing the body's capacity to fight illness. It can also affect health indirectly by instigating behaviours and coping responses that weaken the body's defenses or lead to exposure to pathogens, toxic agents that can produce physical illness. People under stress tend to drink more alcohol, smoke more, sleepless, and exercise less than their peers.

Exercise is an example of a preventive measure that can directly reduce both stress and illness. Unfortunately, people frequently fail to carry out health-promoting behaviours for a variety of reasons. They may, for example, lack the knowledge or resources, or be unrealistically optimistic about their chances for avoiding major health problems (such as believing that others, not themselves, will develop heart disease from smoking). They may also face institutional incentives for waiting until the machinery is broken before fixing anything, such as health plans that cover visits to the doctor but not to the nutritionist, or, the gym.

Stress and Immune System

The **immune system** is the body's surveillance and security system, responsible for detecting and eliminating disease—causing agents in the body such as bacteria and viruses. Three important types of cells in the immune system are **B cells, T cells,** and **natural killer cells**. B cells produce **antibodies,** protein molecules that attach themselves to foreign invaders and mark them for destruction. Some T cells search out and directly destroy invaders, while others (T-helper cells) stimulate immunological activity. T-helper cells are the primary target to HIV, the virus that causes AIDS. Natural killer cells fight viruses and

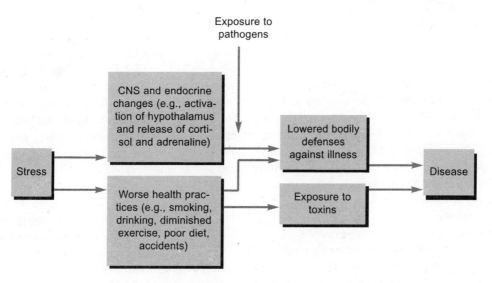

Fig. 10.12 Pathways linking stress to infectious diseases

tumors. Both acute and chronic stress can affect the efficiency and availability of cells in the immune system and hence the body's capacity to fight off disease.

When a group of people are exposed to an infectious disease, such as respiratory illness, only some of them actually become sick. Consequently, one way to explore the effects of stress on the immune system is to see whether people under stress are more likely to suffer from infectious diseases. The evidence suggests that they are. One study investigated the relationship between academic pressure and immunologic functioning (specifically, the secretion of an antibody called Immunoglobin A, or IgA). During periods of the academic calendar rated by both the researchers and participants as most stressful, the secretion rate of IgA was lower—that is, the immune response was reduced.

Stress and Health-Seeking Behaviour

Stress can influence health in a more subtle way by influencing the way the person interprets bodily symptoms. When symptoms are unambiguous and ominous, such as severe stomach pain accompanied by bloody stools, people tend to seek help immediately. However, many symptoms of physical illness are ambiguous. This

ambiguity can lead to several alternative responses. The person may ignore symptoms such as chest pains or take a "wait and see attitude." In some instances, this reflects an effort to cope with the emotion that would be generated if the person took the symptom seriously (in this case, as a possible sign of a failing heart). By deciding that "it's probably nothing," the person essentially reduces his distress—but may ultimately be sealing his fate if indeed the symptom was a warning of an impending heart attack. In other instances, this "wait and see" approach can reflect the inferences people make in the context of recent stressors. For example, a person who has lost a job within the last few months may decide that "it's just stress" and hence fail to seek medical attention.

At other times, and for other people, stress can have precisely the opposite effect, causing people to seek medical care for one minor complaint after another, and leading them to fear that each new bodily complaint could be a sign of a serious disease. In fact, people who are depressed, anxious, or recently stressed by experiences such as job loss tend not only to have more physically illness but also to interpret their illnesses more seriously and to experience the pain as greater. Thus, stress can lead people either to take their health too seriously or not seriously enough.

Stress, Health, and Personality

Whether a person under stress remains healthy or becomes ill also depends on the person's enduring personality dispositions. Personality can influence stress and health through the motives the person pursues, the way individual chronically appraises circumstances (for example, easily becoming angry or sad), or the way the person characteristically copes with stress (such as through drinking, cigarette smoking, avoiding doctors, suppressing emotions, and so forth). For example, in one study, participants kept a daily dairy of their moods and the events of the day (*Suls*, 1998). The higher participants were in neuroticism—the tendency to experience negative affects such as depression or anxiety—the more daily problems they reported, the more reactive they were to stressors, and the more they were distressed by bad things that happened to them.

An understanding of the relation between stress and personality reinforces an important point: Stress is not something that happens to a person; it reflects an interaction between the person and the situation. Recent research on the genetics of personality and stress highlights some of the complexities involved in the relations among stress, environmental events, and genes. Genetics can influence stress in two ways: by influencing the probability a person will place herself in stressful situations, and by influencing her vulnerability to the stressors she encounters. For example, comparisons of monozygotic and dizygotic twins find that the likelihood of being robbed, assaulted, or confronted with financial difficulties is moderately heritable, with heritability estimated between 30 and 40 percent. The tendency to take risks is itself heritable—in large part because people who are fearful take fewer risks, and those who are more pleasure-driven take more—which could account for findings such as this. Once a person experiences a stressful event, the tendency to experience negative affect, which is also heritable, can then amplify the individual's distress.

Type A behaviour pattern and hostility

One of the most thoroughly researched links between personality and health is between heart disease and the type A behaviour pattern. Type A individuals, first identified by two cardiologist (*Friedman & Roseman*, 1959), are impatient, hard-driving, ambitious competitive, and hostile. Type B individuals are more relaxed, easy-going and less easily angered.

Optimism/Pessimism

Another personality dimension related to immune functioning and health is optimism/pessimism. One study found that coronary artery bypass patients who reported higher levels of optimism on a questionnaire recovered more quickly and returned to normal life more easily than pessimistic participants. Another study found that college students with a pessimistic explanatory style (a tendency to explain bad events in negative, self-blaming ways; experienced more days of illness and visited physicians more frequently than other students.

People who are pessimistic do not take as good care of themselves, do not cope as well, and appear to have depressed immune functioning, all of which lead to greater illness.

COPING

People get sick or experience unpleasant emotions in response to stress should come as no surprise. What may seem more surprising is that most people who experience life crises remain healthy. This resiliency in the face of stress reflects the ways people deal with stressful situations, or ways of *coping*.

Coping mechanisms

Researchers often distinguish two or three basic types of coping strategies. Strategies aimed at changing the situation are called *problem-focused* because they try to deal with the stressor itself. Two types of strategy—efforts to alter thoughts about the situation, and efforts to alter the unpleasant emotional consequences of stress—are called *emotion-focused,* because their aim is to regulate the emotions generated by a stressful experience. In other words, if a person cannot change a stressful situation directly, he can try to change his perception of it or the emotions it produces.

Efforts to cope by changing the situation typically involve problem solving. The individual may try to remove the stressor, plan ways of resolving the situation, seek advice or assistance from others to change the situation, or try to avoid the stressor altogether by planning ahead. People high in problem-solving ability and who have a problem-solving orientation (a tendency to define potential problems as challenging and to confront them directly) tend to report less stress and fewer psychological symptoms than other participants. Individuals with a problem-focused orientation tend to endorse questionnaire statements such as, "I am the kind of person who takes action rather than just thinks or complains about a situation," Children whose mothers have a problem-focused coping style tend to be better adjusted and more socially skilled than their peers.

Coping by changing one's cognition or appraisal of the situation often involves reframing an event mentally to make it seem less threatening. For example, a person who is anxious about giving a speech may say to himself, "Come on now, this is ridiculous you are just talking to a bunch of people who are interested in what you have to say."

A number of studies suggest that religious faith often helps people cope with stressful events, such as contracting a terminal disease or losing a child, by allowing them to ascribe meaning to the event or strengthening their sense of closeness to the divine.

When a stressful situation cannot be avoided, people often try to relieve the associated emotional state, as when a person smiles nervously to try to regulate anxiety. Alcohol and drug use are common mechanisms for escaping emotional distress, as is distraction. An AIDS patient, in describing his efforts to cope with distressing emotions, confided, "I used to depend on drugs a lot to change my mood. Once in a while, I still find that if I can't feel better any other way, I will take a puff of grass or have a glass of wine, or I use music. These are certain recordings that can really change my mood drastically. I play it (music) loud and I dance around and try to clear my head." (*Taylor*, 1992).

Social support

An important resource for coping with stress is **social support,** the presence of others in whom one can confide and from whom one can expect help and concern (Strobe & Strobe, 1996). Social support is important for maintaining physical and mental health. A high level of social support is associated with protection against a range of illnesses, from hypertension and herpes to cancer and heart disease (*Spiegel*, 1996).

In humans, the number of social relationships a person has, and the extent to which the individual feels close to other people, is a powerful predictor of mortality.

Two hypotheses have been advanced to explain the beneficial effects of social support, both of which have received empirical support,. The *buffering hypothesis* proposes that social support is a buffer or protective factor against the harmful effects of stress during high-stress periods. In a classic study, urban woman who experienced significant life stress were much less likely to become depressed if they had an intimate, confiding relationship with a boyfriend or husband. The alternative hypothesis views social support as a continuously positive force that makes the person less susceptible to stress in the first place. In this view, people with supportive relationships are less likely to make a primary appraisal of situations as stressful, and they are more likely to perceive themselves as able to cope. Taking a new job is much more threatening to a person who has no one in whom to confide and no one to tell her, "Don't worry, you'll do well at it." In either case, an important aspect of social support is likely to be the opportunity for emotional disclosure, which, as we saw earlier in this chapter, promotes physical health at least in part by strengthening the immune system.

The relations between social support and stress are not, however, simple or uniform. For example, stress can erode social support, leading to vicious cycle, particularly if the person under stress responds with anger or helplessness.

Individuals have different kinds of social needs that are not interchangeable. Coping with death, for example, requires time to adjust to the loss of a particular person, not a quantity of social support. ■ ■

Attitudes

Attitudes

An **attitude** is normally defined as a perceptual orientation and response readiness in relation to a particular object or class of objects. How much we like or dislike something has much to do with determining our behaviour toward that something. We tend to approach, seek out or be associated with things we like and we avoid, shun, or reject things we do not like. Attitudes are simply expressions of how much we like or dislike various things. They represent our evaluations—preferences—towards a wide variety of attitude "objects."

THE NATURE OF ATTITUDES

An **attitude** is an association between an act or object and an evaluation. To put it another way, an attitude—whether toward Pepsi, Reebok, or Rahul Dravid—is a tendency to evaluate a person, concept, or group positively or negatively. To say that alcohol (the attitude object) leads to major social problems (evaluation) is to express an attitude.

Social psychologists distinguish three components of an attitudes: a *cognitive component* or belief (alcohol leads to major social problems); an *emotional* or *evaluative component* (alcohol is bad); and a *behavioural disposition* (alcohol should be avoided). At first glance, attitudes seem relatively straight forward—a person is either for abortion or against it, favourable or unfavourable toward affirmative action, or more positive toward Nike than Reebok or vice versa. Recently, however, researchers have discovered a number of ways in which attitudes vary that make them far more complex than they might

first appear (*Eagly & Chaiken, 1998*).

Attitude Strength

One dimension on which attitudes vary is their strength. **Attitude strength** refers to the durability and impact of an attitude. An attitude is durable if it tends to persist over time and is resistant to change. An attitude has impact if it affects behaviour and influences the way the person thinks and feels.

Attitude retrieval

Attitudes are stable "things" housed in a mental warehouse and hauled out of storage when someone asks to see them. In reality, like all thoughts and memories, attitudes are constructed "online" at any given moment, by combining representations and associations stored in memory with perceptions and feelings at the moment. A person may believe—even strongly—that capital punishment is wrong but construct the momentary attitude that a particular child molester deserves death after hearing the sordid details of the case. In this instance, the emotion of the moment over rides longstanding dispositions or tendencies. At other times, the attitude a person constructs regarding a new object will depend on the extent to which other attitudes are activated. Consider a person who strongly believes in free enterprise but also has strong feelings about protecting children. When asked about his attitudes toward regulating tobacco advertisements to minors, he may report very different attitudes if asked about the issue at a chamber of commerce meeting than at a PTA meeting simply because different values, feelings, and beliefs have been activated by the context.

For an attitude (such as *free enterprise is good*) to have an impact on ongoing thought and behaviour, it must be cognitively accessible. **Attitude accessibility** refers to the ease with which an attitude comes to mind. High accessible attitudes come to mind rapidly and automatically when primed by environmental events.

As with emotions, motives, and cognitions, social psychologists are increasingly recognizing the importance of distinguishing between explicit (conscious) attitudes and **implicit attitudes**—associations between attitude objects and feelings about them that regulate thought and behaviour unconsciously and automatically. Someone who has just attended a lecture on alcohol-related fatalities is unlikely to stop at the bar on the way home because a conscious attitude is active. He may well, however, overindulge at a happy hour a few days later when his implicit attitudes toward alcohol—which reflect years of associations between drinking and enjoyment—become active. In fact, implicit attitudes of this sort play a more important role in predicting drug and alcohol use than people's conscious attitudes (*Stacy*, 1997).

Cognitive components

The cognitive components of an attitude—beliefs—vary on a number of dimensions. These beliefs can be relatively specific or general. They can also differ in their complexity.

Researchers have used some ingenious methods to try to access the complexity of people's attitudes. One method is to read political speeches and code them for the extent to which they reflect complex thinking. Using this kind of analysis, researchers have found that people on both political extremes—far right and far left—tend to be less complex in their thinking than people who are politically more moderate.

People in the middle may actually know less about many political questions than those with more extreme views, but they may be better able to weigh arguments on both sides than people committed to one extreme or another. Although complex thinking is more likely to produce better judgements, it does not always lead to conclusions that, in retrospect, appear to have been the right ones.

Attitudes also differ in the extent to which they are interconnected with other attitudes. Someone who has strong positive attitudes toward feminism is likely to hold a number of related attitudes: that abortion is a woman's right, that women deserve equal or equivalent work, that violence against women should be taken more seriously than it is, and so forth. In contrast, a woman who is relatively conservative politically but has been the victim of rape may strongly believe that violence against women should be taken more seriously but not believe in abortion. Attitudes, like other representations and concepts, can be hierarchically ordered; thus, an important dimension on which attitudes vary is the extent to which they are embedded in broader value systems and ideologies. (*Feather*, 1996)

Evaluative components

The evaluative components of attitudes vary as well. Two important evaluative dimensions are intensity and ambivalence. Some attitudes are associated with strong emotional reactions. Whether the income disparity between rich and poor increases or decreases, however, is not a matter of indifference to me because I am committed to certain ideals, and these ideals are associated with strong feelings.

Another dimension is the extent to which attitudes involve conflicting feelings. For many years researchers measured attitudes by asking respondents to rate the extent to which they were for or against abortion, and so forth. Periodically, however, attitude researchers have wondered whether this really captures the complexity of people's evaluative judgements. The idea that positive and negative feeling can be placed on a single bipolar continum from negative to positive makes intuitive sense, but this is a good example in which science has overturned common sense. As we saw in chapter on emotion, positive and negative affect are somewhat independent and rely on different neural circuits. Thus, a person could associate single attitude object with both positive and negative feelings.

Researchers studying **attitudinal ambivalence**—the extent to which a given attitude object is associated with conflicting evaluative responses—argue that attitudes include two evaluative dimensions, positive and negative, that are relatively independent. These components can each be relatively weak or relatively strong. Low positive/low negative attitudes will have minimal impact on behaviour because the person does not care much either way about the attitude object. These weakly held attitudes are very different from highly ambivalent attitudes—high positive/high negative—that typically yield precisely the same (moderate) scores on bipolar attitude measures that assume that attitudes run from negative to positive. For example, one study compared people who were low on both positive and negative attitudes toward blood donation with those who were high on both (ambivalent). Those who were essentially indifferent were less willing to donate blood than those who were ambivalent, presumably because the latter were able to harness their social values to overcome their classically conditioned squeamishness.

Although researchers have largely focused on positive and negative affect in attitudes, it seems likely that attitudes also differ in the specific feeling associated with them. Some research on conflict between groups (such as nations) suggest, in fact, a very important difference between attitudes associated with disgust and contempt on the one hand, when tend to lead to avoidance of people from that group or country, and those associated with feelings such as fear, anger, and jealousy, which are associated with escalating conflict and attack.

Coherence

A final dimension on which attitudes vary its attitudinal coherence—the extent to which an attitude is internally consistent. Logically, the cognitive and emotional aspects of attitudes should be congruent because an emotional evaluation of an object should reflect a cognitive appraisal of its qualities; that is, we should like things we believe have positive consequences. In fact, however, the beliefs and feelings comprising an attitude frequently develop separately and can change independently.

From a cognitive perspective, coherent attitudes, in which beliefs about the object are strongly associated with feelings about it, are likely to be particularly strong and influence the way people act.

THE MEASUREMENT OF ATTITUDES

The scientific study of attitudes requires that they should be measured. Attitudes are most commonly measured through analysis of patterns of response to questionnaires and other *self-report* techniques.

By far the most common method of measuring attitudes is *self-report method,* in which people are asked to respond to questions by expressing their personal evaluations. But self-report methods have a drawback. As we know from the study of social conformity, people may respond in terms of how they think others respond or how they think they "ought" to respond. The accuracy of the measurement is lowered if a person's public response differs from his or her private attitude. Social psychologists have sought to solve this problem by finding indirect, behavioural measures of attitudes that are not directly under voluntary control physiological measures of one sort or another.

Self-report methods

Whenever you are asked to express your preferences to an interviewer or to write your evaluations of something on a long questionnaire, you are involved in a self-report method of measuring your attitude.

Public Opinion (Attitude) Polling

Public opinion polls are used either to predict something or to provide information. They are used to predict the outcomes of elections, the likelihood of buying a product, or the degree of public support for implementing new policies. They can also be used to provide information about the percentage of the population that supports (or opposes) the use of marijuana, the death penalty or a low-cost housing project. The complexities of opinion polling can be reduced to four steps:

1. Selecting a sample of respondents.
2. Constructing the attitude.
3. Administering items to the sample, and.
4. Tabulating the results.

Although our focus will be on the measurement decisions required in step 2, we will briefly comment on the other steps.
The best way to predict how an election will come out is to ask everyone who will vote what candidate they favour. Opinion polls, however, do not work this way. In the first place, there is no way to know ahead of time, who will and who will not vote. The *target population* cannot be accurately determined. In the second place, it is usually too expensive to contact an entire target population. Polls, therefore, draw samples of people from the population of interest. If the sample is perfectly representative of the population, its result will accurately reflect the results for the entire population. There are many ways to sample a population. The key to accurate sampling is its randomness. **Random sampling** means that each person in the target population has an equal chance of being selected in the sample. The accuracy of polls depends upon the precision of the sampling procedures employed.

The accuracy of polling results can be affected by the clarity of the questions asked. One should obviously avoid using difficult words, double negative ambiguous words, and confusing sentences. Despite such precautions, it is still possible to ask seemingly simple questions that are not understood in the way they were intended.

A question that means different things to different respondents cannot provide accurate polling results.

Attitude Scales

An attitude scale attempts to obtain a precise measure of the extremity of people's attitudes. The accuracy of the measurement can be increased by using many items that are all related to the same issue. Attitude scales use such items. There are, however, only a limited number of ways one can directly ask about any attitude topic. After asking "How much do you favour (or like) X?" there is not much room for additional items. The items on the attitude scale, therefore, inquire about things that are known to be related to the attitude topic. Typically, these involve a person's beliefs, or opinions, about the attitude object. People who are favourable toward something usually have a belief structure that is different from people who hold an unfavourable attitude.

Many standard attitude scales have been developed to measure attitudes concerned with the family, education, religion, health, sexual behaviour, and international affairs. *Robinson and Shaver* (1973) present details on over 120 such scales. Many attitude scales are also constructed for specific purposes.

Involuntary behavioural measures

Self report measures are accurate only to the extent that respondents are willing or able to report their attitudes correctly. While this may well be the case in most situations, accuracy could be increased if attitude indicators were discovered that were not under the voluntary control of the respondent. The search for such measures has often led to studying the body's physiological responses to attitude objects.

Physiological Measures

The Galvanic Skin Response (GSR) was one of the first measures tried out. The GSR measures the electrical resistance of the skin. As described earlier, this resistance decreases when a person is emotionally aroused. Although some research has been successful in relating GSR changes to the extremes of attitudes, it has never been possible to distinguish extremely favourable from extremely unfavourable attitudes; both extremes produce changes in the GSR. The issue is further clouded by the fact that other factors, such as novelty, can result in GSR changes.

Perhaps other indicators of arousal, such as the size of the pupil of the eye, might be used to gauge a person's attitude. Our eyes are reputed to be the "windows to our souls," perhaps pupil size indexes the evaluations going on behind the "window". In early work, expansion of the size of the pupil was found to accompany exposure to favourable stimuli, while contraction of the pupil was linked with exposure to unfavourable stimuli. However, successful demonstrations of the validity of this technique were soon outnumbered by research failures. Pupil size has not yet been established as a good way to measure attitudes.

The most recent, and most promising, physiological measure involves electromyographic (EMG) recording from the major facial muscles. The EMG records minute muscle movements. Drawing on work which showed that different patterns of facial-muscle activity were associated with different emotions, Cacioppo and Petty that EMG activity at different facial-muscle sites produced a pattern that distinguished positive from negative reactions to persuasive messages. Whether or not EMG recordings can distinguish degrees of positiveness and negativeness remains to be determined.

ATTITUDE THEORIES

A number of psychological theories have been suggested to explain how attitudes form and why they change. The theories most frequently employed can be categorized as either (1) learning theories, (2) consistency theories, or (3) cognitive-response theories. These different approaches are not contradictory but simply focus on different factors which may affect the way attitudes develop and change.

Learning theories

One of the first investigators to suggest that learning principles could be applied to attitudes was *Doob* (1947). He proposed that the principles of classical and instrumental conditioning could be used to explain the formation and change of attitudes in much the same way that they have been applied to overt behaviour. Consider classical conditioning. On successive occasions, a neutral stimulus is paired with an unconditioned stimulus. Over time, the previously neutral stimulus may begin to elicit a response similar to that produced by the unconditioned stimulus. Objects, people or events associated with pleasant experiences may take on favourable evaluations, while those associated with unpleasant experiences may be evaluated negatively. For example, in a series of trails, a word associated with the ending of a brief electrical shock will be rated more favourably than will a word associated with the onset of shock. If the association with a particular object is irrelevant, our attitude can be "illogical." *Griffitt* (1970) had people interact in small groups in either a comfortable room or one which was hot and uncomfortable. When asked to rate how much they liked the other people present in the room, individuals in the hot room reported liking the others less than did individuals in the comfortable room. In the manner, attitudes can be formed simply by association.

Instrumental conditioning, in which the reward consequences of any behaviour shape its subsequent enactment, is obviously relevant to attitude formation and change. If you express an attitude to a friend who then provides positive reinforcement (by smiling, nodding, or expressing approval), your attitude is likely to be strengthened. On the other hand, if your friend provides punishment (by frowning, disagreeing, or expressing disapproval), your attitude is likely to be weakened.

Instrumental conditioning is especially important in socially influential situations involving interactions with others. Membership and acceptance in particular groups is often contingent upon the attitudes one expresses.

Consistency theories

A second group of attitude theories focuses on the individual's attempt to maintain consistency among the numerous attitudes he or she holds.

Balance theory

In its simplest form, *balance theory* involves the relations between a person and two attitude objects. The three elements are connected by either favourable (good, liking or positive) attitudes or infavourable (bad, disliking or negative) attitudes. The structure formed by the relations among the elements may be balanced or unbalanced. To illustrate these points, we have drawn some attitude structures that might occur in the mind of someone called Mary. Mary and her friend (favourable link), Bob, are discussing their attitudes toward candidate X (fig. 11.1). In the first diagram, Mary is favourable toward X and learns that Bob is also favourable. In the second diagram, both Mary and Bob are unfavourable toward candidate X. In both instances, Mary's attitude structure is balanced because she holds the same attitude as someone she likes. In general, a balanced state is one in which the elements fit together harmoniously. In the same way, if you have two friends who are not acquainted, you probably assume that they will like each other once they are introduced. Or if you dislike someone, you will assume your friend will also dislike that person.

The basic tenet of balance theory is that there is a tendency to maintain or restore balance in one's attitude structures. Unbalanced structures are somehow uncomfortable or unpleasant. The third diagram in figure illustrates an unbalanced state. Mary and her friend now hold different views of candidate X. In this instance, balance theory predicts that Mary will try to restore balance by changing one or more of her attitudes. She may change her attitude toward candidate X, or she may decide she no longer likes Bob. She may also attempt to restore balance by trying to persuade Bob to change his attitude toward candidate X. Balance theory predicts how attitudes will change in order to create a balanced structure. It also recognizes some solutions other than attitude change to the problems of unbalanced

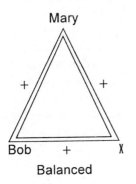
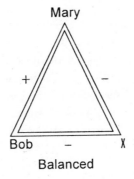
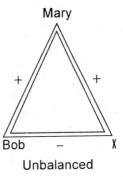

Fig. 11.1 Balanced and unbalanced attitude structures

structures. Balance theory, for instance, would be satisfied if Mary and Bob merely agreed not to discuss candidate X. Agreeing to disagree is a time-honoured way of minimizing the tension of unbalanced states by rendering them irrelevant to the interpersonal relationship.

Balance theory does not predict that imbalance will always be resolved—only that there is a *tendency* toward balance and that unbalanced structures produce tensions and discomfort.

Cognitive Dissonance

According to *Leon Festinger* (1957, 1962), who developed cognitive dissonance theory, attitude change can occur when various objects of thought, which he called "cognitive elements," are logically inconsistent—that is, when they are dissonant with one another. These objects of thought can be attitudes, behaviours, new information—virtually anything a person can think about. Thus, if a person holds the belief that smoking is dangerous (element 1) but does not smoke (element 2), she does not experience dissonance; the two cognitive elements are consistent. If, on the other hand, she knows that smoking is dangerous (element 1) but also knows she smokes (element 2), she experiences cognitive dissonance—a perceived discrepancy between an attitude and a behaviour or between an attitude and a new piece of information.

According to Festinger, this discrepancy leads to a state of psychological tension similar to anxiety. The tension, in turn, motivates the individual to change the attitude, the behaviour, or the perception of the inconsistent information to eliminate the discrepancy and the accompanying tension. For example, if the person knows that smoking is bad but she smokes anyway, she may change the belief component of her attitude toward smoking ("it's not really that dangerous—I don't know anyone who has died of lung cancer from smoking") or she may quit smoking. Alternatively, she may add some additional cognitive element that resolves the dissonance (e.g., "I don't plan to smoke that many years, so it won't hurt me").

Dissonance reduction

Cognitive dissonance theory is essentially a drive—reduction theory in which an attitude change is reinforced by reduction of an uncomfortable emotional state (a drive). Suppose, for example, Samantha has been dating Sam for a few weeks. She was really interested in him when they began dating, but he has seemed somewhat indifferent, often preferring to go out with his buddies on weekends. Whether Samantha is free to date other people is ambiguous; they are involved enough to suggest otherwise, but Sam's level of commitment hardly seems to imply an exclusive relationship.

The plot thickens when another man James asks her out for saturday night. James seems like a nice enough guy, and Samantha has no intention of spending the evening at home while Sam spends another night out with the boys, so she accepts. Then she begins to worry whether she has made the right choice—a phenomenon called *post-decision regret*. The tension she experiences may lead her to convince essentially justifying a choice she has made that is inconsistent with another choice, dating Sam. She may also talk with her friends about the situation in a way that solicits a particular answer—for example, talking only to friends who dislike the way Sam has treated her, or "talking up" Jame's virtues. These are examples of *post-decision dissonance reduction*—or dissonance reduction after the fact.

Cognitive dissonance can also arise when people carry out an act contrary to their attitudes, which frequently leads to attitude change. In a classic test, Festinger and Carlsmith (1959) had participants perform monotonous tasks for an hour. The experimenters told participants that the aim of this procedure was to test their performance, but the actual purpose was to create a negative attitude toward the tasks. The investigators then instructed some participants to tell the next "participant" (who was really a confederate of the experimenter) that the experiment was enjoyable. They paid the participants either $1 or $20 for their compliance.

One might expect that people who received $20 for hyping a boring task would feel more positive toward the task than those paid only $1. In fact, just the opposite occurred. Those who received only $1 rated the experimental tasks more enjoyable, and they more frequently agreed to participate in a similar experiment again. While these results seem counterintuitive, they exquisitely matched the predictions of dissonance theory: To say that a boring task is interesting for a meager payment creates considerable dissonance. Participants who received only $1 either had to change their attitude toward the task or acknowledge that they had sold their souls rather cheaply. In contrast, those who received $20 reduced their dissonance and thus avoided the need to change their attitude because they could readily explain their behaviour in terms of the payment, a considerable amount in the late 1950s. In Festinger's terms, participants in both conditions ($1 and $20 payment) experienced a discrepancy between what they believed (cognitive element 1, "the task is boring") and what they did (cognitive element 2, "I told this poor sucker that the task is interesting"). When participants in the $1 condition tried to explain this to themselves, they had *insufficient justification* for their action, and hence had to change their attitude toward the task. In contrast, participants paid $20 could add a third cognitive element ("I told the guy it was interesting because they paid me a lot to do it") which relieved the logical inconsistency between what they believed and what they said.

Two variables that influence the extent to which dissonance arises and requires resolution are the perception of choice and the size of rewards and punishments. A person with a gun to his head will not feel much pressure to cling to attitudes he publicly professed at the time.

The Festinger and Carlsmith's study shows that smaller the reward or punishment, the greater the attitude change because larger incentives minimize dissonance. This paradoxical finding, that a smaller reward leads to greater attitude change, has obvious implications for teaching children, who must often be induced to perform tasks that do not at first appear intrinsically compelling, such as practicing multiplication tables. Rewarding children too generously for activities they might come to enjoy spontaneously can actually lead them to attribute their enjoyment to the rewards and hence to find the task itself intrinsically unrewarding. This is much more likely to occur with simple, routine tasks, however, than with more complex or creative ones.

Alternative explanations

The original formulation of cognitive dissonance theory explained the results of these experiments in terms of the motivation to reduce dissonance. Not all researchers agree, however, that motivation is necessarily involved. An alternative nonmotivational explanation, derived from behaviourism, is **self-perception theory**. Self-perception theory holds that individuals infer their attitudes, emotions and other internal states by observing their own behaviour (Bem, 1972). Thus, if they see themselves telling someone that they like a task and they have only received $1 for doing so, they conclude that they must have liked it or they would not be saying so. If they slander their country at gunpoint, they conclude that they did so to avoid dying, not because they truly dislike their country. According to self-perception theory, the attitudes people report depend on their behaviour; so their behaviour changes (because of changes in reinforcement contingencies), so again will their attitude. No motivation, tension, or perceived inconsistency is involved.

Other theories provide alternative motivational explanations other than dissonance reduction to explain the findings of dissonance experiments. A **self-presentation** explanation focuses on the way people try to present themselves to others. According to this view, what appear to be changes in attitudes in dissonance studies are really changes in reported attitudes. Because subjects do not want to look foolish to the experimenter by behaving inconsistently, they report attitudes they do not really hold. Another motivational explanation maintains that people feel guilty, ashamed, or lacking in integrity after doing something that conflicts with their values, such as lying about a task. Thus, they change their attitudes to minimize their discomfort and preserve their self-esteem.

Experiments measuring physiological responses demonstrate that encountering conflicting information can produce emotional arousal that people experience as uncomfortable, and that these feelings can indeed be reduced by changing a belief—or by other emotion—regulation strategies, such as watching a funny movie, "cleansing their emotional wounds" with alcohol, or misattributing the cause of their discomfort to something irrelevant like a pill they have recently taken. Unpleasant feeling states are most likely to lead to attitude change when the person has done something that leads to shame, guilt, or anxiety, such as looking foolish to someone else or breaking a moral standard.

Cognitive-response approaches

Cognitive-response approaches focus on the fact that the recipient does more than react to the external information; the recipient also generates thoughts about the information. These thoughts can increase, neutralize, or even reverse the intended impact of the information.

Although various social psychologists have suggested that a recipient's cognitive responses are important determiners of attitude change, it was *Greenwald* (1968) who gave the label cognitive response analysis to these approaches. Greenwald suggested that when people receive a persuasive message, they relate the information in the message to their existing store of knowledge. From this point of view, recipients do not merely process information passively, they actively react to the information with their own personal thoughts. It is, of course, just as impossible to observe another person's inner thoughts as it is to observe his or her private attitude. In order to measure thoughts, Greenwald asked the subjects in his experiments to write down their thoughts immediately after hearing a persuasive communication. These thoughts were then coded. For example, how many thoughts favoured the communication, and how many opposed it? In general, as the number of favourable thoughts increased, so did the degree of attitude change. The physiological measures have also been used to measure cognitive responses to various communications.

Cognitive-response approaches also emphasize the role of the person's cognitive organization in determining how information is interpreted, remembered, and retrieved. This approach appears to be extremely promising in adding to our understanding of attitude processes.

PERSUASION

People often have a vested interest in changing others attitudes, whether they are selling products, running for political office, or trying to convince a lover to reconcile one more time. **Persuasion** refers to deliberate efforts to change an attitude.

Central and peripheral routes

People sometimes change their attitudes after considerable conscious reflection. Other times they change their attitudes with little thought. Correspondingly, researchers have identified two routes through which people can be persuaded. The first, or **central route,** involves inducing the recipient of a message to think carefully and weigh the arguments. The second, or **peripheral route,** appeals to less rational and thoughtful processes—by passing the cortex and often heading straight for points south, such as the limbic system, the heart, or the gut.

According to one model, the **elaboration likelihood model** of persuasion, knowing how to appeal to a person requires figuring out the likelihood that they will think much about (or elaborate on) the arguments (Petty & Cacioppo, 1986).

Rational appeals are more likely to change people's attitudes when they are both motivated to think about a topic (that is, when they care about the issue) and when they able to think about it (when they have time to consider the arguments). In other words, when elaboration likelihood is high, appeals to logic are most likely to be persuasive. These appeals are not, of course, always successful; the recipient of the message may think about the arguments and find them unpersuasive. Nevertheless, attitudes changed via the central route, which involve high-effort cognitive processing, tend to be stronger.

Much of the time, however, people do not have the time, interest, or ability to weigh every argument about every possible attitude object that crosses their paths. People often use simple heuristics (cognitive shortcuts or rules of thumb) to make judgements about attitude objects, such as following the majority opinion (hence laugh tracks on television shows, which tell people that the jokes are funny, in case they did not notice on their own) or passively accepting appeals to unknown experts (e.g., "nine out of ten dermatologist prefer...").

The distinction between central and peripheral routes to attitude change parallels the distinction between explicit and implicit judgement and decision making. Whereas explicit attitude change (the central route) requires conscious deliberation, implicit attitude change (the peripheral route) can occur in several ways. One is through classical conditioning of an object with an emotional response. Advertisers use a catchy slogan and humour so that people will associate their product with a positive feeling, or they populate their commercials with beautiful women, implying that using their product will increase consumer's success. These kinds of conditioning processes can occur outside of awareness.

Other nonrational appeals can also be persuasive. Simply repeating a message enough times can make people believe it. This appears to occur for several reasons. One is simple familiarity: People tend to prefer things that are familiar, which is why advertisers tend to run highly redundant ad campaigns, with familiar faces and jingles. It is also why political campaigns often rely heavily on bumper stickers, which convey absolutely no information. A second reason is that repeating a message linking an attitude object with a feeling strengthens the connection between the two through simple mechanisms of association.

Third, one cue for credibility of a message is the number of times a person hears it. Over time, people tend to forget the source and remember the message. This is no revelation to managers of political campaigns, who often repeat false messages about opposing candidates—usually in highly emotional terms—in order to bias public opinion.

Changing someone's attitude then requires attention to several variables. If the attitude really matters to the person, if the recipient of the message is knowledgeable about the subject, if the recipient has time to evaluate the arguments, and if the attitude was initially generated rationally by weighing costs and benefits, then the best appeal is to the head (central processing). In this case, the persuader should avoid distractions (glitzy campaigns, jingles, and hoopla) that impede conscious, rational processing and annoy the receiver. If, however, the attitude is not strongly held and is based on minimal knowledge, the best route is usually to the heart or the gut—or at any rate, as far from the frontal lobes as possible (peripheral processing).

Components of persuasion

Long before modern psychology, Aristotle described *rhetoric*—the art of persuasive speaking—as a combination of *ethos* (characteristics of the speaker), *pathos* (the appeal of the message), and *logos* (the logic of the argument). Psychologists have expanded Aristotle's view to identify several components of persuasion, including the source, message, channel (the medium in which the message is delivered), context, and receiver.

Source

Speakers tend to be more persuasive when they appear credible (expert and trustworthy), attractive, likable, powerful, and similar to the recipient of the message. For politicians, particularly in countries such as the United States where presidential candidates must appeal directly to voters, winning votes is often a balancing act in which the successful candidate must seem likable but authoritative, powerful yet able to understand the concerns of every citizen.

Message

The type of appeal (e.g., presenting one side of the argument or both) and the way it is delivered also affect change. As we have seen, the match between the recipient's willingness and ability to think about the message and the way the message is delivered is crucial for persuasion.

Fear appeals—efforts to induce fear to try to change attitudes—can sometimes be effective, but they can backfire if they induce too much fear, leading people to stop attending to the message and instead to focus on managing their anxiety. For example, messages about AIDS may fall on deaf ears if they are so frightening that people simply deny the realities. Fear can, however, be useful in inducing attitude change if the recipients of the message believe the danger applies to them and that they can do something to avoid it.

Channel

The channel of persuasion is the means by which a message is sent—in words or images, verbally or nonverbally in person or through media such as telephone or television. Choosing the right channel can be as important as selecting the right message. Turning someone down for a date is much more difficult face to face than on the telephone. Emotional appeals to contribute to emergency relief funds are similarly more effective when the target of the communication can

see starving children with distended stomachs rather than simply hear about their plight.

Context

The context in which a message is presented can also influence attitude. Distraction (such as washing the dishes while discussing a political issue) can also affect the impact of a persuasive appeal, either increasing its impact by preventing counterarguments or decreasing its impact by reducing attention to it.

Persuasion is often complicated by the fact, that someone else has a vested interest in the opposite outcome. Reebok's loss is Nike's gain. Psychologists and advertisers have devised many methods to increase resistance to contrary appeals. One is to get there first: Being the first to make a pitch renders a persuasive appeal more effective. Another method for countering an opposing appeal, called attitude inoculation, involves building up the receiver's "resistance" to an appeal, much as a vaccine builds the body's defenses through exposure to small, inert amounts of a virus. The speaker presents weak and easily assailable arguments supporting the other point of view or forewarns of a strong attack by the other side, prompting the person to develop counter-arguments that serve as attitudinal "antibodies." Salespeople frequently use this technique when they know a customer is about to visit a competitor.

Receiver

Receiver characteristics—qualities of the person the communicator is trying to persuade—also affect the persuasiveness of a communication. People base their information processing in order to preserve attitudes they do not want to change. Coffee drinkers, for example, discount messages about the dangers of caffeine. Prior attitude strength also influences the impact of an appeal; people with weaker opinions are obviously easier to persuade. Moreover, some individuals are simply more resistant to attitude change in general.

People also vary in the extent to which they

are likely to attend to, elaborate, and reflect on careful arguments—that is, to rely on the central route to attitude formation and change. This does not mean, however, that people who focus on the substance of the arguments form "better" attitudes.

Behavioural Change

One of the most effective strategies for changing attitudes is inducing people first to change their behaviour, convincing a person with a snake phobia to get closer and closer to the slithery reptile can change the person's attitudes toward snakes (from intensely fearful to neutral) as well as toward himself (inducing a greater sense of self-efficacy). A persuasive strategy that similarly targets behavioural change is the **foot-in-the-door technique**, based on the principle that once people comply with a small request, they are more likely to comply with a bigger one.

ATTITUDES AND BEHAVIOUR

Logic would suggest that attitudes should predict behaviour. For example, student's attitudes toward cheating should be closely related to how much they cheat. Once again, however, the empirical Aviner is mightier than the logical Davin. Broad attitudes predict behaviour, but not very well. Students attitudes toward cheating are not very useful predictors of the probability that they will cheat, any more than religious attitudes predict attendance at religious ceremonies.

A striking early demonstration of the incongruence between attitudes and behaviour was a study published in 1934 in which a psychologist interested in prejudice wrote to 251 hotels and restaurants to see if they would serve Chinese patrons (La Piere, 1934). Nearly all said no—yet nearly all of them had actually served the investigator and a young Chinese couple travelling with him several months earlier.

Given that people are often passionate about their attitudes, how could their attitudes have so little effect on the way they behave?

Several factors appear to be at work. First, people's attitudes do predict their actions if the attitude and action are at the same level of generality, and particularly if both are relatively specific. Asking people their attitude toward protecting the environment does not predict whether they will recycle, but asking their attitude toward recycling does.

Second, and perhaps most importantly, people's attitudes are only one of many influences on what they do. From a behaviourist perspective, behaviour is under the control of environmental consequences. An ecologically minded person who buys one small bag of groceries a week might reuse her own canvas shopping bag each week and thus contribute to the longevity of tropical rain forests. An equally environmentally conscious person who totes groceries for her family up six flights of stairs might find the convenience of plastic bags such over-whelming reinforcement that she contributes instead to the longevity of landfills. From a cognitive perspective, much of behaviour is controlled by implicit procedures, or habits, that people develop through experience, rather than by their explicit (conscious) attitudes. As in other areas of research, it seems likely that people's explicit attitudes guide their behaviour primarily when they are consciously reflecting on them.

Because attitudes are only one of the factors that influence behaviour, they may not be useful in predicting who a person will vote for in a particular election, but over the long run, they will in fact predict the party the individual tends to endorse at the ballot box. Human behaviour is so complex that a single variable is rarely likely to predict what a person will do in a specific circumstance. By aggregating (averaging) across behaviours, however, researchers get a clearer picture of a person's behavioural tendencies. Attitudes, like personality traits, predict behaviour over the long run. And as with both intelligence and personality, some attitudes are relatively general whereas others are specific.

Third, the recognition that attitudes vary along a number of dimensions points to some previously unrecognized complexities in the way attitudes affect behaviour. For example, as we will see, people's explicit racial attitudes are often much more liberal than their implicit attitudes. Explicit attitudes predict some behaviour, but much of the time implicit attitudes, which are more automatic, explain the way people act.

Finally, the way attitudes are acquired influences their impact on behaviour. Attitudes shaped by personal experience are especially likely to influence action. One study examined student's attitudes toward a campus housing shortage that forced many to sleep on cots in makeshift quarters for weeks. Both the affected students and their more comfortably housed peers had negative attitudes toward the situation and the way the university handled it; however, those who were personally affected were much more likely to act in accordance with their attitudes by writing letters, singing petitions, and the like.

BEHAVIOUR AND ATTITUDES

The road between attitudes and behaviour is actually a two-way street. Daryl. *J. Bem* (1965) was the first to suggest that we sometimes deduce our attitude positions by direct observation of our own behaviour. Bem reasons that if we cannot locate a cause for our behaviour in the environment, we assume the behaviour occurred because of some internal motive or personality disposition.

Bem argues that in the absence of a strongly held attitude and without the existence of strong environmental incentives, we use self-observation of our own behaviour to decide our attitude positions. If you were asked "Do you like movies?" you would think to yourself, "I must like them because I go for so many movies" or "I must not like them because I rarely go for the movies."

It is Bem's contention that dissonance research can best be understood if we view it as instances of self perception. Consider, for example, the dissonance finding that people who are promised large incentives for counterattitudinal role playing, change their attitude less than do those who are promised small incentives.

Bem argues that the attitude issues used in dissonance research are of little importance to most subjects; thus they cannot serve as an internal cause of the behaviour. Instead, dissonance effects depend upon whether situational incentives are high or low. Subjects who are promised large rewards for advocating positions counter to their own will attribute their behaviour to the large rewards. Their behaviour represents a desire to earn rewards, and their private attitudes remain unchanged. Subjects who engage in the same counterattitudinal advocacy for small rewards cannot use the rewards to justify their behaviour. They are more likely to think "I must be advocating this position because it represents my attitude." Their attitudes are subject to change. ■ ■

Study of the Human Life: Birth, Infancy and Childhood

RESEARCH IN HUMAN DEVELOPMENT
— Sources of knowledge
— Descriptive research
— Experimental research
— Ethics in research

THEORIES OF HUMAN DEVELOPMENT
— Psychodynamic view
— Behaviourist view
— Organic maturation views
— Humanistic view
— Holistic developmental view

PSYCHOSOCIAL DEVELOPMENT OF THE FETUS
— Visual responses
— Auditory responses
— Other prenatal activities

THE NEONATE
INFANCY: NEUROMUSCULAR DEVELOPMENT
— Skeletal system
— Muscular system
— Neurological system

DEVELOPMENT OF PERCEPTION DURING INFANCY

COGNITIVE DEVELOPMENT DURING INFANCY
— Piaget's sensorimotor stage

PSYCHOSOCIAL DEVELOPMENT DURING INFANCY
— The Process of Attachment
— Emotional development during infancy
— Adjustment problems during infancy

DEVELOPMENT OF THE TODDLER AND THE PRESCHOOLER
— Cognitive development of the toddler and the pre-schooler
— Attention
— Language development
— Social development
— Adjustment problems in early childhood

DEVELOPMENT DURING LATER CHILDHOOD
— Cognitive development
— Social development
— School achievement
— Adjustment problems in later childhood

Study of the Human Life: Birth, Infancy and Childhood

The process of human development is influenced by three interacting forces: biophysical endowment, psychosocial environment and self-creation. The first two factors affect our lives even before we are born. Each individual receives a unique genetic makeup at the moment of conception that establishes the substrata of biophysical potentials, cognitive abilities, special talents, and, some believe, temperament that thus sets a ceiling on ultimate levels of development. However, the existence of biological propensities does not imply that behaviour is reflexive, predetermined, or immutable.

Our psycho-sociocultural heritage is just as powerful an influence as our biological heritage. Actualization of genetic potentials, or self-fulfillment, depends on the nurturing and opportunities available for expressing and developing one's potentials. Variables such as the neighbourhood in which our family lives (urban or rural, suburban or ghetto), economic level, basic attitude of our parents toward us (i.e. were we wanted, understood, loved?) religious orientation, educational and cultural opportunities, size of our family, and availability of medical care all influence the formation of our attitudes, personality, and skill repertoire. Even the political climate, cultural philosophies, geographic location, and ethnic affiliation have their impact.

Each person is a unique expression of the total combination of hereditary and environmental factors that touch his or her life, not the sum of each, but the result of their interactions. This does not mean, however, that we are at the mercy of heredity and environment, only that these two factors provide the raw materials out of which we uniquely create our self, our approaches and our responses to life. Each of us chooses what to attend to from the multiple stimuli in the environment, and we create our own unique understanding of events. Each person chooses where to focus one's energies and how to approach life's challenges. Thus, we actively construct our knowledge of the world and ourselves.

RESEARCH IN HUMAN DEVELOPMENT

As people began to appreciate and value children, they realized that a better understanding of childhood and human development would (1) contribute to the development of theories of human behaviour that could be used both to interpret and to predict behaviours and (2) that this knowledge could contribute in a practical way to improving the quality of life on both the individual and societal levels.

Sources of knowledge

Each individual develops hypotheses about human behaviour. The major source of knowledge is **experience**. Because people have observed or participated in an event, they hold tenaciously to their own views. Unfortunately, this source of knowledge is severely limited and biased. What people fail to consider is that every other person who observed or participated in the same or similar event also formulated a hypothesis and is equally convinced of its truth. Because events are uncontrolled, like the experience of the blind men and the elephant, their theories may bear little, if any, resemblance to "The Truth." The contribution of experience should not be underestimated, but knowledge gained through experience must be validated before it can be accepted without question.

A more reliable source of knowledge is the opinion or the experience of an **expert** in the field. Identifying with the name or theory of a respected researcher offers more credence to personal observations or theories. However, even the most astute authority is not infallible.

A third source of insight is through **a priori** or intellectual approach, which states that a theory is developed through reasoning. One proceeds logically from a known fact to an assumed effect. A theory may be developed through **deductive reasoning**, in which a specific idea is extracted from a general concept through logical reasoning. In **inductive reasoning**, specific observations are logically combined to develop a more general theory or viewpoint. These methods are useful, but they are not always reliable. Two qualified people may come to equally supportable but opposite viewpoints. The history of science reveals that the understanding of phenomena has frequently been impeded by the acceptance of "obvious" assumptions that are not true.

The most valid and reliable knowledge is obtained through the use of a **scientific approach** to explaining phenomena, described here in four steps. First, as an individual interacts with the environment, he or she becomes aware of a problem. Over a period of time, the **problem becomes more clearly identified**, and critical factors are delineated. Second, through inductive reasoning, the individual **formulates these factors into a theory**, a statement that explains and predicts. Theories are developed to cover the greatest number of facts as simply as possible. Third, further observations or experiments are performed to **test** the hypotheses that are derived from the theory (deductive reasoning). Fourth, **the data are evaluated** for the degree to which the research supports each hypothesis. If the data collected do not support the hypothesis, then the theory must be re-evaluated. The scientific approach, when used properly, is a continuous process with self-corrective mechanisms.

Descriptive research

Critical to the effective use of a scientific approach is the adequate identification of the problem with its parameters and variables. This identification necessitates adequate attention to data gathering through observations.

Contrived observations can be made by placing and observing individuals in restricted environments or by posing specific problems to elicit a response. Piaget used (and most assessment tools today use) this method to evaluate cognitive and physical skills of young children.

Surveys

In 1891, *G. Stanley Hall* pioneered the technique of systematic study of large group of children by the use of a questionnaire. This method was an example of a **cross-sectional** research design (many individuals of different ages are evaluated for differences between age groups and for the identification of norms for each age group). In a **longitudinal** design, the same individuals are evaluated several times to identify changes that occur with maturation or aging.

Ex Post Facto Studies

Many problems in education, medicine, and human development do not lend themselves to experimental research. Consequently, relationships between variables must be identified through careful history taking. Case studies fall into this category. Because the researcher has no control over the variables, no correlation between factors can be offered as absolute proof of a cause-effect relationship.

Correlational Research

When a large number of variables have been identified as potentially related to a problem, a researcher, through detailed study and high-level statistical evaluation, may attempt to identify the degree to which two or more factors are related to each other. Like the ex post facto design, this method offers no proof of causal relationships, only a description of the strength of the relatedness. Both factors may actually be under the influence of an as yet unknown third variable.

Experimental research

Experimental designs test the ability of a theory to generate hypotheses that can predict a result. As such, they can assess the possible existence of a causal relationship.

The true experimental design is identified by two criteria. First, the experimenter must have **control** over the variables that are significant to the research. Environmental consistency is essential for the interpretation of the results. Second, there must be **randomization** in (1) selection of subjects (for external validity), (2) assignment of the subjects to groups (for internal validity), and (3) assignment of treatment to the group. Each group is offered a different condition on one factor (independent variable) while the target behaviour (dependent variable) is measured for differences between groups. Single-subject research designs can also prove powerful cause-effect relationships even though the second criteria cannot be met.

Ethics in research

Much human research remains in the descriptive category because of the technical and humane problems inherent in experimenting with humans. One cannot deliberately subject a pregnant woman to severe stress to see if it will cause birth defects in the offspring; neither does one deliberately avoid all talking to infants to discover "natural" language.

The right to privacy and informed consent have become critical issues. In the case of children, parents or legal guardians must give permission, but the child must also be informed as much as possible about the research design.

Many hypotheses that cannot be adequately tested in humans because of ethical and financial problems or the constraints of time may be successfully tested in animals.

THEORIES OF HUMAN DEVELOPMENT

No one theory has yet been created to encompass all aspect of human development. Theorist go one step beyond description by attempting to identify meaningful relationships. Complex behaviours are reduced to simple frames by the identification of core problems, tasks, or developmental foci for each phase of life.

Theories reflect the culture and the life experiences of those who develop them. Two respected theories may be diametrically opposed. People tend to lean toward a particular theory because it helps them to understand their own past experiences or it blends with their philosophy of life.

The theorist of human development differ in two major ways. First, they differ, in their position on the origin of behaviour; thus, Rousseau's and Locke's views still provoke controversy in theory development and child-rearing practices today. Should nature be allowed to take its course, or should adults actively shape a child's development? A third view on the origin of behaviour involves the issue of self-generativity: Do heredity and environment shape us, or do we shape ourselves in the context of hereditary and environment factors? Is the individual a passive or an active leaner?

Developmental theories attempt to explain both change and consistency over time. The second major area of controversy concerns how the theorists explain the nature of changes. Although all theories recognize orderly, sequential changes from simple to more complex behaviours, some theories characterize these changes as smooth and continuous. **Continuity** views focus on **qualitative** changes that occur gradually over time until the target behaviour is achieved (successive approximations). By **development**, immature skills are strengthened or modified into more complex skills.

Discontinuity views focus on abrupt changes in behaviour patterns. The organization of behaviour becomes **qualitatively** different from one period of the life span to the next through *growth*. Many behaviours may change simultaneously, heralding the entrance to a new level of functioning. Each new stage integrates past and present experience into new, more complex response patterns. The behaviour patterns for each stage can be described and interrelated around a core problem or task. Incomplete resolution of the problem or tasks interferes with the quality of growth at the next stage. During transition periods, an individual may exhibit behaviours of two successive stages. The stages are sequentially arranged so that the order cannot be changed, nor can a stage be skipped if the final level is to be reached. However, it is acknowledged that the speed of passing through various stages may be accelerated or delayed as a result of genetic or environmental factors, and the person may "revisit" a stage under stress or voluntarily for more effective resolution.

Psychodynamic view

Psychodynamic theories view people as basically affective (emotional and irrational). The energy to act and react originates in genetically or biologically determined passions and impulses (instincts). Even the infant's growth is motivated by unconscious, pleasure-seeking urges. According to the psychodynamic views of human development, we are neither active nor passive in shaping our personalities; we merely attempt to balance the internal and external forces in such a way that we can live adaptively with them. This dynamic process of balancing or maintaining homeostasis continues throughout life on the unconscious level. The adjustment process helps

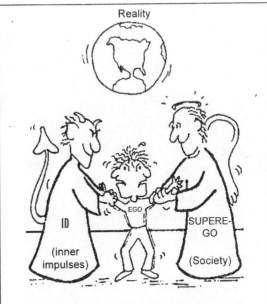

Fig. 12.1 According to psychodynamic theory, the self, or ego, must balance the impulses of the id with the constraints of the superego to meet the realities of everyday life

to change personality structures so that the person interacts differently with the environment in the future. Through this constant process of disequilibrium and homeostasis, identity is formed.

Behaviourist view

The theories of the behaviourists were developed in direct rebellion against the global, intangible theories presented by the psychodynamic theorists. How can one observe, measure, and validate trust, inferiority, anxiety, or other mental processes and instincts? they asked. Their objective approach restricted attention to behaviours that could be directly observed and measured.

The behaviourist theory is quite simple: all behaviour is under the control of environmental contingencies. The antecedent (stimulus or need) sets the occasion for behaviour. Behaviours are maintained by the consequences (contingencies) supplied by the environment when the behaviour

Fig. 12.2 According to behaviourist theory, a person emits a certain behaviour because of the reinforcement received after performing that behaviour

Organic maturation views

The maturationalist postulates that there is an autogenetic, species-typical path canalization, that all members of a species follow given a "normal, expected environment. Individuals have strong self-righting tendencies if the environment is atypical. Biological maturation serves as the impetus for the emergence of social and cognitive skills. Functionalists study structure and activities from a biological perspective and focus on adaptation. Cognitivists concentrate on information processing and cognitive structuring.

Individuals (conciously and unconciously) internally organize, integrate, and transform themselves to maintain meaningful adaptive interaction with the environment. The individual actively guides his or her own growth and development through (1) possession of genetically endowed sensitivities or skills for initial interactions with the environment, (2) determining one's own orientation to both self and the world and thereby constructing their own experiences, (3)

is performed. A basic presupposition of behaviourist theory is that people are pleasure-seeking creatures and behave in ways that result in pleasant consequences. If the consequence is seen as desirable, then the behaviour is increased in frequency or intensity. If the environment does not respond or if the behaviour results in unpleasant consequences, then the behaviour gradually decreases until it becomes extinguished.

The behaviourists offer no comprehensive framework of human development except that knowledge of an individual's responses in past situations can be used to predict responses in the future. Heredity and physical maturation are under-emphasized, primarily because they are uncontrollable. The behaviourists are more concerned with systematic research to discover the mechanics (how and why) of learning than with a description of evolving phases (what or when). Their carefully designed research methodology has proved to be extremely valuable in developing scientific, effective teaching and parenting strategies.

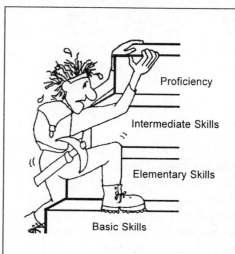

Fig. 12.3 According to the organic maturation views, individuals proceed through a series of increasingly complex skills as body systems' mature and opportunities become available to practice these skills.

organizing one's inner world to interact meaningfully with the outer world, and (4) actively seeking experiences to actualize genetic potentials. Mastery of skills is seen as self-generative toward higher levels of achievement.

Theory of piaget

Jean Piaget's theory of cognitive development assumes that an individual's basic goal in life is to learn to master the environment (both external and internal). The pleasure received from mastery spurs increased curiosity, problem solving, imitation, practice, and play activities. His assumption is that human nature is essentially rational and that human knowledge is self-created.

Piaget proposes four major cognitive processes : (1) a **schema**, which is a unit or category of thought, a mental classification for an object or an action; (2) **assimilation**, the process whereby stimuli are recognized and integrated into an already existing schema; (3) **accomodation**, the creation of a new schema or the modification of an old one to account for newly recognized differences in a behaviour or stimulus; and (4) **equilibration**, the balance a person maintains between assimilation and accomodation. Equilibration is a self-regulating process which prevents overloading or underloading of a system by the search for, or avoidance of, novel experiences.

In Piaget's theory, cognitive development is divided into four developmental levels, each of which is characterized by specific interaction patterns with the environment. During the **sensorimotor** stage (birth to age 2), understanding proceeds from the reflexive activities of the neonate through sensorimotor solutions to problems. The child in the **preoperational** stage (2-7 years) solves simple motor problems internally through the use of symbols and language. The **concrete operational** child (7-11 years) is able to provide logical solutions to specific, practical, concrete problems. Between 11 and 15 years, the child develops the ability to think scientifically about complex and abstract issues. Once **formal operations** (mature

thought processes) are developed, quantitative, but not qualitative, changes in intellectual functioning occur.

Humanistic view

Humanists looked for normal, healthy subjects to interview and analyze in developing their theory of the healthy, self-actualizing individual who is constantly growing toward successively higher levels of personal integration. They contend that the "will to health" or the incentive toward growth is innate. The basic drive is to grow, to find meaning in life, unity in experiences, and to actualize one's innate potentials. The humanist contends that behaviour is ambiguous or confusing unless its meaning and intent are understood from the point of view of the particular individual. For example, one person may cry as an expression of intense joy, another, as an expression of pity, pain, fear, or relief. Attempts to describe and analyze behaviour apart from feelings, beliefs, values,

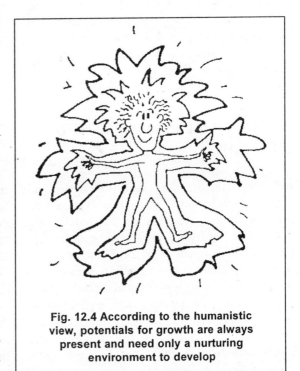

Fig. 12.4 According to the humanistic view, potentials for growth are always present and need only a nurturing environment to develop

thoughts, and aspirations artificially bisect the individual and insult the integrity of the person as a holistic unit.

Humanistically oriented psychologists emphasize the distinctively human characteristics of choice, will, creativity, values and self-realization. The uniqueness of each individual, rather than the norm, is a primary focus. Each individual is endowed with "value" and "dignity". From the humanistic viewpoint, each individual, regardless of the degree of innate potential, has the right to develop his or her potentials to be maximum.

Holistic developmental view

Clara Schuster, (a developmentalist with backgrounds in nursing, education, exceptional children, and developmental psychology) developed a set of generic, culture-free tasks to provide a more holistic description of developmental phases. She observed that the stimuli, opportunities, and contingencies of the environment are crucial in helping the young child to organize adaptive responses. She believes that biophysical, psychosociocultural, and self-generating factors all play significant roles in growth and development. However, the self-generating skills of the young child are weak and need a synchronized, nurturing, contingent environment to maximize potentials.

PSYCHOSOCIAL DEVELOPMENT OF THE FETUS

It is not yet known how much the physical and maternal psychosocial events that occur during intrauterine life directly affect the psychosocial development of fetus. *Gesell* postulated that biophysical development, movement, and responses in utero lay a foundation for reflexive and voluntary movements or responses after birth. These behaviours lay the foundation for social interaction and skill competence and thus, emotional development. Through the use of ultrasound, researchers have probed the secret universe of the prenatal world to discover that some psychosocial

behaviours (such as sensuality or withdrawal) show continuity from the 12th week of gestation through the preschool years. Some would contend that "mother's state of mind before birth can affect the child and can go on doing so into adult life." Questions remain, however: (1) What is genetic and what is environmental? (2) Do hormones from the mother affect the fetus' development? (3) Is there some mechanism by which the mother's attitude is transmitted to the developing child, preparing it to adapt to the postnatal environment of acceptance, hostility, sensuality or neglect?

Available studies are limited to those parameters that can be measured objectively, biological and sensory events. Consequently, studies of infant behaviour—particularly in the affective domain—are primarily limited to the moment of birth as the point of departure. However, a few pioneers are looking at how prenatal events may help to mold affective, cognitive, and language development.

It has been shown that a woman's emotional state can influence fetal motility and that fetal hyperactivity is related to neonatal hyperactivity. Infants born to stressed mothers during world war II were noted to exhibit disturbed affective behaviours and hyperactivity. Seventy-five percent of the offspring of mothers who experience critical stress during pregnancy suffered from a serious illness at some time during the first 3 years of life; only 28% of infants of nonstressed mothers experienced similar serious illness. *Brazelton* notes that infants who suffer from intrauterine growth retardation seem to have more difficulty organizing neuromuscular responses and are frequently labeled as "colicky" by mothers. Babies of stressed mothers tend to be more active before birth and tend to have increased irritability, hyperactivity, frequent stools, and feeding problems after birth.

Visual responses

Beginning with the 16th week of life, a light placed directly on the mother's abdomen startles the fetus or causes it to move away.

Auditory responses

The ability to hear may occur as early as the 16th week of fetal life. Changes in the fetal heart rate indicate that the fetus can discriminate between sounds and habituate to a sound.

Other prenatal activities

By the 7th week of gestation, the fetus has sufficient cutaneous receptors to respond to the touch of a hair around its mouth. Touch receptors spread to the rest of the face, the palms, and the soles by the 11th week, the trunk by the 15th week, and all surfaces by the 20th week of gestation. Brain stem and thalamus pain pathways are completely myelinated by 30 weeks. During the third trimester, some fetuses may arch their backs against the side of the uterus when the mother's abdomen is gently rubbed.

THE NEONATE

The *neonatal* (newborn) period is the first 4 weeks after birth. This is a time of transition from the total dependency of prenatal life to a more independent, creative existence. It is a time when rhythms of breathing, feeding, sleeping, and elimination are established and when babies and parents make some critical adaptations to one another.

Neonates are born with abilities to perceive and respond to some parts of their world in an organized and effective way. For example, reflexes that are in place at birth permit the neonate to grope, or "root," for the breast to suck when an object is placed in its mouth and to swallow milk and other liquids. These three reflexes are obviously essential to feeding. Other inborn reflexes with obvious adaptive value are breathing, blinking, coughing, sneezing, vomiting, and withdrawing from painful stimuli. Another class of reflexes is attributed to the immaturity of certain parts of the brain. One example is the **Moro reflex:** When support is suddenly removed from the back of its

head, the neonate will fling its arms to the side, extend its fingers, and bring its arms inward in a sort of embracing movement. The Moro reflex and other reflexes in this category normally disappear in early infancy, as the brain matures. If these reflexes persist for too long, it may mean that there is a problem with the infant's developing central nervous system.

Neonates show positive reactions to certain sweet tastes and negative reactions to certain sour, bitter, or salty tastes. They turn their heads to avoid some strong odours; and they turn in the direction of certain sounds, including human speech.

Some of the most exciting findings about neonates involve their visual abilities. They not only orient toward light but they can, under the right conditions, actually follow a light or an object placed directly in their line of vision.

Some surprising findings of a study conducted by *Meltzoff* and *Moore* (1977) suggested that neonates are even capable of imitation. The research, appeared to show that babies as young as 2 or 3 weeks can mimic certain adult behaviours, such as facial expressions.

In the first few weeks of life outside the womb, glimmers of "personality" can be seen in the temperament babies display. For example, some babies are "difficult" even in the first weeks after their birth. They may show irregularities in their sleeping, feeding, or elimination patterns. They may be easily distressed and irritable, and prone to cry. Evidence suggests that youngsters who show this "difficult-child syndrome" are more likely than are other infants to develop behaviour disorders in their later life. Genetic and other biological factors seem to influence such characteristics of temperament.

The baby's development is thus shaped by the interplay of its inborn characteristics and its parents' behaviour. This is one example of the interaction between heredity and environment—nature and nurture.

INFANCY: NEUROMUSCULAR DEVELOPMENT

The tissues that compose the muscular and skeletal systems provide structure and allow movement of the infant's' rapidly growing body.

Skeletal system

In general, connective tissue becomes cartilage and then gradually is replaced by bones. Except for the bones of the face, cranium and the shaft centers of long bones (which are ossified during fetal life), all other bony structures undergo gradual hardening *after* birth. If this immature soft bone is subjected to trauma, "green-stick" or incomplete fractures may result. While ossification is occurring, bones continue to grow in length and width and consequently change shape. The bones of girls usually grow and mature faster than those of boys.

Muscular system

During infancy, muscular growth is due mainly to hypertrophic growth of the already formed muscle fibers, although some hyperplastic growth continues. The growth rate of muscle is about twice as fast as that of bone during the period of time from 5 months to 3 years. During these early years, pituitary growth hormone, thyroid hormones, and insulin all play a role in the growth of muscle tissue.

The sequence of motor skill development is more critical than the specific age of its emergence. Children who "skip a stage" frequently experience motor refinement problems later in development. For example, babies need a prolonged crawling experience to strengthen the shoulder girdle muscles. Children frequently experience difficulty with fine motor development (e.g., ball throwing accuracy and writing skills) if the muscles are not strong enough to stabilize the shoulder joint when using the arm. Therefore, *parents should encourage the baby to crawl as long as possible* rather than encourage early walking.

Neurological system

Nearly one-half of the brain's postnatal growth is achieved by the end of the first year. Most of the growth in size occurs in the *cerebral cortex,*

		Gross Motor Skills	Fine Motor Skills
1	MONTH	Head lags when baby is pulled from a supine to a sitting position. When prone, baby may lift head occasionally, but unsteadily. Will turn head from side to side. Will make crawling movements when prone. Is able to push feet against a bare surface to propel self forward. Assymetrical tonic neck reflex (ATNR) present. Moves arms asymmetrically. Dancing or stepping reflex when held upright. Symmetrical Moro reflex.	Hands are held predominantly in fists. Demonstrates a tight reflex grasp. Head and eyes move together. Rooting and sucking reflexes present. Follows persons with eyes and head.
2	MONTHS	Head righting reactions emerging (tonic labyrinthine reaction) but not strong enough to keep head upright in sitting position. When prone, can lift head and chest off firm surfaces to 45°. Kicks feet alternately. Rolls from side to back.	Hands begin to open. May hold a toy placed in hand for a brief time. Uses *primitive palmar grasp* (e.g., grasps objects with finger and palm of hand, with no thumb opposition). Hand to mouth activity. Good visual regard. Follows movements of objects with eyes from side to midline. Social smiling in response to various stimuli.

	Gross Motor Skills	Fine Motor Skills
3 MONTHS	When prone, lifts head to 90° when propped on forearms. Stepping and crawling reflexes absent. When supported, sits with rounded back and flexed knees, leaning forward. Holds head at midline. May roll from front to back. ATNR reflex disappearing as the STNR reflex appears.	Brings hands to midline. Bats at and reaches toward bright objects with one arm, but will obtain them only by chance. Is able to carry an object from hand to mouth. When supine, moves eyes and turns head 180° to follow moving object or person. Follows with eyes past midline. Looks from one object to another. Grasping, rooting, and sucking reflexes begin to fade.
4 MONTHS	Symmetrical arm and leg movements and posture. Hands to knees. Head midline. Strong head-righting reactions. Rolls from back to side. Bears weight briefly when held upright. Will sit upright if supported at hips. No head lag when pulled to sit. Moro reflex disappearing.	Hands held predominantly open. Spreads fingers to grasp. Fingers and plays with own hands at midline. Reaches for objects with both hands in supine position and will briefly hold on to and shake small objects. Uses *ulnar—palmar grasp* (object held against palm with little and ring finger). Will bring hands to midline and watch them for prolonged periods of time.
5 MONTHS	Will hold back straight with no head lag when pulled to sitting position. Reaches for objects in supported sitting. Rolls from back to side, and front to back. Feet to mouth.	Brings toys to mouth to explore. Able to grasp objects voluntarily. Follows objects with eyes without head movement. Uses "mitten grasp" (i.e., grasps with whole hand. All fingers except thumb hold object against palm) or *palmar grasp*. Reaches for objects with both hands, symmetrical movement. Can transfer small object from hand to hand.
6 MONTHS	Pushes up onto extended arms, with chest and abdomen cleared of floor. May pull self up to a sitting position. Sits independently propped on hands or with arms in high guard position to facilitate trunk stability. Forward protective responses appear. Can turn completely over in either direction. Pivots in prone. Some babies may hitch (propel self backward in sitting position, using arms and legs to move body). When held in standing position, bears almost all of weight.	Can hold two objects at once. Bangs objects on table surface. Will unconsciously release one object to reach for and grasp another object. Uses *radial-palmar grasp* (all four fingers in opposition to base of the thumb) for grasping. Uses raking motion to scoop up a raisin with hand. Much mirroring or overflow behaviors seen in opposite hand/arm. May grasp feet and suck on toes.
7 MONTHS	Lifts head as if attempting to sit up when supine. Sits well. Pushes up onto hands and knees and rocks. Bear full weight on feet. Enjoys bouncing when sitting or held in a standing position. Moves from sitting position to prone or quadraped (hands and knees). Protective sideways responses appear.	Reaches for toy with straight elbow and grasps with one hand. Uses *radial-digital grasp* (the tips of all fingers against the thumb) to hold a small object. Will bring feet to midline and watch them for prolonged periods of time.
8 MONTHS	May stand while holding on. Raises on foot while standing. Moves from prone to quadraped to sit. Crawls backward and forward (abdomen on floor, body propelled with arm movement, legs dragging).	Uses *inferior pincer grasp* (index and middle fingers in opposition to the thumb). Spontaneously releases objects. Bangs two blocks together at midline. Pulls large pegs from pegboard. Holds bottle and places nipple in mouth as wanted.

	Gross Motor Skills	Fine Motor Skills
9 MONTHS	May creep (trunk is above and parallel to floor, with both hands and knees used in locomotion). Pulls self to stand holding on to something for support. Stepping movements but may not move from spot.	Complete thumb opposition. Uses *lateral grasp* (thumb and side of index finger) for small objects. Manipulates objects by pushing, pulling, sliding, squeezing. Purposefully releases objects (if the skill of creeping has developed). Takes objects out of containers.
10 MONTHS	Stands briefly independently. Can cruise, or walk sideways holding on to something. May cry when unable to sit down without assistance. Sits by falling down. Walks with hands held. Protective backward responses appear. Pivots in sitting position.	Uses isolated index finger to poke at objects. Feeds self finger foods (e.g., crackers). Can bring hands together and play "pat-a-cake" and "peek-a-boo." Enjoys throwing and dropping objects. Releases objects into larger containers.
11 MONTHS	Can stand erect while holding on to some form of support with one hand. Creeps rapidly. Will walk holding on to adult hand. Lowers self to floor while holding on. May take one-two steps independently with arms in high guard position.	Picks up tiny objects, such as raisins, with *neat pincer grasp* (very precise opposition of thumb and tip of index finger). Can hold marker (to make a mark on paper). Releases objects into small-mounted container. Supinates (rotates) forearm.
12 MONTHS	Stands alone well. May walk alone (some before 1 year; some after). May sit down from standing without assistance or holding on. Kneels.	Begins to use objects as tools, such as spoon, cup, comb. Gives toy on request. Removes lids from containers. Can turn pages in a book, several at a time. Can drink holding cup, but needs assistance.
13 MONTHS	Walks without support. Climbs stairs well on hands and knees. Throws ball while seated, whole body in motion. Stoops to pick up an object. Climbs into sofa, chairs.	Holds adult's hand while being spoon-fed. Will position body to assist with dressing. Places large pegs in peg board. Builds 2 block tower.
14 MONTHS	Steps off one step well with help. Creeps down steps. Walks backwards.	Pats picture in books. Holds spoon to feed, but needs assistance. Inverts a container to get block. Drinks independently from cup with occasional spills. Points with index finger.
15 MONTHS	Creeps up stairs. May not be able to walk around corners or stop suddenly without losing balance. Walks sideways. Fast walk-run. Gets up to standing from middle of floor. Bends over to look through legs. Pulls toy behind self while walking.	Builds a tower of 3 to 4 blocks. Opens most boxes, pokes fingers into holes and playdough (clay). Scribbles spontaneously.

Fig. 12.5 Neuromotor Development during Infancy

which is associated with sensory perception, motor functioning, speech, and cognitive activities (such as processing, organizing, storing, and retrieving information). The *brain stem,* is relatively well developed at birth compared to the other structures of the CNS. The brain stem primarily controls survival functions (such as temperature control, respiration, digestion, and heart rate) and the other activities of the autonomic nervous system. These vital functions continue to be irregular through the early months of infancy, indicating that brain stem development is. incomplete. The *cerebellum,* located behind the brain stem, shows an increase in weight throughout the first decade. The cerebellum coordinates movement and equilibrium.

Head Circumference

During infancy the head grows at a relatively rapid rate. Skull growth closely parallels brain growth. The measurement of head circumference and the assessment of fontanelle status are ways to monitor this growth. The head circumference increases from an average of 34 cm (approximately 13½ inches) at birth to 44 cm by 6 months, and to 47 cm by 1 year. The posterior fontanelle closes during the third month of extrauterine life. The anterior fontanelle may increase in size until the body is 6 months old; then it begins to diminish and is closed by 18 months.

DEVELOPMENT OF PERCEPTION DURING INFANCY

One research study of depth perception was conducted by *Gibson* and *Walk* in 1960. To judge whether infants can read the perceptual cues that adults use to judge depth, these researchers used the visual cliff. It involved an apparent drop-off made safe by a clear glass cover. Despite the cover, *Gibson* and *Walk* found that none of the 6 to 14 months old infants they tested would cross the "deep" area to get to their mothers. Yet all 36 of them

eagerly crawled to their mothers when the moms were stationed on the "shallow" side. This strongly suggests that even 6-month old infants have depth perception. But what about babies who are too young to crawl and thus unfit for the Gibson-Walk test? In a clever extension of the visual-cliff experiment, *Campos, Langer*, and *Krowitz* (1970) simply placed infants too young to crawl on either the shallow or the deep side and then measured changes in their heart rates. Even 1½ month old infants showed increased heart-rate when they were placed over the deep side. They were evidently responding to depth cues.

COGNITIVE DEVELOPMENT DURING INFANCY

Jean Piaget (1970), a Swiss biologist, philosopher, and psychologist, developed the most detailed and comprehensive theory of cognitive development. Piaget called his approach genetic *epistemology.* **Epistemology** is the study of the nature and acquisition of knowledge; Piaget's approach was "genetic" in the sense that it focused on origins (genesis) and development.

According to Piaget, the processes of assimilation, accomodation, and equilibration operate in different ways at different age levels. One result is that our ways of thinking about, or knowing, the world pass through certain predictable stages.

Piaget's sensorimotor stage

The young child does not use the same discriminators as those used by older children or adults to categorize their world. During Piaget's sensorimotor stage (birth to 24 months), the infant experiences the world only as it interacts with the senses and understands it only as far as he or she is able to exert control of events.

Piget observes that the baby's activities progress from organized reflex action to trial-and-error learning.

Substage I: Reflex Activity (Birth to 1 Month)

Piaget hypothesizes that the neonate exists in a state of complete egocentrism, unaware that any other viewpoints exist. When the neonate is stimulated, innate reflexes mediate responses. When an object is put into the neonate's mouth, it is sucked; when an object is placed on the palm, it is grasped; when another human cry is heard, the baby joins the chorus. The infant in this substage cannot differentiate between objects or stimuli.

SENSORIMOTOR STAGE (FIRST 2 YEARS)

Characterized by incorporation of reflex patterns into intentional movements designed first only to repeat, later to maintain, and then to produce new changes in the environment increasing understanding of means-end relationships. Object constancy is achieved, and the beginning of true "thought" and internalized problem solving are seen; but the child still operates very much in the here and now.

PREOPERATIONAL STAGE (2 TO 7 YEARS)

Characterized by unsystematic reasoning. Impressive development of internal representations and language. Thought characterized by egocentrism, animism and faulty reasoning about cause-effect relationships.

> *Preconceptual Substage (2 to 4 years)*
> Rapid development of language. Begins to engage in symbolic play. Tends to use classes inaccurately (for example calls all men "Daddy").
> *Perceptual, or Intuitive, substage (4 to 7 years)*
> "Reasoning" appears but remains centered on appearances rather than implications. Tends to center on the most noticeable aspects of things observed and therefore fails to "conserve" identities in volume, number and mass. May discover true relationships through trail and error but is unable to think in flexible ways that involves reversibility. Confuses reality and fantasy but tries to test which is what.

CONCRETE OPERATIONAL STAGE (7 TO 12 YEARS)

Systematic reasoning appears; thought processes are logical and reversible but limited to a child's area of concrete experience. Alternative strategies are invented (for example, two ways of getting to the store). Can coordinate part-whole, hierarchical classifications. Comprehends conservation of number, mass, and other properties.

FORMAL OPERATIONAL STAGE (12 YEARS ONWARD)

Characterized by logic, reasoning from hypothetical propositions, evaluating hypotheses through testing all possible conclusions. Present reality seen as only one alternative in an array of possibilities. Can think about thinking and uses theories to guide thought.

Fig. 12.6 The stages of cognitive growth according to Piaget

Thus it would seem that most activity during this first month is *assimilated* or incorporated into the primitive schemata of ready-made reflexes. Because reflexive behaviour can enable the neonate to survive, it is adaptive.

Substage II: Primary Circular Reactions (1 to 4 Months)

During substage II, the reflexes begin to be modified as a function of experience and neurological maturation. The infant reproduces behaviours that were previously achieved by chance (through random activity). Building on reflexive sucking action, an infant discovers that inserting the thumb in the mouth brings pleasure and comfort, so it is repeated again and again. The baby will suck on almost anything if it provides sucking pleasure. Thus, the young baby assimilates each object into the sucking schema.

The baby begins to show recognition of objects or *object concept*. For instance, when the breast or feeding bottle is presented, there will be signs of eager anticipation. During substage II, the infant will immediately and purposefully repeat his or her own behaviours that bring sensual pleasure (such as kicking).

Substage III: Secondary Circular Reactions (4 to 8 Months)

Previously, the infant's behaviour was directed primarily toward the self and what physically felt good or pleased the senses. Five-month olds begin to learn to control their environments by making use of visually directed reaching (sighting an object, reaching for it, and making contact with it)—a skill the infant could not accomplish neurologically until this stage.

In this substage, a behaviour is repeated and prolonged for the response that results. Behaviours begin to expand or combined under cognitive control. Thus grasping and holding now become shaking and banging.

During substage III, the infant will imitate the behaviour of others if the skill is already within the infant's repertoire (e.g., coughing or kissing sounds, table patting, or head shaking).

Substage IV: Coordination of Secondary Schemata and Their Application to New Situations (8 to 12 Months)

The entrance into substage IV is heralded by the emergence of **object permanence,** or the knowledge that an object exists independently of one's current perceptions. This is the first evidence of expressive memory.

The baby who is 8 to 10 months old will not only protest the disappearance of a desired object, but will search for the object. Thus, if a desired toy is hidden under a blanket or cup while the baby is watching, the baby will easily retrieve the toy by reaching under the barrier. The baby now demonstrates an awareness that objects still exist when they disappear from view.

Once object permanence emerges, it is a fragile skill. If the desired object is moved from one hiding place to another (e.g., under another cup, pillow, or blanket), the infant of this age does not always search for objects where they disappeared, but where they were found the last time. This is known as *stage IV error*. The original hiding place assumes an independent status as "hiding place."

By this substage, changes have occurred in how the baby approaches the solving of a problem. By the end of this substage, the baby uses primarily those actions that worked in previous situations. This suggests that the baby possesses memory and is beginning to do some mental processing of problems before acting. By using responses that have been previously mastered, the infant can now solve simple problems and begins to use the behaviours to achieve more complex goals. An unwanted toy, for example, will be moved out of the way to reach a more desirable one.

During substage IV, the infant modifies and extends skills and will imitate the behaviours of others if the skill is similar to skills already mastered. For example, the baby learns to wave bye-bye, clap hands, or will imitate hitting a spoon on a dish.

Substage V: Tertiary Circular Reactions— The discovery of New Means Through Active Experimentation (12 to 18 Months)

During substage V, the infant actively attempts to discover and understand cause-event relationships. One of the more common scenarios involves a minor trauma. The toddling child will accidentally fall, hitting his or her head on a chair or door frame, creating a novel sound. The child will look surprised, cautiously and purposefully hit the head against the same spot to recreate the same effect, look pleased (at having discovered the relationship), and then will often look around for the parent before emitting a cry of feigned pain. For the moment, curiosity eclipsed the emotional response to the discomfort. Once a cause-effect relationship is discovered, the infant will attempt to apply the new information to find another solution to an old problem.

During this substage, stage IV error disappear and the infant begins to search for objects in the area of the last visible displacement. However, the ability to search for objects that are hidden while the child is not looking (invisible displacements) does not occur until substage VI, which is considered to be well into toddlerhood.

The infant in substage V will physically manipulate events to test their effect, but does not evidence the ability to mentally manipulate the event before it happens. This is especially evident in the child's ability to place puzzle pieces. There is much guessing, trial-error, slipping and sliding of pieces, and attempts to force pieces into slots.

PSYCHOSOCIAL DEVELOPMENT DURING INFANCY

Most theories of emotional and social development contend that the early mother-child relationship is pivotal to the quality of social relationships and emotional maturity in the adult years. The infant begins life as an asocial being. The parent facilitates development by orchestrating a social context that supports the infant's potentials and efforts. Through mutual focusing on interactions that capture the infant's attention and interest, the infant gradually begins to establish a meaningful relationship with the primary caregiver, to develop social communication skills, and to learn how to learn. This puts a lot of responsibility on the parents for the successful development of their infant.

The infant is a gregarious person from the moment of birth. Inadequate attention to the affective and social needs of the young infant can have serious consequences. The biophysically normal infant who suffer even minor deprivation or inadequate synchronization of the social environment may experience negative cognitive, physical, and social consequences.

The infant is an active and reactive participant in the social process, sometimes the recipient of an interaction and at other times the initiator. Both the baby's and the parent's behaviours change rapidly over the course of the infancy period as they accommodate to one another.

The terms mother, parent, and care-giver are used interchangeably to indicate the primary person whose actions and interactions are associated with the nurturing role.

The Process of Attachment

Attachment, a term coined by Bowlby in 1958, refers to the selective emotional ties that one person (in this case the infant) has for another person or persons, for a pet, or even for objects. This focused relationship develops over time as the child experiences repeated contacts. Attachment behaviours are those activities that serve to obtain or to maintain contact or proximity with the attachment object (e.g., visual tracking, grasping, reaching, smiling, babbling, clinging, crying).

Attachment gives the child a security base, which at first provides a source of strength and identity and later provides a point of differenti-

Substage	Approximate Age	Developmental Unit	Behavioral Example
I	0 – 1 month	Exercising ready-made sensorimotor schemata	Baby improves efficiency of neurological reflexes (e.g., rooting, sucking, swallowing) by beginning to initiate some at will (e.g., thumb suck)
II	1 – 4 months	Primary circular reactions	Baby repeats own behavior for sensual pleasure (e.g., repetitive kicking, fingering of an object placed in or near hand, sucking for a long period of time); begins to modify a reflex (e.g., adjusts swallow to different textures of food). Early coordination of selected reflexes (e.g., sucking and swallowing, reaching and grasping).
III	4 – 8 months	Secondary circular reactions	Behavior becomes "international." Baby repeats behaviors that produce novel, pleasing, and interesting effects on the environment (e.g., to elicit laughter from caregiver or sound from a musical toy). Increased voluntary coordination of motor skills enables exploration (e.g., mouthing objects in environment by combining grasping and sucking). Imitates skills already in repertoire. Early understanding of cause-effect relationships. Cognitive object constancy appears at about 5 months.
IV	8 – 12 months	Coordination of secondary reactions (schemata) and applications to new situations	Infant consciously uses an action that is a mean to an end (e.g., uses reaching ability to obtain many new an interesting objects); begins to solve simple problems. Object permanence appears at about 8 months. Imitates simple behaviors of others. Active search of cause—effect relationships. Repetitive explorations.
V	12 – 18 months	Tertiary circular reactions	Infant shows early experimental approaches to knowledge gathering and problem solving by varying approaches to an old situation or applying old approaches to new problems. Much trial and error learning. Must physically solve a problem to understand cause—effect relationship. Imitates simple novel behaviors.
VI	18 – 24 months	Invention of new means through mental combinations	Child first shows "intelligent behavior" by manipulating objects mentally before acting. Begins to predict events and results. Much trial and error problem solving. Can solve detour problems; can predict effects from observing causes, and can also infer a cause when only the effect is seen; is able to follow an invisible displacement. Early symbolic play. Both immediate and deferred (delayed) imitation of actions and words noted.

Fig. 12.7 Summary of Piaget's Sensorimotor Stage

ation or separation. Most infants form multiple attachments. Although attachments are similar in quality, they differ in intensity and are not freely interchangeable.

The establishment of a meaningful emotional/social relationship is seen as the cornerstone of all future development because early attachment facilitates the following:

1. Differentiation between self and others
2. Exploration of the environment
3. Development of conscience
4. Harnessing of energies

5. Development of self-discipline
6. Emergence of empathy
7. Coping with stress and frustration
8. Development of self-reliance
9. Reduction of fear and anxiety
10. Dissipation of jealousies and rivalries
11. Development of autonomy
12. Attainment of self-confidence
13. Development of self-acceptance
14. Development of later social and emotional relationship
15. Sense of caring for the self

Sensitive period

Infants more than 5 months of age who change caregivers (e.g., because of maternal illness, return to work, or adoption) evidence extreme stress. This behaviour indicates that selective attachment has been established during the first 6 months of life. Even though disruption of a relationship is traumatic, once a child has learned to trust and attach to one person, it is easier to attach to a second person. Children who have never attached to another person experience great difficulty with this process.

Need satisfaction

Early theories emphasized physiological need satisfaction as the basis for the infant's development of attachment to, and meaningful relationships with, others. In 1958, *Harry* and *Margaret Harlow* proved that there is more to attachment behaviour than just being fed adequately. They raised infant monkeys in cages with two very different surrogate mothers. One "mother" was covered with soft terry cloth, the other was composed of hard wire mesh and had a feeding apparatus. The baby monkeys did not spend much time with the wire surrogate mother that fed them, but clung to the cloth surrogate that did not feed them. The need theory was shattered; the provision of food was not the basis for attach-

ment. Comforting potential was a much stronger basis.

When the infant monkeys in Harlow's experiment reached adulthood, they demonstrated marked social difficulties and sexual maladjustment. Research with well-cared-for institutionalized children who experienced as many as 50 to 80 caregivers indicates that inadequate attachment experiences in infancy lead to excessive attention—seeking and indiscriminate friendliness by 4 years of age and to impaired relationship with peers and adults during school years. Inadequate, inconsistent, or nonresponsive attachment objects in infancy prevent adequate socialization.

Theories of Attachment

Infants become attached to caregivers who provide a source of consistent, intimate interaction. Several theorists offer explanations of the process. Freud based his theory of attachment on instinctual drives, viewing the infant as a narcissistic organism who attaches to people who can reduce tensions and meet his or her needs.

Mary Ainsworth observed that 12 to 18 month old infants could be classified as a securely or insecurely attached based on their behaviour in an unfamiliar setting. The child is first left with a stranger for three minutes and is later left completely alone in an unfamiliar room. *Securely attached* infants are noted to cry with mild intensity following maternal departure, to greet the mother's return eagerly, and to be easily soothed upon her return. Insecurely attached babies exhibit two patterns of behaviour. *Anxious avoidant* infants show little stress when mother leaves and do not greet her when she returns. *Anxious ambivalent* babies show extreme stress when she leaves, and are not easily soothed at her return. Research bears out Ainsworth's hypothesis that the security of the attachment is correlated with the sensitivity of maternal feedback to the young infant's behaviours.

Jacob Gewirtz, a behavioural learning theorist, suggests that differential reinforcement leads to attachment. He hypothesizes that attachment is a specific pattern of response that evolves as a result of the infant and caregiver learning to exert control over one another's behaviour (a positive stimulus and reinforcer). However, even in the face of severe maltreatment and severe punishment, attachment behaviours may be exhibited by infants and young children.

Although each theorist offers a different explanation, the scenario is the same: Infants who receive warm, consistent, synchronized responses from a primary person appear to develop a specific attachment to that person. The paradox is that the more securely an infant is attached, the easier it is for the child to separate, to move outward to explore the environment, enjoy new experiences, and associate with other people.

Bowlby's theory of attachment

John Bowlby, a child psychiatrist, postulates that attachment is the result of interaction between adaptive predispositions in the infant and behaviours of the parent. He believes that certain types of stimulation elicit certain types of behaviour in the infant, and that infant behaviours elicit particular behaviours in the adult.

Bowlby asserts that infants use attachment behaviours such as sucking, clinging, following, crying, and smiling to elicit parental caregiving.

He believes that feeding plays only a minor role in the development of attachment. Sensitive social reciprocity is a more critical component. Attachment occurs as the infant learns to "distinguish the familiar from the strange."

Bowlby differentiates between the terms *dependence* and *attachment,* which are considered synonymous by some theorists. **Dependence** is the extent to which one individual relies on another to meet needs. Dependent behaviours may be exhibited toward anyone.

Attachment is absent at birth, and increases over time. Bowlby discusses four overlapping phases in the normal development of attachment:

- Phase 1, as orientation and signals without discrimination of figure.
- Phase 2, (3 to 6 months): (orientation and signals directed toward one or more discriminated figures).
- Phase 3, (7 to 36 months): (maintenance of proximity to a discriminated figure by means of locomotion as well as signals).
- Phase 4: (formation of a goal-directed partnership).

Emotional development during infancy

When babies smile, does it mean they are happy? This seemingly simple question is actually very complicated because what looks like an emotion may not always be one.

Factor	Attachment	Dependency
Specificity	1 person	Anyone
Duration	Over time	Transient
Developmental level	All ages	Immature only
Affect	Strong, intrinsic passion	Minimal or no emotional involvement
Proximity seeking	Focused toward specific person	Contact with anyone who can meet/relieve need
Acquisition	Learned; becomes stronger with time	Unlearned; maximal at birth; should diminish over time

Evidently, smiling happens for different reasons at different ages. Some smiling is seen even in newborns, but much of this seems automatic and hardly "emotional." Other early smiles operate like reflexes, as when neonates smile when someone strokes their lips. In the second month, smiles can be brought on by events in the environment—particularly the sound of a human voice or the sight of a human face. A powerful smile evoker is a combination of a voice and a moving face, particularly if the voice is high-pitched. By the third or fourth month, babies smile more for their mothers than for an equally encouraging female stranger. By the beginning of their fifth month, most babies have begun to combine smiling with laughing. By their first birthdays, interesting visual displays, like a human mask, get more laughs.

One interpretation of this developmental change is that emotions like happiness and delight develop hand-in-hand with a child's intellect. Simple pleasures that are not cognitively demanding may please an immature infant; but as cognitive development proceeds, a baby needs to be increasingly challenged intellectually in order to experience pleasure and humor.

Some investigators argue that babies make sense of the world around them by forming mental representations, or *schemas,* of certain kinds of objects. When they see an object and are able to match it to their schema (and thus "recognize" it), the result is pleasure, which is signaled by a smile or a laugh.

Adjustment problems during infancy

Quiet common in the first year of life are infant feeding problem—especially a digestive discomfort known as colic—and vomiting. Constipation and diarrhoea, irregular sleep patterns, and mystifying bursts of crying also occur very often in the first year. Near the end of the first year and well into the second, the problems most often involve a conflict between the baby's growing physical

and mental processes and the parents' efforts to regulate behaviour that seems to them to be aggressive or dangerous. Two of the most common child-behaviour problems parents report at this age are "stubbornness" and "temper" (*Achenbach & Edelbrock*, 1981).

A number of clinical disorders make their first appearance during infancy. Among these are several that are known to be caused by genetic or other biological factors. **Down syndrome**, for example, involves mental retardation and a characteristic physical appearance noticeable even in newborn.

Early signs of the disorder known as **infantile autism** make their appearance during the first year and a half of life. Autistic youngsters fail to show several of the landmark features of infancy. They fail to focus on other people's' eyes, they do not smile regularly in response to people's' faces or voices, and they do not show such key signs of attachment as protest when a parent leaves them. Later, difficulties with social interaction and especially with language will plague these children into their adulthood. Infants suffering from a *failure to thrive* show apathy, a lack of normal social interest, and stunted growth despite seemingly adequate nutrition. What little evidence we now have suggests that this disorder often results when rearing situations leave infants neglected, abused, or poorly stimulated.

DEVELOPMENT OF THE TODDLER AND THE PRESCHOOLER

From the age of about 18 months through the age of 6, the comfortable confines of the child's family give way to the world of peers. In the context of play, children make the transition from sensorimotor thinking to thinking that involves internal manipulation of symbols. The elegant symbol system known as language takes shape at a pace that leaves even experienced parents dazzled. The frequency and intensity of peer interaction force the child to deal with interper-

---

DEVELOPMENTAL TASKS OF INFANCY

*1. Establish a meaningful emotional/ social rela-
tionship:
- recognize primary caregivers
- develop trust in caregivers
- develop attachment behaviors
- evolve refueling skills

*2. Learn how to learn:
- orient to objects and stimuli
- activate curiosity
- evolve exploration skills
- attend to details
- predict and practice obtaining responses
  from the environment (animate and inami-
ate)
- synthesize/integrate input from
  modalities/senses

*3. Develop social communication skills:
- develop vocalization skills
- recognize social signals of others
- participate in synchronized vocal reciprocity
  and social turntaking activities/games
- initiate interactions with others
  develop nonverbal forms of communication
  imitate simple vocal and social behaviors of
  others.

4. Develop voluntary control of neuromuscular
systems:
- antigravitational skills
- eye-hand coordination
- object manipulation
- balance responses
- mobility

5. Establish rhythms for activities of daily living:
- eating
- sleeping
- elimination

6. Recognize self as a person, physically separate
from attachment person:
- engage in physical exploration and
  comparison experiment with separation and
  reunion experiences
- begin to understand and trust own sensation
  begin to see self as capable of meeting own
    needs, e.g.:
    ○ positioning comfort
    ○ self-comforting skills
    ○ obtaining objects
    ○ feeding self

* Tasks deemed most crucial to continued maturation are marked with an asterisk.

---

sonal issues, such as coping with aggressive impulses and learning how to help.

Cognitive development of the toddler and the preschooler

The period between about the ages of 2 and 7 was labeled the preoperational stage by Piaget (1970). By this label, he meant that these years are preliminary to the development of truly logical operations.

What are operations? They are flexible mental actions that can be combined with one another to solve problems.

Piaget's substage VI of Sensorimotor Intelligence

The last subphase of the sensorimotor period of cognition (Piaget's substage VI: *the invention of new means through mental combinations*) extends to the toddler years. It is during this stage (18-24 months) that the toddler makes the transition from the sensorimotor level of intelligence to **representational intelligence** (the ability to picture an event in the mind). Mental representations enable the child to play out in the mind a sequence of behaviours without actually having to participate in the event physically or to manipulate the physical aspects of the event.

In substage VI, because many solutions can be tried out in the mind, the child is capable of inventing new means much more quickly. Furthermore, the child also can remember the actions of others no longer present and imitate them (delayed imitation).

Through the use of this new capacity for mental representations, the toddler can begin to predict many cause-effect relationships accurately. For example, the child begins to have an awareness that some situations may cause physical injury (climbing too high, running down a hill too fast, touching a hot surface) and will withdraw from the danger.

Piaget's Semiotic (Symbolic) Function

When the child is approximately 1½ years old, a cognitive process appears that is fundamental to the development of language, mental imagery, and symbolic gestures. This process, called the **semiotic** (or symbolic) function; consists of the ability to represent something (a *signified* something: object, event, conceptual schema, and so forth) by means of a *signifier,* which is differentiated from other objects and serves a representative purpose.

Semiotic functioning expands and becomes stabilized between 2 and 4 years of age. In addition to changing mental symbols into words to communicate with others, the child also consciously uses one object to represent another in "make-believe" or symbolic play (object substitution) because the two objects have some common feature that is used as an index for both. The index may be shape, colour, movement, or any other salient feature of the object.

Piaget's Preoperational Stage

During Piaget's preoperational stage (2 to 6 or 7 years of age), new cognitive processes allow the child to use mental symbols to think about what might be going on somewhere else at the present moment.

The preoperational stage is divided into two substages: preconceptional thought and intuitive thought. Because toddlers base their thinking heavily on the concrete perceptions and actions of their immediate environment, Piaget labels their thinking *preconceptional.* For example, "Daddy" describes any male voice on the telephone; "Nanny" may be any woman with white hair and glasses.

Intuitive thinking (4 to 7 years of age) emerges as the child begins to realize the ability of words to truly represent objects, events and actions, thoughts, fears, and feelings. The intuitive child can more efficiently differentiate between signifiers (mother getting her pocketbook) and significates (mother going out to the car), realizing that the pocketbook does not necessarily have to be associated with mother leaving or going for a ride.

Egocentrism

The thoughts of the toddler and the preschooler continue to be greatly influenced by what is seen, heard, or otherwise experienced at a given moment.

Although social interaction and empathy increase, the older preoperational child still is not able to see the viewpoint of another person. The only thought in mind is, "This is how the world looks to me." As a result, the preoperational child never questions his or her own subjective perceptions or viewpoints because they are, as far as the child is concerned, the only thoughts possible and consequently must be correct. Since the egocentric child can only think about things in terms of the subjective meanings attached to them, he or she cannot understand and will become angry when others do not understand his or her concrete, idiosyncratic speech and thoughts.

Cognitive egocentrism prevents the child from understanding other's experience, feelings or viewpoint. Piaget says that it is not until the child's thoughts and those of peers conflict in verbal exchange (usually around 6 or 7 years) that the child begins to accommodate to others; egocentric thought may give way under social pressure at this time.

Attention

One of the most critical tasks of the toddler and preschool years is to learn how to harness and focus energies. Focused attention is fundamental to learning. Unless a child attends to the stimulus, he or she will be unable to isolate the properties or indexes that differentiate one stimulus from another. Once a child learns to attend to the relevant features of a stimulus, he or she can learn to **generalize**, or transfer the knowledge learned, to other more difficult tasks.

Harnessing and focusing energies includes the abilities to invest oneself in the targeted activity, to resist distractors (although environmental scanning continues), to persevere at a task (note that there is a big difference between perseverance and perseveration (meaningless repetition of an activity) and maintain attention to a task long enough to master the challenge or at least to recognize one's limitations or alternatives.

Attention span depends on the nature of the materials as well as on the intellectual level and self-confidence of the individual child. The responsibility of the materials becomes a critical factor. Highly responsive materials tend to draw and capture the young child's attention, making it easy for the child to identify cause-effect relationships.

Materials from this category are identified as *fluid materials,* since they respond very rapidly, and in many ways. One of the reasons why children *love* water and sand so much is because of the highly responsive nature of the materials.

Structured materials are those that require precise physical and intellectual skills to make them respond in a positive way. Because of their minimal responsive nature, they drain emotional energy from the young child. Puzzles and learning to tie one's shoes fall into this category.

The highly responsive nature of fluid materials draws attention and maintains attention through multiple successful reactions. Children learn how to learn through the use of these materials. The sense of voluntary control of the results energies the child to repeat the activity.

Language development

Language expert *Noam Chomsky* (1968) proposed that there are universal grammatical rules used by all children everywhere and that this universal grammar is stimulated by an inborn language—acquisition device. More recent evidence, though (*Braine,* 1976), indicates that children may not really use the same underlying grammatical rules the world over. However, children do seem to follow some remarkably similar steps as they begin to combine words in order to express ideas.

One can view the course of language development as either continuous or discontinuous. Language development looks more discontinuous, or stagelike, when we focus on **syntax**—the formation of grammatical rules for assembling words into sentences.

The ages shown in the table are approximate; they even overlap in places. This is because there are large differences among children in their rate of development and because children (like adults) do not always use their most advanced forms of language. In many children, syntactic development actually begins before stage 1 in the table. *Halliday* (1975) showed that even before their first real English word, children can often communicate with their parents by using private expressions such as *bi* for bird, and *moosh* for milk.

When the first legitimate words are learned, stage I emerges quickly. Theorists used to argue that even the single-word utterances of young children reflected a knowledge of syntax. They called single-word utterances **holophrases**, meaning that single words stood in for entire phrases or sentences. But if children really understand the concept of sentence, what keeps them from combining the single words into sentences? Certainly, their memory spans, vocabulary, and attention are sufficient to allow them to use sentences earlier than they do. Theorists now believe that single-word utterances do not encode syntactic relations, although they do, in combination with gestures and intonation, communicate more than simply the meaning of the individual word.

Children usually move so rapidly through the next four stages of syntax that by age 4 they are using grammar much like that of adults in informal conversation.

The recurring conflict between active and passive views of the developing person can be seen in the study of language development. Some theorists, notably *B.F. Skinner* (1957), have argued that children learn language by trying various combinations of sounds and being rewarded (for example, with praise and attention) by their parents and others for those sounds that represent true language. Others, such as *Piaget*, have argued that children create their language by constructing their own rules and revising them as needed. There can be little doubt that some of children's language acquisition comes from being rewarded or encouraged by others; all of us have seen this process in action. Yet it also is hard to deny that children are active builders of their own language. One line of evidence often used to support this view is the erroneous language that children use—language that reveals rules the children have constructed but that is not likely to have been rewarded. Children who

AGE	SKILL
0 – 2 months	Vocalization become more differentiated as cries become recognisably different. Fussing and vegetative sounds also present. Some random sounds, occasionally in "response" to adult vocalization.
2 – 4 months	Shows more control over sounds as cooing (single vowel sounds) appears. Vowels are also sometimes combined with other sounds to create trills. Chuckling and laughing also are evident.
5 – 6 months	Lolling (chains of vowel sounds) appears. Pitch intonations appear. Babling begins although only marginally. Single consonant sounds appear.
7 – 9 months	True babbling (consonant-vowel combinations) is evident. Reduplicated babbling evident. Can imitate familiar sound patterns. Baby can "yell."
10 – 12 months	Sound patterns become more complex. Nonreduplicated babling. Intentional communication, first in the form of protolanguage, appears. First words, most commonly single nouns, may appear.
12 – 18 months	Slow vocabulary growth. At 18 months, the average vocabulary is about 30 words. Some normal children will not yet be talking.
18 – 24 months	More rapid vocabulary growth. Some children will experience a sudden "vocabulary spurt." Normal vocabulary ranges from 50-400 words at 24 months. Children will begin combining words into sentence, with 2 and 3 words sentences usually appearing between 18 and 24 months.
2 – 4 years	Production becomes increasingly sophisticated as grammatical morphemes (e.g., plural forms) begin to appear, vocabulary grows (to an average of about 1500 words at age 4), and syntax becomes more complex. There are still many miscommunications, however, due to the child's egocentrism and limited understanding of the precise meaning of words. Pronunciation is still noticeably immature.
Over 4 years	Pronunciation problems continue into school years. Language becomes more adult like although not all forms (e.g., metaphors and irony) will be used and understood until late school age or adolescence. Specilised language, including slang, usually does not appear until early adolescence.

Fig. 12.9 The development of expressive language skills

have found out that the plural of *dog* is *dogs* and that the plural of *box* is *boxes* are apt to decide on their own that more than one mouse should be called *mouses*. Children who do this are showing they have understood a rule governing grammar; they are obviously not just repeating what they have been rewarded for saying, nor are they imitating an adult model. Far from being discouraged by such errors, parents should take heart from the knowledge that their child has mastered a rule.

Social development

Along with the increasing mobility and accelerating language skills of the preschool child comes in an expanding social world. The process by which the child's behaviour and attitudes are brought into harmony with that of the world is called socialization.

Freud's theory focused mainly on the child's socialization with respect to parents during this period. *Freud* believed that during the anal stage, roughly the second year of life, key interactions center around toilet training. The child takes physical satisfaction from stimulation in the anal region of the body, and social issues including self-control and orderliness are confronted. During the phallic stage, roughly ages 3-6, children find physical satisfaction in stimulation of their sexual organs and are attracted to the parent of the opposite sex. Out of the experiences of this stage, Freud believed that children forge a lasting identity with their same-sex parent.

Erikson saw the second year of life and the

Stage of Development	Nature of Development	Simple Utterances
1. Sentence like word (12 to 18 months)	The word is combined with non-verbal cues (gestures and inflections).	"Mommy" "Mommy!" "Mommy?"
2. Modification (18 months to 2 years)	Modifiers are joined to topic words to form declarative, question, negative, and imperative structures.	"Pretty baby. (declarative) "Where Daddy?" (question) "No play" (negative) "More milk!" (imperative)
3. Structure (2 to 3 years)	Both a subject and a predicate are included in the sentence types.	"She's a pretty baby." (declarative) "Where Daddy is?" (question) "I no can play." (negative) "I want more milk!" (imperative)
4. Operational changes (2½ to 4 years)	Elements are added, embedded, and permuted within sentences.	"Read it, my book" (conjunction) "Where is Daddy?" (embedding) "I can't play" (permutation)
5. Categorization (3½ to 7 years)	Word classes (nouns, verbs, and prepositions) are subdivided.	"I would like some milk." (use of "some" with mass noun) "Take me to the store." (use of preposition of place)
6. Complex structures (5 to 10 years)	Complex structural distinctions made, as with "ask-tell" and "promise."	"Ask what time it is." "He promised to help her."

Fig. 12.10 Six stages in children's syntactic development

toilet-training experience as a time of conflict between autonomy, on the one hand, and shame and doubt, on the other. During the next 3 or 4 years, Erikson argued, the child's core conflict is between the urge to be industrious in school and elsewhere and the risk of feeling inferior.

The parent-child Relationship

With the increasing physical powers, intellectual power, and language skill the child becomes less complaint and manageable than before. This transform the nature of the parent-child relationship.

In addition, a major task of socialization must be confronted: toilet training. Parents who have been largely nurturers and caretakers of their children become teachers and enforcers, active agents of socialization.

In addition to teaching specific skills the parent during this period called upon to be a disciplinarian. But how should parents go about telling their child no? Research findings offer some guidelines.

First, a combination of general parental warmth and specific explanations for specific prohibitions seems to promote effective discipline. Parental warmth seems to make the child eager to maintain the parent's approval and to understand the parent's reasons for the prohibition. Giving reasons, in turn, helps the child form concepts of what is appropriate—concepts that can then generalize to new situations. Second, consistency—over time and between parents—is very important. Many studies have shown that parental inconsistency and conflict are linked to maladjustment in children, especially to aggression and delinquency.

A third guideline concerns the question of how controlling parents should be with their children. Baumrind's study, like several other investigations in this area, suggests that parenting which combines warmth with moderate restrictiveness and an authoritative style will foster independence and social maturity in children even as early as the preschool years.

Baumrind's (1980) research also suggests

that identical parental styles may foster different behaviour patterns in boys and in girls. For instance, boys with punishing fathers seem to have difficulty in forming good peer relationships, but girls with such fathers seem especially likely to be independent and self-reliant.

A longitudinal research indicates that children may be born with "styles" of their own in the form of basic temperament patterns. Parental style may influence the way these patterns are expressed; but parental style is also partly a response to the child's style. Parent behaviour and child behaviour influence one another in an ongoing cycle. To view the parents as "the cause" and the child as "the effect" would certainly be a serious mistake, just as it would be a mistake to think that every troubled child is a product of poor parenting.

Sex roles

Children's identification with their parents influences their ideas about sex roles. Children of *both* sexes may initially adopt many traditionally feminine and maternal behaviour patterns (Sears, 1965); but by the age of 4 or 5, boys have already begun to show traditional male types of behaviour. The toys they choose and the roles they play in games become increasingly masculine. At about the same age, girls intensify the feminine sex-typing of their play. One reason for the divergence of boys and girls is that children pick up sex-typed behaviour through *observational learning*—that is, boys observe and imitate males, particularly their fathers, while girls observe and imitate females, particularly their mothers.

Why does such differential imiation of males and females not show up strongly until children are 4 or 5 years old? One reason seems to be that children's awareness of sex differences is influenced by their cognitive development. Before the age of 4 or 5, as we saw in the preceding section on cognitive development, most children do not understand the **principle of identity**—that is, they do not recognize that certain characteristics of objects remain fixed even when the appearance of the object changes. In the same way, young children do not recognize that one of their own key characteristics—their gender identity—remains fixed even though their appearance changes.

Evidently, cognitive development and observational learning both contribute to sex-typed behaviour. In addition, a broad range of environmental influences can be identified. For generations, parents have tended to treat boys and girls differently, differentially rewarding them for "sex-appropriate" behaviour and even decorating boys' rooms with "educational" materials while decorating girls rooms with dolls and ruffles (*Rheingold & Cook, 1975*).

Play

Play is an essential ingredient in a child's cognitive development. Through activities which adults view as play, the child learns how to control and refine both gross and fine motor movements and how to approach and solve problems. Play is a *child's work*. The child learns and practices new skills through play which are or will be essential to the activities of daily living.

Piaget incorporates this initial work activity into his theory of cognitive development as an **accomodation** activity. The child is actively changing his or her approach and is consciously creating new schemata to be successful at the skill.

Once a child figures out the cause-effect relationships or physical movements necessary to master a task, the skill is replicated multiple times and in different settings or with alternative materials. Thus, the child may walk all over the house or on and off the sidewalk; may button and unbutton his or her own clothes and those of others; may cut paper, hair, clothes, or the curtains; and may try to put puzzles and any other shapes together. This practicing phase is essential for assuring the child that he or she is able to control events and to develop the physical and intellectual skills to the point where the activity no longer requires concentrated thought and has become a habit firmly entrenched in the child's repertoire of skills.

During this practicing phase, the skill will be unstable in its appearance as the child continues to work at accomodation.

Once the child has mastered a skill the activity becomes easy and fun to perform. Piaget says that at this point **assimilation** is the cognitive activity involved. The child's relaxed face and approach are external indicators of the decreased concentration required for success. The activity is no longer an end in itself, but becomes a tool for mastering the next task or to meet new challenges—to get to a specific place as quickly as possible, to dress oneself for the day, to cut out a specific shape for an art project, or to fit objects together in as small an area as possible (e.g., packing a suitcase). Thus, adults may identify all of a child's activities as play because they would be easy, relaxing, or fun for the adult. But, the activity is work for the child during the learning process, and does not become play until it can be accomplished easily by the child. All the play activities help the child gain the skills that will be needed for school and general adaptation to life.

Initially, children engage in **solitary play**. They may show a preference for being near other children and show some interest in what those others are doing, but their own individual play runs an independent course. Solitary play is eventually replaced by parallel play, in which children use similar materials (such as, a pail and toy) and engage in similar activity (such as, digging oil), typically near one another; but they hardly interact at all. By age 3, most children show at least some cooperative play, a form that involves direct child-to-child interaction and requires some complementary role taking (for example, games of "Mommy and Daddy" or games of "Doctor").

Aggression

In early childhood, boys and girls face an important new task: learning to express unpleasant feelings in socially acceptable ways. Often the feelings are vented in the form of aggressive behaviour. Why do children show aggression, and why does it take the forms that it does? Many have argued that frustration provokes aggression, and that the forms it takes will depend on the child's previous learning. This has led to some concern about the possible effects on children of the aggressive and violent behaviour they see on television programs.

Aggressive behaviour may be fostered not only by observational learning but also by direct reinforcement, or reward. In many settings where children play, the aggressive children often triumph over others, have easier access to preferred toys, and even get extra attention from adults who are encouraging them to be less combative. Many youngsters are also rewarded for their aggressive behaviour at home. Parents often respond to such behaviour by paying special attention to the child and even by giving in to the child's demands "just to get a little peace and quiet" (*Patterson*, 1976).

Prosocial Behaviour

Preschoolers can be aggressive, but they can also be touchingly helpful, generous, and comforting. Such behaviour is called *prosocial*. It is often seen in the same children who tend to be aggressive. Some have argued that these children, are motivated to be involved with other children, and whether the involvement is aggressive or prosocial will depend upon the situation. Others argue that aggressive children, who themselves are easily upset, "find it easier to empathize with others who are upset."

According to *Hoffman* (1976), children pass through four predictable stages in the development of empathy that makes prosocial behaviour possible. In the first stage, infants have trouble differentiating self from others. Their behaviour is triggered by, and often looks like, the strong emotional displays of others. They often cry when others cry and laugh when others laugh.

After the first year, children gradually develop a sense of self as different from others, and at that point they enter a second stage. Although they have come to recognize that another person is in fact another person, their egocentric thinking leads them to "help" the other person in ways that they themselves would want to be helped. So, a boy whose mother is upset may bring her his favourite blanket or his teddy bear. In the third stage, children recognize that a distressed person may have feelings and needs that are different from their own. Their efforts to help become aimed at figuring out what the distressed person really needs, even if the need is different from the child's own personal preference. During this stage, which lasts through early childhood, children are limited to empathy for others who show specific expressions of emotion. Their empathy is situation-specific. It is only in later childhood, when the fourth stage is reached, that children come to relate one expression of distress to another and to be concerned for the general condition of others. It is only in this fourth stage that children are likely to empathize with and seek to help, say, an unpopular child who seems generally morose or withdrawn.

It may have occurred to you that television viewing can have good as well as bad effects—that it can enhance prosocial behaviour through positive observational learning. There may be several positive effects of television watching in early childhood, but the effects found in research thus far have not been dramatic or clear-cut.

Adjustment problems in early childhood

In the preschool years, children acquire a risky combination: mobility, language, and immature judgement. Their limited powers of reasoning make it hard for them to fore-see the consequences of their physical activity. They are physically able to cross the street but unable to envision all the dangers that crossing the street poses. Preschoolers also use their newfound language skills with a distinct lack of restraint. Their cognitive egocentrism prevents them from taking the perspective of their listener; the result can be painfully honest comments such as, "Hello, fat lady" or "you have yellow teeth."

Surveys of parents shows that fears are among the most common behaviour problems of early childhood, but what children fear changes markedly during this period. Fears involving thought and imagination increase sharply during the preschool years; in contrast, the percentage of fears related to concrete, physical sensations generally declines. This illustrates the shift away from the sensorimotor "thought" of infancy and toward the internalized, representational thought of early childhood.

The other problems mentioned most often in parent surveys reflect their children's unsocialized use of physical and verbal powers. "Overactive, shows off, talks too much, temper, argues, disobedient," and "resists bedtime," are terms that appear often in these surveys. Some of these problems are common throughout the preschool years.

Some of these problems become exaggerated enough in some children to require clinical intervention. Two of the most common causes of clinic referral are unsocialized behaviour and phobias. Speech problems are a third major reason for clinic referral, especially in the 2 to 5

DEVELOPMENTAL TASKS OF THE TODDLER PRESCHOOLER

*1. Recognize self as a person, psychologically separate from attachment person:
  - tolerate separation from attachment person
  - recognize and express own ideas, feelings, needs, and will
  - develop self-entertainment skills
  - reinvest separation anxiety energies

*2. Learn how to harness and focus energies:
  - identify short-range goals
  - invest in activity at hand
  - increase attention span
  - persist at tasks
  - resist distractors
  - listen actively

*3. Learn prosocial behaviors (to be socialized):
  - imitate and practice roles, responsibilities, and relationships
  - observed in the family and culture
  - share attention
  - begin to postpone own gratification in difference to the needs of others
  - respect rights of others
  - work and play cooperatively with others
  - observe basic social skills
  - develop and express empathy/sympathy for others

*4. Adopt collective communication skills:
  - develop receptive comprehension skills
  - develop expressive communication skills
  - use a language for sharing ideas, feelings, observations

*5. Develop basic self-control skills:
  - evolve awareness of feeling states
  - learn culturally acceptable ways to express feelings, frustration, and anger
  - cooperate with adult guidance

obey simple rules without adult reminding
develop safety awareness and self protection behaviors

*6. Learn to live with consequences of own choices:
  - recognize simple cause—effect relationships
  - make simple decisions regarding activities of daily living project decisions into the near future

7. Coordinate body movements for skill mastery:
  - develop awareness of body-space relationships
  - achieve independent mobility within the immediate environment
  - manipulate objects and tools
  - meaningfully refine gross- and fine-motor skills

8. Learn basic values and mores of the family and culture:
  - deference
  - etiquette
  - roles
  - cultural myths and identities

9. Function independently in basic activities of daily living:
  - eating
  - dressing
  - toileting
  - simple chore mastery

10. Seek information and understanding:
  - ask questions
  - experiment with events
  - verify knowledge and understanding
  - practice skills

---

* Tasks deemed most crucial to continued maturation are marked with an asterisk.

year age group. Poor hearing, faulty brain functioning, or mere lags in development can interfere with children's ability to understand speech or to produce it. Stuttering can also begin in early childhood. Sometimes it can be traced to common early problems in pronunciation that lead children to worry about their ability to talk. At other times, the cause is harder to find. Stuttering usually fades out with development, but in some cases it lingers throughout life. In some cases difficulties in producing language sounds or other anxiety-laden circumstances in a child's life can lead a youngster to stop speaking altogether, a problem called elective mutism. Finally, infantile autism, which we discussed in the section on infancy, may not be actually identified until it shows up in certain speech peculiarities in early childhood. One example is echolalia, a tendency to repeat, or "echo," what another speaker has just said rather than to use speech for true communication. Many researchers who study autism now believe it is especially ominous if a child reaches the age of 5 and still cannot use speech to communicate.

DEVELOPMENT DURING LATER CHILDHOOD

The elementary school years, the years 6 to 12 in a child's life, are sometimes referred to as the latency period. However, in many areas of development, these years are actually action-packed, not latent at all. They are filled with both motion and emotion as the child confronts the diverse demands of school and entry into a rule-bound society. A capacity for increasingly intimate social relationships promises important rewards but poses real risks as well. And children acquire intellectual tools during these years that give them an unprecedented grasp of the way the world is put together.

Cognitive development

The intellectual tools that children develop in this period were labelled *concrete operations* by Piaget, and that is also the name he has given to this stage of development. This stage involves a major advance in the power of the child's reasoning.

In the period of concrete operations, children are no longer fooled, for example, by Müller-Lyer illusion lines. They recognize that the length of a particular stick will remain fixed so long as nothing is added or taken away from it. Thus, they have learned one of nature's constants: the principle of conservation of length. They believe in this principle because their mental actions now show *reversibility*. Their reversible operations also help them understand, for the first time in their lives, that subtraction reverses and compensates for division. In this way, a variety of mental activities are seen *in relation* to one another. When these mental activities can be used in flexible ways (for example, with reversibility) and understood in relation to one another, they qualify as true operations.

In many ways, the concrete-operational child's thinking shows a power and versatility that would have been literally unthinkable in the pre-operational period. But even this more advanced level of thought has its limitations. The operations are concrete in the sense that they are tied to the real world of objects and events. The children can think clearly about things that are real, but not very clearly about more hypothetical propositions such as, "suppose that people hatched from eggs." It is also hard for concrete-operational child to grasp the broad meaning of abstract concepts such as freedom, integrity, or truth. These limitations mean that intellectual growth in later childhood, though impressive, is still incomplete.

Social development

As their social world expands to include classmates and teachers, children's ways of thinking about people show a corresponding change. Studies of "person perception" show that a child even as old as 6 or 7 will describe others in egocentric ways, referring to what the other people do to or for the child. Descriptions at this age also focus on concrete, observable characteristics of others, such as their physical appearance or their outward behaviour.

During the next few years, children begin to use more and more descriptive statements involving psychological characteristics—statements that require some inference about the other person. Note that psychological inferences (italicized) made by this 8-year-old.

> *He is very dull. He does silly things and is very stupid. He has a long nose and always chews his pencil and picks his nose and I think he is disgusting.*

Friendship

In the early preschool years, children have momentary playmates but not ongoing, reciprocal friendships. Some time between the ages of 4 and 9, most children develop an ongoing friendship, or perhaps several. Their first friendships tend to be self-serving; a friend is someone who "does what I want." Later, during the elementary school years, friendships become not only outgoing but reciprocal as well; friends are seen as people who "do things for each other" (*Selman*, 1980). Friendships are almost exclusively boy-boy and girl-girl in elementary school.

Groups

Groups have certain defining characteristics: goals shared by its members, rules of conduct (often merely implied or understood), and a hierarchical structure. There are leaders at the apex and followers at the lower levels; each individual member has some identifiable relationship to other members. Psychologists have tried to learn what conditions cause group structures to take shape in later childhood.

A classical camp study by Sherif and others (1961) showed that group formation in preado-

lescent is stimulated by the experience of living together, sharing pleasant experiences, cooperating in ventures that involve shared goals, and especially, competing with other groups. The Sherif study, like others focused on this age range, suggests that shared adversity and joint problem solving can stimulate group formation and reduce antagonism between groups.

School achievement

Formal schooling in almost all countries begins around the age of 6 or 7. By that age, the major limitations of preoperational thought have been left behind, language has matured to a point where a teacher can communicate with children in groups, and the perceptual and motor skills needed for such activities as writing with a pencil are in place. During the early school years, most children develop a broad array of basic skills.

Learning in school can be very different from informal, everyday learning. In the later, children often learn by immersion; they jump in feet first, try their best, learn from their mistakes, and try to "get the hang of it"—often without learning any general rules until much later. Most of us learned to ride a bicycle well before we could state a rule for how to do it. Most of us followed some basic grammatical rules before we could articulate what these rules were.

In school learning, the process is often reversed: the teacher presents a general rule first, and the children later figure out how the rule applies to concrete examples in real life.

Studies suggest that in addition to teaching specific cognitive skills, schools are particularly good at teaching problem-solving techniques (*Fischer & Lazerson, 1984*); such techniques as labeling the parts of a problem and constructing a general solution rule can give the schooled youngster a real edge in tackling new and unfamiliar problems.

Adjustment problems in later childhood

School experience can be exhilarating for a child who "fits in" academically and socially; but it can be sheer misery for children who do not. Children from lower socioeconomic levels may feel out of place and uncomfortable in these settings. Half of all children from the lowest socioeconomic level drop out before they finish high school. Person-to-person comparison becomes intense during the elementary school years; children who do badly in their schoolwork may have a pretty good idea, by the third or fourth grade, where they rank in relation to their peers. With this knowledge comes a newfound capacity for feelings of inferiority. This is particularly difficult for children who suffer from cultural-familial mental retardation. Because their retarded functioning is not caused by any known physiological disorder, their intellectual problems may not be noticed until they enter school.

For some children, the social demands of school are harder to satisfy than the academic demands. Often the setting seems to call for impressing one's peers and teacher; this may help to explain some of the most commonly reported problem behaviours of this age— "argues, brags, shows off, talks too much, self-conscious." These problems are continuations of behaviours seen in preschool. Clusters of these problems taken to extremes, can lead parents to refer their children to clinics for special professional attention.

At the other extreme are children who respond to the social demands of school with self-consciousness carried to the point of social withdrawal.

A problem known as school phobia is seen early in the school years. It is an extreme form of normal school anxiety—school-phobic boys and girls often panic and even show physical reactions like vomiting when it is time to go to school. Many psychologists now agree that the phobia is often a fear of separation from the parents rather than a fear of school itself and that a quick reentry into school is usually the best treatment.

School phobias combined with generalized anxiety, sadness, or shyness can form an ongoing pattern called internalizing problems. Aggressive behaviour combined with other kinds of antisocial behaviour and attitudes can form an ongoing pattern called externalizing problems. Persistent internalizing or externalizing patterns can lead to many long-term difficulties, but the externalizing patterns pose the most serious threat to long-term adult adjustment (*Robins*, 1979).

Two other common problems during later childhood are learning problems and hyperactivity. The most frequent learning problem is *dyslexia,* difficulty with reading. Other children are said to have *learning disabilities* or *specific development disorders.*

Such problems often accompany hyperactivity. Youngsters with this problem are impulsive and over-active. In some settings, these children are diagnosed as having an attention deficit disorder. Many are taken to physicians and given drugs to calm them down and help them pay attention in class. Critics note that many overactive children are able to manage their problems without being indicated if they are given careful training in self-control. ■ ■

Study of the Human Life: Adolescence, Adulthood and Old Age

Study of the Human Life: Adolescence, Adulthood and Old Age

Three of the most dramatic life transitions that occur in peoples' lives will be discussed in this chapter. One of these is the transition from childhood into adolescence. In a stunningly short time, the child takes on an adultlike physique and intellect and is dubbed a "teenager." A second transition we will consider is the movement into the responsible world of the true adult—the world of careers, marriage, and family. Finally, we will consider the aging process and the period we call old age. This period, as we shall see, involves some kinds of decline; but it also offers the prospect of intellectual mellowing and a special quality called "wisdom."

ADOLESCENCE

Adolescence is the term used to identify the period of transition from childhood to adulthood and includes the marked changes occurring in all five domains. Adolescence is recognized as the period of life during which the individual is forging a sense of personal identity and gaining emancipation from the family unit. As such, it is primarily a cognitive sociological, affective, and spiritual process, rather than a physical phenomenon. Adolescence has no clear-cut beginning or end. However, the age from 11 to 19 represent the period of adolescence, with the specific understanding that the boundaries can be extended or collapsed at either end to encompass the variations in development found in individuals. Some persons may continue to function as adolescents for many years beyond the twentieth birthday.

Technically, *adolescence* is the period from the beginning of sexual maturity (*puberty*) to the completion of physical growth.

Biological development and puberty

In a physical sense, the events of puberty mark the transition from childhood to adult. During early childhood, males and females have small amounts of both estrogen (female hormone) and androgen (male hormone). At about age 7 to 8 years, both of these hormones begin to increase gradually until **pubescence** (the first half of the pubertal period, which precedes the onset of external puberty). During pubescence, females experience a rapid increase in the production of estrogen, whereas males have a rapid increase in the production of androgens.

The mechanics that initiate the pubertal process are as yet poorly understood. It appears that the maturation of the hypothalamus initiates the process through secretion of neurohumoral releasing factors (chemicals released into the hypophysial portal vessels and neurons connecting the hypothalamus and pituitary). This causes the anterior pituitary gland to release GnRH and **follicle—stimulating hormone** (FSH), which in turn stimulates the gonads to release **leutenizing hormone** (LH). Gradually, an effecting positive feedback system is established, and increasing amounts of FSH are released.

Two other hormones secreted by the anterior pituitary are *pituitary* **growth hormone** (GH) and **thyroid-stimulating hormone**

(TSH). Growth hormone levels remain relatively constant throughout life. The main function of GH appears to be the stimulation of deoxyribonucleic acid (DNA) synthesis and hyperplastic cell growth, particularly of the bones and cartilage. Since the increased androgen levels that accompany puberty in both males and females are antagonistic to GH, increased androgen levels are partially responsible for the decrease in the rate of body growth.

Adequate thyroxin levels are essential throughout life for (1) hypertrophic and hyperplastic cell growth of all body systems, especially the brain and skeletal systems, and (2) primary and secondary sexual development. During the pubertal period, there is an increase in thyroxin secretion by the thyroid under the influence of TSH. Thyroxin levels directly increase body metabolism. The increased metabolic rate leads to a higher body temperature, which frequently causes teenagers to complain of feeling too warm.

During the pubertal process, imbalances in hormonal levels are common. Because of their intimate relationship to the hypothalamus, emotional states in an individual, such as fear or anxiety, can directly affect the efficiency of the total process. Normal maturation depends on a complicated and sensitive balance among the endocrine glands. (Fig. 13.1)

The pubertal period

The *pubertal period*—the period of maturation of the reproductive system—includes all the primary and secondary sexual developments precipitated by the endocrine changes in the individual. Sexual maturation has been held in abeyance since fetal life when the hypothalamus was "imprinted" to respond to male or female hormones. Before the second birthday, the hypothalamus reaches a very sensitive "set point," which establishes a negative feedback system to inhibit production of sex steroids. The pubertal period is initiated when the hypothalamus matures sufficiently to reset or override the inhibitory effects of the gonadostat which has suppressed the release of *gonadotrophin— releasing hormone* (GnRH). Readjustment of

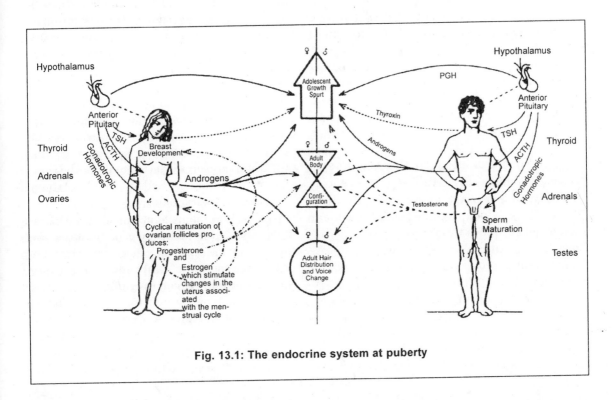

Fig. 13.1: The endocrine system at puberty

the set point allows for higher concentrations of sex hormones and the establishment of a positive feedback control mechanism. This leads to maturation of the reproductive system and changes in other body cells. The pubertal period may last 8 to 10 years although 3 to 5 years is more common. **Primary sexual development** includes the maturational changes occurring in all those organs directly related to reproduction (e.g., penis, testes, ovaries, breasts, uterus). **Secondary sexual development** includes the physiological changes that occur in other parts of the body as a direct result of changes in hormonal balance (e.g., development of facial and pubic hair, voice changes, fat deposition).

Cognitive/Intellectual Development

Along with the bodily changes of adolescence come major intellectual changes. Remembering your own leap from child to teenager, you may have tried to solve ethical problems by relying, more and more, on abstract moral principles. You may also have grown much better at solving complicated riddles or "posers," playing games like bridge or chess by planning several moves in advance, and figuring out answers to purely hypothetical questions. Many of these features of adolescent thought can be understood from the perspective of Jean Piaget's theory of intellectual development.

Piagets' Theory of Intellectual Development
The most complete theoretical account of cognitive development is that proposed by *Jean Piaget*. Piaget is not concerned with the content of thought or "body of knowledge" per se but the operational structure used for processing information. He proposes an invariant sequence of four qualitatively different stages, the last of which, "formal operational thought," emerges during adolescence. Piaget saw the late adolescent and young adult years as a time for refining the formal operational approach to problem solving. He asserted that any cognitive advance-

ment beyond the acquisition of formal operations represented quantitative rather than qualitative change; that is, the same cognitive operations are applied throughout adulthood to an ever expanding and more complex array of experiences and problems.

The adults started reasoning and integrating the mental steps involved in problem solving. The alternative solutions to a situation are evaluated, prioritized, and synchronized with one's past experiences, value system, and goals. The end result is a unique product for each person, even though the processes used are the same. The adult, because of reduced egocentrism, is able to approach issues more objectively, enabling him or her to draw more effectively on education and experience as well as on all the cognitive operations available.

Because of inadequate environmental stimulation or intellectual limitations, some people fail to master formal operational thought. Others may not master the skills until the adult years when faced with more complex and frequent issues that require hypothetical—deductive thinking. Once acquired, the use of formal operational thought may be limited or even abandoned, depending on a person's response to environmental challenges.

Cognitive processing is also influenced by one's physical and emotional status. Formal operational thought takes much energy. Reduced physical or emotional health reduces energies available to process more complex issues and problems, a factor that may be significant in precipitating accidents or other "stupid" decisions and behaviours.

Piaget notes marked differences in the levels of development attained by people. During adolescence, individual differences in education, experience, aptitude, motivation, talents, and interests begin to become significant in shaping the direction of formal operational thought. Piaget feels that these differences influence a person's career choice. Thereafter, he feels that the working environment contributes to one's knowledge base and to the use of nonuser of formal operations. Law students build their career on their ability to apply precise logic to abstract concepts. Auto mechanics and physicians alike build their careers on the ability to hypothesize the source of a problem and then to systematically intervene to "cure" the ill. It is important to note that although career *choice* may be based on one's interests, motivations, special talents, education, and competence, job *success* is largely determined by attitude, emotional maturity, and interpersonal relationship skills.

Although Piaget's framework for describing the processing of information appears to have universal applicability, the individual's data base is heavily influenced by culture and life experiences. A person who may be considered "intelligent" in one society may be thought to be quite naive in a cultural context that requires a different knowledge base and adaptational skills.

MORAL DEVELOPMENT

Morality, a dynamic process extending over a lifetime, calls primarily upon the cognitive and affective domains for decisions regarding "right" and "wrong" behaviour. However, the moral aspects of life involve a unique interface of all five domains of human experience. Moral decisions are influenced by familial and cultural values, by one's understanding of and sensitivity to the implications of one's behaviour on the personage or rights of others, and on one's levels of personal maturity and self-discipline. The crisis and chaos of a generation of devalued living have precipitated a new concern for the ultimate questions (and answers) of morality and the life's meaning.

Moral development is one of the dimensions of the "identity crisis" as elaborated by Erikson. According to *Erikson*, seeking inspiration from others and seeking help from someone higher than self are activities essential for the establishment of an ideology.

Types of Morality

Moral behaviours are the responses that individuals make throughout life to ethical pressures. If these responses are consistent with societal standards of "good," they are regarded as moral; if they contradict those expectations, they are considered immoral. Experiences of rejection, neglect, or abuse during developmental years can create an attitude of detachment from objects and people, and a total disregard for commonly accepted values. One result is the **immoral** person, who is aware of cultural codes of right and wrong, but willingly chooses to violate or ignore many of the values of society to meet his or her own needs and impulses. Immoral behaviour often has a component of hostility and disregard for negative consequences on others. A less common outcome of early rejection, neglect, or abuse is an attitude of **immorality.** The person has been so badly damaged during early emotional development that he appears to have no conscience, and no awareness of the rightness or wrongness of an attitude or action. Such a person is not reached by appeals to reason or emotion to abide by commonly accepted standards of behaviour. No *social agents provide a source of identification for this person, consequently there is no valuereferent to serve as a motivator or guide for moral behaviour or attitudes.*

Kohlberg's theory of moral development

Lawrence kohlberg, one of the leading theorists in moral development, recognized the contribution of cognitive structuring to moral development. He recognized, however, that although moral development is influenced by cognitive structures, it does not parallel cognitive development.

Stages of Moral Development

Kohlberg proposes eight stages of moral development. Moral decisions become increasingly differentiated, integrated, and universalized at each successive stage. Justice is the goal of moral judgement. The individual seeks equilibrium at progressively higher stages as cognitive and affective domains mature.

Preconventional level (premoral level)

The first three stages are characterized by cognitively limited and very biased egocentric thinking.

Level Stage	Age	Underlying Principles
Preconventional (Premoral Level)		
0	0 – 2	Do what pleases me
1	2 – 3	Avoid punishment
2	4 – 7	Do what benefits me
Conventional (Maintain Expectations of others)		
3	7 – 10	Avoid disapproval
4	10 – 12	Do duty, obey laws
Postconventional (Maintain Internal Principles)		
5	13 –	Maintain respect of others
6	15 –	Implement personal principles
7	18 –	Live by eternal, universal principles

**Fig. 13.2: Kohlberg's levels of
moral development**

Conventional level (externally mediated moral guidelines)
Socially mediated moral reasoning becomes possible as concrete operational thought emerges. The new social sensitivities of the school-age child increase awareness of other's feelings. Maintaining expectations is valuable/crucial regardless of the consequences.

Postconventional level (internally mediated moral guidelines)
The last three stages represent morality based on inner principles and reasoning rather than external pressure or emotions. Many people never realize these stages, or may acquire them late in life. One must employ Piaget's formal operational thought to master these stages.

THE QUEST FOR IDENTITY

The central crisis of one's life, the fifth rung of Erikson's ladder of social—emotional development, is the issue of **identity**. It is not until adolescence that the individual develops "the prerequisites in physiological growth, mental maturation, and social responsibility to experience and pass through the crisis of identity. All the previous crises lead toward the development of a unique identity. Those who have incompletely or negatively resolved the previous crises may take a maladaptive stance of fanaticism or rejection of cultural standards, or may find safety in a passive stance resulting in bewilderment or **role confusion**.

Erikson's identity development theory

In Erikson's theory, identity development is a life-long process. Each previous stage contributes to one's sense of selfhood. During the school-age years, the well-developing person explored and mastered multiple skills and roles, each of which contributed to an identity based largely on concrete descriptors of one's physical characteristics and competencies. The new cognitive skills of abstraction and hierarchical organization enable one to consolidate these multiple concrete identities into a more abstract, conceptual and internalized sense of self.

This awareness of conceptual identities (e.g., leader, dramatist, artist, problem solver, poet, mathematician, comedian) and characteristics (dependable, optimistic, creative, and so forth) enables the adolescent to begin to systematically and realistically identify career options, focus energies, expand skills, and modify personal characteristics to actuate a chosen, desired self.

During adolescence, Erikson's four earlier stages assume new forms and are reworked as an integral part of the identity crisis.

Stage I (Trust): Temporal Perspective Versus Time Confusion

Adolescents find it difficult to trust time. There is a great temptation to take shortcuts or make premature commitments to marriage, career, or parenthood. Ironically, these premature commitments tend to delay self-discovery and identity resolution. A second aspect of the reworked trust crisis is that the trust learned in infancy is now refocused in the trusts of adulthood—the search for a self-chosen love, the capacity for faith, or an in-depth religious experience.

Stage II (Autonomy) : Self-certainty Versus Self-consciousness

In the search for autonomy in problem solving, identity, and value formation, the adolescent often rejects the guidance of authority figures such as parents, teachers, and society, substituting the peer group as the authority. Self-discipline is exerted to achieve one's goals and to squelch impulsivity.

There is a marked increase in personal agony, which can be covered up by arrogance to hide one's sense of insecurity. The adolescent "is mortally afraid of being forced into activities in which he would feel exposed to ridicule or self-doubt..." He would rather act shamelessly in the eyes of his elders, out of free choice, than be forced into activities which would be shameful in his own eyes or in those of his peers.

Stage III (Initiative): Role Experimentation Versus Role Fixation

The grandiose ideas and plans of adolescence are frequently unmatched by their skills or perseverance. The adolescent may play the role of an aristocrat one day, and a recluse the next.

Freud observed that adolescents express a range of relationships, from forming passionate love relationships one day to breaking them the next; from an overpowering longing for solitude to throwing themselves enthusiastically into the life of the community; and from being a whiny kid one day to a sophisticated, mature person the next. Such contrasts are as confusing to adolescents as to the adults living and working with them. However, there is a tendency to choose "safe" roles set by others to avoid embarrassment, disorder and guilt.

Stage IV (Industry): Apprenticeship Versus Work Paralysis

The adolescent begins to focus on the more sophisticated social and career skills needed for successful adulthood. The industry of adolescence demands a lot of enthusiasm, hard work, and self-discipline. Adolescents need opportunities for gainful employment in the community as they explore interests and abilities, develop work habits and social relationships, and increase independence from their families.

State V: Identity Versus Role Confusion (Adolescent)

Identity refers to the "Who am I?" and "What am I going to do with my life?" questions of adolescence. Difficulty in answering such questions leads to a role confusion. A favourable ratio of identity to role confusion leads to a sense of consistency.

State VI (Intimacy): Sexual Polarization Versus Bisexual Confusion

Sexual activity undertaken during adolescence is seen by Erikson as "the self-seeking, identity-hungry kind; each partner is trying only to reach himself." Physical intimacy without psychosocial intimacy may cause foreclosure of identity development and confusion of values because the pursuit of physical affirmation and excitement eclipses the emotional intimacy so essential to knowing and being known, to sorting values, establishing priorities, strengthening self-discipline, and developing social and negotiation skills—all requisite components in the task of identity homework. If one's identity is not clear, one can become a "chameleon" in social relationships, losing one's identity to that of the other.

The adolescent must begin to share viewpoints, concerns, and feelings to get sufficient feedback to see the self more clearly.

Stage VII (Generativity): Leadership and Followership Versus Authority Confusion

The adolescent is already beginning to reveal allocentric orientation through involvement in projects that benefit others without concern for self-enhancement. The healthy adolescent is not a "blind follower" but a conscientious volunteer or cooperative follower. There is an awareness of self-expression in the opportunities to work with others.

Stage VIII (Integrity): Ideological Commitment Versus Confusion of Values

Most people identify what they are against before they are able to clarify what they are for and why. The adolescent "must repudiate some 'foreign' values in order to focus his or her beliefs on some chosen identity." The healthy adolescent begins to stand up for or against something based on a chosen identity and values. Ideologies at this point tend to be simplistic views that will be modified or fleshed out through the rest of life. But they provide a compelling power and source of commitment that contribute to vital involvement in life. Without commitment, people become pawns of the environment, and values lack integrity.

Negative identities

Approximately three fourths of adolescents negotiate this life phase fairly successfully. The remaining quarter experience problems of delinquency, drug or alcohol dependency, school failures, sexual involvements conflict with parents, and generalized expressions of depression. When a person believes that expectations of the self, peer, or parents cannot be met, a negative identity may develop. Adolescents may feel that they are not good enough, expect failure, and therefore give up trying to achieve the culturally desirable roles. Some may assume a rebellious stance, acting out, or exhibiting behaviours in direct defiance of authority figures as a way to maintain self-esteem and control. The culturally undesirable or dangerous roles may appear to be the most realistic. Thus, a child with devotly religious parents may engage in stealing, taking drugs, or other anti-establishment behaviours. The young person may focus energies on "being the best at being bad," to achieve self-satisfaction, control, or attention.

Social development

Because it marks the transition from childhood to adulthood, adolescence requires the redefining of some basic social relationships. Relationships with family members at this time involve increasing independence for the adolescent and usually involve increased conflict, too. Relationships with peers may become much more intimate and vital than they were in childhood. Finally, relationships with the opposite sex have new overtones of sensuality.

Family Relationships

Teenagers see themselves becoming adults, and they press for the freedom and privileges of true adulthood. These are signs of the adolescent's cognitive growth and should be respected as such. Parents who respond to disagreements with open discussion are encouraging their children to do the same and thus to practice a valuable social skill. Some studies suggest that self-reliance, independence, and social responsibility are most effectively promoted by parents who are flexible and encourage discussion.

Teenage girls report more conflicts with their parents than do teenage boys, and the conflicts they report more often involve emotional flareups. Parents seem to place more restrictions on their teenage daughters than on their teenage sons; they worry more about their daughter's safety and especially about their sexual activity and risk of pregnancy. Their daughters, unfortunately, do not see these restrictions as "protection." One of the most common explanations teenage girls give for their conflicts with their parents is that their parents do not respect their maturity (*Konopka, 1976*).

Boy's conflicts with their parents tend to involve more objective issues of authority and privilege, such as access to the family car. Boys are more likely than are girls to report that they are disciplined primarily by their fathers and that they receive affection primarily from their mothers.

With the puberty completed, boys seem clearly more influential in family decision making than they were prior to puberty.

BASIC CONFLICT	OPTIMUM OUTCOME
1. Basic trust vs. basic mistrust (infant)	Trust is the faith that things will be "all right." It develops from good care provided by reliable others. A favorable ratio of trust to mistrust results in hope.
2. Autonomy vs. shame and doubt (toddler)	Without a sense of self-control (autonomy), children feel shame and doubt. A favorable ratio of autonomy to shame-and-doubt results in self-direction with self-esteem.
3. Initiative vs. guilt (preschooler)	Initiative adds to autonomy the quality of doing things just to be doing them. A sense of guilt is often experienced over things contemplated or actually done. A favorable ratio of initiative to guilt results in a sense of purpose.
4. Industry vs inferiority (schoolchild)	Grade-school children learn to win approval by making things and doing things approved of the the culture. In literate societies, they learn to read; in preliterate societies, they learn the skills necessary for survival. Failure to produce or do valued things leads to a sense of inferiority. A favorable ratio of industry to inferiority leads to sense of competence and pleasure in work.
5. Identity vs. role. confusion (adolescent)	Identity refers to the "who am I?" and "What am I going to do with my life?" questions of adolescence. Difficulty in answering such questions leads to role confusion. A favorable ratio of identity to role confusion. A favorable ratio of identity to role confusion leads to a sense of consistency.
6. Intimacy vs. isolation (young adult)	Here the task is to establish lasting and loving relationships with other people. Love is the outcome of a favorable ratio of intimacy to isolation.
7. Generativity vs. stagnation (middle adult)	Generativity includes productivity and creativity, but here it refers primarily to preparing the next generation for life in the culture. Care is the outcome of a favorable generativity-to-stagnation ratio.
8. Ego integrity vs. despair (older person)	Ego integrity has many facets. In part, it refers to one's acceptance of one's life as what it had to be. Despair, on the other hand, includes the feelings that life is too short to do much and that integrity cannot be achieved. A favorable ratio of ego integrity to despair brings wisdom and the ability to face death calmly.

Fig. 13.3: Erickson's psychosocial developmental stages

Peers

With increasing age, adolescents spend more time with peers and less time with parents. They find peer interactions relaxing and a source of entertainment, as well as a challenge. Because peers usually come from the same social environment—the same neighbourhood, similar ethnic and cultural heritage, and the same socio-economic status—peer groups tend to reflect the values of the parent culture. This tendency to affiliate with friends who share values thus reinforces many values instilled by parents. Although the desire to affiliate with same-gender friends is strong throughout adolescence, the desire to affiliate with opposite-gender friends grows with increasing age.

Value of peers

The importance of peers can vary significantly from adolescent to adolescent. Peers influence matters of taste, dress, speech and leisure activity. When there is a stressful, unsupportive, or chaotic environment at home, the adolescent's peer group may gain prominence over the parents in identity nurturing. The peer group is perhaps best viewed as an auxiliary to the family, a bridge between the dependence of childhood and the independence of adulthood.

One major function of peer groups is to provide a context in which adolescents can learn and test their developing interpersonal and social skills. In the peer setting, adolescents learn what to expect from friends; shape their identities by comparing themselves with peers; experiment with roles and behaviour; practice leadership and conformity skills; gain and give social support to others learn how to cope with social rejection and failure; resolve interpersonal problems; and learn how to hold themselves and others in esteem. In essence, peer groups serve a major socialization function in the life of the adolescent.

Adjustment problems in adolescence

Adolescence is a time of real vulnerability. Nowhere is this truer than in the area of adolescent sexuality. Although sexual activity has increased dramatically over the past decade or two, sex education has not. Adolescent girls (not to mention boys) are sadly unaware of such crucial basics as how to figure out the high-risk period of conception. A majority of teenage girls now use contraceptive devices when they have intercourse, but a majority of them did not at the time they first had intercourse. Girls who delay the use of contraceptives beyond their early sexual experiences are about three times as likely to get pregnant as girls who use protection from the beginning. Most of these pregnancies end in abortion. In the remaining cases, the result is a new teenage mother.

Sexually active adolescents who manage to avoid pregnancy still face risks of veneral disease, risks that have increased sharply over recent years. In addition to the diseases that are treatable with antibiotics, there is a new strain of gonorrhoea that is not. There is also herpes simplex virus, type 2, otherwise known as genital herpes; it is thus far incurable.

The beginning of adolescence can mean facing up to some very adult psychological problems. One of these is *depression,* which is characterized by feelings of guilt, a loss of interest in activities, sleep problems, and even suicidal thoughts. Another life-threatening disorder that surfaces in adolescence is **anorexia nervosa,** a form of self-starvation. Still other adolescents have an escalating sense of confusion about things around them; they feel that "things are not real" or that they are actually outside of themselves. Distortions in thinking may develop into irrational belief systems **(delusions)** or into perceptual experiences that seem to be, but are not, real **(hallucinations).** These and other problems can combine to form schizophrenia.

YOUTH

Keniston in 1970 proposed yet another "life phase": youth. **Youth** is essentially a period of "studenthood"; it exists only for those who move on to post-secondary education before settling into fulltime work. Whatever the length of the period, the time it affords can be valuable. It can serve as a kind of lull, a time for serious experimentation without the need for a long-term commitment to a single course of adult life. Because the peer group is no longer such a dominant influence the individual has a new freedom to develop individually—to shape a personal perspective on life and a sense of direction before tackling the challenges of true adulthood.

MIDDLESCENCE

The physical vigor of youth may have passed, but most middlescent nevertheless continue to experience and enjoy a healthy body throughout midlife. "Middlescence," a term synonymous with both middle-age and midlife, means being in the middle of the age continuum, arbitrarily that period of life between 40 and 60 years of age.

Even though middlescence is characterized by changes in the way the body looks and works, these bio-physical changes vary in how and when they appear, being more obvious in some individuals than others. Primary (normal) ageing refers to universal changes inherent to the process of ageing. Secondary (pathologic) aging results from illness, disease, and other environmental factors that may hasten the ageing process.

The quality and quantity of health maintenance behaviours through childhood and early adulthood (e.g., nutrition, treatment of disease, and exercise) directly affect the level of wellness that the middlescent experiences. Those who have cared for their bodies during the early adult years are more likely to enjoy continued good health during middlescence. Likewise, the middlescent who takes proper care of the body during midlife generally is healthier during late adulthood.

DEVELOPMENTAL TASKS OF ADOLESCENCE

*1. Appreciate own uniqueness:
- identify interests, skills, and talents
- identify differences from peers
- accept strengths and limitations
- challenges own skill levels

*2. Develop independent and internal identity:
- value self as a person
- separate physical self from psychological self
- differentiate personal worth from cultural stereo-types
- separate internal value from societal feedback

*3. Determine own value system
- identify options
- establish priorities
- commit self to decisions made
- translate values into behaviors
- resist peer and cultural pressure to conform to their value system find comfortable balance between own
- and peer/cultural standards, behaviors, and needs

*4. Develop self-evaluation skills
- develop basis for self-evaluation and monitoring
- evaluate quality of products
- access approach to tasks and responsibilities
- develop sensitivity to intrapersonal relationships
- evaluate dynamics of interpersonal relationships

*5. Assume increasing responsibility for own behavior:
- quality of work/chores
- emotional tone
- money management
- time management
- decision making
- personal habits
- social behaviors

6. Find meaning in life
- accept and integrate meaning of death
- develop philosophy of life
- begin to identify life or career goals

7. Acquire skills essential for adult living:
- acquire skills essential to independent living
- develop social/emotional abilities and temperament
- refine sociocultural amenities
- identify and experiment with alternatives for facing life
- acquire employment skills
- seek growth-inducing activities

8. Seek affiliations outside from family of origin:
- seek companionship with compatible peers
- affiliate with organizations that support uniqueness
- actively seek models or mentors
- identify potential emotional support systems
- differentiate between acquaintances and friends
- identify ways to express one's sexuality

9. Adapt to adult body functioning:
- adapt to somatic changes
- refine balance and coordination
- develop physical strength
- consider sexuality and reproduction issues

*Tasks deemed most crucial to continued maturation are marked with an asterisk.

Biological changes in adulthood

Strength, agility, reaction time, and manual dexterity; all four attributes decline gradually, but most people are reasonably healthy and physically sound into their fifties and sixties. Muscular strength, for instance, peaks between the ages of 25 and 30, but there is only about 10 to 15 percent loss of strength by age 60.

Weight is redistributed, hairline may recede, hair grays, skin texture changes as drying and wrinkling begin, and often the structure of the face becomes modified. In women, one of the most dramatic physical changes is *menopause,* the cessation of menstruation. This usually occurs between the ages of 45 and 55; it signals the climacteric—the end of ovulation and the termination of reproductive capacity. There is no parallel event for men; men can produce viable sperm at all ages, but their reproductive capacity does decline gradually over their adult years.

Generally the physiological changes that accompany early and middle adulthood seem not to have major effects on work or other behaviour, except where physical performance expectations are very high, as in professional athletics.

Psychosocial development during middle adult years

During middlescence, arbitrarily the years between 40 and 60, most adults have passed the stage of youthful idealism, must acknowledge the reality of the passage of time, respond to present opportunities, and begin to make plans for the future. The individual who actively developed his or her value system and identity during the earlier years finds the changes that accompany middlescence merely one more step in the evolving understanding and expression of the self. This continuation of "identity homework" assists the middle-age adult to realistically assess expected and unexpected life events. Uncertainty, differences, tragedies, and other stressors are tolerated with greater equanimity.

Middlescence is not too late to resolve one's identity homework. One has multiple opportunities to actively examine what has been and what is yet to be. As life is reevaluated, midcourse adjustments can be made. Consequently, these years can be a time of crisis, reversal, constriction, and disintegration, or one of stability, expansion, healing, renewal, and self-actualization, depending on the person's willingness and ability to face life's exigencies.

Piagetian Perspectives on Cognitive Development

One study found that most adult women in a supermarket are unable to solve formal-operational reasoning problems. This is true even when the content of the problems is relevant to shopping—for example, figuring out which of two deodrant offers is the better to buy. On the other hand, some research suggests that when older and younger people are matched carefully for educational level, there is little difference in their use of formal operations (*Blackburn,* 1984).

The question of whether cognitive structure changes after formal operations has stirred real excitement among developmental psychologists. Piaget (1970) did not identify any stage levels beyond formal operations, but he did note that reasoning may operate differently in adults than in adolescents. Adolescents often have the luxury of using hypothetical reasoning "playfully", to solve hypothetical "What if . . ." problems—the essence of pure formal operations. Adults, on the other hand, often have to fit their reasoning into the dimensions of real life. As a result, they may often think in ways that are less abstract and less purely logical. That is, they may combine abstract thinking with realistic thinking about the way life actually works.

Some researchers (for example, *Labouvie–Vief,* 1982) have suggested that the adult's integration of abstract logical principles with realism represents a real advance that goes beyond formal operations. Others have begun to study this kind of integration, focusing, for example, on how adults think when they serve on juries.

Peck's Developmental Tasks of Middle Age

Robert Peck concluded that reassessment of self is the prevailing theme of middle age. He thought Erikson's stages of intimacy and generativity were more crucial to young adulthood, while Erikson's last stage, integrity, represented the major issue of life after age 30. Feeling that the latter half of life deserved as much attention as the earlier years, he looked for additional tasks faced during middle and old age.

Peck's first task of middle age is **valuing wisdom versus valuing physical powers**. Biological changes are inevitable, causing physical powers such as strength, stamina, and youthful attractiveness to decline. From his analysis of thousands of business people (mostly men), he observed that most reach a critical transition period somewhere between the late thirties and early forties where "middle age depression" can occur if physique continues to be a major source of identity. If, however, this source of identity is replaced by deeper values and judgement, the individuals gain the necessary wisdom (emotional stability, motivation, and intellectual ability) for solving life problems.

Mastery of Peck's second task, **socializing versus sexualizing** in human relationships, emphasizes redefining men and women as individual personalities rather than as sexual objects. Mastery provides the potential for added depth and understanding in interpersonal relationships.

As his third task, Peck defines **cathectic or emotional flexibility versus cathectic impoverishment** as the capacity to shift emotional investments from one person or activity to another. The potential for crisis exists because, as parents and friends begin to die and children grow up and leave home, they need to be replaced adaptively by investing in new interpersonal pursuits.

Peck's fourth task of middle age is **mental flexibility versus mental rigidity**. As the mature person faces new problems in life, he or she creatively seeks new solutions and actively explores options offered by others. Immature adult continue to face problems with the same solutions used in the past. They become rigid, inflexible, close-minded, and set in their ways. "But this is the way we have always done it."

The opportunities of middlescence

Flowering

The self-evaluation and self-discipline skills developed during adolescent years and strengthened through young adulthood continue to be significant through middle-life. Improvements in judgement, increased tolerance, heightened self-understanding, and a better grasp of realities become reassuring aspects of middle adulthood. Women often feel a firm sense of identity for the first time in their lives and delight in the self-discovery. Men can enjoy an increased sense of expressiveness and compassion. Although men and women may move in opposite directions in middle-life, they move toward the same goal, wholeness or completion.

Productivity

Human experience and relationships are appreciated more; prestige, power, physical appearance, and physique, less. Life may be valued more deeply because of an awareness of death, and life's potentials may be appreciated in a new way.

Lessening of earlier restrictions, increased free time, and newfound energy provide freedom and spontaneity to extend oneself to the larger community. Erikson proposes that a basic strength of generativity results in a widening commitment to *take care* of persons, products, and ideas. All the basic strengths from earlier developmental phases (hope, will, purpose, skill, fidelity, and love) are essential as one redirects energies to being concerned about, caring for, and contributing to the welfare of the next generation. As one becomes a parent in the broader sense, the productive and creative opportunities for self-actual-

ization and generativity increase.

Creativity

New interests or those left dormant during early struggles to establish a family and career now can be developed or expanded. Hobbies or talents can blossom into serious work. New energies are released with the development of creative abilities.

Creativity also includes satisfaction with life as it unfolds and a confident attitude toward the future. Motivation no longer comes from the desire to please others, but to please oneself. The result is increased self-reliance. Spontaneity often complements creativity as one experiences the joy of life.

Expand Beyond Me and Mine

Although one becomes introspective in middle age and shows less concern for what others think, the need to be generative propels many into leadership and decision-making positions. Whether within the family or the larger community, healthy middlescent use their skills and experience to help and guide the younger generation. Competency, a feeling of being in control of one's life and actively involved in the larger world, is an obvious trademark of middle age.

Developmental tasks of adulthood

The developmental tasks of adulthood are many and varied. Here we will consider a few of them.

Entering Young Adulthood

Erikson depicted young adulthood as a time of tension between isolation and intimacy. If the tension is handled well, mature love can result. Erikson stressed that commitments to others can ultimately help society flourish. Traditionally, this is accomplished through intimate heterosexual relationships that are socially sanctioned through marriage and expanded with the birth of children.

When one partner, or both, cannot sustain an unselfish relationship of mutual sharing—or when an individual cannot experience such a relationship—the result can be a sense of isolation, "*aloneness.*"

The transition of Middle Adulthood

According to Erikson, adults in their middle years confront a core conflict between generativity and stagnation. The generative adult is productive, creative, and involved in preparing the next generation for life within the culture. The adult who fails to generate in these ways may show a stunting of personal growth, a sort of psychological shriveling that Erikson called "*stagnation.*"

Vocational Development

Most working adults spend more time at their occupations than at any other activity. The jobs held by the parents largely determine the family's social status, place of residence, how often they move, who cares for the children, when family members sleep and eat, and when (and how much) they are together.

How do people select *one* from among the 25,000 or so different occupations that exist today? Personality factors seem to play a role in

this. In an effort to make this picture more clear Holland (1973) studied the vocational preferences of high school and college students and developed a personality—environment model for career selection: The model includes the six personality types, with each type suited to a particular kind of work environment. For example, people who are energetic, talkative, ambitious, and otherwise enterprising are said to be inclined toward careers that reward people for achieving power, status, and money—careers such as sales.

Work Choice, Work Change, and Life Satisfaction

One reason that early career choices are considered important is that each time we open one career door, we, in effect, close others. When we choose to sharpen one set of skills, we leave other skills undeveloped.

Adults who shift careers voluntarily reflect a combination of personality and situational factors. Some research has suggested that personality factors such as risk-taking tendencies and a sense of control over one's own destiny may contribute. Other evidence has pointed to situa-

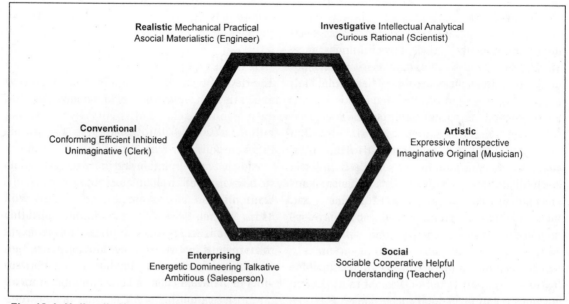

Fig. 13.4: Holland's Hexagonal model, showing personality types (bold), associated traits, and a sample career choice which might be appropriate for each type.

tional factors such as increasing disenchant-ment with one's present career (or "burnout"), discovery of an alternative occupation that promises greater satisfaction, and pivotal events (such as, divorce or death of a loved one) that lead one to shift life goals and priorities.

People may differ in their patterns of job commitment and success overtime, but these individual differences are not necessarily relat-ed to their overall adjustment and satisfaction. Work, while it is an important part of life, is only *one* part. When careers fail to provide a full measure of gratification, some change jobs, but others stay in the job and find satisfactions out-side the world of work.

Intimate Partnerships

For many, the greatest satisfactions in life come from their intimate relationships. Partners tend to be similar in their physical characteris-tics, their intelligence and education, their social and ethnic backgrounds, their religion, their temperament, and their life outlook. The more similar partners are in these ways, the more stable their marriages tend to be.

Satisfaction with marriage is apt to depend in part upon on how well the expectations and preferences of the two partners match up.

Parenthood

As marital partners become parents, a new process of growth begins. Learning to care for infants and young children is a developmental task of enormous magnitude. Infact, couples tend to rate the arrival of their first child as at least "moderately stressful" (*Hobbs & Cole*, 1976). Parenthood usually means a decline in the couple's sexual activity and in most other one-to-one adult interactions. It also often means movement toward a more traditional household, with the wife setting her career aside for a time and entering the world of chil-dren and housework. Despite such potentially stressful changes, couples often put children at the top of their list of marital satisfactions.

As children mature into adolescents and

eventually have their own lives and move away from home their parents face the prospect of an "empty nest." The experience can be painful and depressing for some parents. The empty nest allows nurturance to be redirected; husband and wife can offer each other much of the support and companionship that had been focused on their children when all the family members lived together.

Adjustment problems in adulthood

When families remain intact despite multiple problems, individual members may suffer any-way. Children may simply be underattended. Children enter their empty homes alone everyday after school, while their parents are still working. In more serious cases, parents struggling to make good earning and trying to cope with personal problems may neglect their children emotionally or physically, abuse their children physically, or they do violence to one another.

There are increasing reports of parent abuse by teenagers and of grandparents abuse by younger family members. Family life, a source of strength and security for many, can be a source of anxiety and danger for others.

Besides, the risk of family problems, the adult years include risks outside the family. Many peo-ple simply do not make a success of adult life. Sometimes these failures are linked to serious thought disorders such as schizophrenia, to sub-stance-abuse problems such as alcoholism, or to long-standing personality disorders—all of which become more common in the adult years.

OLD AGE

The boundary between middle and old age is not clearly marked by any physical or intellectual transformation. Both subjective and objective def-initions of old age emerge as one seeks answers to the question: "When does late adulthood begin?" Sometimes, the answer lies in the chronological age of the persons offering the definition. Many persons in their sixties and seventies may not see themselves as "old". However, the adolescent or

---

DEVELOPMENTAL TASKS OF MIDDLESCENCE

*1.
- Find self-confidence in inner identity, values Reevaluate and solidify or modify personal convictions
- Differentiate between self-worth and external problems
- Separate personal value from career success or financial status

*2.
- Balance or come to grips with discrepancies among dreams, goals, and realities Readjust goals as necessary
- Put experiences into context of continuities of life
- Make proactive midcourse adjustments

*3.
- Develop a philosophy for dealing with own mortality
- Expand avenues for spiritual development
- Resolve meaning of death

*4.
- Identify and share factors that give life meaning and continuity
- Identity and develop active and latent talents and interests
- Evaluate keys to personal success
- Share traditions, culture, folklore, and skills with younger generations
- Provide formal and informal mentor relationships
- Assume leadership roles

*5.
- Extend sense of caring and responsibility beyond the immediate
- Families of origin or creation
- Neighborhood
- Church and organizations
- Immediate community
- Extended community (state, national, international)

6.
- Develop wisdom
- Separate affective from cognitive domain for decision making
- Appreciate needs and views of others

Evaluate issues in the context of time

7.
- Establish new relationships with other people
- Revise bonding and commitment to family of creation
- Encourage independence in offspring
- Integrate new persons into family system
- Rebalance power and responsibility as family memberships and needs change
- Adjust to aging and death of parents
- Enjoy an active social life with persons of all ages
- Maintain a confidant(e) relationship

8.
- Find satisfaction in career or job
- Share expertise with younger workers
- Discover ways to improve knowledge and competence
- Plan for retirement

9.
- Adapt to changes in physical domain
- Climacterium
- Decreased strength and stamina
- Physical appearance
- Biological changes

10.
- Assume active responsibility for maintaining high-level wellness in all five domains
- Develop self-renewing ability
- Seek new information to maintain currency and promote continued development
- Assume prophylactic health maintenance habits
- Seek consultation as necessary
- Balance work and leisure time
- Balance family and self time
- Develop meaningful leisure-time activities

---

* Tasks deemed most crucial to continued maturation are marked with an asterisk.

---

young adult may categorize anyone over 40 or 50 as "old." The question generally is addressed from three perspectives: One is to look at biological aging as it is defined by scientists and gerontologists; another is to look at subjective and objective definitions of aging; the third and most common approach is to look at arbitrary categories based on chronological definitions.

Definitions of aging

Aging is defined objectively as a universal process that begins at birth; but, subjectively, aging is associated with chronological age or the older adult years. Children generally do not identify themselves as "aging," but they delight in announcing "how old" they are. They usually view birthdays as a positive experience that will admit them to additional opportunities, privileges, and responsibilities. During adulthood, however, aging is negatively associated with "being old" (which may imply "no longer useful" or "infirm"). Thus "old age" is often defined as an age that is several years or a decade beyond one's current age. Consequently, it is not uncommon to hear people of 75 years or more refer to "old people" as if they were a species different from themselves.

People identify age as the length of time that has elapsed since one's birth. As such, chronological age often serves as an objective basis of social organization. For example, societies establish chronological age criteria for certain activities, such as education, driving, military service, and the collection of retirement benefits. To participate legally in these activities, individuals must provide documentation of chronological age.

Physical changes

Many of the physical changes that come with age are familiar. Hair whitens and becomes sparse; skin dries and wrinkles; gums recede, and teeth are lost—more than half of the elderly have none of their own teeth; the facial configuration shifts; the spine bows. Sensory capacity declines as well. After age 50, most people need glasses. Impaired hearing is five times as common among 65 to 79-years-olds as among 45 to 64-years-olds. Aging even has subtle effects on autonomic nervous system arousal.

In older adults, arousal may still peak quickly, but it fades slowly. Thus the older adult remains "wired" longer and may seem overly nervous, vigilant, or cautious when events are moving quickly.

Psychosocial development in old age

Any attempt to understand and appreciate the adult in old age necessitates a life-span developmental perspective because the individual, at any given point of the life span, is a partial product of all the developmental processes and forces, events, and determinants that constitute his or her life history. Previous events, experiences, and choices continue to exert an impact on the quality of life. Memories, habits, knowledge, expectancies, and self-concept provide a basic continuity in the lives of adults.

However, this continuity is not total because individuals are also a partial product of the developmental processes and forces, events, and determinants that currently impinge on them. To the extent that earlier development allows and current circumstances encourage, require, or dictate new adaptations, adjustments, and behaviours, individuals will, at any given point in the life span, be capable of marked change. In contrast to the stereotype about increasing rigidity in old age, many new and highly positive behaviours often appear for the first time during the later years of life! Old age can continue to be a period of renewal and expansion, discovery and growth.

Piagetian Perspectives

Much of the research evidence has shown that the elderly do not do as well on many tests as do adolescents and younger adults. In fact, some studies even showed poorer performance by the elderly than by older children on conservation tasks. The easy conclusion to draw from such findings is that as people grow old, they regress cognitively—that is, they slip back to earlier, less adequate levels of thinking. Some have drawn this conclusion, and they may be right.

On the other hand, some have raised questions about what Piagetian tests really tell us about the elderly and whether these tests are really appropriate ways of measuring ability in older people. Piagetian tests were designed for children. They use child-oriented materials (for example, wooden blocks, balls of clay) and child-oriented language. The tests may seem silly or uninteresting to some adults and unfamiliar or confusing to others. As a result, older adults who take the tests may not do so well at first, despite adequate ability. One way to explore this possibility is to give older adults practice with some Piagetian measures and then test them with other, similar Piagetian measures. When such training was provided, older people generally showed marked improvement in their performance (for example, *Hornblum & Overton*, 1976). The performance of the elderly seemed to be quite improvable.

Another question raised by some investigators is whether the health problems and educational limitations of older adults may have hampered their performance on Piagetian tests. One investigator (*Blackburn*, 1984) tried to control for this problem. He selected adults aged 63-75 who were all healthy, all college-educated, and all currently taking college-course work. When these elderly adults were compared to college students aged 19-24, there were *no* significant differences between the groups on nine different tests of formal-operational thinking.

Learning and Memory

Although older adults can certainly learn via classical and instrumental conditioning, some kinds of classical conditioning take longer in older people than in younger adults. This may be due partly to the fact that older people tend to have more problems with their sight, hearing, and other sensory functions.

In verbal learning—learning lists of words, for example—adults over 60 generally do not perform as well as do young adults, but experts are now debating whether these performance differences reflect real differences in learning ability. Some attribute the inferior performance of older adults to pacing problems. It is on timed tasks that older people perform most poorly. This, in turn, may be related to their cautious style of responding, which we discussed earlier. Older adults tend to make errors of omission rather than to give incorrect responses; perhaps they are just being careful— taking a lot of time to make sure their answers are right—and this lowers their score on tests where speed is crucial.

Overcaution and pacing problems may also contribute to some of the memory-performance deficits older people demonstrate (*Salthouse & Kail*, 1983). These deficits are not found in all aspects of their memory but are largely confined to what is called secondary memory, a term applied to our system for processing information. Secondary memory includes three processes: (1) encoding, putting the to-be-remembered material into our memory systems; (2) storage, retaining the material until it is needed; and (3) retrieval, pulling the information out of storage. Older people show deficits in the first and the third processes: encoding and retrieval. They are less effective than are younger adults in coming up with good strategies for organizing and rehearsing the memories out of storage (Erber, 1982).

Life-Span Research on Intelligence—Test Performance

Assessing intellectual functioning in the same adults as they grow older, these investigators have reached some important, though tentative, conclusions about true age effects (*Schaie*, 1983). First, true intellectual declines before the late fifties are unusual; when declines do occur before 50, they usually reflect some pathological process, such as an illness or a degenerative disorder. Second, from the late fifties on, there is often a decline in abilities that involve speed of response. Third, beyond age 80, performance declines of some sort become the rule rather than the exception.

The fourth and perhaps most intriguing conclusion is that many of the intellectual limitations found in older adults reflect absolescence, not decline. In other words, big generational differences exist in the approaches people take to the tasks of processing information and solving problems. Many older people seem to use the same reasoning strategies they used in their younger days, but these strategies are often not so effective as those used by more recent generations.

Developmental tasks of old age

Erikson's View

In Erikson's (1963) account of the life course, old age brings on a core developmental conflict: integrity versus despair. To achieve *integrity,* in Erikson's sense of this term, means to integrate one's attitudes, beliefs, motives, and experiences in such a way that they fit together comfortably and form a coherent whole. One result is a feeling of satisfaction with a life well lived. Without this integrity, the older person feels a growing sense of *despair,* a fear that time is running out before the pieces of life's puzzle can be assembled in a satisfying way. This despair can show up in various ways—as perpetual irritability and disgust or as a nagging fear of death—but at its core is a sense of incompleteness, of a life that is not yet whole.

Retirement

Retirement means vastly different things to different people. It may signify the abrupt and unsought termination of one's livelihood, a welcomed relief from the tedium of a boring job, or the natural conclusion of a successful career and job well done. It may provide more time to pursue already established and pleasurable activities, enough time to engage in activities that were previously "out of the question," or release unlimited amounts of unoccupied time. Retirement may be associated with a broadening or expansion of one's lifestyle or signal the beginning of severe "cutbacks." Whatever the specific, subjective and objective meanings of retirement, it involves "separation from a sphere of activity that has provided social order, economic remuneration, and some degree of personal identity and prestige for the greater part of the adult years.

The transition into and through retirement can be usefully divided into stages or phases that reflect and indicate the changing nature of the individual's concern about retirement. In the **pre-retirement period**, the individual begins to consider retirement issues including time management and finances. In the early or *remote phase* of this period, both the notion of someday retiring and the thoughts about what it will be like are rather vague; but in the *near phase,* the individual begins to actually prepare for retirement by adopting new attitudes towards the work role and by entertaining fantasies about life in retirement. After the **retirement event**, there is a *honeymoon phase,* in which the individual begins to actualize these fantasies. A *disenchantment phase* then sets in for most retirees, its onset determined by the realization that personal fantasies and actual resources (reality) are incongruent. The true **postretirement period** begins with the *reorientation phase,* when more realistic routines for day-to-day living are established. The next phase is that of *stability,* which is characterized by the maintenance of work, decision-making strategies, and satisfying routines. The majority of the postretirement years are lived in this phase. Increases in illness, disability, and dependence on others make it increasingly difficult to continue carrying out the retirement role that had been established. Consequently, a final or *termination phase,* may emerge as the individual abruptly or gradually releases the postretirement routines and relationships.

Wisdom

Those who do achieve a sense of wholeness and integrity may develop one of the hallmarks of successful ageing: wisdom. Many cultures traditionally rely on selected elderly people for advice about complex life problems. One reason may be that older people who have been attentive to their life experience often have a perspective on reality that is richer and more informed than the view most younger people take.

Some have also suggested that the wise person is one who has a "balanced investment in self as well as in others" and who combines "experience, reflectiveness, and emotional balance" (*Birren & Renner,* 1980).

Grand Parenthood

One of the special delights of old age is having grandchildren. The role of grandparent may differ from one family to the next.

There are various ways of filling the grandparent role. Yet across the many variations in its form, the grandparent-grandchild relationship remains one of the most important institutions in human society. It is a bridge across generations, one that is valued by grandchildren even after they mature into adulthood (*Robertson,* 1976). For grandparents, the relationship can provide one path to the kind of generativity discussed by Erikson (1963)—that is, an opportunity to "pass the torch" to younger members of the family team.

Coping with Loss

One of the painful occurrences in old age is that one partner will lose the other and face the pain of bereavement. Because women live longer than men (and often marry men older than they are in the first place), the surviving partner is usually female.

It is difficult to develop and sustain a warm, intimate relationship with a single partner but, it can be even more difficult to face life without that partner.

The difficulties can be serious for both widows and widowers, but women in general seem to cope better than men. Although women tend to cope better than men in general, some groups of women are especially at risk for problems. In particular, middle-class women with a strong investment in their roles as wives report "strong disruption after the death of the husband." However, women who, in addition to their marriages, have had active lives in the community or workplace report loneliness but relatively less disruption in their lifestyle. There is also evidence that older widows, particularly those who had advance warning of their husband's impending death, adjust better than do younger widows and those for whom the death was unexpected. Some widows and widowers eventually cope with their loss by remarrying.

Whatever the coping strategies an older man or woman adopts for dealing with the death of a spouse, one implication of that death is difficult to deny: The surviving spouse, too, is undergoing an ageing process that will culminate in death. Facing up to this process and the inevitability of one's own death is the final aspect of old age.

Facing Death

Facing up to the inevitability of death is a major developmental risk of old age. Psychiatrist *Elisabeth Kübler-Ross* (1969, 1975) proposed that the psychology of the dying process involves five stages:

1. The first is denial; informed of a terminal illness, the individual reacts with shock and disbelief ("No, this can't happen to me").
2. The second is rage and anger, particularly over the idea that others will live while he or she will not.
3. Stage three involves bargaining; the person

accepts the inevitability of death but pleads for a bit more life, sometimes trying to "negotiate" with God for a few extra months.
4. The fourth stage is depression, a kind of anticipatory self-mourning.
5. The fifth and final stage is called acceptance; the person becomes quietly expectant—not happy about death, but ready for it nonetheless.

Kübler-Ross originally proposed that these five states always occur, and in the same order, for every person who knows that he or she is dying.

Regardless of whether a particular elderly person experiences these stages or not, acceptance of death is likely to come easier if he or she can reflect positively on a life well lived. This capacity is one part Erikson's (1963) notion of ego integrity.

Adjustment problems in old age

Inadequate financial planning can leave older people "newly poor" shortly after retirement and thus poor for the rest of their lives. Like other age groups, the elderly like to have friends of their own age and recreation to enjoy with those friends. However, retirement communities that offer these attractions are mostly for the financially secure. Other elderly people may live in substandard housing and on substandard diets.

The aging body is highly vulnerable to various diseases and injuries. Among these are diseases that attack the brain—**Alzheimer's disease** and **Pick's disease**, for example, both of which cause disorientation, poor judgement, and death within 5 years and their is no known cure for either. **Senile brain disorders** cause tissue loss and shrinkage in the brain, which in turn triggers mental and physical deterioration. **Cerebral arteriosclerosis**, or hardening of the arteries in the brain, blocks the supply of oxygen and nutrients to the brain; brain tissue thus degenerates, and severe intellectual slippage follows. In addition to these physiologically based disorders, the psychological stressors of old age can provoke various psychological disorders, but one that deserves special attention here is *depression*. In elderly bleak circumstances and internal state that Erikson referred to as despair can combine to make life seem not worth living.

DEVELOPMENTAL TASKS OF LATE ADULTHOOD

*1. Find satisfaction in reduced or nonemployment activities:
  - Leisure time
  - Volunteer work
  - Family relationships
  - Continue to share job and career related expertise

*2. Validate value, meaning, and responsibilities of life lived:
  - Take pleasure in memories of personal successes
  - Place contributions in context of history
  - Accept own humanness in the failures and disappointments of life
  - Share events and stories of earlier years with younger generation
  - Share observations, values, and wisdom learned from continuities of life

*3. Prepare for own death:

  - Adapt to death of peer, siblings, and spouse accept own mortality

  - Gradually transfer social and civic responsibilities to others
  - Arrange for distribution of personal possessions solidify concept of life after death

4. Pace activities with physical ability and endurance:
  - Seek assistance as necessary
  - Continue health maintenance practices
  - Separate self-worth from issues of forced dependency
  - Continue proactive, high-level involvement in life

5. Maintain maximal independence in activities of daily living:
  - residence
  - self-care
  - decision making
  - financial management

---

* Tasks deemed most crucial to continued maturation are marked with an asterisk.

Man is a model exposed to the view of different artists, everyone surveys it from some point of view none from every point.

—Helvetius

Personality

Personality

The word, "**Personality**", has been derived from the Latin word, '**Persona**', which was used for the "mask" utilized by the actors to change their appearance but in Roman times it was taken as a particular character itself. Since then the word, Personality, is used for not only for one's character but also to those aspects of individual's behaviour that set him apart from other individuals.

VARIOUS DEFINITIONS OF PERSONALITY

It is not easy to define personality. *Turkat* and *Levin* (1984) while examining the literature on definitions of personality noted that they were unable to identify a unifying definition. Years ago *Gordon Allport* (1937) recounted as many as fifty definitions of personality. According to Allport (1961), "*personality* is the dynamic organisation within the individual of those psychophysical systems that determine his characteristic behaviour and thought." This is one of the most comprehensive definitions that takes into account the biological as well as the psychological variables involved in the development of the individual's personality. The words, "Dynamic Organisation", in the above definition, imply that the individual is an everchanging and developing organism as a result of new experiences and new goals. They also further imply that an individual goes on changing and developing but at the same time maintaining coherence. The word, "psychophysical" imply that personality is neither exclusively a psychological nor an exclusively physiological phenomenon. Both these aspects interact and influence each other and in this process our behaviour including our thoughts, feelings, emotions, attitudes and other aspects of our inner self are shaped into a pattern that becomes, 'characteristics' of a particular individual. By the word, "characteristic," is meant that each individual is unique in itself, however, similar the experiences of two or more people might be. This definition though not oriented towards any particular theory emphasizes heavily on the individual being or represents the person—concerned approach. In contrast to this definition let us examine another definition presented by well known learned theorist, *Walter Mischel* (1976). According to him, personality can be defined as, "the distinctive pattern of behaviour, including thoughts and emotions that characterize each individual's adaptation to the situations of his or her life. This definition implies that personality is largely confined to terms of the adaptation of an individual to his surroundings. By the word, "characteristic," Mischel meant that each individual was unique and that personality was a relatively stable feature of a given individual. His stance largely represented the situational approach because it learned heavily on the role environment.

Recently *Hall* and *Lindzey* (1985) noted that all definitions of personality can be grouped into five categories. The first was largely used by layman where personality tended to have an evaluative connotation. It was a measure of a person's social skills or the reflection of his or her most outstanding characteristic. The other four categories of definition reflected the most common theoretical orientations regarding the structure and functioning of human personality. These four categories of definition are biosocial, biophysical, omnibus and integrative. The biosocial definition emphasized the social factors that played an important role in determining an individual's personality. Mischel's definition discussed above falls in this category. The biophysical group of definitions emphasized the organic, inherent components of personality. The omnibus definition listed every concept considered of importance in describing the person, where as an integrative definition held that personality was what gave order and congruence to many different behaviours in which a person engaged. Allport's definition discussed above falls into this last category.

> *Personality refers to the enduring patterns of thought, feeling, motivation, and behaviour that are expressed in different circumstances.*

TYPE THEORIES

One of the first type theories that we know of was proposed about 400 B.C. by Hippocrates, a Greek physician now known as the father of medicine. He grouped people into four temperament types: sanguine—cheerful, vigorous, confidently optimistic; melancholic—depressed, morose; choleric—hot-tempered; and phlegmatic—slow-moving, calm, unexcitable. Since the time of Hippocrates, countless other ways of grouping people into types have been tried.

A *type* is simply a class of individuals said to share a common collection of characteristics. For example, introverts could be described as people who share a common collection of characteristics. For example, **introverts** could be described as people who share characteristics such as shyness, social withdrawal, and a tendency not to talk much; while **extroverts** share a tendency to be outgoing, friendly, and talkative.

Eysenck's hierarchical theory

One of the best-researched type theories was developed by *Hans Eysenck* (1967). Eysenck distinguishes traits and types, with *types* representing a higher order organization of personality. In this view, individuals produce specific behaviours, some of which are frequent or habitual (that is, they are habits). A trait is a group of correlated

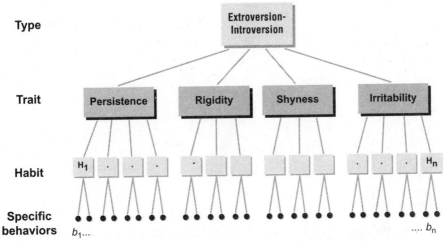

Fig. 14.1: Eysenck's model of personality

habits; that is, a person who has one of these habits tends to have the other habits that constitute the trait. For example, avoiding attention in a group, not initiating conversation, and avoiding large social gatherings are habitual behaviours of people with the trait of shyness. A type is a group of correlated traits. People who are shy, rigid, and inward looking are introverts.

On the basis of thousands of studies conducted over the last half century, Eysenck identified three overarching psychological types: extroversion—introversion, neuroticism—emotional stability, and psychological—impulse control. **Extroversion** refers to a tendency to be sociable, active, and walking to take risks. Introverts, who score at the low end of the extroversion scale, are characterized by social inhibition, seriousness, and caution. **Neuroticism** defines a continuum from emotional stability to instability. It is closely related to the construct of negative affect. People high on neuroticism report feeling anxious, guilty, tense, and moody, and they tend to have low self-esteem. **Psychoticism** is an oddly named scale whose opposite pole is impulse control. People high on psychoticism are aggressive, egocentric, impulsive, and antisocial. People low on psychoticism are empathic and able to control their impulses.

TRAIT THEORIES

Trait theories were largely derived from the words people use to describe themselves and others in their everyday lives, beginning with adjectives like *shy, devious, manipulative, open,* or *friendly.* **Traits** are emotional, cognitive, and behavioural tendencies that constitute underlying personality dimensions on which individuals vary.

According to *Gordon Allport* (1937), who developed the trait approach to personality, the concept of trait has two separate but complementary meanings. On the other, a trait is an inferred underlying personality disposition that generates this behavioural tendency. Presumably, a tendency to be cheerful (an

observed trait) stems from an enduring pattern of internal processes, such as tendency to experience positive affect, to think positive thoughts, or to wish to be perceived as happy (an inferred disposition).

How does one measure traits? The most straightforward way is the same way people intuitively assess other people's personalities: Observe their behaviour over time and in different situations. Because extensive observation of this sort can be very cumbersome and time consuming, however, psychologists often use two other methods. One is to ask people who know the subject well to fill out questionnaires about the person's personality. The second, more commonly used method is to ask subjects themselves to answer self-report questionnaires.

To describe personality from a trait perspective, one must know not only how traits but also which ones to measure.

Allport and *Odbert* (1936) complied a list of some 18,000 words from Webster's unabridged dictionary that could be used to distinguish one person from another. Many of these words denote similar characteristics, however, so over the years trait psychologists have collapsed the list into fewer and fewer traits. *Raymond Cattell* (1990) reduced the list to just 16 traits, such as warm, emotionally stable, intelligent, cheerful, suspicious, imaginative, sensitive, and tense.

Allport's trait theory

Gordon Allport

Allport (1961) believed that the rich collection of trait like terms provided a way of capturing the uniqueness of each individual. He believed that this uniqueness could be described well in terms of the individual's traits, or "personal dispositions," at three levels of generality.

Cardinal traits he defined as those which are so dominant that nearly all of the individual's actions can be traced back to them. These broad, highly influential traits are often called by names drawn from key historical figures. For instance, one person might be described as Christ-like. Each term describes a trait so broad and so deep in its impact that it overshadows the influence of other traits in the same individual. Allport believed that most people have *no* true cardinal traits but that when someone does have a cardinal trait it shows itself in virtually all of the person's behaviour.

For most people, who are without a cardinal trait, central traits become crucial. **Central traits** he described as characterizing an individual's behaviour to some extent but not in such a complete way as cardinal traits.

Finally, the least generalized characteristics of the person he labeled **secondary traits**. These are traits such as "likes chocolate" or "prefers foreign cars"—traits that are influential but only within a narrow range of situations. Allport recommended that cardinal, central, and secondary traits be used to assemble what he called psychological life histories and that information about these traits come from materials produced by the individuals themselves—materials such as letters, diaries, or personal journals.

Contributions and limitations of trait theories

The trait approach to personality has several advantages. Traits lend themselves to measurement and hence to empirical investigation through questionnaires. Without the trait approach, we would not have been able to assess the heritability or consistency of personality. Further, trait theories are not committed to theoretical assumptions that may be valid for some people but not for others. Psychodynamic and cognitive-social theories offer universal answers to questions such as "Are humans basically aggressive?" or "Are people basically rational?" Trait theories, in contrast, offer a very different answer: "Some people are, some aren't, and some are in between."

Trait approaches, however, have a number of limitations:

- First, they rely too heavily on self-reports; people often cannot or will not give an accurate assessment of themselves. For example, people who consider themselves psychologically healthy may deny statements about themselves that are true but threaten their self-concept.

- Second, trait theories can be no more sophisticated than the theories of personality held by lay people and particularly by college students, who serve as subjects for most studies, because the basic terms of trait theory come from everyday language. Trait theory may be less a theory of personality than a theory of the way everyday people think about personality. Where do concepts developed by experts such as defenses or expectancies fit it? One could argue that relying almost exclusively on self-reports is like asking a physicist to depend on the observations of untrained observers.

- Third, as in factor-analytic studies of intelligence, the factor structure that emerges depends in part on the items that are included and a number of highly subjective decisions made by the factor analyst. Although most personality researchers have converged on the FEM, others have repeatedly found three or four factors and some have found seven.

- Finally, trait theories often provide more insight into the *how much* of personality than the *how* or the *why* (Block, 1995). They describe and even predict behaviour but do not explain it. A person may rank high in aggressiveness, but this says little about the internal processes that occur when the person is behaving aggressively or why he behaves aggressively in some circumstances but not in others.

PSYCHODYNAMIC THEORIES

Sigmund Freud developed the first comprehensive theory of personality. As a neurologist practicing in the 1880s before the advent of psychiatry and clinical psychology, Freud encountered patients with a wide range of psychological disturbances. A particularly perplexing disorder was **hysteria,** in which a number of patients, most of them women, suffered from paralysis, numbness, and fainting spells, with no apparent biological origin. In seeking a treatment for the disorder, Freud was particularly influenced by the work of *Jean Martin* Charcot. Charcot, a French neurologist, demonstrated that hysterical symptoms could be produced—and alleviated, at least temporarily—through hypnosis. Paralyzed patients could walk again under the influence of a hypnotic suggestion, but the symptoms usually returned before long. These patients *wanted* to walk, but something seemed to override their conscious determination or will, much as many individuals today with bulimia cannot stop binging and purging.

Freud reasoned that if a symptom is not of physiological origin and the patient is consciously trying to stop it but cannot, then opposing the conscious will must be an unconscious counter-will of equal or greater magnitude. This basic assumption was the centerpiece of Freud's theory of psychodynamics, analogous to dynamics among physical forces. According to Freud, psychological forces such as wishes, fears, and intentions have a direction and an intensity. When several such motives collide and conflict, the balance of these forces determines the person's behaviour, as in the case of a patient suffering from a hysterical paralysis, whose will to move her leg is unconsciously overridden.

Freud's model

Sigmund Freud

Why would a counter-will be unconscious? And what balance of unconscious forces could lead to paralysis or to a need to starve or drink oneself to death? Freud tried to answer these questions throughout his career by developing a series of models, which he never entirely reconciled with one another.

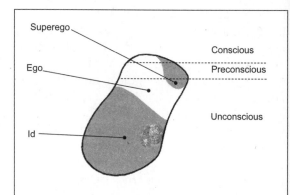

Fig. 14.2 The components of personality, in psychoanalytic theory, can be imagined something like this figure.

Topographic Model

Freud's first model, the **topographic model** (1900), used a spatial metaphor (the mind as split into sectors) that divided mental processes into three types: conscious, preconscious, and unconscious. Conscious mental processes are rational, goal-directed thoughts at the center of awareness. Preconscious mental processes are not conscious but could become conscious at any point, such as knowledge of the colour of sparrows. Finally, unconscious mental processes are irrational, organized along associative lines rather than by logic. They are inaccessible to consciousness because they have been repressed, that is, kept from consciousness to avoid emotional distress.

Unconscious processes, while barred from consciousness, are not inert. Because they are not consciously acknowledged, they may leak into consciousness and affect behaviour in unexpected and often unwelcome ways, as in slips of the tongue. For example, a woman in her late thirties who was talking to a boy several years her junior was asked about the age difference. She replied, "Oh, I don't think it really matters." Apparently, a part of her was not so sure.

Freud used the topographic model to understand dreams, distinguished between their story line (the manifest content) and their underlying message (the latent content). For example, a 30-year-old male virgin considering having his first sexual encounter reported in psychotherapy a recurring dream of dipping his feet into a polluted river. From a psychodynamic perspective, the dream appeared to express conflicting feelings and wishes about sexuality—will and counter-will. He wanted to get his feet wet, so to speak, but he was reluctant because he considered sex unclean. The connection of sexuality, wetness and pollution, in his view, is not accidental and was supported by many statements the patient made in this and other sessions.

Drive Model

Freud's topographic model addressed conflict between conscious and unconscious motives. His second model, the **drive model,** tried to explain why people pursue the motives they do. Influenced by the work of *Charles Darwin,* Freud stressed the continuity of human and nonhuman behaviour. He hypothesized that humans are motivated by drives and instincts, like other animals. *Freud* (1993) proposed two basic drives: sex and aggression. He defined the sexual drive or **libido,** more broadly than its colloquial usage. Libido refers as much to pleasure seeking, sensuality, and love as it does to desires for sexual intercourse. Expressions of libido may be as varied as day-dreaming about sex or romance, dressing to attract romantic partners, or selecting a career likely to attract a potential spouse because of its status or income potential.

People also express aggression in various ways, some socially acceptable and others not. We see aggression on the sports field, in the corporate boardroom, and in just about every video game on the market. Freud would not have been surprised by the two criteria used to determine whether television shows and movies are acceptable for general viewing—the amount of sex and the amount of aggression—because these are the same things that individuals regulate and censor in themselves.

Developmental Model

Freud (1933) considered the development of the libidinal drive the key to personality development, and hence proposed a **developmental model,** or theory of **psychosexual stages.**

The psychosexual stages reflect the child's evolving quest for pleasure and growing realization of the social limitations on this quest. At each stage, libido is focused on a particular bodily region, or erogenous zone.

To understand these stages, one must view them both narrowly and broadly. That is, the stages describe specific bodily experiences, but they also represent broader psychological and psychosocial conflicts and concerns (*Erikson,* 1963). Freud's psychosexual stages may sound preposterous at first, but if you try to imagine yourself a child at each stage—sucking your mother's breast for nourishment, fighting with your parents about toilet training (a fight that can go on for a year), or sobbing and shrieking as your parents leave you alone at home room—the broader the issue may seem less absurd than at first glance.

Oral stage

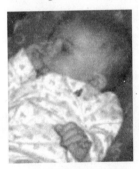

Fig. 14.4: An Infant in the Oral stage

During the oral stage (roughly the first 18 months of life), children explore the world through their mouths. Many parents observe that their infants literally put anything that is not nailed down into their mouths. During the oral stage, sucking the breast or bottle is the means by which infants gain nourishment, but it is also a prime avenue for *social* nourishment, that is, warmth and closeness.

From a broader standpoint, in the oral stage children develop wishes and expectations about dependence because they are totally dependent on their care takers. Difficulties (such as chronic dissatisfaction or discomfort) during the oral stage—or any of the

STAGE	AGE	CONFLICTS AND CONCERNS
Oral	0 – 18 months	Dependency
Anal	2 – 3 years	Orderliness, cleanliness, control, compliance
Phallic	4 – 6 years	Identification with parents (especially same sex) and others, Oedipus complex, establishment of conscience
Latency	7 – 11 years	Sublimation of sexual and aggressive impulses
Genital	12+ years	Mature sexuality relationships

Fig. 14.3 Freud's Psychosexual Stages.

stages—can lead to **fixations,** conflicts or concerns that persist beyond the developmental period in which they arise. People with fixations at the oral stage may be extremely clingy and dependent, with an exaggerated need for approval, nurturance, and love. More concretely, the soothing and pleasure associated with mouthing and sucking during this stage may lead to fixated behaviour such as thumb sucking and cigarette smoking.

Anal stage

The anal stage (roughly ages 2 to 3) is characterized by conflicts with parents about compliance and defiance, which Freud linked to conflicts over toilet training. Freud argued that these conflicts form the basis of attitudes toward order and disorder, giving and withholding, and messiness and cleanliness. Imagine a toddler, who has scarcely been told "no" to anything, who finds himself barraged by rules during his second year, with the ultimate insult of being told to control his own body. This is the age during which the child learns to do unto others what they are now constantly doing unto him: saying no.

More concretely, *Freud* proposed that in the anal stage the child discovers that the anus can be a source of pleasurable excitation. Within a few short years the anal region is experienced as so disgusting that we cannot even touch it without the intervention of a piece of paper.

People with anal fixations exhibit a variety of behavioural tendencies. On the one hand, they may be overly orderly, neat, and punctual or, on the other, extremely messy, stubborn, or constantly late. They may have conflicts about giving and receiving or about compliance versus noncompliance with other people's demands. Children can also regress to anal issues particularly in times of stress. **Regression** means reverting to conflicts or modes of managing emotion characteristic of an earlier stage, as when young children whose parents are undergoing a divorce suddenly start soiling themselves again (an anal regression).

Phallic stage

During the **phallic stage** (roughly ages 4 to 6), children enjoy the pleasure they can obtain from touching their genitals and even from masturbating. During this stage children also become very aware of differences between boys and girls and mummies and daddies.

More broadly, during the phallic stage the child identifies with significant others, especially the same-sex parent. **Identification** means making another person part of oneself : imitating the person's behaviour, changing the self-concept to see oneself as more like the person, and trying to become more like the person, by adopting his or her values and attitudes. Much of adult personality is built through identification, as the child internalizes motives, behaviours, beliefs, and ideals—from the importance of achieving in school to the proper way of doing a particular thing.

Identification has many roots. Freud emphasized its link to the **oedipus complex,** named after the character in Greek tragedy who unknowingly slept with his mother. According to Freud, little boys want an exclusive relationship with their mothers, and little girls want an exclusive relationship with their fathers. From a young boy's perspective, for example, "Why should Mommy spend the night alone with Daddy? Why can't I go in there instead?" (Many children manage a compromise by finding ways to spend the night in the middle).

Freud argued that because children learn about love and sensual gratification from their parents, they desire an exclusive sexual relationship with the parent of opposite sex (bearing in mind the broad meaning of "sexual" in Freud's theory). At the same time, these wishes are so threatening that they are quickly repressed or renounced (consciously given up). Boys unconsciously fear that their father, their ultimate rival, will castrate them because of their desires for their mother (the **castration complex**). The fear is so threatening that they repress their Oedipal wishes and identify with their father. In other words, they internalize a moral prohibition against incest as a way of preventing themselves from acting on their wishes, which would be dangerous, and they instead become like their father in the hopes of someday obtaining someone like their mother. Girls; too, renounce their secret wishes toward their fathers and identify with their mothers because they fear losing her love.

During the phallic stage, according to Freud, **penis envy** emerges in girls, who feel that because they lack a penis they are inferior to boys. Taken on a metaphorical level, penis envy refers to the envy a girl develops in a society in which men's activities seem more interesting and valued (*Horney*, 1956).

Latency stage

During the **latency stage** (roughly ages 7 to 11), children repress their sexual impulses and continue to identify with their same-sex parent. They also learn to channel their sexual and aggressive drives into socially acceptable activities such as school, sports, and art. Whereas people fixated at the phallic stage may be preoccupied with attracting mates or take on stereotypical characteristics of their own or the opposite gender, individuals fixated at the latency stage may seem totally asexual.

Genital stage

During the **genital stage** (approximately age 12 and beyond), conscious sexuality resurfaces after years of repression, and genital sex becomes the primary goal of sexual activity. At this stage, people become capable of relating to and loving others on a mature level and carrying out adult responsibilities such as work and parenting. Prior elements of sexuality do not disappear—most people's foreplay continues to have oral and anal components—but these "pregenital" elements become integrated into patterns of sexual activity involving genital satisfaction. This stage was probably least elaborated by Freud, who believed that the major aspects of personality become firmly established in childhood and may require considerable effort to change thereafter.

Structural Model

The final model Freud developed was his **structural model** (Freud, 1923, 1933). In it, he shifted his understanding of conflict, from conflict between conscious and unconscious forces, to conflict between desires on the one hand and the dictates of conscience or the constraints of reality on the other.

Id, Ego, and Superego

The structural model posits three sets of mental forces, or structures: id, ego, and superego. The **id** is the reservoir of sexual and aggressive energy. It is driven by impulses and, like the unconscious of the topographic model, is characterized by wishful, illogical, and associative thought (called **primary process thinking**). To counterbalance the "untamed passions" of the id (Freud, 1933), the **superego** acts as a conscience and source of ideals. The superego is the parental voice within the person, established through identification. The **ego** is the structure that must somehow balance desire, reality, and morality, a task Freud described in terms of serving three masters: the id, the external world, and the superego. Unlike the id, the ego is capable of **secondary process thinking**, which is rational, logical, and goal directed. The ego is thus responsible for cognition and problem solving (Hartmann, 1939). It is also responsible for managing emotions and finding compromises among competing demands.

Neo-Freudians

From the start, Freud's theories drew a wide range of responses, from admiration to repulsion and derision. A group who came to be known as neo-Freudians accepted the nation of unconscious process and conflicts among psychological forces but rejected Freud's drive theory, particularly the central role of sexuality. Swiss psychiatrist *Carl Jung* (1875-1961) and Austrian psychiatrist *Alfred Adler* (1870-1937) were the first psychodynamic theorist to defect from the Freudian camp; in some ways, they were less neo-Freudians (that is, people who developed a new Freudian—inspired approach) than dissenters who went their own separate ways and started their own schools of thought.

Jung's analytical psychology

Carl Gustav Jung

Carl Gustav Jung (1928), had a very different opinion about psychoanalysis and he took the direction of *analytical psychology*. One of the main differences between the theorists was that Jung thought childhood psycho-sexual development to be not nearly so important to adult

adjustment as Freud did. Jung placed much less emphasis than Freud on sexual and aggressive impulses arising from past conflicts and much more emphasis on people's future-oriented goals, hopes, and plans. Both had quite different ideas about the nature of the unconscious.

From childhood, Jung was extremely interested in dreams and fantasy. Some of Carl's most powerful dreams involved religious images and symbols. These dreams were often laced with forbidden and sacrilegious overtones—for example, a godlike figure that looked like a gaint penis. Such boyhood dreams helped give Jung, the theorist, his lifelong fascination with the content and meaning of dreams and visions in people's lives.

In developing his theory, Jung drew on both his own dream and fantasy material and that of his patients; but he also drew on findings from such experimental techniques as the word—association test, in which people were read a standard array of 100 terms (for example, "head, to sin, to pray, bride, to abuse") and instructed to respond to each term "as quickly as possible with the first word that occurs to you." In addition to content of the test taker's associations, Jung recorded how long it took them to respond and whether certain words led particular patterns of breathing or even perspiration. Stimulus terms that resulted in long delays, an inability to respond, or certain other key signs were thought by Jung to be parts of what he called complexes. He defined a complex as a network of ideas bound together by a common emotion or set of feelings.

In using his word-association test to diagnose complexes, Jung believed he was exploring the unconscious. Yet Jung's findings with his own techniques led him away from Freud's ideas in several respects. Jung split with Freud over Freud's emphasis on libido because he felt that Freud viewed the brain as "an appendage of the genital glands" (Jung, 1961). Furthermore, although Jung accepted the existence of unconscious processes, he proposed that people also have **collective unconscious**, a repository of ideas, feelings, and symbols shared by all humans and passed genetically from one generation to another. According to Jung, certain basic symbols arise in all cultures because they reflect innate tendencies originating from the collective unconscious. These **archetypes**, or mythological motifs that emerge in dreams and cultural practices, express basic human needs, such as the image of a mother or a wise elder. Within all men, he argued, is a feminine archetype or **anima**, just as women possess an unconscious masculine side, or **animus**. Because of each archetype involves strong emotion, Jung believed that people's emotion—generated behaviour could often be explained by identifying the key archetype that was influencing them.

In addition to the collective unconscious, Jung credited each individual with a *personal unconscious* which developed out of any of the individual's conscious experiences that had been repressed. Psychologically healthy people were said to gradually come into contact with the unconscious parts of their personalities, integrating the unconscious or "shadow" side with their "conscious ego". In this way, all major components of the personality could eventually work in concert to form a fully realized, purposeful self. This process of harmonizing one's conscious and unconscious components happened in a unique pattern of behaviour. Jung called this process **individualization**; he saw it as the means by which each of us becomes an individual distinct from others.

Adler's Individual Psychology

Alfred Adler was a colleague of Freud and Jung. He also took issue with Freud's libido theory, eventually replacing it with a theory based on the "will to power" and "social interest"—loosely analogous to the distinction between motives for agency and relatedness. According to Adler, mature, well-adjusted people have needs for power, control, mastery, and personal growth as well as needs to participate in a large community. Adler maintained that people are motivated by a lifelong need for superiority in order to overcome feelings of inferiority developed in

childhood (Adler, 1929). He also paid more attention to people's conscious goals and values than Freud, who emphasized unconscious determinants of behaviour.

Alfred Adler

According to Adler, each individual creates his or her own personal approach to living; this highly individualized style grows out of the individual's unique sense of his or her inferiorities and the strategies they develops to overcome these inferiorities. This concept together with the concept of the subjective nature of individual goals, led Adler to label his theory **individual psychology.**

Adler's theory also pays a close attention to birth order as an influence on personality development. First-borns said Adler, begin life as the exclusive focus of their parents' attention and then are often abruptly dethroned with the birth of their first siblings. The result may be that the child feels cheated and later becomes an unruly misfit. A more positive possibility is that first-borns may develop a style of life in which they behave like a parent toward their siblings and become particularly responsible adults. Adler described other possibilities for second-born, last-born, and only children. Many of his specific ideas have not been borne out, but his ideas did help stimulate some important research. According to the research, first-borns do have especially intense relationships with their parents and that they tend to be more achievement-oriented and self-controlled than do later-born children. While later-born children tend to be less conforming, more sociable, and more popular.

Horney's Psychoanalytic Interpersonal Theory

Karen Horney (pronounced "horn-eye"), took sharp issue with Freud on some of his views about "feminine psychology." For example, she argued

Karen Horney

that "penis envy" was not a normal development in females but rather an unusual and pathological occurrence. She also countered that some of her male patients envied women *their* capacity for pregnancy, childbirth, motherhood, breast development, and sucking. Her views on females, sex differences, and Freud's theory were compiled in the book, *Feminine Psychology* (1967). Horney did not deny the existence of sex differences altogether, but she stressed the striking similarities of the two sexes as members of the human race facing similar challenges; she proposed that what psychiatry and personality theory needed was a "psychology of persons."

Two major components of her "person" psychology were the twin notions of basic anxiety and basic hostility (Horney, 1937).

Basic anxiety, is what arises in childhood when the child feels helpless in a threatening world. Children learn that they are relatively weak and powerless, dependent on their parents for safety and satisfaction. Loving and reliable parents can create a feeling of security (even serenity), but erratic, indifferent, or rejecting parents may sharpen the child's sense of helplessness and vulnerability. This sets the stage for basic anxiety.

In Horney's view, **basic hostility**, usually accompanies basic anxiety and grows out of resentment over the parental behaviour that led to anxiety in the first place. Because the hostility cannot be expressed directly to parents, it is typically repressed, which only increases the child's anxiety. Children caught in this bind—dependent on their parents, anxious because of their parents, turn hostile toward their parents, and unable to express their true feelings directly—tend to rely heavily on one of three modes of social behaviour, each of which might well carry into adulthood.

- *Moving toward others*—involves excessive compliance. Security is sought by making oneself indiscriminately complaint, subject to the will of others, and inclined to do whatever they wish in order to gain their approval and affection. The result may be a kind of security, but a costly kind that involves total repression of basic hostility and leaves the individual feeling depleted, exploited, and unhappy.

- *Moving against others*—involves pursuit of satisfaction through ascendance and domination of others. Self-protection is provided via one's power over others. Basic hostility may be expressed, but basic anxiety is usually denied. As a result, feelings of weakness and vulnerability are neither explored nor resolved.

- *Moving away from others*—is self-protection by withdrawal. Some people avoid the risk and pain of social relationships by avoiding relationships in the first place. This strategy does provide some protection, but it also cuts short any real prospect for growth in the social realm.

Horney believed that normal people use all three modes of social interaction at times but in a relatively balanced and flexible manner, adjusting their approach to situational demands. According to Karen Horney, the neurotic patterns seen in a society, such as endless striving after material goods or difficulty committing to intimate relationships, are similarly shaped by cultural forces.

Defense mechanisms

When people confront problems in their lives, they typically draw on problem-solving strategies that have worked for them in the past, rather than in inventing new solutions to every problem. The same is true of emotional problem solving. According to psychodynamic theory, people regulate their emotions and deal with their conflicts by employing defense mechanisms—unconscious mental processes aimed at protecting the person from unpleasant emotions (particularly anxiety) or bolstering pleasurable emotions.

Repression

This is an involuntary denial of instinctual wishes, feelings, and experiences, so that associated anxiety will not be experienced. A similar mechanism is *denial* (suppressing awareness of other things, people, events, or consequences that could arouse anxiety or threaten one's psychic integrity). In denial, a person refuses to acknowledge external realities (such as having cancer) or emotions (such as anxiety) rather than thoughts. Denial is at work when an individual notices a peculiar skin growth but concludes that "it's nothing." Much of the time it is nothing, but this defense can lead to failure to seek a potentially life-threatening treatment.

Projection

Attributing negative wishes, feelings, and impulses to other persons while denying that they originate in oneself. For instance, a hard-driving businessman who thinks his competitors, suppliers, and customers are always trying to cheat him may in fact be the one with questionable ethics. To recognize his own greed and lack of concern for others would conflict with his conscience, so instead he sees these traits in others. Recent research suggests a cognitive mechanism through which projection may occur. Paradoxically, keeping a thought out of awareness keeps it chronically activated at an implicit level; to stop a thought from attaining consciousness, the mind essentially sets up an automatic mechanism to "keep a lookout" for the thought, but this process has the unintended byproduct of keeping the thought active.

Thus, when a person is trying not to see himself as dishonest, the concept of *dishonesty* remains active implicitly. When someone else then behaves in a way that could be interpreted as either accidental or dishonest, the concept of *dishonesty* is already activated and is thus more likely to be used to interpret the person's behaviour. As a result, the individual sees in others what he is trying hard not to see in himself.

Reaction Formation

Another defense mechanism, in which the person turns unacceptable feelings or impulses into their opposites. For example, at the same time that a man was preaching the evils of sex to millions, he was regularly seeing a prostitute. His conscious repulsion toward sexuality, and particularly illicit sexuality, apparently masked a tremendous need for it.

Sublimation

Involves converting sexual or aggressive impulses into socially acceptable activities. A young boy may turn his feelings of competition with his father or brother into a desire to excel in competitive sports or to succeed in business when he is older.

Relationalization

Means explaining away actions in a seemingly logical way to avoid uncomfortable feelings, especially guilt or shame. A student who plagiarizes her term paper and justifies her actions by saying that passing the course will help her earn an another degree and serve the community is using rationalization to justify her dishonesty.

Intellectualization

Related to rationalization is intellectualization, another defense mechanism which involves reasoning. In *intellectualization,* however, the intensity of the anxiety is reduced by are treat into detached, unemotional, abstract language. Professionals who deal with troubled people may intellectualize in order to remain helpful without being overwhelmed by sympathetic involvement. For example, a nurse may describe in an intellectual fashion an encounter with a dying or angry patient.

Displacement

Displacement is the shifting of emotional energies from the object, idea, person, or situation to another that is less threatening and cannot retaliate. When a new baby is the centre of attention, an older child may become jealous; prevented from harming the baby, the child demolishes a doll. Thus by displacing aggression, the child finds a substitute outlet.

Regression

In the face of a threat, one may retreat to an earlier pattern of adaptation, possibly a childish for primitive one. This is called regression. Faced with the upsetting arrival of a new baby or going to school for the first time, a 5-year-old may have toilet accidents, revert to "baby talk", demand cuddling, or suck her thumb.

Just as people tailor their problem-solving efforts to specific situations, so too do people typically use defenses is by definition incomplete. Using defenses is neither abnormal nor unhealthy. In fact, some degree of defensive distortion may be useful, such as the tendency for people to see themselves more positively than is warranted by reality. A bit of denial can also be essential to surmounting seemingly insurmountable odds, as when an aspiring novelist persists despite repeated rejection and suddenly gets a break. Defenses become dysfunctional when they inhibit adaptive functioning rather than foster it.

Defense mechanisms are generally considered properties of individuals, but they often require collusion from other people. An alcoholic who denies his alcoholism will have a much easier time maintaining his defense if his wife and children adopt a code of silence.

LEARNING AND BEHAVIOURAL THEORIES OF PERSONALITY

These theories emerged from experiments in classical conditioning, instrumental conditioning, and cognitive learning.

Psychologists who build their theories on learning and behavioural principles share some important assumptions and practices. One shared assumption is that many of the behaviours that make up personality are conditioned, or learned. This means, first, that many such behaviours originate some where in the learning history of the individual, often as early as childhood. A second assumption is that current condition in the individual's environment help maintain these behaviours. Thus learning theo-

rists seek to understand people's behaviour by studying their learning history, their current environment, or both.

Early social learning theory: Dollard and Miller

Neal Miller

Learning theorists *Neal Miller*, an experimental psychologist, and sociologist *John Dollard* tested the basic idea that individual and social behaviour can be explained by means of basic learning principles. They even tried to translate Freud's psychoanalytic concepts into the language of learning theory and to test his concepts in the laboratory—with rats as their subjects! As we noted above, Freud believed that neurotic, disturbed behaviour involves conflict between id demands and ego/superego restraints. Dollard and Miller drew an analogy between this conflict and the conflict between approach and avoidance tendencies.

They argued that we may act indecisive and "neurotic" when we are torn between approaching and avoiding a certain course of action—as, for example, when we want to get a tooth filled but we fear the pain. In such cases, the tendency to approach (get the filling, for example) is often stronger than the avoidance tendency at first; but the closer we get to the "moment of truth," the more likely it is that the avoidance tendency will win out and we will retreat from the planned action (we will cancel out our dental appointment, for example).

John Dollard

Dollard and *Miller* (1950) applied ideas like this to a variety of human problems. Their aim was to engineer, if not a merger, atleast a bridge between the dynamic and learning perspectives on personality.

Skinner's radican behaviourism

B.F. Skinner's approach is exclusively instrumental or operant—that is, it deals only with the processes by which reinforcement (reward) and punishment influence the likelihood of behaviours. Ruled out of Skinner's analysis wherever possible are such "unobservables" as drives, motives, and emotions. Also ruled out are the trait and type notions discussed earlier. What, we might ask, is left to constitute the human personality?

B.F. Skinner

For Skinner, the answer seems to be that what most people call personality is actually a collection of reinforced responses. We are the persons that we are because of the reinforcement contingencies we experience. Skinner prefers to focus on the reinforcement that accompanies behaviour.

With such accounts of people's behaviour, described entirely in terms of objectively observable events, Skinner generated what some consider a "personalityless" view of personality. Many are offended by Skinner's efforts to reduce the seeming richness of human personality to nothing more than a set of responses strengthened by reinforcers. Others see Skinner's work as refreshing because it is an effort to be clear, precise, and rely on the smallest possible number of theoretical concepts and assumptions.

Later social learning theory: Bandura and Walters

Albert Bandura and *Richard Walters* (1963) saw the animal-derived principles of Dollar, Miller, and Skinner as simply too limited to account for important aspects of real human behaviour. For example, they thought the animal experiments involved artificially "safe" laboratory situations. In real life, they argued, people (and rats, for that matter!) often do not have the luxury of learning through instrumental or operant conditioning—trial and error learning in a protected laboratory where only "correct" responses get rewarded. In real life, it is often too costly to risk "incorrect" responses because an "incorrect" response would have serious consequences, including a risk of death.

Albert Bandura

The approach that Bandura and Walter took focused on the highly efficient form of learning known as observational learning, or imitation. They viewed observational learning as requiring no direct reinforcement to the learner. Observational learning generally takes place in a social situation involving a model and an imitator. The imitator observes the model and experiences the model's behaviour and its consequences vicariously; this process is called vicarious reinforcement. Bandura maintains that nearly all learning that can take place directly with instrumental learning procedures can also take place vicariously through modeling.

The powerful influence of observational learning is evident in both clinical and everyday settings. Observational learning has also been used to treat troubling problems, such as phobias and to explain a variety of both normal and abnormal personality patterns.

HUMANISTIC THEORIES

During the 1950s and especially during the 1960s, an approach to personality emerged as an alternative to psychoanalysis and behaviourism. Humanistic approaches to personality hold that within each individual is an active, creative force, or "self," that seeks expression, development, and growth. Thus, the aim of the psychologist should not be to search for unconscious processes or environmental contingencies but to understand how individuals experience themselves, others, and the world and to help them actualize their potential. Thus, many humanistic psychologists argue that scientific methods borrowed from the natural sciences are inappropriate for studying people, whose actions reflect the way they understand and experience themselves and the world. Two of the most influential humanistic theorists are *Carl Rogers* and *Abraham Maslow*.

Roger's person-centered approach

Carl Roger

The most widely used humanistic theory of personality is Carl Roger's **person-centered approach** (1951, 1959). Philosophically, Rogers descended from the French philosopher *Jean–Jacques Rousseau*, who two centuries earlier wrote that "man is born free but everywhere he is in chains." Rousseau meant that people are innately free and compassionate to their fellows, but somehow in the course of growing up, they become mean-spirited, selfish, and trapped by convention. Rogers similarly believed that human beings are basically good but their personalities become distorted by inter-personal experiences, especially in childhood. In his view, psychology should try to understand individual's **phenomenal experience**—that is, the way they conceive of reality and experience themselves and their world. According to Rogers and other humanistic psychologists, we should not be studying people as *objects* of our investigations but as *subjects* who construct meaning. Thus, the fundamental tool of the psychologist is not a projective test, an experiment, or a questionnaire, but **empathy**, the capacity to understand another person's experience cognitively and emotionally.

Rogers, like other, humanistic theorists, postulated that individuals have a true self—a core aspect of being, untained by the demands of those around them—but that they often distort this into a **false self**—a mask they wear and ultimately mistake to be their true psychological "face". According to Rogers, the false self emerges because of people's natural desires to gain the positive regard of other people. As children develop, they learn that to be loved they must meet certain standards. In the process of internalizing these **conditions of worth,** they distort themselves into being what significant others want them to be.

Rogers defines the self, or **self-concept**, as an organized pattern of thought and perception about oneself. When the self-concept diverges too much from the **ideal self** (the person's view of what she *should* be like), the individual may distort her behaviour or the way she sees herself to avoid this painful state. Thus, people's internalized expectations of what others want them to be may lead them to abandon their own talents or inclinations and ignore their own needs and feelings. The artistic students who becomes an accountant because that is what his father always wanted him to be is, in Roger's view, sacrificing his true self to meet internalized conditions of worth.

Rogers proposed that the primary motivation in humans in an **actualizing tendency,** a desire to fulfill the range of needs that humans experience, from the basic needs for food and drink to the needs to be open to experience and to express one's true self. These needs were similarly described by *Maslow*, another humanistic psychologist. Opposing the actualizing tendency, however, are the needs for positive regard from others and for positive self-regard, which often require distorting the self to meet imposed standards.

Maslow's self-actualization theory

Abraham Maslow

In 1951, Maslow met Kurt Goldstein (who introduced him to the idea of self-actualization) and began his own theoretical work. It was at that time he began his crusade for a humanistic psychology—something ultimately much more important to him than his own theorizing. One of the many interesting things Maslow

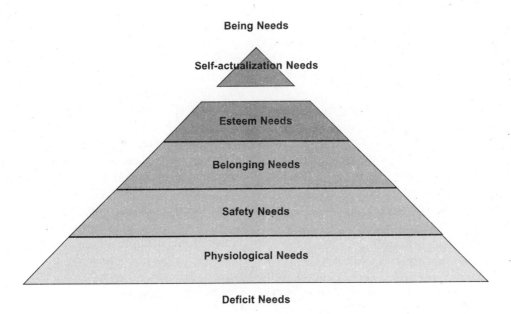

Fig. 14.5: Hierarchy of Needs.

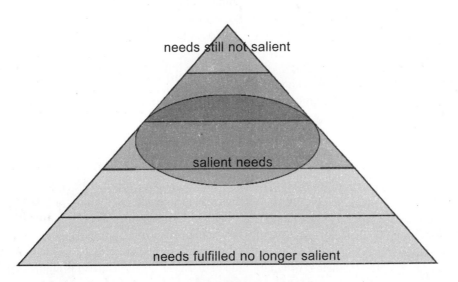

Fig. 14.6: Salient needs.

noticed while he was working with monkeys early in his career, was that some needs take precedence over others. For example, if you are hungry and thirsty, you will tend to try to take care of the thirst first. After all, you can do without food for weeks, but you can only do without water for a couple of days ! Thirst is a "stronger" need than hunger.

Maslow took this idea and created his now famous **hierarchy of needs**. Beyond the details of air, water, food, and sex, he laid out five broader layers: the physiological needs, the needs for safety and security, the needs for love and belonging, the needs for esteem, and the need to actualize the self, in that order.

The physiological needs

These include the needs we have for oxygen, water, protein, salt, sugar, calcium, and other minerals and vitamins. They also include the need to maintain a pH balance and temperature. Also, there's the needs to be active, to rest, to sleep, to get rid of wastes (urine and feces), to avoid pain, and to have sex.

The Safety and Security Needs

When the physiological needs are largely taken care of, this second layer of needs comes into play. You will become increasingly interested in finding safe circumstances, stability, protection. You might develop a need for structure, for order, some limits.

Looking at it negatively, you become concerned, not with needs like hunger and thirst, but with your fears and anxieties. For example, a home in a safe neighbourhood, a little job security and a good retirement plan and so on.

The Love and Belonging Needs

When physiological needs and safety needs are, by and large, taken care of, a third layer starts to show up. You begin to feel the need for friends, a sweetheart, children, affectionate relationships in general, even a sense of community. Looked at negatively, you become increasingly susceptible to loneliness and social anxieties. For example, desires to marry, have a family, be a part of a community. It is also a part of what we look for in career.

The Esteem Needs

Next, we begin to look for a little self-esteem. Maslow noted two versions of esteem needs, a lower one and a higher one. The lower one is the need for the respect of others, the need for status, fame, glory, recognition, attention, reputation, appreciation, dignity, even dominance. The higher form involves the need for self-respect, includ-

ing such feelings as confidence, competence, achievement, mastery, independence, and freedom. Note that this is the "higher" form because, unlike the respect of others, once you have self-respect, it's a lot harder to lose!

The negative version of these needs is low self-esteem and inferiority complexes. In modern countries, most of us have what we need in regard to our physiological and safety needs. It's a little respect that often seems so very hard to get!

All of the preceding four levels he calls **deficit needs,** or **D-needs.** If you don't have enough of something—i.e., you have a deficit—you feel the need. But if you get all you need, you feel nothing at all ! In other words, they cease to be motivating. As one says, "you don't miss your water till your well runs dry!"

He also talks about these levels in terms of **homeostasis.** Homeostasis is the principle by which a furnace thermostat operates: when it gets too cold, it switches the heat on; when it gets too hot, it switches the heat off. In the same way, our body, when it lacks a certain substance, develops a hunger for it; When it gets enough of it, then the hunger stops. Maslow simply extends the homeostatic principle to needs, such as safety, belonging, and esteem, that we don't ordinarily think of in these terms.

Maslow sees all these needs as essentially survival needs. Even love and esteem are needed for the maintenance of health. He says we all have these needs built in to us genetically, like instincts. In fact, he calls them **instinctoid—** instinct like needs.

In terms of overall development, we move through these levels a bit like stages. As newborns, our focus (if not our entire set of needs) is on the physiological. Soon, we begin to recognize that we need to be safe. Soon after that, we crave attention and affection. A bit later, we look for self-esteem.

Self-actualization

The last level is a bit different. Maslow has used a variety of terms to refer to this level: He has called it growth motivation (in contrast to deficit motivation), being needs (or **B-needs,** in contrast to D-needs), and **self-actualization**.

These are needs that do not involve balance or homeostasis. Once engaged, they continue to be felt. In fact, they are likely to become stronger as we "feed" them! They involve the continuous desire to fulfill potentials to "be all that you can be." They are a matter of becoming the most complete, the fullest, "you"—hence the term actualization.

The question becomes, of course, what exactly does Maslow mean by self-actualization. Fortunately, he did this for us, using a qualitative method called **biographical analysis.**

He began by picking out a group of people, some historical figures, some people he knew, whom he felt clearly met the standard of self-actualization. Included in this august group were *Abraham Lincoln, William James,* and soon. He then looked at their biographies, writings, the acts and words of those he knew personally, and so on. From these sources, he developed a list of qualities that seemed characteristic of these people, as opposed to the great mass of us.

- Reality-centered, which means they could differentiate what is fake and dishonest from what is real and genuine.
- Problem-centered, meaning they treated life's difficulties as problems demanding solutions, not as personal troubles to be railed at or surrendered to.
- Different perception of means and ends. They felt that the ends don't necessarily justify the means, that the means could be ends themselves, and that the means—the journey—was often more important than the ends.
- The self-actualisers also had a different way of relating to others. First, they enjoyed solitude, and were comfortable being alone. And they enjoyed deeper personal relations with a few close friends and family members, rather than more shallow relationships with many people.
- They enjoyed autonomy, a relative independence from physical and social needs. And they

resisted enculturation, that is, they were not susceptible to social pressure to be "well-adjusted" or to "fit in"—they were, in fact, nonconformists in the best sense.

- Unhostile sense of humour—preferring to joke at their own expense, or at the human condition, and never directing their humours at others.
- Acceptance of self and others, by which he meant that these people would be more likely to take you as you are than try to change you into what they thought you should be.
- Spontaneity and simplicity: They preferred being themselves rather than being pretentious or artificial.
- Humility and respect towards others—meaning that they were open to ethnic and individual variety, even treasuring it. They had a quality Maslow called Human Kinship or Gemeinschafts-gefühl—social interest, compassion, humanity. And this was accompanied by a strong ethics, which was spiritual but seldom conventionally religious in nature.
- Freshness of appreciation, an ability to see things, even ordinary things, with wonder.
- Finally, these people tended to have more peak experiences than the average person. A peak experience is one that takes you out of yourself, that makes you feel very tiny, or very large, to some extent one with life or nature or God. It gives you a feeling of being a part of the infinite and the eternal.

Maslow doesn't think self-actualisers are perfect, of course. There were several flaws or imperfections he discovered along the way as well: First, they often suffered considerable anxiety and guilt—but realistic anxiety and guilt, rather than misplaced or neurotic versions. Some of them were absentminded and overly kind. And finally, some of them had unexpected moments of ruthlessness, surgical coldness, and loss of humour.

Contributions and limitations of humanistic theories

Humanistic psychology has made a number of

contributions to the study of personality. Perhaps the most important is its unique focus on the way humans strive to find meaning in life, a dimension that other approaches have failed to address. In day-to-day life this need may not be readily observable because culture confers meaning on activities, relationships and values. The salience of this aspect of personality emerges, however, in times of personal crisis or loss, when life may seem capricious and meaningless. The search for meaning also becomes apparent in times of rapid cultural change, when a culture's values and worldview are breaking down and no longer fulfill their function of making life predictable and meaningful.

The humanistic approach has at least two major limitations:

- First, it does not offer a comprehensive theory of personality in the same way that psychodynamic and cognitive—social theory do. It does not, for example, offer a general theory of cognition, emotion, behaviour, and psychological disorder, although different theorists at times address many of these.
- Second, with some notable exceptions (Rogers, 1959), humanistic psychology has largely failed to develop a body of testable hypotheses and research, although this failure reflects its rejection of empiricism as a philosophy of science.

THE GENETICS OF PERSONALITY

The oldest issue in psychology is perhaps **nature versus nurture.** A recent view of genetic research noted that "investigators who have studied . . . .twins are unanimous in concluding that personality is more affected by environment than any other area of human functioning (*Farber,* 1981). Nonetheless some investigators have asked whether genetic endowment might not also play an influential role? The answer seems to be a cautious yes, but we are still trying to learn how much genes influence personality and the specific ways in which they make their mark.

One line of research concerns *temperament*—the aspect of personality that includes mood, activity level, and emotion, and the variability of each. Studies with animals have shown that selective breeding can heighten or diminish characteristics like emotionality over successive generations. Twin studies with humans also seem to show a genetic influence.

Moving beyond child temperament, we can find some evidence of a genetic contribution to a large number of adult trait dimensions and to at least one topology. The average correlations obtained across several studies of MZ and DZ pairs show that, MZ correlations average much higher than DZ correlations. These correlations do not show, conclusively, that personality traits have a genetic basis; one reason is that MZ twins are often more similar in *environment* than are DZ twins because parents tend to treat their identical twins alike, to dress them alike, and so forth. However, at least one study (*Loehlin & Nichols,* 1976) showed that similarity of upbringing was not a major cause of higher correlations among MZ twins; this, of course, strengthens the case for genetic influence.

H.J. Eysenck, proposed that traits related to his introversion—extroversion type dimension are linked to inherited characteristics of the *reticular formation,* the part of the brain that influences an individual's level of arousal. Eysenck believes that introverts inherit more of a tendency to be aroused, "revved up," than do extroverts and that they have a basic need to inhibit, or "damp down," their arousal. As a result, introverts tend to avoid extreme excitement; seek out calm, quiet conditions; and shy away from the activation caused by social interaction. Extroverts, on the other hand, genetically predisposed to be *under* aroused, are attracted to excitement and social interaction. Tests of introversion—extroversion do show fairly strong evidence of heritability.

In addition to similarities in their test scores, identical twins show a remarkable number of subtle behavioural similarities. Even twins who have been reared apart tend to laugh alike, smoke similar numbers of cigarettes per day, and show similar nervous mannerisms (*Farber, 1981*).

Genes may influence personality in more diverse and dramatic ways than most have thought.

IS PERSONALITY CONSISTENT ?

The concept of personality traits described thus far implies that personality has some degree of consistency. If John is an honest person, one assumes he is likely to behave honestly in various situations and to be honest two years from now. No one is honest all the time, however, and people do change. Thus, two questions arise: Is personality consistent from one situation to another? And is personality consistent over time?

Consistency across situations

In 1968, *Walter Mischel* touched off a 30-year debate by arguing that people's behaviour largely reflects situational variables—the circumstances in which they find themselves—rather than enduring aspects of their personalities. He marshaled considerable evidence of the inconsistency of people's behaviour across situations and showed that most personality tests had only modest correlations with behaviours in the real world. For example, trait measures tended to be far less predictive of whether a psychiatric patient would require future hospitalization than the weight of the patient's psychiatric chart!

Mischel almost single-handedly slew the mighty field of personality. If personality is not consistent, psychologists have nothing to measure, so they might as well pack up their questionnaires and go home. Indeed, the field of personality languished for years after Mischel's critique. Several psychologists, however, challenged Mischel's arguments. *Seymour Epstein* (1997) pointed out that any single behaviour has multiple causes, so that trying to predict a single behaviour from a personality trait is virtually

impossible. No measure of "honesty", for example, can predict whether a child will cheat on an exam on a *particular* occasion. However, averaging across multiple occasions, measures of honesty do predict whether or not a child will cheat.

Other psychologist argued, further, that psychologists cannot predict all of the people all of the time, but they *can* predict some of the people some of the time.

Consistency over time

Researchers have now also documented considerable consistency in many aspects of personality over long periods of time. One example is *inhibition to the unfamiliar,* a cluster of attributes in children that includes shyness and anxiety in the face of novelty.

Inhibition to the unfamiliar appears to be an aspect of **temperament,** that is, a basic personality disposition heavily influenced by genes. Infants who are inhibited show a distinct pattern of crying and motor behaviour as early as four months when confronted with unfamiliar stimuli. In fact, infants classified as inhibited at four months show more fear responses than uninhibited children at 9, 14, and 21 months when confronted with novel stimuli (such as an unfamiliar room, application of painless electrodes to the skin, or application of liquid through a dropper to the mouth or eye).

Complex view of personality and consistency

If personality shows substantial consistency across situations and over time, was *Mischel* simply wrong? Yes and no. He clearly overstated the case for the role of situations in behaviour and understated the case for personality variables. A 21-year-old man who was impulsive and undercontrolled at age 3 is more likely to be aggressive when someone accidently bumps into him on the street and to steal from a store than a similar man who was better adjusted in preschool. In many respects, that is quite remarkable.

On the other hand, *Mischel* forced personality psychologists to move beyond simple statements such as "John is an aggressive person" to more complex statements about the *circumstances* under which John will be aggressive. In other words, Mischel's critique of traits led to a recognition of **person-by-situation interactions,** which simply means that people express particular traits in particular situations. In fact, in his most recent statements of his approach, Mischel argues that personality lies in if-then patterns— stable ways in which particular situations trigger specific patterns of thought, feeling, and behaviour (*Mischel & Shoda*, 1995).

Mischel's recent research, like that of a line of other psychologists who have been tracking down the nature of person-by-situation interactions, supports a contention of early trait theorists that seemed to get lost for many years: Consistency is most likely to emerge in similar situations. Like Spearman's distinction between s-factors and g-factors in intelligence, some personality traits are specific to particular situations, whereas others are probably general or global in some individuals.

PSYCHOSOMATIC DISORDERS

> *Psychosomatic means mind ('psyche') and body ('soma'). A psychosomatic disorder is a disease, which involves both mind and body.*

All illnesses can be considered to be psychosomatic. That is, they inevitably involve the mind's reaction (psyche) to a physical (soma) illness. However, in some illnesses, psychological factors seem to play a particularly important part. They can influence not only the cause of the illness, but can also worsen the symptoms and affect the course of the disorder. It is these illnesses that are termed psychosomatic disorders. Because psy-

chological factors are important in every illness, there is lack of agreement as to what should be considered as a psychosomatic disorder. Many doctors believe that illnesses such as duodenal ulcers, irritable bowel syndrome, bronchial asthma, eczema, psoriasis, high blood pressure and heart attacks are strongly influenced by psychological factors. Sometimes psychological factors can cause ill health without actually causing a disease. As a result of unhappiness, anxiety or stress due to personal problems, physical symptoms may develop. We are all familiar with the headache that develops as a result of stress. Similarly, other physical symptoms can develop. These include nausea, abdominal pain and chest pain, breathlessness, diarrhoea and giddiness and muscle pains.

How does a Psychosomatic Disorder Occur?

Illness can be due to many factors. It can occur as a result of social or environmental factors. It may also happen as a result of genetic or hereditary reasons : a tendency for a certain condition to run in families. Some families also tend to suppress feelings : any emotion then tends to be expressed by physical symptoms. Children can learn this behaviour that may continue to adult life. Some people think that it is our personality that is a major factor in determining which illness we develop. For example, people with what is known as Type A personality tend to be ambitious, impatient, and set themselves high standards. They seem more likely to develop heart attacks. Quiet, introverted individuals, who tend to conceal their feelings and fears and suppress emotions, may be more likely to develop cancers.

It is well known that the mind can cause physical symptoms. For example, when we are afraid or anxious we may develop: a fast heart rate, palpitations, feeling sick, shaking (tremor), sweating, dry mouth, chest pain, headaches, a 'knot in the stomach', fast breathing. These physical symptoms are due to 'an overdrive' of nervous impulses sent from the brain to various parts of the body, and to the release of adrenaline into the bloodstream when we are anxious.

However, the exact way the mind can cause certain other symptoms is not clear. Also, how the mind can affect actual physical diseases (rashes, blood pressure, the extent of heart disease, etc) is not clear. It may have something to do with nervous impulses going to the body, which we do not fully understand. There is also some evidence that the brain may be able to affect certain cells of the immune system, which is involved in various physical diseases.

Why Does a Psychosomatic disorder Occur

Why the illness occurs at a particular time is often a mystery. It could be that a combination of the factors mentioned above triggers off the illness. Should there be untoward stress due to personal problems at home or at work, or bereavement, then an illness may result. We know for instance that certain life events such as moving house, getting divorced or suffering bereavement can precipitate physical illness. Similarly, an existing illness may worsen as a result of these stresses.

Treatment Involved for a Psychosomatic Disorder

Increasingly doctors are recognizing the importance of dealing with psychological and social factors in relation to physical disease. As a result, many doctors now try to deal with the whole person. This means taking all these factors into consideration. By doing this, it is important to realize that the doctor is not playing down or ignoring the physical disease. Many people with so-called psychosomatic disorders feel that their doctor does not take them seriously. They feel that the doctor believes that it's all in the mind. The doctor will always attempt to treat the physical illness with appropriate medical treatment if necessary. But he will also be interested to understand more about the person who has the illness. This will in turn help him and the patient to understand the illness better. Sometimes psychotherapy or talking treatment can help. Patients are given the opportunity and time to talk about their feelings and emotions. This will help provide them with an insight into themselves and help them understand their illness better. During the course of the psychotherapy, sometimes the patient may feel that he is not being understood. It is important to share these feelings with the therapist or doctor.

Sometimes it is helpful to look at the whole lifestyle of the person involved. This may require looking at how the stress is dealt with, teaching techniques for stress management, as well as examining factors such as diet and exercise.

Each disease has its own treatment options. For physical diseases, physical treatments such as medication or operations are usually the most important. However, healthcare workers will usually try and treat a person as 'a whole' and take into account mental and social factors that may be contributing to a disease. So, treatments to ease stress, anxiety, depression, etc, may help if they are thought to be contributing to the physical disease. People with psychosomatic disorders need the support and understanding of their family and friends. No special expertise is required. A person who will listen and provide support at times of crisis is all that is required. ■ ■

Dreams and Dreaming

Dreams and Dreaming

What are dreams? Why do we have dreams and what do they mean? These questions have for centuries been the subject of a debate.

Dreaming is a subjective experience of imaginary images, sounds/voices, words, thoughts or sensations during sleep, usually involuntarily.

Dreams are full of imagery. This imagery ranges from the normal to the surreal; in fact, dreams often provoke artistic and other forms of inspiration. The scientific discipline of dream research is called **oneirology**. Forms of dream include the frightening or upsetting nightmare and erotic dream with sexual images and nocturnal emission.

For a long time true dreaming had only been positively confirmed in Humans, but recently there have been research reports supporting a view that dreaming occurs in other animals as well. Animals certainly undergo REM sleep, but their subjective experience is difficult to determine. The animal with the longest average periods of REM sleep is the armadillo. So, animals do dream!

HISTORICAL BACKGROUND

The view that dreams, despite being enigmatic, 'mean' something, has reappeared in age after age, in many cultures. The dreams recounted in the Bible, for example, were believed to be messages from God, and thereby were assumed to have meaning.

The Greeks

The writings of the ancient Greeks show a con-cern with questions about sleep and dreams that remain unresolved today: Why do we sleep, and why do we dream? How is our thinking during sleep and dreams like waking-life thinking, and how is it different? Do our daytime wishes manifest in dreams? What role does the memory of daytime events play in dreams? How does illness influence dream content? What do dreams mean?

Aristotle indicated that dreams give a magnified construction to small stimuli arising during sleep. Men think, he wrote, that they are walking through fire and are tremendously hot, 'when a small heat is produced about certain parts.' From this circumstance he drew the conclusion that dreams may very well betray to the physician that first signs of some bodily change which has not been observed in waking.

A most interesting approach of the Greeks to dreams involved the practice of incubation, which, as Aristotle said, was a therapeutic method. Incubation was a means of encouraging healing dreams sent by a god or saviour, especially by *Asclepius,* a divine physician.

The essential feature of the incubation was that the sick person would have the right dream while asleep. In such a dream Asclepius would appear to the sick person and prescribe a treatment or appear to perform a surgical procedure upon the sick person's body.

Clearly, the belief in healing dreams presupposed that those dreams had meaning. In fact any historical review of the literature of dreams consists of accounts and examples of dreams that were thought at the time to have meaning. Dreams that were thought at the time to have meaning have generally not appeared in histories of dreams.

STAGES OF SLEEP

Since the early 20th century, human sleep has been described as a succession of five recurring stages: four non-REM stages and one REM stage. A sixth stage, waking, is often included. Waking, in this context, is actually the phase during which a person falls asleep. Rapid eye movement (REM) sleep is marked by extensive physiological changes, such as accelerated respiration, increased brain activity, eye movement, and muscle relaxation. People dream during REM sleep, perhaps as a result of excited brain activity and the paralysis of major voluntary muscles.

Sleep quality changes with transition from one sleep stage into another. Although the signals for transition between the five (or six) stages of sleep are mysterious, it is important to remember that these stages are, in fact discretely independent of one another, each marked by subtle changes in bodily function and each part of predictable cycle whose intervals are observable. Sleep stages are monitored and examined clinically with polysomnography, which provides data regarding electrical and muscular states during sleep.

Waking

Waking stage is referred to as relaxed wakefulness, because this is the stage in which the body prepares for sleep. All people fall asleep with tense muscles, their eyes moving erratically. Then, normally, as a person becomes sleepier, the body begins to slow down. Muscles begin to relax, and eye movement slows to a roll.

Non-REM Sleep

The period of non-REM sleep (NREM) is comprised of Stages 1-4 and lasts from 90 to 120 minutes, each stage lasting anywhere from 5 to 15 minutes. Surprisingly, however, Stages 2 and 3 repeat backwards before REM sleep is attained. So, a normal sleep cycle has this pattern: waking, stage 1, 2, 3, 4, 3, 2 REM. Usually, REM sleep occurs 90 minutes after sleep onset.

Stage 1

Stage 1 sleep, or drowsiness, is often described as first in the sequence, especially in models where waking is not included. Polysomnography shows a 50% reduction in activity between wakefulness and stage 1 sleep. The eyes are closed during Stage 1 sleep, but if aroused from it, a person may feel as if he or she has not slept. Stage 1 may last for five to 10 minutes.

Stage 2

Stage 2 is a period of light sleep during which polysomnographic readings show intermittent peaks and valleys, or positive and negative waves. These waves indicate spontaneous periods of muscle tone mixed with periods of muscle relaxation. Muscle tone of this kind can be seen in other stages of sleep as a reaction to auditory stimuli. The heart rate slows, and body temperature decreases. At this point, the body prepares to enter deep sleep.

Stages 3 and 4

These are deep sleep stages, with Stage 4 being more intense than Stage 3. These stages are known as slow-wave or delta sleep. During slow-wave sleep, especially during Stage 4, the electromyogram records slow waves of high amplitude, indicating a pattern of deep sleep and rhythmic continuity.

REM Sleep
Stage 5

REM sleep is distinguishable from NREM sleep by changes in physiological states, including its characteristic rapid eye movements. However, polysomnograms show wave patterns in REM to be similar to Stage 1 sleep. In normal sleep (in people without disorders of sleep-wake patterns of REM behaviour disorder), heart rate and respi-

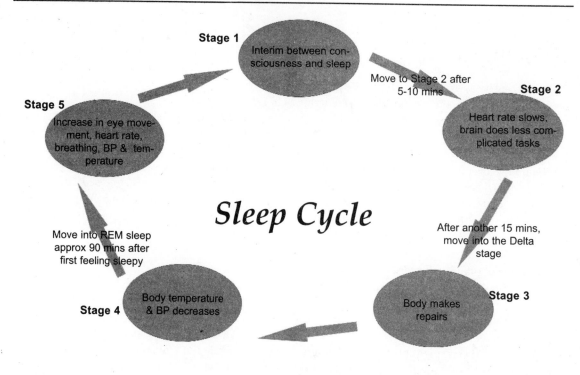

Fig. 15.1 Sleep Cycle

ration speed up and become erratic, while the face, fingers, and legs may twitch. Intense dreaming occurs during REM sleep as a result of heightened cerebral activity, but paralysis occurs simultaneously in the major voluntary muscle groups, including the states of excitement and muscular immobility, it is sometimes called paradoxical sleep. It is the dreams that occur during this intensely cerebral stage. The first period of REM typically lasts 10 minutes, with each recurring REM stage lengthening, and the final one lasting an hour.

SLEEP CYCLE

The five stages of sleep, including their repetition, occur cyclically. The first cycle, which ends after the completion of the first REM stage, usually lasts for 100 minutes. Each subsequent cycle lasts longer, as its respective REM stage extends. So a person may complete five cycles in a typical night's sleep.

Factors that Affect Sleep Stage and the Sleep Cycle

The sleep cycle is variable and is influenced by several agents. Sleep cycles subsequent to the first one in a night's sleep typically feature less slow-wave sleep, as Stages 3 and 4 shorten. Slow-wave, deep sleep is longest early in a night's sleep. Generally, sleep disorders affect the quality, duration, and onset of sleep. Sleep deprivation, frequently changing sleep schedule, stress, and environment all affect the progression of the sleep cycle. Rapid eye movement latency (the time it takes a person to achieve REM sleep) may be affected by a sleep disorder like narcolepsy. Psychological conditions like depression shorten the duration of rapid eye movement. Also, treatment for psychiatric conditions often positively affects sleep, typically including some desired change in sleep habit. For example, antidepressants usually quicken sleep onset and lengthen REM stages. People who take antidepressants often benefit from the effects they have on the quality and duration of the sleep cycle.

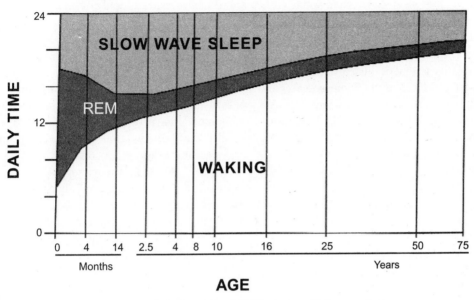

Fig. 15.2 Relationship of REM sleep with increasing age.

Age

The percentage of REM sleep is highest during infancy and early childhood, drops off during adolescence and young adulthood, and decreases further in older age. Of course, infants require the greatest amount of sleep. As parents know, total sleep time typically becomes shorter during childhood and may become longer again in adolescence. The stage-respective dimensions of sleep change relative to age. Stages 3 and 4 in the first sleep cycle shorten even more dramatically in older people than they do during a typical night for everyone else, so older people get less total deep sleep than younger people do. Also with age comes the lengthening of the first REM stage. Older people commonly enter REM sleep quicker and stay there longer.

PHYSIOLOGY OF DREAMING

While asleep, all human beings, starting in intrauterine life, cyclically enter into a rapid eye movement (REM) sleep period. In an adult, this cycle is approximately 90 minutes. If woken from REM sleep, 6 to 9 times out of 10, adults will report a dream—that is, a story with incidents and characters—told mainly by visual images. We know that most adults have about four or five periods of REM sleep every night, comprising about 25% of all sleep. The results of many studies involving awakening from all stages of sleep indicate that REM reports tend to be dream-like. Whereas the usual non-REM report is vague, fragmented and thought-like.

Sleepers usually forget events that occur during REM sleep unless they wake up soon afterwards. Theories about the meaning of dreams are based upon a small fraction of events taking place in REM sleep that people have recalled after waking up. Both nightmares and night terrors involve the experience of fear and a raised heart rate and respiratory rate: nightmares are dreams and occur in REM sleep, whereas night terrors occur predominantly during NREM sleep. The time between onset of sleep and of the first REM period of the night is shorter in patients with major depressive disorder than in normal people.

Newborn babies sleep more than older children and adults, and a higher proportion of their sleep is REM sleep. The earlier in gestation a premature baby is born, the higher its proportion of REM sleep relative to that of the baby born at term (*Dement,* 1976). Consequently some researchers have speculated that REM sleep is needed for the development of the nervous system by the stimulation of neural activity during REM. This is unlikely to be the only function of REM sleep, since it continues past childhood and persists throughout life.

Hobson and **McCarley** proposed their "*activation-synthesis*" theory of dreaming in 1977. Hobson later called this a "*psychophysiological theory* of how dreams are formed" (Hobson, 1988). This theory proposes, that the experiences of dreaming (REM sleep) are due to activation, by brainstem circuits, of forebrain cognitive structures which are normally used in our analysis of the external world. The forebrain synthesizes from the signals generated and from information stored in memory what we experience as a dream. The theory proposes that, in dreams, visual hallucinations, for instance, correspond to activation of visual brain-circuits. If the type of signal that stimulates the visual cortex in waking life with eyes open stimulates it in sleep, the visual cortex 'reads' the signal as if it had come from the outside world. Without external cues with which to orient itself, the brain or mind construes what it is experiencing as real. Although this theory was partly refuted by *Vogel* (1978) it has considerable experimental support.

Hobson (1988) was interested in the *formal* properties of dream content, but not in the content of individual dreams. Scientific knowledge is, he thinks, unhelpful in interpreting such dreams.

In Hobson's view a complete description of either brain or mind would be a complete description of the other. He assumes a "formal isomorphism," an equality of form, between the psychology of dreams and the physiology of the sleeping brain. Signals generated internally differ in intensity and pattern from external ones, which is why dreaming experience is so odd: persons, places, and times change suddenly or combine in impossible ways, and gravity is overcome. Intense feelings in dreams are due to activation of emotional brain centres, probably in the area known as the limbic system. The forgetting of most dreams plausibly results from their being stored temporarily in a short-term memory system without a 'remember' instruction. Although speculative, 'the mind-brain parallels' that Hobson has proposed are of great interest.

Besides offering theories and conjectures, Hobson has made valuable observations. For instance, he drew attention (1988) to the *uncertainty* that dreamers experience about dreamed events: it is often unclear who someone in a dream is and when or where things are occurring. This, as well as the discontinuities and incongruities of dreams, is what makes dreams 'dreamy'. Hobson has not proposed an intention or purpose for dreams; and his approach does not require that they have any. Rather, he has been concerned with the mechanism and causes of dreams.

Hobson's and *McCarley's* hypothesis is attractive since it has certain consequences which can be tested by dream researchers. One consequence is that damage to certain cortical cognitive structures will lead to an alteration in specific dream imagery. There is some evidence to support this. *Llinas* and *Pare* (1991) reported dreams of faceless subjects in a patient who had damage to the structures involved in facial recognition.

These theories propose that, with the change for NREM to REM sleep, cholinergic cells in the reticular midbrain formation, particularly those of the central tegmental field, the giganto-cellular tegmental field, and the tegmento-reticular nucleus, fire. This produces some activation of the cortex and stimulation of the pontine oculomotor system. At the same time, the noradrenergic brainstem systems of the raphe nuclei, the parabranchial zone and the *locus coeruleus* are switch off. Thus, the noradrenergic drive to the cortex is reduced. The noradrenergic drive to the cortex normally sharpens and enhances both the flow of peripheral information to the cortex and its analysis.

With the switching to REM, there is a reduction in input of external information to the cortex and a dependency on spontaneous activation of cortical cognitive modules from intrinsic stimuli. The closer these intrinsic stimuli are to those of the normal world, the more real will be the perception of our dreams. Hobson has suggested that when stimulation of the cortex, during REM, contains noise elements, the cognitive dream world becomes more bizarre.

Llinas and Pare take these ideas further and, in an excellent review paper (1991), but forward the hypothesis: (a) that 'REM sleep can be considered a modified attentive state in which attention is turned away from the sensory input, towards memories', and (b) that 'wakefulness is nothing other than a dream-like state modulated by the constraint produced by specific sensory inputs.'

These theories are similar in their basic concept: dreaming is an intrinsic function of the brain produced by activation of the cognitive units that we use during the day. Dreams will thus contain daytime residue from memory, as well as spontaneous excitation of cortical cognitive units. Brain damage may therefore lead to dream damage.

CHARACTERISTICS OF DREAMS

Colour in dreams

One dream-study from the pre-laboratory era indicated the occurence of colour in 29% of 3000 spontaneously recalled dreams, with women reporting colour more often (31%) than men (24%) (*Hall*, 1951). A later study found than 83% of reports from subjects questioned in detail about their dream experiences after wakenings from REM sleep contained colour.

Dreams of blind people

There is evidence that people who become totally blind before the age of five do not have visual dreams as adults, whereas people who become totally blind after seven years of age have visual dreams even after an interval of 20 or 30 years. When total blindness occurs between the ages of five and seven, the occurrence of visual dreams in adulthood varies in frequency (*De Manaceine*, 1897).

Berger and colleagues (1962) showed that no rapid eye movements occurred during REM sleep in subjects who were blind from birth. Similar electrographic studies in 1965 revealed some rapid eye movements during REM sleep in five subjects blind from birth which were, however, of low amplitude (*Gross*, 1965). These eye movements were independent of visual imagery, since the subject's dreams were non-visual.

A comparison of the dreams of blind and sighted subjects showed that, except for the absence of visual imagery, the dreams of the congenitally blind were as complex as those of the sighted. This suggests that complexity in dreams does not depend upon dreaming of seeing.

Dream sensations

A study of transcripts of 635 dream reports of young adults in America showed that dreaming consciousness 'is a remarkably faithful replica of waking life.' In all the reported dreams, visual imagery occurred, and auditory imagery induced bands playing, rain falling on the roof, and dogs barking. Touch and taste were present in 1% of the dreams and smell in an even smaller number. The experience of pain is most unusual in dreams.

LUCID DREAMS

The awareness while dreaming that we are dreaming has come to be called *lucid dreaming*. During ordinary *non-lucid* dreaming, as in waking life, we usually do not wonder whether we are awake or asleep: We assume that the world we are experiencing is real; we believe that we and our bodies are located within that real world, and are relating to persons and objects in much the way we do when awake. However, there are dreams in which we are aware of our true situation: that we are asleep and dreaming. These are lucid dreams.

In an ordinary dream, events carry us along, and we are unaware of whatever is determining the path that the dream takes. In a lucid dream, the dreamer can often guide the course of the dream. At times, while dreaming lucidly, a dreamer can decide to do something and, while still dreaming, do it. The lucid dreamer can also change features of the dream environment. Even in lucid dreams, figures may appear and events occur that are outside the dreamer's control. However, the dreamer can often choose how to respond to these.

Particularly valuable for dream research is the fact that, while awake, someone can play to investigate properties of the dream state and then, while dreaming lucidly, recall the plan and conduct the investigation. Needless to say, this ability is vouchsafed only to lucid dreamers who are experienced and skilled enough to achieve considerable control over their dreams.

Theories About the Purpose of Dreaming

Many theories try to answer the question, why do people dream? One theory is that dreams are necessary for sanity. *Fisher* has said that 'dreaming permits each and every one of us to be quietly and safely insane every night of our lives.' Or do dreams in some way compensate for stresses of daily life? Was *Kierkegaard* right when he said that he was 'so unhappy' then that in his dreams he was 'indescribably happy'? Do dreams contain valuable information, as *Lichtenberg* suggested when he commented that, if people would recount their dreams truthfully one might divine character more correctly from dreams than from faces.

Among the functions that have been proposed for dreaming are the assimilation of anxiety, the gratification of impulses, catharsis, synthesis, mastery, rehearsal for the future, education and waste disposal.

Waste disposal

An investigator could learn much about someone by rummaging through his or her rubbish bins. Would that information have meaning? Some things in the rubbish bins would contain information of a sort that formerly had implied intention or purpose. For instance, initially, letters, accounts, bills, and bottle labels were composed intentionally. Yet whoever had thrown them out, along with the food scraps and ashes, would hardly have intended thereby to convey information. No one would use rubbish as a means of sending a message, unless they were prevented from communicating in an ordinary way.

Rubbish represents a leading approach to dreams. The 'rubbish' theory of dreams has appeared twice in modern times. In 1886, *Robert* in a pamphlet quoted by Freud, said that the hidden purpose of dreams, is to 'excrete' a 'great mass of uncompleted, unworked-out thoughts and superficial impressions.' If not for dreaming, these would 'accumulate in the brain' and lead to 'mental derangement.'

In Robert's view the functions of 'dream-work' were 'to eliminate from the mental system impressions which cannot be properly assimilated; and to deepen the understanding of other impressions so that they are lastingly incorporated in the memory. Dreams thus form a "safety valve." And the therapeutic function associated with sleep should really be attributed to dreams.

Reverse learning theory

In 1983, molecular biologists *Francis Crick* and *Graeme Mitchison* put forward virtually the same theory as had Robert: dreams are deliberately discarded waste. *Crick* and *Mitchison* (1986) proposed that REM sleep, the state in which most dreams occur, has a 'biological' purpose—to avoid overloaded neural nets. In REM sleep we 'unlearn' or in the authors' peculiar expression, 'reverse learn' disturbing thoughts. In their 1983 paper they suggested that we dream in order to forget. Without REM sleep, they alleged, we would suffer waking-life 'delusions,' 'obsessions,' 'hallucinations' and 'a state not unlike (that in) some schizophrenias.' In their second paper on this subject

(1986), they withdrew the phrase 'dream in order to forget' and replaced it by the suggestion 'we dream to reduce fantasy' or 'we dream to reduce obsession.'

Robert (1886) had argued that the dreaming mind somehow discriminates between different 'impressions': those that are to be excreted, so to speak, and those that are to be preserved. Crick and Mitchison did not mention a discriminating faculty. They stated that 'the process is somewhat paradoxical, since it has the general character of forgetting . . . and yet improving memory.' They suggested that reverse learning is an automatic process with no 'supervisor to determine which fragments of memory should be damped down and which should be left untouched or strengthened.' Yet, shortly after, they proposed that some supervisor in the loose sense' must be necessary. The nature of such a supervisor remains obscure and, without the operation of a discriminatory or supervisory faculty, it is difficult to understand the process by which some mental events undergo 'reverse learning', while others do not.

The theory of Crick and Mitchison (1983, 1986) did not suggest how dreaming could aid forgetting. Nor did they present evidence that it does. That dreams aid forgetting seems improbable. If we recall a dream, we are likely to think about any waking life events that the dream reminds us of, thereby rendering those events more memorable. There is no empirical evidence to support the theory of Crick and Mitchison and some contradicts it. Crick and Mitchison were unconcerned with whether useful information can be obtained from rummaging through dreams. However, their theory implies that dreams are meaningless, as a person is unlikely to derive significance from rubbish that he or she is discarding.

Dreams as the guardians of sleep

Freud believed that dreams are the guardians of sleep. Dreams, he thought, weave the wishes which instigate dreams into dream narratives. The dream represents the wish as fulfilled, allowing the dreamer to stay asleep, rather than respond to the demands that the wish be gratified, which would require waking up. If Freud were right, then all dreams from which the dreamer woke up would represent failures, of this process; if the process had succeeded, the dreamer's sleep would have continued undisturbed.

THE MEANING OF DREAMS

The question of whether dreams mean anything; is an issue separate from the function of the brain activity that accompanies or generate dreams.

Much modern sleep research has been unconcerned with the usefulness of dreams. It has investigated the neurophysiology, biochemistry, pharmacology, endocrinology and pathology of sleep and of the REM state—in humans of all ages, including in utero, and in animals. It has been interested in the physical characteristics of the state in which dreams occur.

REM sleep apparently supplies favourable conditions for dreaming. However, it seems like that REM sleep fulfills its purpose with or without the recall of dreams. Sleep researchers remain uncertain as to why we dream. Some would consider that dreams are a mere by product of a brain process. They would suggest that in dreams we glimpse the products of that process, which continues regardless and independently of those glimpses and REM sleep fulfills its function, whether or not dreams are recalled, and whatever the content of the recalled dreams.

Träume sind schäume ('Dreams are foam')

Many people familiar with the work of Freud and Jung have remained unconvinced that dreams have meaning. They would still agree with the German folk-saying Träume sind schäume ('dreams are foam'). For instance, Medawar wrote that 'the content of dreams may be totally devoid of "meaning"' and that many dreams may "convey no information whatsoever" (Medawar, 1969).

Do dreams mean anything?

The answer is 'yes'—but if, and only if, a dream can be shown to offer information or knowledge that waking consciousness lacks, and to do so self-evidently, without requiring control and elaborate interpretation. Further, it must do so in such a way that the presence of the information or knowledge cannot be ascribed to chance, but is there apparently because of some intention or purpose on the part of the dream.

Many people assume that dreams contain hints for self-understanding or for self-improvement. This assumption implies that dreams have information, knowledge, or even wisdom, albeit expressed in metaphor, that waking consciousness lacks.

But do dreams really have information, knowledge, or wisdom that waking consciousness lacks? Interpreters of dreams seem to presuppose that dreams do. This presupposition is non-scientific. It is impossible to test the idea that a particular dream chosen at random has a meaning because it cannot be proven that it does not. A dream that lacks any apparent meaning may do so because no one has yet had sufficient insight to find it.

Faced with a dream, a person risks making either the mistake of ignoring an important message or the mistake of reading a message into what is mere nonsense. Interpreting a dream can be compared with finding a message in a group of markings written in an unknown language. Suppose that someone deciphers a message that plausibly corresponds with those markings. Criteria exist for ascertaining the validity of the deciphering. It is possible to decide whether the deciphered message was there from the start, that is whether the author of the markings intended it. Offered a dream, a resourceful interpreter can almost always find a message. But was the message really there or did the interpreter invented a message in the course of looking for one? The question might be hard

to answer in the case of a particular dream and its interpretation.

Content analysis

One leading approach to dream interpretation searches for relationships between dream content and the kind of person the dreamer is. It treats dream contents as traces left by the dreamers and assumes lawful relationships between dream content and traits of the dreamers. Its method is analogous to looking for links between animal footprints and animals. Much can be learnt about an animal from its footprints. An animal that leaves footprints does not intend thereby to supply information. In the course of going from here to there, it happens to lay down information about itself. The footprints are traces, but they are not messages.

Pioneered by *Calvin S. Hall* (1953) and his co-researchers, *Robert Van de Castle, Bill Domhoff,* and *Vernon Nordby* and by *Milton Kramer* (1969), the technique called **content analysis** consists of gathering hundreds or thousands of dreams and comparing their contents, according to the gender of the dreamers, their age, race, psychiatric diagnosis, country of national origin, and so on. A large literature is based upon such findings.

Cognitive psychologists have carried out a number of studies on the structure and organization of dreams. In particular, *Cipolli* and *Poli* (1992) investigated the story structure of dreams (mental sleep events) by provoked awakening during REM sleep. Their evidence suggests that story-like organization is produced by the dream rather than reconstructed on wakening. They showed that the first dream report of the night was shorter than subsequent ones and that verbal complexity was greater in dream reports in the second half of the night. *Montangero* (1991) has stressed that, except in young children, dreams usually consist of sequential representations actions and scenarios changing in succession. He suggested that dreams must therefore be produced by mechanisms regulating their organization.

Freud and 'The interpretation of dreams'

Freud believed that the contents of all dreams represent the fulfilments of wishes. He assumed that the meaning of a dream was self-evident once the wish that allegedly lay behind it became manifest. He also believed that wishes are the *motives* for dreams. In interpreting a dream, which for him meant finding the wish underlying it he thought he was also explaining how the dream had come into being. He thereby linked the meaning of a dream to its cause.

Freud linked the meaning of dreams to the 'meaning' of hysterical symptoms. He reported having gained knowledge of the 'scientific procedures' for interpreting dreams in the course of his psychoanalytic studies of hysteria. In those studies, he alleged he was 'unravelling' the 'psychopathological strucutres' of hysteria, which, he wrote, 'coincides with removing them.'

His hysterical patients had been 'pledged' to communicate to him 'every idea or thought that occurred to them in connection with some particular subject.' Among other things they told him their dreams, and so taught him 'that a dream can be inserted into the psychical chain that has to be traced backwards in the memory form a pathological idea.' It was then only a short step to treating the dream itself as a symptom and to applying to dreams the method of interpretation that had been worked out for symptoms.

If the analogy between dreams and hysterical symptoms is as close as Freud alleged, then correctly interpreting someone's dreams should lead to the person no longer dreaming, just as unravelling the meaning of hysterical symptoms reportedly led to their removal.

Freud's attempt is perhaps the most ambitious one to show that dreams have meaning. He said he would bring forward proof that there is a psychological technique which makes it possible to interpret dreams, and that, if that procedure is employed, every dream, reveals itself as a psychical structure which has a meaning and which can be inserted at an assignable point in the mental activities of waking life.

Upon hearing a dream account, Freud usually set about interpreting the dream by proposing that the dreamer kept elements from the dream in mind as a starting point and associated to them freely. He maintained that doing so provided access to the same thoughts that had been active during sleep and that had played a part in the formation of the dream. He did not, however, prove this crucial assumption of his theory. Instead, he offered his and other dreamers' free associations as evidence for the relevance of the associations. He made the mistake of presupposing in his line of argument a premise that depended upon his conclusion.

Freud gave many examples of his method of interpreting dreams. However, he proved not that his interpretations were valid, but that he was ingenious at making them. We know of no evidence, either from Freud, his followers or anyone else, that free associations reliably reveal the meaning of a dream. Of course, it is possible that some of his interpretations may happen to have been valid.

For Freud, then, dreams had meaning, but fulfilled their function whether or not they were recalled and, if recalled, whether or not they were interpreted. That the dreamer may gain access in the dream too new information was, for Freud, irrelevant to the purpose of the dream. In this regard Freud's view resembled that of modern sleep researchers. Yet they reject both of his explanations of why we dream: their evidence suggests that we do not dream in order either to fulfill wishes or to stay asleep.

Freud left a basic question unresolved; do dream interpreters find meanings actually present in dreams or, alternatively, do they invent meanings in the course of looking for them? Do they interpret dreams because they have found them to have meaning, or do they presuppose that dreams have meaning in order to interpret them?

William Blake said 'The truth can never be told so as to be understood', William Blake said, 'and not believed' (Blake, 1793). That many people who understand Freud still disbelieve that dreams have meaning, suggests that he did not satisfactorily demonstrate the truth of his views.

Jung's theory about dream

That dreams are goal-oriented and purposeful was also central to the approach of *Carl Jung* (1974), though the goals or purposes he postulated were very different from those of Freud. Jung did not believe that dreams necessarily involve concealment of motivation. On the contrary, he saw dreams as oracular, as the work of farseeing mentors, whose primary concern was the fulfillment of the dreamer's life and restoring balance to the dreamer's attitudes. Jung believed in looking to dreams for hints, warning, and messages—not only about the dreamer's state of mind, but also about the dreamer's future.

He too, relied on the free associations of the dreamer, though he also encouraged the interpreter to associate freely to a dream. Jung recommended that dream interpreters 'amplify' dream images by drawing upon parallels from mythology, folklove, and religion. This is because he believed that dreams express *archetypal* themes from the 'collective unconscious', by which he meant instincts from the most primitive levels of nature.

Hypermnesic dreams

In 'The Interpretation of Dreams' Freud reported a curious class of event. 'It may happen that a piece of material occurs in the content of a dream which in our waking state we do not recognize as forming part of our knowledge or experience. We remember, ofcourse, having dreamt the thing in question, but we cannot remember whether we experienced it in real life. We are thus left in doubt as to the source which has been drawn upon by the dream and are tempted to believe that dreams have a power of independent production. Then at last, often after a long interval, some fresh experience recalls the lost memory of the other event and at the same time reveals the source of the dream. We are thus driven to admit that in the dream we knew and remembered something which was beyond the reach of our waking memory.'

This is a description of what has come to be known as a *hypermnesic* dream. Some (though not all) such dreams, we believe, fit our criteria of having meaning.

Problem-solving dreams

In the course of psychotherapy people often relate their dreams to the therapist and invite comment. That is because most psychotherapy patients, as well as their therapists, assume that dreams contain hints for self-understanding or self-improvement. This assumption implies that dreams have information, knowledge, or even wisdom, albeit expressed in metaphor, that waking consciousness lacks. Is the assumption justified?

Being familiar with historical anecdotes by testifying to dreams having reportedly solved artistic problems, *Schatzman* chose to try to collect some problem-solving dreams himself. He decided to challenge people with brain-twisters and suggest that they might solve them in dreams. A few years ago, Schatzman asked a young medical doctor friend to try to solve this problem in a dream: Which two English words begin and end with the letters 'HE'?

The friend thought for a few minutes, but could not find the answer. During the course of the day, he remembered from time to time that he had this problem to solve. In the afternoon, sitting in the back seat of a car, he fell asleep briefly and, while asleep, felt the problem disturbing him. He woke up, and decided that the best thing to do was to remind himself of the problem while falling asleep that night—and in fact that is what he did.

Around 2 a.m. he went to sleep, awoke six hours later, and remembered a dream. Instantly he saw how it had given him the answer whereupon he wrote down the dream.

Excerpt from the dream account
'. . . I get an intense pain in my chest and fall

over. Juliet, my wife, comes out of the house laughing. Her laugh is not her usual one, but is a squeakly "He...he.. he". Her laughter hurts and puzzles me, since I want her sympathy.

She calls an ambulance, into which I'm carried and taken to hospital. I tell the driver to hurry as the pain is severe. I ask him why it's taking so long. He says the road is blocked—a brain has fallen out on to the road and must be removed before the traffic can proceed.

We arrive at the hospital, the stretcher is placed on a trolley, and I am wheeled through the front door of the hospital. Many people have gathered there, all laughing the same way as Juliet was. I try to cover my ears, but I can't bring my fingers together to keep the sounds out. I'm in the ward. A doctor comes. "I know what's wrong with you", he says.

"Then take away my pain," I reply.

"I can," he says, "but I won't. You must tell me what is wrong with you, and then you'll be better and can go home."

"I have had a coronary," I say.

"Jargon isn't good enough," he says.

"I'm a doctor and I'm being precise and technical," I say.

"I have been forbidden to discharge you," he says, "until you tell me in plain language what your problem is." All this time, behind his hand he's laughing with a high-pitched "He... he.. he."

I get very angry. "You're infuriating!" I say.

"Why do you keep laughing? I could have my pain forever. You could call it anything, even heartache."

He stops laughing. "You can go home now."

I still feel pain, but now I don't know where it is.

"I'm not quite better," I tell him.

"You must see another doctor, a word specialist," he replies.

I leave the hospital and Morton Schatzman appears.

"I hear you're not quite well," Morton says.

"I told you there were two things wrong with you."

"I just want to go to sleep", I say, "and not think about it."

"You can go to sleep anytime you want", he replies, "but you must learn to juggle words and pains."

"Riddles give me headaches," I tell him.

My, pain goes away completely, and I feel well . . .

The dream ended and the dreamer awoke, delighted to know the answer: 'HEartacHE' and 'HEadacHE'.

Much later, the dreamer re-read his account of his problem-solving dream and recognized something that neither he nor Schatzman had previously realized: Juliet's 'he ... he' laugh early in the dream, which in a way hinted at the problem, also contained the two-letter word 'He', another word beginning and ending with the letters 'He'. That was correct answer, but the dream had apparently overlooked it, or felt dissatisfied with it, as it had gone on to other solutions.

The dream provided the answers to the problem, but no clue as to how the dreamer's mind had actually discovered them. It seems reasonable to suppose that the process must have involved the dreamer searching his memory for words beginning or ending with the letters 'HE' and checking whether they were suitable answers, and that this process had gone on entirely outside his awareness.

This example illustrates, that at last some dreams are not mere mental doodling, but have meaning, in the sense of having purpose. The same can be said for many lucid dreams and for hypermnesic dreams.

In dreams we can experience light, colour, sound, temperature, touch, movement and even taste and smell. The quasi-sensory experiences of dreams often closely resemble the sensory experiences of waking life: unless lucid, the dreamer assumes that he or she is interacting with real persons and things. William C. Dement (1975), asked how does the brain produce a comprehensive perceptual experience in the complete absence of structure neural input from all the sensory pathways, an experience that essentially duplicates the real world in terms of completeness, detail, continuity, etc? This, until we begin to understand and account for it, is the miracle of dreaming.' To create a quasi-perceptual world may be even more difficult than to perceive one that already exists.

Somewhere in the brain, neural activity must ingeniously produce an effect similar to that created in waking life by energy impinging on sensory receptors. Even more remarkably, in at least some dreams, quasi-perceptual events convey to the dreamer information which has meaning. ■ ■

Annexure – I

ILLUSION	DELUSION	HALLUCINATION
Illusion is a perception of something objectively existing in such a way as to cause misinterpretation of its actual nature; especially optical illusion. Illusions are misperceptions that are perceived by most people, and are based on a specific stimulus received under certain conditions. Some experiments with animals indicate that several species of mammals and birds are "fooled" by illusions in much the same way as we are.	Delusion is a false belief regarding the self or persons or objects outside the self that persists despite the facts and occurs in some psychotic states. Delusions are different from both illusions and hallucinations. They are beliefs, not perceptions. Like hallucinations, they tend to be found in people who are mentally ill. A person may have delusions of grandeur (believing that he or she is a very important or famous person) or delusions of persecution (believing someone or something is out to harm them) when the facts clearly do not support these beliefs.	Hallucination is a perception of something (as a visual image or a sound) with no external cause and usually arising from a disorder of the nervous system (as in delirium tremens or in functional psychosis without known neurological disease) or in response to drugs (as LSD). Hallucinations are usually seen by only one individual. Most often they are experienced by people who suffer from specific kinds of mental illnesses, or who are influenced by drugs or extreme amounts of alcohol. Hallucinations are false perceptions that occur in the absence of appropriate external stimuli, whereas illusions are misinterpretations of external stimuli that are, in fact, present.

Annexure – II

Psychological Therapies

PSYCHOLOGICAL THERAPY	ASSUMED CAUSES OF DISORDER	BASIC THERAPY METHODS

Psychoanalysis	• Repressed anxieties about unresolved childhood conflicts
	• "Schizophrenic mother" or schizophrenic family system
		• Help the person to get in touch with repressd feelings & conflicts in order to gain **insight**; once the person understands that he/she can resolve the conflict.
		• Techniques include:
		  i) free association to overcome resistance
		  ii) interpretation of dreams
		  iii) analyzing transference

Humanistic Therapies	• Evironmental stressors
	• Lack of social support or friends
		• Person-centered therapy
		  i) unconditional positive regard
		  ii) active listening
		• Gestalt therapy

Behavioural Therapies	• Peculiar reinforcement history • Overgeneralization	• Classical conditioning systematic desensitization & aversive conditioning • Operant conditioning token economics
Cognitive Therapies	• Irrational belief systems • Learned helplessness & attributions of self-blame	• Rational-emotive therapy • Cognitive-behavioural therapy for depression

PSYCHOANALYSIS

Psychoanalysis assumes that the past experiences cause current psychological problems. Because these past experiences were emotionally upsetting, negative and hurtful, the person represses memory of these experiences into the unconscious. Therefore, the therapist talks with the person to reconstruct or uncover these past experiences. However, since the memories are unconscious, the therapist must use indirect methods to discover these repressed memories. Furthermore, since these unconscious memories are painful, the person is likely to use defense mechanisms to resist discovering these painful past experiences.

The indirect methods that a psychoanalyst uses includes:

- *Free association*—the therapist says several words and the person says the first thing that comes to mind in response to each stimulus word.
- *Dream interpretation*—unconscious conflicts are believed to be symbolically represented in dream content. Recurring dreams or emotionally changed dreams are especially important for uncovering unconscious memories.
- *Transference*—the therapist tries to be a stand-in or substitute for other persons in the person's life who caused the past emotional stress. For example, if a person has an unresolved anger toward his/her father, the therapist encourages the client to see the therapist as a father-like substitute-and transfer the angry feelings into the client-therapist relationship. Now, the therapist can help the client with expressing, managing and resolving conflicts associated with these feelings.

BEHAVIOURAL THERAPIES

Behavioural therapies assume that the behaviour is the problem and that there are no unconscious conflicts or underlying problems of self-esteem. Instead, psychological disorders are behaviours that have been learned-sometimes under extreme or unusual circumstances. If disordered behaviour is learned, then it can be unlearned or extinguished. *Classical conditioning* and *Operant conditioning* theories each offer variations of behavioural therapies.

Classical Conditioning Therapies

1) *Systematic Desensitization*—This therapy has been especially effective for treating phobias. It is based on the idea that an individual cannot be relaxed and anxious at the same time. First, the situations that trigger anxiety are identified and rank ordered based on how much anxiety each situation triggers. Second, the person is taught relaxation techniques. Next, the person imagines the least anxiety provoking situations and practices the relaxation techniques. Several trails of relaxing while imagining the anxiety situation may be needed until the situation triggers a relaxation response instead of an anxiety response. This process is repeated with the next situation on the hierarchy, then the next, and the next. Eventually, the person will practice relaxation techniques in the real situations until there are no more anxiety response in those situations.

2) *Aversive Conditioning*—This therapy has been used most with undesirable compulsive behaviours, such as alcoholism or child molesting. It is also based on the idea that a fear response cannot occur at the same time as a pleasurable or arousal response. This stimulus that has provoked a positive response is paired with an aversive stimulus. For example, alcoholic drinks are laced with another drug that induces vomiting. Several trials of drinking and vomiting should extinguish the undesirable behaviour. Unfortunately, aversive conditioning has the same problems associated with using

punishment as a learning tool. A client may learn not to drink in the presence of the therapist, but drinking in the neighbourhood bar is still OK.

Operant Conditioning Therapies

1) *Token Economies*—A system of rewards points is created to reward positive or desirable behaviours. Rewards or points are lost when the person performs undesirable behaviours. Token economies work best when they are used in institutional settings or group-homes where there can be frequent monitoring of behaviour and frequent rewards. As the person gets used to the token economy, time intervals between rewards can be increased. Eventually, points or rewards also need to be replaced with naturally occurring positive or negative consequences.

COGNITIVE THERAPIES

Cognitive therapies recognize the importance of disordered behaviour patterns, but also that one's thoughts and feelings about oneself, relationships, and so forth, affect psychological disorders. In particular, a symptom of many disorders is negative thought about the self such as **self-blame.** Another negative thought process common in many psychological disorders is *overgeneralization.* Often self-blame and overgeneralization are accompanied by an *external locus of control* or the belief that the self cannot influence his or her own experiences.

Self-blame is the belief that everything that goes wrong is one's own fault. For example, many women who are physically beaten by relationship partners blame themselves for the partners' violent behaviour. The woman thinks that she is not enough loving or that she is a bad cook or that she nags too much and provokes the beating. Similarly, she may believe that she does not deserve a better relationship partner or that she could not live independently, so she stays in the abusive relationship.

Overgeneralization is extending beliefs about one situation to many other unrelated situations. For example, a student who fails a calculation class will also believe that she is bad at all math—statistics, algebra, geometry, etc. Furthermore, the student may believe that she is just a bad student regardless of the subject and that she will probably flunk out of college, will have problems finding or keeping a job, and that no one would want to have a relationship with a failure like her.

External locus of control is the belief or perception that fate, destiny, or other environmental factors determine what happens to an individual and the individual's "free-will" or "self-determination" have little or no impact on what happens to the individual. If this belief is exaggerated, a person may fall into a pattern of *learned helplessness*, where a person feels helpless, hopeless and no expectation of being able to do anything to improve his situation. Learned helplessness (or lack of personal control) is common among people with mood disorders, anxiety disorders, and substance abuse problems.

1) *Rational-Emotive Therapy* (RET)—This therapy directly challenges the logic of an individual's self-blaming, overgeneralizing, learned helplessness, and other irrational beliefs. It assumes that there is a thought or belief system for every behaviour; for maladaptive behaviours these beliefs are irrational or illogical (*Albert Ellis, 1974*).

An example of an irriational belief system would suggest that:

"Because I want something it is not only desirable or preferable that it exist, but it absolutely *should* exist and it is *awful* when it really doesn't. It is so *awful*, that I just can't stand it!"

The therapist often restates the person illogical believes in extreme, absurd terms . . . so absurd that the person is likely to disagree with the therapist. The therapist contradicts irrational beliefs or statements by the person. Persons are often given "homework" to take risks or do things that they are afraid of and take notes about all the bad things that did not happen. The therapists often uses strong, confrontational language with the person.

2) **Cognitive Therapy (cognitive-behavioural therapy)**—This therapy is commonly used with depressive disorders and generally is effective. The focus of therapy is to identify, the dismantled negative self-thinking and replace these negative thoughts with more positive thinking. Some cognitive therapies use humanistic techniques (e.g., unconditional positive regard) to accomplish goals similar to those of RET.

HUMANISTIC THERAPIES

Person-centered therapy—the therapist focuses on the person's conscious self, listens to the person without judging or interpreting comments, and expresses **unconditional positive regard** for the person.

- active listening
- paraphrase
- invite clarification
- reflect feelings

BIOMEDICAL THERAPIES

Generally, biomedical therapies (also called somatic therapies) essentially accept Hipprocrates theory—that psychological disorders are physical disorders. Something must be 'wrong' with normal biological or physiological processes and this causes the psychological problems. Therapy for the psychological problem must include some kind of medical intervention or treatment for the body.

1) **Drug Therapy** (psychopharmacology)—In the 1950s, biochemists developed Thorazine, a psychoactive drug that helps control symptoms of schizophrenia. This allowed many individuals to leave psychiatric hospitals and live with family, friends, in supportive care facilities, or on their own. Since the 1950s, dozens of new drugs have been developed to treat a range of psychological symptoms.

Psychoactive drugs may mimic the normal effects of neurotransmitters, or increase the amount of the neurotransmitter being released (agonist), or block receptors sites (antagonist), etc. However, no psychoactive drug is a perfect replacement for normal brain functioning. Also, there are side effects—these are the extra effects of the drug that are not needed or wanted.

2) **Electro-convulsive Shock Therapy** (ECT)—This is used only with depressed clients who are dangerously suicidal and who have not responded to other forms of treatment.

3) **Psychosurgery**—Brain tissue is removed or destroyed. More common in the past, today this is a rarely used as a treatment for psychological disorders. ■ ■

Annexure – III

Homoeopathy and Psychology

After going through the various chapters in the book each reader must have known "what is psychology and its various other aspects?" Now the question that arises "what is the need of having the knowledge about the subject of psychology by the homoeopathic students?"

RELATIONSHIP OF PSYCHOLOGY AND HOMOEOPATHY

The first psychological laboratory was established by Wilhelm Wundt in the year 1879 in Leipzig. And years back in 1810, Dr. Samuel Hahnemann wrote the first edition of Organon "*Organon of rational art of healing*" which is now in its sixth edition, known as the "*Organon of medicine.*" In his "Organon of medicine" our Master Dr. Samuel Hahnemann, has talked about the subject of psychology in various aphorisms (even before the subject of psychology came to the recognition of the entire world as such). Dr. Hahnemann was a genius, and he has very well written about the mental diseases and also about their treatment with homoeopathic medicines as well as the other methods of dealing with such patients.

The subject of psychology is the most closely related subject to homoeopathy; rather I would say both the subjects are interwoven with each other.

Some references from the "organon of medicine" where Dr. Hahnemann talks about mind, mental health and mental diseases.

In aphorism 3 Dr. Hahnemann says
"If the physician clearly perceives what is to be cured in diseases, that is to say, in every individual case of disease (knowledge of disease, indication), ...".

So, in order to have the knowledge of disease completely one must have the knowledge of the symptoms of body as well as the mind too. And for having the complete knowledge of the psyche of the patient; a physician must possess the knowledge of the subject of psychology along with the knowledge of other subjects like medicine, preventive health, etc.

Again, in aphorism 5 Dr. Hahnemann writes
"Useful to the physician . . . . due to a chronic miasm. In these investigations, the ascertainable physical constitution of the patient (especially when the disease is chronic), his moral and intellectual character, his occupation, mode of living and habits, his social and domestic relations, his age, sexual function, etc., are to be taken into consideration."

Here in this aphorism he talks about moral and intellectual character of a patient and his social and familial relationships; this is again related to the subject of psychology directly. Dr. Hahnemann has given immense importance to the psychological aspects of the patients.

In aphorism 96, it is written

"Besides this, patients themselves differ so much in their dispositions, that some, especially the so-called hypochondriacs and other persons of great sensitiveness and impatient of suffering, portray their symptoms in too vivid colors and, ... describe their ailments in exaggerated expressions."

In this aphorism Dr. Hahnemann talks about hypochondriacs, and their ways of presentations to the physician. This again is related to the subject of psychology as well.

Dr. Hahnemann has defined the mental diseases, and has also laid down the methods of treating these diseases (aphorisms 210 to 230). He has also talked about mania, insanity, fears etc., also in these aphorisms.

In aphorism 228 he specially talks about the way of dealing with the patients suffering from mental diseases.

"In mental and emotional diseases resulting from corporeal maladies, which can only be cured by homoeopathic antipsoric medicine conjoined with carefully regulated mode of life, an appropriate psychical behaviour towards the patient on the part of those about him and of the physician must be scrupulously observed, by way of an auxiliary mental regimen. To furious mania we must oppose calm intrepidity and cool, firm resolution—to doleful, querulous lamentation, a mute display of commiseration in looks and gestures—to senseless chattering, a silence not wholly inattentive—to disgusting and abominable conduct and to conversation of a similar character, total inattention.

We must merely endeavour to prevent the destruction and injury of surrounding objects, ... in the homoeopathic system the small doses of the appropriate medicine never offend the taste, and may

consequently be given to the patient without his knowledge in his drink, so that all compulsion is unnecessary."

IMPORTANCE OF THE KNOWLEDGE OF PSYCHOLOGY FOR THE HOMOEOPATHIC PHYSICIANS

- It will help in the diagnosis of the disease (mental diseases as well as the psychosomatic diseases).
- It will help in predicting the prognosis of the disease progress.
- It will help in making a true totality of symptoms, by ignoring or ruling out common symptoms of the disease.
- It will also help in the selection of the medicine to be prescribed.
- It will also help in treating as well as counseling the patients.
- Some of the other great stalwarts like, Dr. Kent who has given so much importance to the symptoms of mind in his repertory; so much so that the chapter on the rubrics of mind contains the maximum number of rubrics in his repertory. For using those rubrics, and for knowing the meaning of those rubrics, the knowledge of psychology is of tremendous help.
- Again much importance is given to the 'dreams', in the repertories as well as by some of the physicians, who only prescribe on the basis of dreams and their interpretations. To know 'what dreams are?', and 'how they can be helpful to us in prescription?' a physician must acquire the knowledge of the subject of 'PSYCHOLOGY'. ■■

Annexure – IV

Summary of the Major Elements of the Human Psyche

ELEMENT	FUNCTION
Conscious Mind (Wernicke's area)	Has capacity to consciously experience stimuli, and to formulate thoughts, images, & decisions related to them.
Will	Agent of the *conscious mind* in interacting with other systems.
Rational Mind (Left pre-frontal lobe)	Formulates thoughts relating to plans and the organization of activities to satisfy needs and desires in a rational and socially acceptable manner, and to resolve problems.
Intellect	Agent of the *rational mind* in interacting with other systems.
Spirited Mind (Angular gyrus)	Formulates feelings and thoughts related to perceived stimuli.
Human Spirit	Agent of the *spirited mind* in interacting with other systems.
MEMORY SYSTEM	Composite of memory systems that identify stimuli, and store events, knowledge, language, thoughts, beliefs, feelings, and motor programs.
Sensory Memory System	Stores sensory data by type of stimulus. Used for real-time identification of people and things, and to stimulate thoughts and feelings about them.
Personal History Memory System (PHMS)	Stores all the events, knowledge, thoughts, and feelings of a person.
Event Memory System	Part of PHMS that chronologically stores events and related thoughts and feelings.
Knowledge Memory System	Part of PHMS that stores knowledge, facts, beliefs and plans.

Belief System	Part of knowledge memory system that stores beliefs, and generates thoughts indicating propriety of expressing actions and thoughts of the conscious mind.
Hemispheric Memory System	Stores sensory memory system and PHMS data in hemisphere specialized for processing the data.
Temporary Storage System	Stores non-priority thought and feeling impulses until they can be processed.
Motor Memory System	Effects motor responses to stimuli, and stores the motor programs involved.
STIMULUS RESPONSE SYSTEM (SRS)	Controls and coordinates all physical responses of the brain to internal and external stimuli.
Stimulus Response System Coordinator	Brain structure (hypothalamus) responsible for operation of the SRS.

Right brain vs. Left brain

Left Brain	Right Brain
Logical	Random
Sequential	Intuitive
Rational	Holistic
Analytical	Synthesizing
Objective	Subjective
Looks at parts	Looks at wholes

Annexure –V

Syllabus of psychology
(by Central Council of Homoeopathy)

1. Definition of Psychology—as a science and its differences from other sciences. Concept of mind—contemporary schools of psychology with special reference to behaviouristic and psychoanalytic approaches.

2. Scientific study of behaviour, intelligence, cause—effect relation—behaviourists (Pavlov, Watson, Skinner) and dynamics of behaviour (Freud and Neo-Freudians).

3. Basic concepts of sensation, perception, illusion, hallucination, delusion, image, intelligence, aptitudes, attitude, attention, thinking and memory.

4. Emotion, motivation, personality, anxiety, conflict, frustration, psychosomatic manifestations and dreams.

5. Developmental psychology—normal developments since birth to maturity (both physical and psychological) and deviations—its effect on later behaviour. ■ ■

Bibliography

The Human Psyche and the Nature of Man
Herbert R Rinder
Saunders Elsevier Science Limited

What is psychology
Andrew M. Colman
University of Leicester, England

Psychology, Mind, Brain and Culture
Weston
The Princeton Review

Essentials of Physiological Psychology
W. Arnold
Harper & Row Publishers, New York

Study of the Human Life Span
Clara S. Schuster
Simon & Schuster, Inc.

A Textbook of Psychotherapy in Psychiatric Practice
Alexander F, French T.M.
Churchill Livingstone Medical Division of Longman Group UK Limited

The Brain and Emotion
Edmund Rotts
Oxford University press Inc. New York

Dreams and Dreaming
Morton Schatzman and Peter Fenwick
Collier-Macmillan New York

Encyclopedia of Psychology
H.J Eysenck and W. Arnold
The Seabury Press New York

Thinking and Problem Solving
Peter Singer
Elsevier New York

Psychosomatic Disorders
P.J. Shoenberg
Elsevier New York

Psychotherapy with Special Groups
P. Wilson and S. Grant
Tavistock Publication, London

Symptoms in the Mind, An Introduction to Descriptive Psychopathology
Prof. Andrew C.P. Sims
Saunders Elsevier Science Limited

The Psychotherapies and their application to Psychiatry
J. Holmes, R.T. Vett
Churchill Livingstone Medical Division of Longuman Group UK Limited

Organon of Medicine, Sixth Edition
Dr. Samuel Hahnemann
B. Jain Publishers (P) Ltd. Delhi

Homeopathic psychology personality profiles of the major constitutional remedies
Philip M. Bailey
B. Jain Publishers (P) Ltd. Delhi

Introduction to Psychology
Clifford Thomas Morgan & Richard A. King
McGraw Hill Higher Eudcation.

■ ■

What are dreams? Why do we have dreams and what do they mean? These questions have for centuries been the subject of a debate.

Dreaming is a subjective experience of imaginary images, sounds/voices, words, thoughts or sensations during sleep, usually involuntarily.

Dreams consist of imagery. This imagery ranges from the mundane to the bizarre. In fact dreams are a rich source of... and other forms of inspiration. The scientific discipline of dream research is called oneirology. Forms of dreams include the frightening or upsetting nightmare, and erotic dreams with sexual imagery, and nocturnal emissions.

For a long time dreaming was regarded only as positively confirmed in humans, but recently there have been research reports supporting the view that dreaming occurs in other animals as well. Animals certainly undergo REM sleep, but their subjective experience is difficult to determine. The animal with the longest average periods of REM sleep is the armadillo. So animals do dream!

HISTORICAL BACKGROUND

The view that dreams, despite being enigmatic, mean something, has remained in age after age, in many cultures. The dreams recounted in the Bible, for example, were believed to be messages from God, and thereby were assumed to have meaning.

The Greeks

...cern with questions about sleep and dreams that remain unresolved today. Why do we sleep, and why do we dream? How is our thinking during sleep and dreams like waking life thinking, and how is it different? Do our daytime wishes manifest in dreams? What role does the memory of daytime events play in dreams? How does illness influence dream content? What do dreams mean?

Aristotle indicated that dreams give a magnified construction to small stimuli arising during sleep. Men think, he wrote, that they are walking through fire and are tremendously hot, where a small heat is produced about certain parts. From this circumstance he draws the conclusion that dreams may very well betray to the physician the first signs of some bodily change which has not been observed in waking.

A most interesting approach of the Greeks to dreams involved the practice of incubation, which, as Aristotle said, was a therapeutic method. Incubation was a means of encouraging healing dreams sent by a god or someone, especially by Asclepius, a divine physician.

The essential feature of the incubation was that the sick person would have the right dream while asleep. In such a dream, Asclepius would appear to the sick person and prescribe a treatment or appear to performed surgical procedure upon the sick person's body.

Clearly, the belief in healing dreams presupposed that those dreams had meaning. In fact any historical review of the literature of dreams consists of accounts and examples of dreams that were thought at the time to have meaning. Dreams that were thought at the time to have meaning have...

Index